The Native American Renaissance

American Indian Literature and Critical Studies Series

The Native American Renaissance
Literary Imagination and Achievement

Edited by

ALAN R. VELIE and A. ROBERT LEE

UNIVERSITY OF OKLAHOMA PRESS : NORMAN

Library of Congress Cataloging-in-Publication Data

The Native American renaissance : literary imagination and achievement /
edited by Alan R. Velie and A. Robert Lee.
    pages cm. — (American Indian Literature and Critical Studies Series ;
Volume 59)
    Includes index.
    ISBN 978-0-8061-4402-3 (paperback : alk. paper) 1. American fiction—Indian
authors—History and criticism. 2. Indians of North America—Intellectual life.
3. Indians in literature. I. Velie, Alan R., 1937– editor of compilation. II. Lee, A.
Robert, 1941– editor of compilation.
    PS153.I52N378 2013
    813.009'897—dc23

                              2013017327

The Native American Renaissance: Literary Imagination and Achievement is
Volume 59 in the American Indian Literature and Critical Studies Series.

The paper in this book meets the guidelines for permanence and durability of
the Committee on Production Guidelines for Book Longevity of the Council on
Library Resources, Inc. ∞

Contents

Acknowledgments

Much appreciation is owed to the University of Oklahoma Press stalwarts who have given professional steering to this volume. Our thanks to acquisitions editor Alessandra Jacobi Tamulevich, manuscript editor Steven Baker, and freelance copyeditor Ursula Smith.

A. Robert Lee owes every debt in this as in other projects to Josefa Vivancos Hernández.

Alan R. Velie thanks his wife, Sue Velie, for her love and support.

The Native American Renaissance

Introduction

ALAN R. VELIE AND A. ROBERT LEE

When, in 1983, Kenneth Lincoln published *Native American Renaissance*, his title quickly gained currency as the term to describe the efflorescence of literary works that followed the publication of Scott Momaday's *House Made of Dawn* in 1968. Indians, Native Americans, in fact had been publishing works in English since the eighteenth century—early autobiography, works of fiction, poetry, drama, oratory, and, increasingly, rosters of discursive writing and essay-work. But, in relative terms, they were few. In the case of the novel, symptomatically, there were only nine novels published by Native authors before Momaday made his bow with *House Made of Dawn*. By the time Lincoln wrote, there were scores; now there are hundreds. These take their place alongside a matching output of all the other genres, a body of Native authorship now as wide in compass as it has been bold in imagination.

As the term "Native American Renaissance" became familiar and increasingly used, it referred overwhelmingly to the literary phenomenon. But as changes in other aspects of Indian life and culture manifested themselves, it acquired far more inclusive meaning. Richard B. Williams, president and CEO of the American Indian College Fund, writes, much to the point, in his introduction to *Indian Country Noir* (2010): "For centuries Indian people faced extinction, brutality, and racism. . . . That horrible existence finally began to change in the 1960s. Since then we have seen a resurgence of Native pride. People are returning to their Indian culture for a sense of who they are. This renaissance is captured powerfully in the work of these authors."[1] By "renaissance" Williams means the changes in economics, politics, and public presence, as well as literature and other arts, that have contributed to the increased prosperity and sense of achievement among Indians. This is not to underplay setbacks, poverty-line subsistence on certain reservations, city drift, alcohol and its fetal alcohol syndrome (FAS) consequences, school dropout rates, and domestic violence. But the changes in Indian Country, and Indian life beyond, amount to a genuine renaissance, a widespread economic and cultural rebirth.

Political sovereignty, economic development, and high-stakes gaming have materially changed things in Indian Country, and it is now apparent that the outpouring of literary works has been part of the larger phenomenon. The term "renaissance" is indeed appropriate, for like the European Renaissance of the fourteenth through the seventeenth century or the American Renaissance of the nineteenth century, the Native American Renaissance has involved changes in all aspects of life, political and material as well as cultural. In Europe the Renaissance encompassed the Reformation, the rise of the nation-state, and the development of capitalism as well as changes in painting, sculpture, drama, and poetry. The Native American Renaissance has seen similar transformations, most importantly the recovery of sovereignty in matters of tribal governance. Other manifestations have been at once various and consequential, whether seen in the revival of traditional tribal religions, the emergence of the American Indian Movement (AIM) as a political activist movement, the establishment of the multibillion-dollar casino gaming industry from Connecticut to California, the Choctaw Revolution, or Hopi and Navajo mining.

The literary outpouring has been an integral part of this renaissance, but only one aspect of it. Although this first volume in what will become a Native American Renaissance series (Volume 2 addresses Native film, the visual arts, and discourse) is devoted exclusively to literature, a recognition of the role of other arts, economic activity, and politics is necessary by way of context. The earliest stirrings of the movement, for instance, that became the Native American Renaissance can especially be seen in Native painting. American Indians had been drawing and painting since infinitely before European contact, be it rock petroglyphs or birchbark pictographs, tepee decoration, bead and basket work, or sand designs. To all of these can be added their adaptations of Western influence. As the tribes were obliged to settle on reservations, paper, and especially ledger books, replaced hides, and with encouragement from Anglo mentors like Oscar Jacobson at the University of Oklahoma in the 1920s and Dorothy Dunn in Santa Fe in the 1930s, Native artists have gone on to produce and sell a great deal of easel art.

What triggered the renaissance in Indian art in the 1950s and 1960s was the desire on the part of Native artists like Joe Herrera (Cochiti), Oscar Howe (Sioux), and Fritz Scholder (Luiseno) to get away from what Scholder called "Bambi Art" by incorporating a modernist sensibility into their work. The embrace of modernism is especially to be seen in Scholder and the painters of the Santa Fe School. That has also been evident in the visual collages and canvases of Anishinaabe painters like George Morrison and David Bradley. Stylistically the breach was as sharp as the shift from medieval to Renaissance painting, the change from the style of Giotto to that of Masaccio. Scott Momaday, an artist himself, and the son of the distinguished Kiowa painter Al Momaday, was aware of the changes in Indian art, and in literary terms he was much influenced stylistically by moderns like Faulkner, Hemingway, and Isak Dinesen. His success with *House Made of Dawn* helped inspire, and confirm, Native writers like James Welch, Leslie Marmon Silko, and Gerald Vizenor, the last of whom had actually begun publishing in the early 1960s.

At the same time, and with a backward look to each historic setback of poverty and depletion, the tribes began stirring economically. As dramatic an example as any would indeed be the "Choctaw Miracle" in Mississippi. Lyndon Johnson's antipoverty and community development programs of the sixties specifically targeted tribes by defining them as "qualifying units of local government that would themselves administer the programs for their people."[2] This led directly to the "Choctaw Revival." In 1969 the tribe formed a construction company, and in 1971 opened an industrial park. It took a few years to attract businesses, but by the early 1980s the Big Three automakers had opened operations at the Choctaw site, and many other businesses followed. The upshot has been that by the late 1990s Choctaw per capita income had risen from two thousand dollars in 1971 to twenty-four thousand dollars, life expectancy had risen by twenty years, welfare rolls had shriveled, and tribes from all around the country were visiting Mississippi to see how the Choctaws had done it.

Many Americans are aware of the burgeoning Indian prosperity, but they attribute it mostly to high-stakes gaming. While it is true that Indian gaming produces over twenty-five billion dollars a year (consider the Massachusetts Pequots with their massively profitable Foxwoods casino), tribes like the Pottawatomi, Chickasaw, Cherokee, and many others have substantial incomes from sources other than gaming.[3] Politically, the tribes now have much more control over their governance than they did before the Native American Renaissance began—and in light of the Anaya Report in 2012 on land claims in Sioux country, they may come to have even more. Although Chief Justice John Marshall promulgated the doctrine of Indian sovereignty in 1832 in *Worcester v. Georgia*, it wasn't until the 1970s, a century and a half later, that Indians actually felt the benefits. After Marshall handed down *Worcester*, Andrew Jackson purportedly said: "Justice Marshall has made his decision, now let him enforce it." Perhaps the story is apocryphal, but tribes rarely were able to act as sovereigns until the Supreme Court issued *Morton v. Mancari* in 1974.[4]

While the effects of the Native American Renaissance have been felt in manifold aspects of Indian life, since the term was coined to describe a literary phenomenon, this volume limits itself to how that modern and contemporary renaissance of story, poem, and life-writing, along with theory and critique, have made their impact. First, however, due acknowledgement is necessary as to the literary work that preceded the Renaissance. The earliest work of an American Indian in English, Samson Occom's "Sermon Preached at the Execution of Moses Paul, an Indian," was, in the words of Jace Weaver, "an early best seller."[5] Despite this auspicious start, there was not a great deal of known Indian literary activity in the decades immediately following. Names, however, did emerge: notably, John Rollin Ridge, Pauline Johnson, Zitkala Sa (Gertrude Bonnin), Charles Eastman, Luther Standing Bear, Alexander

Posey, John Joseph Mathews, D'Arcy McNickle, Mourning Dove, Will Rogers, John Milton Oskison, and Lynn Riggs. Their effect, even so, and with full ac-knowledgment of all earlier imaginative achievement, was marginal in com-parison to the impact that Scott Momaday made with *House Made of Dawn*, which deservedly won the Pulitzer Prize for fiction in 1969.

The novel reminded America, and indeed the world beyond, that the Van-ishing American, a misnomer from the start, was still very much with us. It also had a greatly salutary effect on the gathering roster of Native writers whose work would be taken up by mainstream publishers like Viking and Harper & Row.[6] As the 1970s gave way to each later decade, that roster has grown both in volume and richness: Leslie Marmon Silko, Louise Erdrich, Gerald Vizenor, Thomas King, Louis Owens, and Sherman Alexie in the novel; Simon Ortiz, Paula Gunn Allen, Linda Hogan, Jim Barnes, Maurice Kenny, Diane Glancy, Luci Tapahonso, Ray A. Young Bear, Carter Revard, Joy Harjo, Jim Northrup, Mary TallMountain, Ofelia Zepada, Roberta Hill Whiteman, Wendy Rose, and Kimberly Blaeser in poetry; Hanay Geiogamah in drama; key autobiographers like Momaday, Vizenor, Silko, and Janet Campbell Hale; and discursive writers from Vine Deloria and Elizabeth Cook-Lynn to the academic generation of Craig Womack, Jace Weaver, Robert Warrior, Daniel Heath Justice, and David Treuer. There has even been a postmodern author-ship, notably Stephen Graham Jones and D. L. Birchfield, not to mention Vizenor and Alexie as ongoing doyens of the reflexive text.

That the Native American Renaissance has not been limited to novelists is borne out by the fact that almost all of the prominent ones—Momaday, Welch, Silko, Vizenor, Erdrich, Alexie—began as poets. With the exception of Goethe and D. H. Lawrence, it is difficult to think of writers in any lan-guage who have achieved much success as both poets and writers of fiction. Melville has a few poems in large anthologies like the *Norton*, and though his poetry is increasingly winning recognition, it still rarely gets much atten-tion in the classroom. Hemingway and Joyce made their respective efforts at writing verse, but neither was especially masterful. Native American writers, however, have been as adept as poets as they have been novelists, and have continued to publish verse throughout their careers. In addition to addressing fiction and poetry, moreover, we include here essays given to literary-cultural criticism, autobiography, drama, the span of First Nations as well as Native American writing, and a retrospective by Kenneth Lincoln on having written *Native American Renaissance*.

The essays that follow are organized in a way that seeks to highlight pairings and connections by genre, each aimed to edge and nuance the other. In this respect the collection opens with two essays that categorize the nature of criti-cal perspectives to Indian literature. Jace Weaver, Cherokee, makes the case for American Indian literary nationalism. That is, he raises the question: who should be listened to on the matter of how to view Native American writers and writings? The earliest critical writing about Native American literature came from Euro-American scholars, among them, Charles Larson, Alan Velie, A. LaVonne Brown Ruoff, Karl Kroeber, Brian Swann, Arnold Krupat, and Kenneth Lincoln. While acknowledging their contributions, Weaver notes, "What was notably absent was active engagement of Native voices." This changed radically in the 1990s. Louis Owens, Choctaw-Cherokee, published his seminal study of contemporary Indian novels, *Other Destinies: Understanding the American Indian Novel* (1992), and soon many other Indian critics were publishing their critiques. This culminated in a manifesto. Weaver, Craig Womack, and Robert Warrior published *American Indian Literary Nationalism* (2006), asserting nationalism to be not only a legitimate perspective from which to explore Native American works of literature, but also crucial to supporting Native national sovereignty and self-determination.

In "Ethics and Axes: Insider-Outsider Approaches to Native American Literature," James Mackay, a Britisher teaching in Cyprus, surveys the field of Native American literary theory from a European and so, of necessity, an "outsider" standpoint. Considering the questions of identity that have plagued the discipline, he examines the duties and responsibilities of the outsider critic. In answer to the question "How can the non-Native critic contribute work of value in the wake of Indian literary nationalism?" Mackay suggests that there is room for a flexible and heterogeneous criticism that is mindful of both European theory and Native critical concepts like Gerald's Vizenor's "survivance"—with its emphasis on Native self-creativity as enactive story and irony and as a hedge against the stasis of stereotype, be it Noble Savage, Devil, or Victim.

In the ten essays that immediately follow, a gallery of major fiction writers comes under scrutiny for power of imagination in its own right and for helping create a shared sense of literary renaissance. Alan Velie turns to the achievement of Scott Momaday to examine the ways Native American novelists have influenced one another even as they establish their own unique signature. Although Native Indian literature is not a tight-knit movement like Surrealism, launched with position papers, posters, and manifestos, nonetheless to a degree greatly exceeding other American ethnic writers, its authors have shown a long tradition of reading and borrowing one from another. Momaday's success with *House Made of Dawn*, the story of the Pueblo man named Abel who suffers from the traumatizing effects of combat in World War II, encouraged James Welch to publish *Winter in the Blood*, a novel in which Welch uses the myth of the wasteland to tell the story of a Blackfeet protagonist who suffers the same sort of anomie and alienation as Abel, though his condition results from familial rather than military trauma. Leslie Marmon Silko returns to Momaday's subject of a Pueblo victim of post-traumatic stress disorder, but uses Welch's method of undergirding her novel with myths. Silko deploys Pueblo myths very similar to those of the wasteland: traditional stories of sin causing drought, and ritual tasks that bring the freeing of the waters. Momaday, impressed by Silko's use of tribal myths, and cognizant of Gerald Vizenor's *Darkness in Saint Louis: Bearheart*, in which the hero turns into a bear, tells the story of Kiowa painter Locke Setman as a novelization of Kiowa myths of a boy who turns into a bear. Louise Erdrich, having read all of the above-mentioned novels, ends *Bingo Palace* by having her protagonist, Fleur Pillager, turn into a bear.

Rebecca Tillett takes on the challenge of situating Leslie Marmon Silko in contemporary Native American literature. Along with Simon Ortiz and James Welch, Silko has been a key member of the first wave of Native writings to follow N. Scott Momaday's groundbreaking *House Made of Dawn*. Moreover, her work has also helped to create both a popular interest in, and a market for, a whole range of Native women's writing, including that of Paula Gunn Allen, Linda Hogan, LeAnne Howe, Luci Tapahonso, and the internationally acclaimed Louise Erdrich. Significantly, Silko's fictional works are implicitly and often explicitly political. The semiautobiographical familial and communal focus of *Storyteller* (1981) extends beyond the personal to demonstrate and politically situate a specifically Laguna worldview. The localized "witchery" of *Ceremony* (1977), which is identified within the text as including, with witchcraft proper, all forms of exploitation and oppression, is explored on a truly global scale in *Almanac of the Dead* (1991) in order to address multiple grotesque atrocities of an almost unimaginable magnitude. Silko's most recent novel, *Gardens in the Dunes* (1999), filters European and American cultures through the worldview of the Indian child Indigo, alongside a passionate condemnation of Euro-American nature-culture separatism that she sees as having led to massive environmental destruction. Given their prescient vision and their continuing relevance to emerging American and more global political events, Silko's literary works have been not only cutting but truly on the cutting edge.

Within an account of James Welch's overall canvas, Alan Velie focuses on the uses of mythology in *Winter in the Blood, The Death of Jim Loney*, and *Fools Crow*. The novelists of the first decades of the Native American Renaissance—Momaday, Welch, Vizenor, Silko, Erdrich—took pains to incorporate traditional tribal stories into their works. In fact, Kenneth Lincoln makes incorporating tribal lore into contemporary Indian fiction a hallmark of the Native American Renaissance: "The Native American renaissance here targeted . . . is a written renewal of oral traditions translated into Western literary forms." Nowhere is that statement truer than in *Winter in the Blood*, on the surface a gritty, realistic saga of Montana in the 1970s yet possessed of an underlying mythic structure combining Indian, primarily Gros Ventre, but also Blackfeet, legend and ritual together with the Grail Myth that figures so prominently in twentieth century modernism. Welch's second novel, *The Death of Jim Loney*, in many ways a mirror image of *Winter*, makes heavy use of Gros Ventre mythology, particularly the Supreme Being of the Gros Ventre religion, Ixtcibəni:həhat, and his messenger, Bha'a, the thunderbird, the mysterious bird that Loney thinks must be a message from his mother's people, the Gros Ventre. Finally, *Fools Crow* again uses Blackfeet mythology, especially the story of the sinful Feather Woman, whose transgressions have brought suffering to the Blackfeet.

Kathryn Shanley primarily addresses James Welch's *Winter in the Blood* in "The Event of Distance." She argues for it as a "unique vision," the depiction of an American Indian as perhaps never seen before. Through the eyes of the nameless narrator we are enjoined to view the world of northeast Montana as littered with colonial ruin, and through his voice, to hear his reflections as a man struggling to understand his world in a way that allows him dignity as a Plains Indian male of his time. Shanley writes that he does so "out of his own experience as one clothed in the word 'Indian,'" thereby marked yet "simultaneously and paradoxically invisible." "An Event of Distance," a phrase from the novel, stands for a melding of place with time in a distinctly Plains Indian worldview, the dynamic goal of vision questing to renew the world and one's place in it.

Kathryn Hume explores Gerald Vizenor's elevation of imagination as working dynamic to be contrasted with the mere "representation" of "reality." So important does she consider cultivation of the self's imaginative powers that she suggests Vizenor's stance resembles that of religions that put the welfare of the soul or condition of one's consciousness above anything else. The world itself evidently matters but only as it is refiltered through changed understanding. Such a stance can seem insouciant in regard to the world's dips and fragility. But Vizenor is not making naive claims for the power of imagination as a solvent to change the world or the course of history; rather, and with a postmodern (even post-postmodern) flourish, he is looking for new ways to establish both human and tribal value in a deconstructed world. Vizenor's emphasis on tribal network is a possible improvement over the vulnerable and unstable nuclear family favored by Euro-American writers such as Pynchon or the elective affinities upheld by Douglas Coupland. In other words, Vizenor reverses the terms of imagination and real world, suggesting that most of the bad things we have to survive happen inside even if they look like outside events, so that learning to better or to more fully direct the imagination gives us a stronger, not to say, more cheerful kind of survivance—to use his signature term.

Connie Jacobs's essay, "One Story Hinging into the Next," discusses the hugely consequential achievement of Louise Erdrich. In 1985, after reading Erdrich's first novel, *Love Medicine*, Kenneth Lincoln predicted that Erdrich had the potential to become a great American writer, in the league of F. Scott

Fitzgerald, Eudora Welty, and Ernest Hemingway. Today, twenty-eight books later (thirteen fiction, seven children/young adult, three poetry, a short story collection, two nonfiction, and two books coauthored with Michael Dorris), Erdrich's stature as a leading author confirms Lincoln's early assessment. Enthusiasts, both from the reading public and from academia, are drawn to her craft: lyrical language, fascinating characters, abundant humor, innovative narrative technique, compelling stories, steadfast compassion for humans with all their weaknesses, and the abiding power of love in all of its many guises. What distinguishes Erdrich among other well-known American Indian writers is the way in which all of her fiction is connected, is woven into one long story. The narrative pattern established in *Love Medicine* continues to characterize her work with its linking cycle of stories, use of landscape, and overlapping lives and dynasties. Jacobs's essay analyzes the connecting pattern of Erdrich's novels, her own Chippewa equivalent of Faulkner's Yoknapatawpha, crafted from each contributing filament of place, history, and memory.

In "Thomas King: Shifting Shapes to Tell Another Story," Carol Miller argues that the lens of "trickster discourse" through which this mixed-blood Cherokee writer's work has most frequently been viewed is certainly a relevant approach since humor has been a creative strategy for King from the outset. But a fresher and even more productive trope in King's prolifically diverse literary production (literary novels, children's fiction, detective novels, a radio series, Canada's prestigious Massey Lecture Series delivered in 2003, and an in-progress idiosyncratic historical overview) is that of "shape-shifter." Venerable and mysterious, shape-shifters drive both the content and theory that lie at the heart of King's work. They are to be seen as figures who represent the power of story to both heal and yet also injure—and to determine the ethical choices that shape reality. Standing in a long line beginning with Cherokee oral traditions and including the "tellings" of other contemporary Native writers, King's extraordinarily diverse body of work expands the "platforms" of indigenous storytelling in as many directions as his fertile imagination can deploy. This belief in storytelling as "medicine" and King's use of the shape-shifter figure hold throughout his oeuvre, whether in key novels like *Medicine River* (1990) and *Green Grass, Running Water* (1993) or in a discursive text like *The Truth about Stories* (2003), not to mention his *Dead Dog Café Comedy Hour* radio series and spoken-word video, "I'm Not the Indian You Had in Mind."

The work of Louis Owens is carefully explored by Linda Lizut Helstern. She argues that the four novels published between 1992 and his untimely death a decade later grew out of a critical matrix that, since the 1970s, had largely been taken up with ethnic representation, identity politics, and, in the case of Native writers, authenticity, generally understood by the academic critical establishment to mean an explicit connection to Native oral tradition or ritual. Owens entered this conversation not so much to change the subject as to change the slant of the discourse with respect to Native peoples, many of them mixed-bloods like himself. In his fiction, attuned to the danger of representations that trap tribal peoples in their past with no opportunity for change, he adopted a strategy to interrogate and alter the construction of Indian identity on the very ground where Indian stereotypes have been created and perpetuated for some three hundred years—in the discourse of popular culture. Determined, to borrow a phrase from his admiring essay on *The Crown of Columbus*, to "defiantly, even subversively, seize the low ground of American literature,"[7] Owens turned the mass-market thriller to his own uses, creating an avowedly American Indian literature from what is arguably the dominant form of Euro-American cultural production. Each thriller subgenre in turn—murder mystery, supernatural horror story, Western, and war story—became the basis for a subsequent Owens novel. In plot-centered stories that show a surprising affinity with traditional orature, Owens succeeds not only in decentering the thriller's Western cultural foundations, moral, metaphysical, and epistemological, but in privileging such values as communitism and reciprocity, values central to traditional Native culture and contemporary Native lives.

In "'We've been stuck in place since *House Made of Dawn*': Sherman Alexie and the *Native American Renaissance*," John Gamber marks Alexie's career as a new phase of the Native American Renaissance, one that both draws upon and turns away from many of the defining conventions of that movement. Alexie builds on the artistic as well as popular successes of authors such as Momaday, Silko, and Erdrich, particularly in his examinations of issues surrounding (and attempting to define) Indian identities, the repercussions of Native relocations, and intercultural connections among and between Native and non-Native people. Nonetheless, Alexie's work has generally eschewed Native American Renaissance mainstays, including a revered sacred landscape, the homing plot, and a valorization of the mixed-blood protagonist as hope for the future. While Alexie does make use of these tropes from time to time, he refuses to rely on them consistently. Indeed, because Alexie publishes so voluminously in short story and poetic genres, he offers a breadth of work that provides numerous examples of innovation within Native American literature, and literature generally. Finally, while Alexie's recent work has been observed as, if not critiqued for, being overly optimistic (and assimilative), an optimism seen in contrast to reception of his earlier work as overly cynical and/or depressing (for which he has also come in for criticism), the presence of optimism and pessimism, hope and despair, humor and pain exists throughout Alexie's oeuvre in largely equal amounts. His novel *Flight* (2007), with its teenage orphan Native-boy narrator and use of time-travel, gives these elements a fresh bead, a new set of perspectives.

Chris LaLonde tackles what has come to be recognized as the postmodern turn in Native American writing. The pathway was early indicated in the work of Gerald Vizenor and has been followed by names like Louis Owens, Sherman Alexie, Gordon Henry Jr., and D. L. Birchfield. This development, in the words of Linda Hutcheon, affords "a new space for negotiating both identity and difference."[8] For Native writing, this use of the postmodern points to, indeed enacts, a subtle critique of what Vizenor has long indicted as the *indian* (lowercase and italicized) and perpetuated by the dominant culture. The boldly reflexive texts in play, on LaLonde's reckoning, give expression to historical elucidation and healing—not to say tribal-cultural particularity and their own kind of case for sovereignty.

Native poetry receives another pairing, two essays that respectively map the role of memory and of place, not to say their interaction. A. Robert Lee addresses both tribal and individual memory as calling upon new dynamics of voice, image, and design across a selection of writings by Simon Ortiz, Diane Glancy, Luci Tapahonso, Ray A. Young Bear, and Kimberly Blaeser. He argues for the ways in which, by reworking oral traditions as memorial templates— creation myths, trickster stories, songs, stories passed down the generations— along with first-person memory, these Native poets have made new of old, a memory of the present as well as of the past. The upshot has been a body of Native poetry which not only gives evidence of individual powers of imagining but helps augment the sense of a Native American literary renaissance overall. Memory, in these respects, becomes axial: the remembrance not just of time and place but of how the poet's enacting language itself stores and renews Native tradition.

The grounding of Native poetry in natural cycles and concepts of place, including sacred spaces and traditional tribal lands, is given interpretation by Kimberly Blaeser. At the beginning of the renaissance, Native poetry was firmly grounded in the attachment to geographical communities and to the common rhetorical representation of this placement. "We are the land" is the way Laguna-Sioux writer Paula Gunn Allen expressed this foundational understanding.[9] As time passed, various colonial interventions effected Native physical and spiritual displacements, and what Blaeser calls "this easy understanding of place" began to dissolve. Accordingly, in her account, Blaeser examines the shifting thematic and metaphorical relationship of Indian poets to tribal lands. Drawing examples from the work of poets from Linda Hogan to Heid Erdrich, from Simon Ortiz to Sherwin Bitsui, and from Marvin Francis to Joy Harjo, she investigates the ways writers both reimagine their relationship with historic homelands and with past colonial attempts at spatial confinement of Indians. She also reexamines popular conceptions of reservations and city-urban spaces.

Two other genres play alongside fiction and poetry. Native autobiography has won justified recognition for its importance in the formation of a Native

American literary canon. A. Robert Lee's essay seeks to convey both the span of modern life-writing and the virtuosity of some of its best practitioners. To that end, he first sets a context of the issues that have attended the writing of Native autobiography and the different formats in play, whether "as told to" lives, mixed-blood histories, political memoirs, media "Indian" self-portraiture, the brief essay-memoir, or the full-length self-portrait. The perspectives that so arise, from how Native life comports with modernity or the relationship of tribal community to the city and across the world's map, he refracts in close readings of six key texts by Momaday, Silko, Vizenor, Janet Campbell Hale, Carter Revard, and Jim Barnes. If emphasis falls upon the fashioning of discrete and different Native lives, it does so also in necessary recognition of legacy, the presence—wholly inerasable—of Native timeline and culture in the making of the life-writing to hand.

In her essay on Native drama, Gina Valentino argues that many of the features we associate with the Native American Renaissance were anticipated by American Indian drama. A crucial but understudied figure for understanding this legacy is Hanay Geiogamah. In part 1 of the essay, she examines the work of Geiogamah, the Native American Theater Ensemble, and Spiderwoman Theater in order to bring into focus how the dramatic currents of the Native Renaissance connect back to prior Native traditions of performance. In part 2 she explores the significant body of work that has emerged in recent years in Native American drama. One way to understand this development is to recognize that dramatic literature seems to escape the critiques leveled at Native fiction. Specifically, there has been a tendency to see novels and short stories as breaking with Native storytelling, however close the attempts to approximate that legacy. Dramatic texts (though also written), by contrast, require modes of oral and embodied performance that are more continuous with tribal traditions and rituals. Valentino concludes by exploring current trends in Native American theater, including the increasing role of technology, in the creation and dissemination of Native American performing arts.

The Native American Renaissance, rightly or not, has long been a term used to embrace Canada as much as the United States. David Stirrup, accordingly, gives focus to First Nations authors, Canadian Indian writers of fiction, drama, and poetry. He takes note of how tribal groups in North America have long preceded, and have always transcended, the invention of the nation-state with its arbitrary imposition of geographic boundaries. Yet very few major transborder studies of North American indigenous literatures exist. Stirrup's essay seeks to address these limitations by taking account of the burgeoning of writings across all genres by First Nations Canadian writers and thinkers. In doing so, he develops the parameters of Kenneth Lincoln's original thesis to consider the cross-border, hemispheric modalities of indigenous literary production in North America. Just as the conventional discourses of American literary nationalism are being unseated by the transnational frameworks of the "new" American studies, this essay confirms that indigenous writing in the Americas cannot be confined by nation-state ideologies. At the same time it argues that the *presence* of Native literatures, their rootedness in specific geographical and tribal-mythic territories itself, serves as brake to one of the bolder claims of the "new" dogma, that of "deterritorialized" cultural production. Stirrup's coverage looks to four broad categories—life-writing (James Sewid, Lee Maracle, Beth Brant), poetry (Rita Joe, Kateri Akiwenzie-Damm, Joan Crate), prose (Jeanette Armstrong, Eden Robinson), and drama (Tomson Highway, Drew Hayden Taylor, Waawaate Fobister, Daniel David Moses). In each case he takes a comparative approach to the intersections and departures, the "sameness and difference," of First Nations and Native American literatures.

We conclude the volume with a contribution, both personal and literary, from Kenneth Lincoln, whose *Native American Renaissance* first offered terms of reference, a touchstone. The controversies aroused by his study, with writers favored and others not, centered most of all on the critique voiced by Leslie Marmon Silko, Gerald Vizenor, Elizabeth Cook-Lynn, and a number of others that tribal cultures did not spring out of nowhere. Debate joined. On the one hand, what had happened to Native oral and written tradition prior to the canonization, however merited, of *House Made of Dawn*? On the other hand, how to account for the near-global currency of Native writers from Silko, Welch, Erdrich, or Tapahonso to Sherman Alexie and Sherwin Bitsui as subsequently argued for in Lincoln's *Speak Like Singing: Classics of Native American Literature* (2007)? Other critique has emerged, perhaps inevitably. Craig Womack takes on the case for a self-affirming Native aesthetic in *Red on Red: Native American Literary Separatism* (1999) and joins his cohorts Jace Weaver and Robert Warrior in *American Indian Literary Nationalism* (2006). Elizabeth Cook-Lynn trashes "reconciliation" between Natives and newcomers in *Anti-Indianism in Modern America: A Voice from Tatekaya's Earth* (2001).

Who, asks Lincoln, is best situated to read Native writers? Is it to be a domain of chosen privilege, readership by ethnic identity or history? How best for non-Native readerships to proceed? Is there a case for a spectrum of interactive reading communities—nationalist, cosmopolitan, even non-American? None of these questions yields easy resolution. But they underscore, in their cut and thrust, how resilient, and quite wholly ongoing, has been the Native/First Nations literary voice and with it a force of debate as to theory and interpretative reference and ideology. Whether the label "renaissance" does or does not best hold, there can be no doubt that it arises out of a proven truth: Native America's literary renewal marks a spirit of cultural offering for all the people.

NOTES

1. Cortez and Martinez, eds., *Indian Country Noir,* pp. 11–12.
2. Fererra, *Choctaw Revolution,* p. 56.
3. The National Indian Gaming Commission reports revenues of over $27.1 billion. The figure is for 2011, the most recent report available. www.nigc.gov/Gaming_Revenue_Reports.aspx.
4. Kidwell and Velie, *Native American Studies,* p. 61.
5. Weaver, *That the People Might Live,* p. 52.
6. The success of *House Made of Dawn,* initially published in hardback by Harper & Row, inspired Harpers to begin a Native American publishing program.
7. Owens, *I Hear the Train,* p. 250.
8. Hutcheon, "Postmodern Afterthoughts," p. 8.
9. Allen, "Iyana: It Goes This Way," in *The Remembered Earth,* p. 191.

WORKS CITED

Allen, Paula Gunn. "Iyana: It Goes This Way." In *The Remembered Earth: An Anthology of Contemporary Native American Literature.* Edited by Geary Hobson. Albuquerque: University of New Mexico Press, 1980.

Cortez, Sarah, and Liz Martinez, eds. *Indian Country Noir.* New York: Akashic Press, 2010.

Fererra, Peter J. *The Choctaw Revolution: Lessons for Federal Indian Policies.* Washington, D.C.: Americans for Tax Reform Foundation, 1998.

Hutcheon, Linda. "Postmodern Afterthoughts." *Wascana Review* 37:1 (2002).

Kidwell, Clara Sue, and Alan R. Velie. *Native American Studies.* Edinburgh: Edinburgh University Press, 2005.

Owens, Louis. *I Hear the Train: Reflections, Inventions, Refractions.* Norman: University of Oklahoma Press, 2001.

Weaver, Jace. *That the People Might Live: Native American Literatures and Native American Community.* New York: Oxford University Press, 1997.

1
Turning West
Cosmopolitanism and American Indian Literary Nationalism

JACE WEAVER

In 2001, the historian Daniel Richter published *Facing East from Indian Country: A Native History of Early America*. This important monograph examined how, in the first instance, North American indigenes might have attempted to come to terms with the scattered appearances of Europeans during the "Age of Discovery" and the possibility of a new, unknown world across the waters. He writes,

> Hard facts are very difficult to come by. . . . They probably heard mangled tales of strange newcomers long before they ever laid eyes on one in the flesh, and, when rare and novel items reached their villages through longstanding trade and communication, they discovered European *things* long before they confronted European *people*. Rumors and objects, not men and arms, were the means of discovery, and we can only imagine how Native imaginations made sense of the skimpy evidence that reached them."[1]

Richter then explores how, during the later colonial era, when the settler colonizers had firmly settled in, those same indigenous peoples sought to preserve the stability of the shaky and inherently unstable "middle ground"—to use Richard White's term—as they negotiated with and among European metropoles and their North American colonial avatars, even as they became, at the same time, increasingly integrated into the transatlantic economy.[2]

As Richter suggests, certainly since first contact the lives of many Native persons and peoples have been animated, circumscribed, even defined in relation to Europe and Amer-European settler colonizers. Natives have repeatedly been required to face east and react to Europeans, their cultures, their material goods, and their ideas. With the collapse of the middle ground and the rise of the United States as the dominant power in the center of the continent, Natives were encouraged—in many cases, forced—to assimilate into

American culture. The halting closure of the Indian Wars, the establishment of the reservation system, and the creation of boarding schools combined to formalize a system that had begun with the earliest Spanish *reducciones*, or New England "praying towns," or countless other missions: leave the blanket, learn English, embrace Christianity, and, in the process, swap your culture— Cherokee, Muskogee, Apache, Sioux, Comanche, whatever—for a prescribed Euro-Western alternative.

In the late twentieth and early twenty-first centuries, this dynamic again played itself out in a surprising venue—literature. Like Richter's Indians of the colonial era, who increasingly found themselves imbricated in transatlantic economic exchange, Native Americans were increasingly integrated into American economic, educational, and cultural systems even as they maintained the separate sovereignties, however clipped, of their tribal nations and their own cultural practices. Native oral traditions stretch back tens of thousands of years, and Natives have produced literatures written in English since 1763, often with great sophistication. The publication of N. Scott Momaday's novel *House Made of Dawn* in 1968, however, marked the beginning of what has been called the Native American Literary Renaissance, a term coined by Kenneth Lincoln.[3] In 1969, *House Made of Dawn* became the first and thus far only work by a Native American to win the Pulitzer Prize for fiction. There had been a flowering of Native writers in the 1930s. Lynn Riggs, D'Arcy McNickle, and John Joseph Mathews all produced important works. But the boomlet quickly faded. After Momaday's achievement, however, the doors of publishing houses seemed to open wide for Native authors. Through them walked Leslie Marmon Silko, Gerald Vizenor, Simon Ortiz, Joy Harjo, and many others who emerged as major figures in Native American literature. This time the boom did not subside.

The history limned briefly above is well known. What is less discussed is the reception of this literature and the development of criticism about it.

In 1969, Alan Velie became the first English professor in the country to teach a course in Native American literature, doing so at the behest of Indian students at the University of Oklahoma. More classes soon followed, there and elsewhere, and as scholar-readers taught, they read and recovered earlier texts, like those of McNickle and Mathews mentioned above. Early anthologies appeared—like Kenneth Rosen's *The Man to Send Rain Clouds* and *Voices of the Rainbow* and Geary Hobson's *The Remembered Earth*. The first critical work, Charles Larson's *American Indian Fiction*, was published in 1978. Four years later, Velie published *Four American Indian Literary Masters*, followed the next year by Lincoln's era-defining monograph. In 1985, Arnold Krupat served up *For Those Who Come After*. In the process of teaching, reading, and researching, these critics learned about Native cultures and histories. Other non-Natives who made forays into Native literature did not bother. Armed with the confidence of Matthew Arnold's disinterested readers, they thought they could "get at the truth" of the texts without understanding the places from whence they came.[4]

What was notably absent was the active engagement of Native voices. Paula Gunn Allen published her seminal essay, "The Sacred Hoop: A Contemporary Indian Perspective on American Indian Literature," in 1975, following it up with pieces like "A Stranger in My Own Life: Alienation in American Indian Prose and Poetry" (1980) and "'The Grace that Remains'—American Indian Women's Literature" (1981). Geary Hobson wrote a significant critical introduction to his 1979 anthology. And poet and scholar Simon Ortiz issued his compelling challenge, "Towards a National Indian Literature: Cultural Authenticity in Nationalism," in 1981. Yet literary criticism by Natives remained sporadic and spotty, and few non-Native critics, with the notable exceptions of Velie and Lincoln, responded to these Native scholars.

All of this changed radically in the 1990s. In 1992, in his book *Ethnocriticism*, Krupat wrote that "what might be called an 'indigenous' criticism for Indian literatures remains to be worked out."[5] That same year witnessed the publication of Louis Owens's monograph, *Other Destinies: Understanding the American Indian Novel*, and Jeannette Armstrong's edited volume, *Looking at the Words of Our People: First Nations Analysis of Literature*. From that time to the present, the number of Native American literary critics has grown seemingly exponentially every year. The dialogue between them and non-Native critics, on the one hand, and *among* them, on the other, has been spirited. With literary critical circles dominated by postmodernism, postcolonialism, and high theory, many of these new Indian critics felt that they were being "schooled" by non-Natives to continue facing East for their critical models and apparatuses.

During the last two decades, one of the most important debates has been between so-called nationalists and cosmopolitans. The argument has been lively and vociferous. It has also too often been acrimonious with, until recently, very little middle ground between the two sides.

In 1989, in his book *The Voice in the Margin: Native American Literature and the Canon*, Krupat argued that "the canon of American literature must substantially include the literary production of Native American and Afro-American peoples quite as well as those of the Euro-American peoples whose culture came to dominate the United States."[6] He thus made the case for inclusion of Native literature within the American canon. He drew distinctions among what he termed "local," "national," and "cosmopolitan" literatures. The *local* is traditional indigenous or ethnic literatures. *National* literatures are the sum total of all literary productions within the territory of given "national formations." *Cosmopolitan* literature is the totality of national literatures. For Krupat, both national and cosmopolitan literatures necessarily involve "a commitment to dialogism and heterodoxy." He follows Paul Rabinow in defining cosmopolitanism "as an ethos of macro-interdependencies, with an acute consciousness . . . of the inescapabilities and particularities of places, characters, historical trajectories, and fates."[7]

Seven years later, in *The Turn to the Native: Studies in Criticism and Culture*, Krupat wrote that "the sociopolitical values of cosmopolitanism" have been "opposed by some Native American critics whose pedagogical strategies make claims to cultural 'sovereignty' and 'autonomy,' the political implications of which strategies are nationalistic."[8] The trenches began to be dug in Flanders fields. To cosmopolitans, following postcolonial theorists like Homi K. Bhabha and Kwame Anthony Appiah, nationalism was cramped, rejectionist, and exclusionary as opposed to a liberal cosmopolitanism engaged in a globalized conversation.[9] Nationalism reified tribal identities where cosmopolitanism embraced the simple reality of modern cultural hybridity. To nationalists, cosmopolitanism erased tribal sovereignty in that it promoted a freewheeling, rootless postmodern identity. They were being told, they felt, to face East and salute once more. Not much room for common ground there.

The "Native American critics" to whom Krupat was referring in *The Turn to the Native* were principally Elizabeth Cook-Lynn and Robert Warrior. Cook-Lynn, one of the founding doyennes of Native American studies, is a poet, novelist, and literary critic. In her 1993 *Wicazo Sa Review* essay, "Cosmopolitanism, Nationalism, the Third World, and First Nation Sovereignty" (included in her 1996 book, *Why I Can't Read Wallace Stegner*), she declaims against cosmopolitanism and defends nationalism. She writes,

> [T]he violation of nationalistic or Third World models in fiction and criticism should be of legitimate concern to scholars and should become part of the discourse in literary theory as it is applied to the works of Native American writers. . . . Scholarship and art must say something about the real world, mustn't they? As Vine Deloria, Jr., asked the anthropologists in 1970, "Where were you when we needed you?" Indians may now ask of their writers, two decades later, "Where were you when we defended ourselves and sought clarification as sovereigns in the modern world?"[10]

Krupat considered the essay inaccurate and misguided. He nonetheless called it "the strongest and best account of the 'nationalist,' 'nativist,' and anti-'cosmopolitan' position. . . . [N]o supporter of the internationalist or cosmopolitan position should proceed without taking Cook-Lynn's arguments into account."[11]

Two years after Cook-Lynn's essay originally appeared, Robert Warrior published *Tribal Secrets: Recovering American Indian Intellectual Traditions*. A study in intellectual history, the compact monograph was arguably the first book-length intervention in American Indian literary nationalism. John Purdy, in his recent book, *Writing Indian, Native Conversations*, observes, "By

1995 . . . the discourse had expanded to include multiple generations of writers and scholars, and conditions were right for the reconsideration of the assumptions upon which much of the earlier criticism was based."[12]

Warrior compared Vine Deloria and Osage writer John Joseph Mathews on the issue of sovereignty and argued that Native Americans must look to their own internal intellectual resources. To emphasize the point, and as a political statement, he quoted Native writers and thinkers almost exclusively. His most significant contribution to the ongoing discourse in literary scholarship was his coining of the term "intellectual sovereignty." Warrior deliberately left the meaning of the phrase open-ended to "allow the definition and articulation of what that means to emerge as we critically reflect on that struggle [for intellectual sovereignty itself]."[13]

In *The Turn to the Native*, Krupat takes issue with Warrior's argument, pointing out that the twin subjects of his comparative study, Deloria and Mathews, were themselves cosmopolitans. He writes, "[S]urely the thought of Mathews and Deloria can no more be understood without reference to Euramerican tradition than can Warrior's." He continues:

> Further attention to Mathews and Deloria and to, perhaps, John Milton Oskison, Francis La Flesche, Gertrude Bonnin, and a great many other formidable Native American intellectuals might, at this historical juncture, be more important than continued attention to any of a number of non-Native intellectuals. But to consider these Native thinkers as "autonomous," "unique," "self-sufficient," or "intellectually sovereign"— as comprehensible apart from Western intellectualism—is simply not possible. Nor, if it were possible, would it be useful for the purposes claimed. As Appiah has poignantly written, "For us to forget Europe is to suppress the conflicts that have shaped our identities; since it is too late for us to escape each other, we might instead seek to turn to our advantage the mutual interdependencies history has thrust upon us."[14]

Krupat ignores or misses that Warrior himself declared in *Tribal Secrets*, "The framework I have suggested, finally, is not an attempt to define a critical discourse free from influences outside of American Indian experience. By following the path I have suggested here, though, I believe I am placing myself in the same position as every American Indian person who struggles to find a way toward a self-determined future."[15]

In 1997, I entered the fray with *That the People Might Live: Native American Literatures and Native American Community*, a study of Native written literatures in English from 1768 to the present. Building on Warrior's work, I focused on the relationships of Native writers to Native communities. To interrogate these relationships, I coined the word "communitism." I wrote, "Central to this study is the concept of communitism. . . . Communitism is related to Vizenor's 'survivance,' Warrior's 'intellectual sovereignty,' and Georges

Sioui's 'autohistory.' Its coining, however, is necessary because none of these terms from Native intellectuals nor any word from the Latin root *communitas* carries the exact sense implied by this neologism. It is formed by a combination of the words 'community' and 'activism.' Literature is communitist to the extent that it has a proactive commitment to Native community."[16]

Unlike Warrior, I did not refrain from engaging non-Native critics and thinkers. In particular, I both employed and critiqued critical theory. Like Warrior, however, I said that Native American critics must look first to internal American Indian sources. Alan Velie accused me of "pluralist separatism."[17]

The following year, Craig Womack published *Red on Red: Native American Literary Separatism*. Reviewing it in *American Literature*, Patricia Penn Hilden called it "a brave, controversial, and rich argument in favor of establishing a new Native American literary scholarship, driven by Native concerns and written either by Native scholars or by those with language skills, cultural knowledge, and respect that non-Natives must possess if they are to assist with this project."[18] Womack not only argued for drawing upon internal critical sources but went further, arguing for privileging internal readings of Native literature. Largely examining literature produced by Muscogee writers, Womack, himself Muscogee, rejected postmodernism and high theory, arguing instead for tribally specific criticism.

Though Womack did not cite either *Tribal Secrets* or *That the People Might Live*, *Red on Red* was consonant with those works. Those three books came to be seen as a kind of unspoken literary nationalist trilogy, and the three of us were viewed as a troika, the "three W's" of Native American literature, as Clara Sue Kidwell called us.[19] Perhaps because of his advocacy of tribalcentric readings, perhaps because he used the word "separatism" in his title, perhaps because of his barbed, often satirical, style—maybe due to all three—Womack's book seemed to provoke the angriest response from cosmopolitan critics. Indicative of that response is Robert Dale Parker who, in his *The Invention of Native American Literature*, writes, "Just as I do not find Womack's arguments for essentialism convincing or well informed about critical debates around essentialism, so I cannot abide his implication that non-Native critics cannot contribute helpfully to the discussion of Native American literature."[20] As I have written, I do not read *Red on Red* (or anything else Womack has produced) this way: rather I see him as saying simply that in reading literature—of any group—one should privilege internal cultural readings.[21] That does not mean that non-Native critics cannot enter the conversation: it simply means that critics—Native and non-Native—are obliged to consider particular tribal perspectives. It was not Womack's implication but Parker's own highly charged inference.

Because of the close intellectual affinity among our positions and our personal friendships, it was perhaps inevitable that Womack, Warrior, and I would collaborate on a project. That eventuated with *American Indian Literary Nationalism*. The catalyst was Elvira Pulitano's *Toward a Native American*

Critical Theory. Pulitano examined the work of six Native American literary critics—Paula Gunn Allen, Robert Warrior, Craig Womack, Greg Sarris, Gerald Vizenor, and her former professor Louis Owens. The first three she groups as nationalists, and the latter three she denominated as "dialogic." Though she professed to admire the work of all six of her subjects, she obviously preferred the dialogists for their cosmopolitanism. She rebuked her three nationalists for their refusal to face East and engage high theory. She also accused them of essentialism and promoting romantic, purist notions of "Indianness," since they are inextricably imbricated in Western culture and academic discourse. She challenged them to admit and embrace their hybridity. She lumped Warrior and Womack together as being "tribalcentric," despite the patent fact that Warrior was not—unless the term stood in for her as a proxy for "nationalist." She wrote:

> While their work makes an interesting contribution to the overall field of Native American critical theory, their position remains problematic, eliciting severe criticism from those who reject Nativist or nationalistic ideologies. In the attempt to isolate and define a kind of Native American intellectualism rigidly based on an Indian perspective, Warrior and Womack produce a critical strategy that ultimately collapses back in on itself because of failed logic, internal contradictions, and linguistic inconsistencies. By envisioning a Native American theory exclusively grounded in indigenous categories, the product of a unitary, a priori given identity, both critics seem to overlook the complex level of hybridization and cultural translation that is already operating in any form of Native discourse (including their own)—the product of more than five hundred years of cultural contact and interaction.[22]

Such sentiments, though perhaps seeming naïve to anyone familiar with Native American community, mark her as a student of Owens and his particular brand of cosmopolitanism. Unlike her mentor, however, she assumed a prescriptive attitude.

I was not implicated—presumably because I had engaged and employed high theory while maintaining a nationalist position. As Stuart Christie (also a student of Owens) writes, "I [Christie] am . . . not alone in embracing a pluralist approach to an iron-clad indigenous sovereignty. For more than a decade or more, Jace Weaver has been a forceful and articulate proponent of indigenous nationalism, all the while asserting the tenability of a pluralist position."[23] Although I was not a subject of Pulitano's chiding, I felt that a response was needed. I contacted Womack and Warrior, suggesting we collaborate on a book arguing for literary nationalism. The result was *American Indian Literary Nationalism* (the title and the term were Womack's). Our inspiration was Simon Ortiz's challenge in his 1981 essay.

In my introductory chapter to the book, I attempted to show the contours of a literary criticism based on internally derived sources—a turning West—while at the same time not erecting impermeable barriers to outside influences. As Ortiz says, in describing an Acqumeh (Acoma) ceremony celebrating a Catholic saint's day, there is an "overtone" of "Christian ritual celebration," but it is nonetheless an Acqumeh ceremony. He writes, "This is so because this celebration speaks of the creative ability of Indian people to gather in many forms of the socio-political colonizing force which beset them and to make these forms meaningful in their own terms."[24] Or, as Richter says of trade goods in *Facing East*, "As consumers . . . Indians used imported goods in ways rooted in their own rather than European cultures; they were no more decultured by trade than were twentieth-century North Americans who purchased Japanese televisions."[25]

I employed Warrior's rhetorical strategy from *Tribal Secrets*, offering up the term "American Indian literary nationalism" as a kind of empty vessel into which meaning would be poured through dialogue among sympathetic nationalist critics. I invited discussion. While averring that "the final definition of American Indian Literary Nationalism must await a collaborative effort beyond the four corners of [that] book," I did offer some of its elements: (1) it takes as a given settler colonialism; (2) it defends Native literature as a separate discourse and resists incorporation in or appropriation by a national canon; (3) it attempts to serve the goal of tribal national sovereignty. Later, I suggested that nationalist criticism should contribute to the creation of a "new human person"—a new *indigenous* person, speaking of it by pursuing a *via negativa*, that is to say, defining it by what it is not: The new human person we wish to upbuild is (1) not one who pursues an individualistic agenda without commitment to Native people and the ongoing sovereignty of Native nations; (2) not a victim; (3) not one who romanticizes "some halcyon pre-Contact culture and existence"; and (4) not an anti-intellectual. Finally, I wrote that "American Indian Literary Nationalism, which takes seriously Native sovereignty and survivance [to use Gerald Vizenor's term], has indigenous self-determination at its core and decolonization, survival, recovery, development, and transformation in its penumbra."[26]

If I was somewhat oblique in my contribution, Craig Womack was more straightforward. He directly critiqued Pulitano's text in detail, and he did not prescind from defining American Indian literary nationalism. In his second chapter, he offered and discussed ten "flexible tenets for a compassionate American Indian literary nationalism," "a set of principles open to further discussion." In brief, these ten precepts were as follows:

- Literary nationalism can do local work with global implications, thus demonstrating a more profound cosmopolitanism than has been argued for to date.

- Our criticism can grow, and we can learn to interrogate each other's work as much as we celebrate it, while keeping up such a discussion at the level of ideas rather than personal attacks.
- A compassionate criticism, gathering people back together, seats them at the table, feeds them, and they, in turn, give something back.
- Critics can recognize the validity of the work of those who have chosen to work within tribes as much as those seeking to establish Native literature as part of broader multicultural movements in the United States.
- The compassionate nationalist cannot simply walk away from things that are killing us in Native communities.
- A compassionate literary nationalism makes religious studies a key feature of its interests.
- A compassionate literary nationalism must engage in challenging historical work.
- The American Indian literary nationalist serves double duty as an activist.
- Literary nationalists need to demonstrate more close reading strategies.
- We need to scrutinize theory based on what we *do* as much as what we say and write.[27]

In his chapter, Robert Warrior argued for the value of critics to Native community. He did so through what he described as an "intellectual memoir," reflecting on the classes he had with the late Palestinian intellectual, Edward Said, when he was in graduate school.[28] He discussed the impact of Said and those two courses on his work, particularly *Tribal Secrets*. The title of his contribution, "Native Critics in the World," was an homage to Said's book *The World, the Text, and the Critic*.

Central to Warrior's piece is his argument "that dissent is perhaps the primary sign of good health in nationalist discourse," a position he finds "articulated most compellingly by Said."[29] In the chapter he offers critiques of the varied nationalisms of Native scholars and writers Taiaiake Alfred, Laura Tohe, Eva Garroutte, and Spero Manson.[30] Then, in keeping with his support of dissent, he declares, "[F]ollowing Said, I think of myself as a nationalist and a critic, but I don't put the two together. This is a distinction that I am not certain I share with my co-authors, nor do I suspect that it will be well received by some people whom I consider allies in Native Studies."[31]

It is true that some have been critical of Warrior for seeming to want to have it both ways, making such a declaration in a volume announcing "American Indian Literary Nationalism." One should, however, take him at his word: he states that "in deploying this formulation I am not seeking to give comfort and aid to those who would make critical discourse a place devoid of politics."[32] He is simply exercising the dissent he advocates and opting out: he is a nationalist but not a literary nationalist.

American Indian Literary Nationalism received hot fire from those in the nonnationalist trenches. Kenneth Lincoln, first in *Indian Country Today* and then in his book *Speak Like Singing*, decried "purist bloods, ethnic nationalists or academic essentialists," asking, "Aren't these attitudes so many self-defensive gripes or academic rumbles or career aggrandizements, rather than rez issues of land, language, sovereignty, spirit and cultural survival?" Though couched ostensibly as a review of *Red on Red* (nine years after its publication), the original *Indian Country Today* article was clearly sparked by our joint book, published a few months earlier. In both the newspaper piece and *Speak Like Singing*, he wrote, "For ongoing polemics of the drummed up culture wars—debates over real and virtual Natives, rez and academic Indians, oral and literary texts, self-determination and multi-culturalism—see Robert Warrior, Jace Weaver, and Craig S. Womack's recent *American Indian Literary Nationalism* . . . essentially an attack on 'outsider' Elvira Pulitano's *Toward a Native American Critical Theory*."[33]

Criticism of our work by non-Native critics often centered on our efforts to exclude non-Natives from literary criticism of Native literature specifically and Native American studies generally. Helen May Dennis, in her 2007 book *Native American Literature: Towards a Spatialized Reading*, writes:

> While Arnold Krupat has led the field in advocating a cosmopolitan criticism of Native American texts, Nativist intellectuals have argued stridently for a separatist position. I respect the case for a strong tradition of Native literary criticism, and understand why Robert Allen Warrior and Jace Weaver, among others, call for the development of an autonomous Native American intellectual community. European by birth and inclination, I could never pretend to participate in this essential project. At the same time I would feel dismay if the movement towards establishing intellectual sovereignty for America's First Nations were to preclude me from reading published novels. Common sense tells me that my acts of reading and interpretation contribute to a larger sense of community that implicitly supports the current work of Nativist scholars.[34]

In his *Indian Country Today* review, Lincoln was more forceful. Calling the debate between nationalists and nonnationalists, "an academic civil war," he wrote:

> Regardless of motive, xenophobia defeats Native and American cultural discourse.
> Talking stink, as they say on the streets, fouls the common air people share exploring mutually sovereign literacy. Beyond Indian country, can only a Mississippi sharecropper understand race relations in

William Faulkner, an Ohio black singly get local dialect in Toni Morrison or a New Jersey shopkeeper exclusively scan the variable foot of William Carlos Williams? Using cultural monopoly for private witness rules out any other tribal classics than one's own, including the Bible and the Great White Roots of Peace, Homer and the Code of Handsome Lake, Dante and the Popol Vuh, and Shakespeare and the Blessingway Ceremony. Do Native writers want to be appreciated by audiences inside and outside their own kin, or misunderstood behind the screen of separatist privilege?[35]

He concludes by quoting Louis Owens: "The descendant of mixed blood sharecroppers and the dispossessed of two continents, I believe I am the rightful heir of Choctaw and Cherokee storytellers and of Shakespeare and Yeats and Cervantes. Finally, everything converges and the center holds in the margins. This, if we are to go on."[36]

I must confess to being mystified by such reactions. It is true that in *American Indian Literary Nationalism*, I note that "if we assert American Indian Literary Nationalism, there are those critics who will accuse us of a destructive separatism and an effort to suppress all other voices." Just a few pages before, however, I write:

Let me be explicit and I hope (for the last time) coruscatingly clear: I have never said, nor have I ever heard any responsible Native scholar say, that non-Natives should not do Native American studies, much less the study of Native American literature, any more than Natives should prescind from bringing their own insights to literature by anyone else. (The late Louis Owens was, among his other accomplishments as a creative writer and critic of Native literature, a talented Steinbeck scholar.) It is not our intent simply to superinduce Native scholars for white ones. . . . We *want* non-Natives to read, engage, and study Native literature. The survival of Native authors, if not Native people in general, depends on it.[37]

We took issue with Pulitano's book, not because she was an "outsider," but because as a non-Native with no ties to the community she presumed to prescribe how Native critics should do their work. She failed to show the restraint that Helen May Dennis did. As Taiaiake Alfred states, "Our deference to other people's solutions has taken a terrible toll on indigenous peoples."[38]

Other than Lincoln, perhaps the most strident criticism came from Brewster Fitz in his review in *American Indian Culture and Research Journal*. Of my chapter, he writes, "Assuming a voice that blends the preacher and the lawyer, Weaver skillfully . . . attempt[s] to persuade his congregation of readers that they shall not commit the sin of postmodern high theory." Though, of course,

I say nothing of the sort.[39] Doubting my sincerity in stating that Native scholars want non-natives to read and engage Native literature, he cites the passage quoted above, but then notes that I go on to say Native critics don't need "literary *colonizers.*" He italicizes that word for emphasis, though I do not. He continues, "By metaphorically designating the unneeded and unwanted literary theorists as 'literary colonizers,' Weaver opens this allegedly 'coruscatingly clear' statement to readers' inferences about what constitutes literary colonialism. Is it possible for a non-Native scholar or critic to put forward ideas and interpretations based on theoretical understandings of oral and written language that differ from those of Weaver, Womack, and Warrior, without opening herself to the charges being a literary colonizer?"[40] A close reading of my chapter reveals that the answer is clearly, "Yes." As I have stated above, what we object to is simply being dictated to as to methods and sources. "Which is it?" he seems to be asking: "Do you want non-Natives studying Native literature or do you reject literary overseers?" Is the position of literary overseer one to which Fitz aspires?

Referring to the interdisciplinary nature of the scholarship in the book, Fitz concludes, "Owing to their rhetoric, in which religion, politics, law, literature, and criticism are inseparably interwoven, it becomes difficult not to liken their own nationalist discourse to the very ethnocentric colonial discourse they see as misguided." At the end of his review, however, he makes the Nazi analogy. Discussing Lisa Brooks's afterword, he points out that she was educated and teaches in the Ivy League and is the progeny of both Abenakis and a Polish mother who survived the Nazi labor camps. He then writes:

Seemingly the perfect incarnation of the mixed-blood hybridism against which the book inveighs, Brooks favors instead the concepts of self-contained, totally indigenous culture and nationalist literary sovereignty. She rejects poststructuralist thought. Probably alluding to the crimes against humanity committed under German *Nazionalsozialismus* and to the murderous Anglo-American nationalist expansion under manifest destiny, she "admit[s] that talk of nationalism makes [her] wary." Implicit in her essay, however, and in the other essays in this book, is the argument that not all nationalisms are the same and that not all nationalisms give birth to abominable crimes against humanity. In other words, just because some indigenous writers refer to concepts like blood memory, one cannot automatically infer that the literary nationalism espoused by the coauthors of this book is informed by a troubling ideology like that of *Blut und Boden*, which is the German expression for the racist, essentialist, and warlike National Socialist (Nazi) ideology that led to so much bloodshed during World War II. Nevertheless, there are disturbing signs that these five nationalist critics have not understood that the linguistic, literary, and cultural theory that informs their writings is quite similar to that which informs the thought of conservative literary and historical scholars who not only reject high theory but also reject cultural studies of all sorts.[41]

"One cannot *automatically* infer" that literary nationalists are informed by an ideology like that animating Nazism? *Really*? Is *American Indian Literary Nationalism* the literary critical equivalent of *Mein Kampf*? In his defense of troops in the cosmopolitan trenches of Lincoln's academic civil war, Fitz deploys the heavy armor. But it is clear that it is he who has gone "over the top."[42]

Certainly, not every Native American critic is a literary nationalist as Warrior's and Owens's examples—among others—attest. Shari Huhndorf offers a mixed, but largely critical, reading of *American Indian Literary Nationalism* in her review in *American Literature*.[43] In 2006, David Treuer produced *Native American Fiction: A User's Guide*. Treuer, a creative writer with a doctorate in anthropology, correctly argues that one should not look to Native literature for ethnography. He then goes on to use the New Criticism of the early to mid-twentieth century, as exemplified by writers like T. S. Eliot and R. P. Blackmur, to examine Native literary works as self-contained aesthetic creations, focusing on Sherman Alexie, Louise Erdrich, Leslie Silko, and James Welch. John Purdy, in *Writing Indian*, notes the impulse of both students and writers to believe no one before them has had the same insights. With Treuer's book, he writes, "[W]e found ourselves back in critical terrain familiar to [Charles] Larson [in 1978]: trying to define how this canon is distinct and where it is located within a wider aesthetic of Western literary history."[44]

One on the most gratifying outcomes of our work, however, has been the rise of a second generation of literary nationalist critics like Lisa Brooks, Daniel Justice, Sean Teuton, and Tol Foster. It also includes simpatico young, non-Native critics like James Cox, whose 2006 book, *Muting White Noise*, was very much in the nationalist vein. These scholars build upon and extend our work, contributing to and fulfilling the challenge to help define American Indian literary nationalism.

Acutely aware in writing *American Indian Literary Nationalism* that we were three males, and at the gentle prodding of Simon Ortiz, we wanted to include a woman's voice. We asked Abenaki literary scholar Lisa Brooks to contribute an afterword (just as Ortiz provided a foreword). While performing the function of an afterword, her piece went much further. It was itself a full contribution, as she announced herself as a literary nationalist critic in her own right. Her much-discussed "At the Gathering Place" used the metaphor of conversations around a kitchen table, where there is honest give-and-take. Drawing upon her own heritage, she wrote, "[T]he activity of nation-building, in the Abenaki sense, is not a means of boundary-making but rather a process of gathering from within." She admitted, as Fitz points out, "that talk of nationalism" made her wary but that American Indian literary nationalism was "a dynamic model that posits the existence of a field of Native American literature" and advocates (though not exclusively) for scholarship drawing upon Native experience and epistemologies. She envisioned

> a nationalism that is not based on the theoretical and physical models of the nation-state; a nationalism that is not based on notions of nativism or binary oppositions between insider and outsider, self and other; a nationalism that does not root itself in an idealization of any pre-Contact past, but rather relies on the multifaceted, lived experience of families that gather in particular places; a nationalism that may be unlike any of those with which most literary critics and cultural theorist are familiar.

She concluded, "American Indian Literary Nationalism is a model that does not view knowledge as something to be gathered within a vessel and preserved, or as a process of steady accumulation, of ever-growing accuracy or progress. Rather this gathering relies on a process of exchange, which will constantly shape and change the state of the field."[45] She continued to articulate these concerns and values in her 2008 book, *The Common Pot: The Recovery of Native Space in the Northeast.*

Daniel Heath Justice followed Womack in pursuing tribally specific scholarship. His 2006 *Our Fire Survives the Storm* examined Cherokee literature, particularly in regards to its treatment of Removal. He stated:

> To ground one's work within Indigenous ways of knowing is not a necessarily exclusivist act that seeks an idealized cultural purity. . . . Intellectual sovereignty doesn't presume an insistence on tribal-centered scholarship as the *exclusive* model of sensitive or insightful analysis. It does, however, privilege an understanding of community as being important to a nuanced reading of the text. This notion is something rarely questioned in other areas of inquiry—after all, historical and cultural context is generally seen as essential in any substantive understanding of Shakespeare's plays—but the reactionary howl of "essentialism" rises up when we try to apply similar methods to minority literatures.[46]

Sean Teuton, also Cherokee, published *Red Land, Red Power: Grounding Knowledge in the American Indian Novel* in 2008. The book examined the literature of the movement years of the late sixties and early seventies. Like others in the American Indian literary nationalist movement, Teuton rejected seeing these works as ethnostalgia for a halcyon Indian past. Instead, he articulated what he termed "tribal realism." In developing his theory, he drew upon the "postpositivist realism" of Satya Mohanty as a means "to understand minority literatures and serve political action."[47]

Teuton calls "the realist approach to knowledge, identity, and experience" a "trade language." In former times, trade jargons or trade argots enabled both Europeans and Natives to engage in commerce and diplomacy. Teuton explains:

As an Indian scholar, I still rely on trade languages. Like the currency attending wampum or treaties, trade languages enable us to communicate across cultural differences and to trade in intellectual capital, without diminishing our cultural autonomy or "authenticity." The English language has become a trade language, adopted by a vast number of people who wish to trade items and ideas—with no concomitant reduction in their cultural viability. In this book, I draw on a theoretical trade language called "realist theory" in order to exchange ideas with other scholars. My adaptation of this alternative theoretical position, however, does not weaken my tribal viewpoint; in fact, realism might even help expand my intellectual views to strengthen Native critical practice.[48]

In so speaking, Teuton makes an argument consonant with those of Ortiz or Richter, cited above. Or my own in *American Indian Literary Nationalism*. Teuton hopes his approach will answer Elizabeth Cook-Lynn's demand for "a First Nations intellectually based politics," based on the call of the First Convocation of American Indian Scholars in 1970 "for the development by Indians of bodies of Indigenous knowledge." He concludes, "To justify this development, scholars must be theoretically equipped to make normative claims."[49]

Tol Foster describes himself as a "Native regionalist."[50] In the spring of 2008, he published an article about my work in the journal *American Literary History*, entitled "Against Separatism: Jace Weaver and the Call for Community." Taking on the opponents of American Indian literary nationalism, he called the "fear that prioritization of indigenous critical and historical contexts in reading indigenous texts amounts to a repudiation of multiculturalism, or a retrenchment from critical theory to a position of essentialism" as "so overblown." He continued:

What is baffling is the is the misrecognition of scholars . . . that the identity wars they forward have been laid to rest by *That the People Might Live*. Before this book, monographs and articles in the field centered around debates over authenticity and mixed-bloodedness, belonging and dislocation. From Leslie Marmon Silko's attack on Louise Erdrich to Elizabeth Cook-Lynn's attack on Louis Owens, the critical moment seemed obsessed, like the title of Owens's 1997 book *Mixedblood Messages: Literature, Film, Family, Place*, with articulations of *individual* tribal identity, an exercise of little validity once Weaver placed readings of Native concerns back in the realm of the *political* rather than *racialist* concerns.[51]

As personally flattering as that is, Foster underestimates Warrior and the rhetorical moves he makes in *Tribal Secrets*. Nevertheless, Foster was correct in averring that it was my intention that *That the People Might Live* mark a "shift back to politics and history from the cultural and anthropological focus of Paula Gunn Allen's seminal book *The Sacred Hoop* . . . and the focus on mixedblood protagonist individuality in Louis Owens's *Other Destinies*."[52]

Despite his self-ascribed regionalist label, Foster maintains a rigorous literary nationalism, arguing that American Indian literature must be viewed as "something more than a convenient multiculturalist Other to the whitestream or a sad ghetto of mixedbloods neither tribal nor white, so hybridized that their relation to tribal identity can be dismissed as ethnic nostalgia." Parting ways with Teuton, he writes, "This has been an ongoing concern of indigenous scholars—our allies seem not to have much from the theory larder that is of any sustenance in resisting colonialism. Thus Weaver has doggedly engaged in two responses: to dig deeper and to strike out for a uniquely indigenist approach." He concludes that, although American Indian literary nationalist scholars "are accused of separatism, their work demonstrates that it is colonialism and the indifference born of asymmetrical power relationships which separate us, not the articulation and scrutiny of indigenous principles."[53] As of this writing, Foster is completing a book manuscript entitled, "The Enduring Indian Territory: Oklahoma Writers and the Relational Frontier in the Twentieth Century." Among the figures studied are John Joseph Mathews, Will Rogers, Melvin Tolson, Ralph Ellison, and Woody Guthrie.

Despite isolated hostile reactions to *American Indian Literary Nationalism*, even before its appearance in 2006 the lines between the two sides in Lincoln's "academic civil war" were beginning to shift, and trenches were beginning to be abandoned. In *Red Matters* in 2002, it seemed, Arnold Krupat's position began to soften. He declared that the cosmopolitan critic needs the nationalist critic.[54] The publication of our book only accelerated the process. Today, Krupat considers himself fully sympathetic with the literary nationalist project.[55] In *American Indian Literary Nationalism*, Warrior calls it "one of the enduring lessons" he learned reading Said's *The World, the Text, and the Critic*: "That was the idea that it was possible to be a critic, a nationalist, a cosmopolitan, and a humanist all at the same time."[56] And non-Native scholar Stuart Christie, in his book, *Plural Sovereignties and Contemporary Indigenous Literature*, while not going so far as to embrace the literary nationalist agenda, nonetheless admitted, "I, like Pulitano, was a student (and happily so) of Owens. Yet I . . . read the contemporary resurgence of literary nationalism as a probably necessary correction, on the part of materialist critics [as opposed to the constructivism of Owens's followers] who have witnessed the field and its discourses drifting too far from specific communities, their struggles and sovereign sites of resistance."[57]

In fact, the territory between the trenches of cosmopolitanism and literary nationalism and between non-Native and Natives has never been the uncrossable critical "No Man's Land" that some have portrayed it. There have always been those in both camps willing to mingle in that interstitial space. In the spring of 2006, prior to the publication of *American Indian Literary Nationalism*, the Institute of Native American Studies at the University of Georgia hosted "Native American Literature: Nationalism and Beyond," the first conference organized on the subject. The event was jointly keynoted by Simon Ortiz and Joy Harjo. Among the Native scholars in attendance were Robert Warrior, Craig Womack, Lisa Brooks, LeAnne Howe, Lee Maracle, Daniel Justice, and myself. Yet also speaking were Alan Velie, James Cox, and Michael Elliott. Literary nationalism has always been a commodious tent. As I wrote at the conclusion of my chapter in *American Indian Literary Nationalism*:

> We do not see American Indian Literary Nationalism so much as erecting ramparts that must be defended [to continue the martial metaphors] as offering a permeable barrier, neither Veil nor Buckskin Curtain. As an approach that supports sovereignty, it is broad enough to encompass not only Warrior, Womack, and Weaver, but also scholars as disparate [as] Elizabeth Cook-Lynn, Paula Gunn Allen, Gerald Vizenor, Geary Hobson, LeAnne Howe, Jack Forbes, and Daniel Justice, to name only a few. To be sure, we have our disagreements, but they are our own, and that's the point. It can also include sympathetic non-Natives like Elaine Jahner and James Cox, to single out only two. American Indian Literary Nationalism is a set of critical strategies, growing out of the concerns and issues of Natives themselves, that is equally as applicable to analysis of Cooper, Faulkner, and Wiebe as it is to Momaday, Silko, and Sherman Alexie. American Indian Literary Nationalism is separatist, but it is a pluralist separatism. We are splitting the earth, not dividing up turf.[58]

In the above recitation of scholars whom American Indian literary nationalism encompasses is Gerald Vizenor. Among Native Americans, there is no more erudite or cosmopolitan critic than Vizenor. No one is more conversant with critical theory or more adept at deploying it. Yet he is also a nationalist. He has authored the draft constitution for the White Earth Nation of Anishinaabeg; there is no greater act of literary nationalism. In his creative writing, criticism, and activism, he also demonstrates himself to be a nationalist. As I discuss in both *That the People Might Live* and in *American Indian Literary Nationalism*, in his writings Vizenor champions mixed-bloods, but he champions them *as Native* not as "hybrids," and he criticizes Larson for engaging in essentialism as he posits a descent from a racially pure past. In that same body of work, he also champions tribal sovereignty.

The work of the younger scholars discussed above also illustrates clearly that there is no unbridgeable gulf (to shift away from the military) between cosmopolitans and nationalists. Daniel Justice demonstrates that the Beloved Path of accommodation and cooperation advocated by Nancy Ward and the "Chickamauga consciousness" of "physical and/or rhetorical defiance" exemplified by her cousin Dragging Canoe are reciprocal—quite literally an intrafamilial squabble.[59] Sean Teuton uses critical theory, but he does so in service of a nationalist agenda. Tol Foster, with his self-assigned appellation of "tribal regionalist," focuses on the interconnections and interrelationships among tribal peoples and their nontribal neighbors, both African American and Amer-European. And he writes of me, "If we actually *read* Weaver, the concern is toward *greater* cosmopolitanism and *greater* engagement, not less."[60]

Manifestly, I have been identified—including self-identification—as a nationalist, and, unlike Warrior, I link my nationalism with my criticism. I am a literary nationalist. Yet, as Foster points out, I am also in favor of cosmopolitanism. In my current project, without apology, I take a hard cosmopolitan turn. In early 2011, I published an article in *American Indian Quarterly* entitled, "The Red Atlantic: Transoceanic Cultural Exchanges," as part of a special issue I edited on the state of Native American/American Indian studies.[61] The "Red Atlantic" is an obvious corrective to Atlantic World studies in general and Paul Gilroy's "Black Atlantic" in particular, both of which have tended to ignore the participation of indigenes of the Americas in the Atlantic world. The piece examines the movement of Native wealth, technology, commodities, and Native persons themselves around the Atlantic basin. I define a "Red Atlantic" as stretching from the year 1000 C.E., when Norsemen landed in Vinland, until 1927, when Lindbergh's flight ushered in an era of travel that changed forever how people interacted with that body of water.

That article is part of a larger monograph, which is currently under contract with the University of North Carolina Press. The Institute of Native American Studies at the University of Georgia prides itself on being a place where cutting-edge ideas in Native American studies are discussed first. In November 2010, as it had with American Indian literary nationalism, it organized the first conference on this new concept. Arnold Krupat keynoted. An edited volume has grown out of that event, edited by Coll Thrush and me.

Indigeneity is about rootedness in place. Yet Natives in motion around the Atlantic basin provide us with examples of radical mobility. Indians crossed the Atlantic as captives, slaves, diplomats, sailors, soldiers, entertainers, and tourists—sometimes in multiple roles—and in numbers that are surprising to many. Many became cosmopolitans in the process. Both "The Red Atlantic" and the forthcoming book demonstrate once again that the space between nationalism and cosmopolitanism is not as wide as some have contended. Case studies of figures like Oconostota, Attakullakulla, Joseph Brant, Paul Cuffe, and Garcilaso de la Vega demonstrate that these Red cosmopolitans used the intellectual and material tools they acquired by their participation in the Atlantic world for nationalist ends—much like Simon Ortiz's Acqumeh syncretic religious ceremony or Sean Teuton's realism.

In old legal procedure—to put on momentarily another of my professional hats—there was a pleading called a demurrer. By it, a party to an adjudication objected (demurred) to the case presented by the opposing side, admitting generally the facts of the opposition's argument but claiming that they do not sustain the argument itself.[62] Normally, a demurrer only had recourse to evidence presented by the opposing side. There was, however, a specific demurrer known as a "speaking demurrer." Such an objection required the aid of facts not already pleaded. The party, under such a circumstance, was thus permitted to allege the existence of facts not already so pleaded.[63]

What many non-Native critics apparently find difficult to believe is that the demurrer of literary nationalist critics is, in fact, a speaking demurrer. Their charge against us is that we are obdurately rejectionist: we refuse to acknowledge the simple fact of our own hybridity; we absolutely refuse to engage critical theory; we seek to preempt non-Natives and exclude them from the conversation entirely. To plead their case, they cherry-pick. They engage in cramped readings and selective citations. Yet the evidence does not sustain their claim. They do not understand that in our turn to the West we are not turning our backs totally on the East. We are not struthiously closing our eyes and ears and pretending it does not exist. Our objection—our demurrer—is to being prescribed and proscribed in our scholarship.

We recognize the reality of hybridity. Yet we also assert the reality and validity of indigenous sovereignty and through our work seek to support it. We may be separatist. But our separatism is a pluralist separatism or, if you will, an agonistic pluralism. We recognize that we must all live together in this place we share despite our differences. That space is both geographic and academic. We acknowledge this. Do non-Native critics? Or, like the commanders of armies during the Great War after the Christmas truce of 1914, would those who would be literary overseers just have everyone return to the trenches? I would remind everyone that all that followed was four more years of pointless war and more than nine million military dead.

In asserting American Indian literary nationalism, we seek to rely on our own internal cultural resources and draw upon outside theory as we determine useful. We seek simply to drink from our own wells and to share the dipper with friends and those who would be our friends.

NOTES

1. Richter, *Facing East from Indian Country*, p. 11.
2. Ibid., p. 150ff. See also White, *Indians, Empires, and Republics*, p. 50.
3. Actually, Lincoln's book was called *Native American Renaissance*.
4. Arnold, *Mixed Essays*, p. 242.

5. Krupat, *Ethnocriticism*, pp. 44, 186. By "Indian literature," Krupat meant traditional orature, excluding poetry and fiction written in English for publication.

6. Krupat, *Voice in the Margin*, p. 202.

7. Ibid., pp. 198, 202, 215.

8. Krupat, *Turn to the Native*, p. 25.

9. *See,* for example, Appiah, *Cosmopolitanism*, pp. xiv–xv.

10. Cook-Lynn, "Cosmopolitanism, Nationalism, the Third World, and First Nation Sovereignty"; reprinted as "American Indian Fiction Writers" in Cook-Lynn, *Why I Can't Read Wallace Stegner*, pp. 82–83.

11. Krupat, *Turn to the Native*, pp. 3–4.

12. Purdy, *Writing Indian*, Kindle ed., locations 21–25.

13. Warrior, *Tribal Secrets*, pp. 97–98.

14. Krupat, *Turn to the Native*, p. 18.

15. Warrior, *Tribal Secrets*, p. xxiii.

16. Weaver, *That the People Might Live*, pp. xii–xiii.

17. Weaver, Womack, and Warrior, *American Indian Literary Nationalism*, p. 46.

18. Hilden, "Red on Red," p. 888.

19. Weaver, Womack, and Warrior, *American Indian Literary Nationalism*, p. xv.

20. Parker, *Invention of Native American Literature*, p. 196.

21. Weaver, Womack, and Warrior, *American Indian Literary Nationalism*, p. 10.

22. Pulitano, *Toward a Native American Critical Theory*, pp. 60–61.

23. Christie, *Plural Sovereignties*, p. 6.

24. Ortiz, "Towards a National Indian Literature," p. 254.

25. Richter, *Facing East*, p. 175.

26. Weaver, Womack, and Warrior, *American Indian Literary Nationalism*, pp. 38–43, 71–73.

27. Ibid., pp. 168–74. Womack discusses each of these precepts in detail. Though I have edited them for space, all words are Womack's verbatim. Emphasis in original.

28. Ibid., p. 179.

29. Ibid., p. 184.

30. Ibid., pp. 181–84, 208–16.

31. Ibid., p. 192.

32. Ibid., pp. 192–93.

33. Lincoln, "Red Stick Lit Crit"; Lincoln, *Speak Like Singing*, p. 4. In his review piece, Lincoln refers to the "buckskin curtain," a term I borrow from Harold Cardinal. Womack does not employ it in *Red on Red*.

34. Dennis, *Native American Literature*, p. 1.

35. Lincoln, "Red Stick," op. cit.

36. Ibid.

37. Weaver, Womack, and Warrior, *American Indian Literary Nationalism*, pp. 38, 11. Emphasis in original.

38. Alfred, *Peace, Power, and Righteousness*, p. 29.

39. Fitz, "American Indian Literary Nationalism," p. 204. Fitz is a talented close reader, although his review doesn't always demonstrate it here. He uses the preacher/lawyer analogy because, as he notes, I have a law degree and a Ph.D. in religion from Union Theological Seminary. My J.D., however, is from Columbia, not Yale Law School, as Fitz states.

40. Ibid., p. 205.

41. Ibid., pp. 206–207. The five referred to are Simon Ortiz and Lisa Brooks, in addition to Womack, Warrior, and me.

42. Fitz, writing in 2007, could not know that in my latest book, *Notes from a Miner's Canary*, I compare French cosmopolitan Bernard-Henri Lévy and Native American nationalist John Mohawk in their common conclusion that utopianisms, whether Communism or fascism or Christianity, trend toward totalitarianism. Weaver, *Notes from a Miner's Canary*, pp. 385–91.

43. Huhndorf, "American Indian Literary Nationalism," pp. 185–187.

44. Purdy, *Writing Indian*, pp. 25–29.

45. Weaver, Womack, and Warrior, *American Indian Literary Nationalism*, pp. 229, 244–45.

46. Justice, *Our Fire Survives the Storm*, p. 10. Emphasis in original.

47. Teuton, *Red Land, Red Power*, p. 31.

48. Ibid., p. 28.

49. Ibid., p. 85.

50. Tol Foster, personal communication with author, Dec. 21, 2010.

51. Foster, "Against Separatism," pp. 569, 572. Emphasis in original.

52. Ibid., p. 572.

53. Ibid., pp. 572, 575–77.

54. Krupat, *Red Matters*, p. 1.

55. Arnold Krupat, personal communication with author, April 2008.

56. Weaver, Womack, and Warrior, *American Indian Literary Nationalism*, p. 192.

57. Christie, *Plural Sovereignties*, p. 5.

58. Weaver, Womack, and Warrior, *American Indian Literary Nationalism*, pp. 73–74.

59. Justice, *Our Fire Survives the Storm*, pp. 16, 31.

60. Foster, "Against Separatism," p. 570. Emphasis in original.

61. Weaver, "The Red Atlantic."

62. See Phillips, *An Exposition of the Principles*, pp. 273ff.

63. "Demurrer," *Black's Law Dictionary*, 5th ed., p. 390.

WORKS CITED

Alfred, Taiaiake. *Peace, Power, and Righteousness: An Indian Manifesto.* New York: Oxford University Press, 1999.

Appiah, Kwame Anthony. *Cosmopolitanism: Ethics in a World of Strangers,* New York: W.W. Norton, 2006.

Armstrong, Jeannette, ed. *Looking at the Words of Our People: First Nations Analysis of Literature*, Penticton, B.C.: Theytus Books, 1993.

Arnold, Matthew. *Mixed Essays*. London: Smith, Elder & Co., 1879.

Brooks, Lisa. *The Common Pot: The Recovery of Native Space in the Northeast*. Minneapolis: University of Minnesota Press, 2008.

Christie, Stuart. *Plural Sovereignties and Contemporary Indigenous Literature*. New York: Palgrave Macmillan, 2009.

Cook-Lynn, Elizabeth. "Cosmopolitanism, Nationalism, the Third World, and First Nation Sovereignty." *Wicazco Sa Review* 9:2 (1993), 26–36. Reprinted as "American Indian Fiction Writers: Cosmopolitanism, Nationalism, the Third World, and First Nation Sovereignty" in Elizabeth Cook-Lynn, *Why I Can't Read Wallace Stegner*. Madison: University of Wisconsin Press, 1996.

Cox, James. *Muting White Noise: Native and European American Native Traditions*. Norman: University of Oklahoma Press, 2006.

Dennis, Helen May. *Native American Literature: Towards a Spatialized Reading*. London: Routledge, 2007.

Fitz, Brewster. "American Indian Literary Nationalism" (review). *American Indian Culture and Research Journal* 31:3 (2007).

Foster, Tol. "Against Separatism: Jace Weaver and the Call for Community." *American Literary History* 20:3 (2008).

Hilden, Patricia Penn. "Red on Red" (review). *American Literature* 73:4 (2001).

Hobson, Geary, ed. *The Remembered Earth: An Anthology of Contemporary Native American Literature*. Albuquerque: University of New Mexico Press, 1981.

Hundorf, Shari. "American Indian Literary Nationalism" (review). *American Literature* 18:1 (2008).

Justice, Daniel Heath. *Our Fire Survives the Storm: A Cherokee Literary History*. Minneapolis: University of Minnesota Press, 2006.

Krupat, Arnold. *Ethnocriticism: Ethnography, History, Literature*. Berkeley: University of California Press, 1992.

———. *Red Matters: Native American Studies*. Philadelphia: University of Pennsylvania Press, 2002.

———. *The Turn to the Native: Studies in Criticism and Culture*. Lincoln: University of Nebraska Press, 1996.

———. *The Voice in the Margin: Native American Literature and the Canon*. Berkeley: University of California Press, 1989.

Larson, Charles. *American Indian Fiction*. Albuquerque: University of New Mexico Press, 1978.

Lincoln, Kenneth. *Native American Renaissance*. Berkeley: University of California Press, 1983

———. "Red Stick Lit Crit." *Indian Country Today* (April 5, 5007).

———. *Speak Like Singing: Classics of Native American Literature*. Albuquerque: University of New Mexico Press, 2007.

Momaday, N. Scott. *House Made of Dawn*. New York: Harper & Row, 1968.

Ortiz, Simon J. "Towards a National Indian Literature: Cultural Authenticity in Nationalism." Reprinted in Weaver, Womack, and Warrior, *American Indian Literary Nationalism*, p. 254.

Owens, Louis. *Other Destinies: Understanding the American Indian Novel.* Norman: University of Oklahoma Press, 1992.

Parker, Robert Dale. *The Invention of Native American Literature.* Ithica, N.Y.: Cornell University Press, 2003.

Phillips, George L. *An Exposition of the Principles of Pleading under the Codes of Civil Procedure.* Chicago: Callaghan and Company, 1986.

Pulitano, Elvira. *Toward a Native American Critical Theory.* Lincoln: University of Nebraska Press, 2003.

Purdy, John Lloyd. *Writing Indian, Native Conversations.* Lincoln: University of Nebraska Press, 2009

Richter, Daniel. *Facing East from Indian Country: A Native History of Early America.* Cambridge: Cambridge University Press, 2001.

Rosen, Kenneth, ed. *Voices of the Rainbow: Contemporary Poems by Native American.*, New York: Arcade, 1993.

Said, Edward. *The Word. the Text, and the Critic.* Cambridge, Mass.: Harvard University Press, 1983.

Said, Edward, ed. *The Man to Send Rain Clouds.* New York: Vintage Books, 1974.

Teuton, Sean. *Red Land, Red Power: Grounding Knowledge in the American Indian Novel.* Durham, N.C.: Duke University Press, 2008.

Treuer, David. *Native American Fiction: A User's Guide.* St. Paul, Minn.: Graywolf Press, 2006.

Warrior, Robert. *Tribal Secrets: Recovering American Indian Intellectual Traditions.* Minneapolis: University of Minnesota Press, 1995.

Weaver, Jace. *Notes from a Miner's Canary: Essays on the State of Native America.* Albuquerque: University of New Mexico Press, 2010.

———. "The Red Atlantic: Transoceanic Cultural Exchanges." *American Indian Quarterly* 35:3–4 (2011).

———. *That the People Might Live: Native American Literatures and Native American Community,* New York: Oxford University Press, 1997.

Weaver, Jace, Craig Womack, and Robert Warrior. *American Indian Literary Nationalism.* Albuquerque: University of New Mexico, 2006.

White. Richard. *Indians, Empires, and Republics in the Great Lakes Region, 1650–1815.* Cambridge: Cambridge University Press, 1991.

Womack, Craig. *Red on Red: Native American Literary Separatism.* Minneapolis: University of Minnesota Press, 1998.

2

Ethics and Axes

Insider-Outsider Approaches
to Native American Literature

JAMES MACKAY

Rereading Kenneth Lincoln's 1983 volume, *Native American Renaissance,* in 2013 is a somewhat chastening experience.[1] The book is characterized by, among other things, a breadth of scholarship, a generosity of spirit, and an inclusiveness that few contemporary critiques of American Indian writings manage. Lincoln is sure of his purpose: to survey an entire field of literature to as wide an extent as possible; to allow for that field's heterogeneity; to assert a contemporary, fluid sense of Native American cultures that would insist on neither language nor fidelity to custom as criteria; and above all, to promote a group of writers that he sees as in some way of equal stature with both the inventors and architects of the American Renaissance and the creators of the European.[2] The monograph begins with a short, clear positional statement— "Among the Lakota on the northern plains where I was raised" (1)—complementing the facing-page acknowledgement of "My Lakota brother [who] baked bread when I was a boy . . . and taught me more about Native America than all the books" (x), making it clear that this is not the work of a complete outsider, nor one reliant on anthropology or other forms of precoded, institutionally friendly knowledge. Instead, Lincoln is sure that for him the literature is its own primary theorization, and that wherever possible it should be interpreted through tribal experience and without recourse to stereotype. Such straightforward premises anticipate, it seems, both the radical decentering of grand narratives of Indianness proposed by trickster theorists in the 1990s and the contemporary tribalcentric impulse of much nationalist criticism.

That the field of Native American literary criticism has changed both in scope and direction since Lincoln's book was published is natural—no field of literary study remains untouched by the theory wars of the '80s and '90s, nor the steady subsequent decline in standards of literary scholarship. It seems to me, however, that the changes are particularly radical in the wake of *Native American Renaissance.* First, the number of authors has grown exponentially, as have their prominence on the (inter)national scene and the number of texts they have published. In 1983, to take some random examples, Louise Erdrich was yet to bring out *Love Medicine* (1984), and Sherman Alexie's rise to superstardom was years away, while terrifyingly prolific writers such as Robert Conley and Diane Glancy were still to release their first books. Second, though Lincoln begins by quoting Native critics, there was still little in the way of formally stated theory organic to Native literatures in English for his work to draw upon. He summarizes the field as consisting primarily of works inflected with an ethnographic or anthropological slant. These are bolstered by a mere two full-length literary monographs, both by non-Native scholars (Charles R. Larson's *American Indian Fiction* [1978] and Alan R. Velie's *Four American Indian Literary Masters* [1982]); both of these Lincoln largely rejects. Although essays including Paula Gunn Allen's "The Sacred Hoop" (1979), N. Scott Momaday's "The Man Made of Words" (1979), and Simon Ortiz's "Towards a National Indian Literature" (1981) had been published, they had not yet assumed their central position in the discipline. Scholars embarking on a survey similar to Lincoln's today would need to be at least cognizant of, and preferably intimately familiar with, these discussions and a large body of subsequent theoretical work that has revolutionized the way that Native-authored texts are critiqued several times over.

This chapter approaches the thirtieth anniversary of *Native American Renaissance*'s publication by taking stock of that changed critical context. While nobody would deny the debt owed to non-Native scholars such as Lincoln, Elaine Jahner, Karl Kroeber, Arnold Krupat, John Purdy, LaVonne Brown Ruoff and many others (not to mention the editors of this present volume), it might be asked how the non-Native critic might go about work of equal value in the wake of what has been called American Indian literary nationalism. Just as the moment of the Native American Renaissance saw among its effects a new consciousness of the falseness of most outsider depictions of Native cultures, so might the current American Indian critical theory explosion make us aware of the vacuity of some outsider criticism? In Hollywood and in popular novels, the continuance of an inexcusable level of ignorance and stereotype reveals the workings of a colonial state—surely similar blundering criticism could be sustained by an academy itself founded on, in, and by such a state. In this context, what are the strategies that a non-Native writer might follow to best do justice to the literary art of colonized communities? In other words, what is the duty of the non-Native critic?

I will first ask whether the binary division into Native/non-Native is either helpful or accurate, arguing that such absolutist terms should be avoided in favor of the more flexible "insider/outsider critic." Using the insights from this discussion, I will consider the ethical duties of an outsider critic as they have evolved since the Native American Renaissance (NAR), interrogating recent trends in indigenous literary criticism. Finally, I will put forward a set of critical "axes" that seem to me the essential bring-away of Native American literary theory. In all these discussions, it should be understood that my focus is on the critique of imaginative literature—textual acts of the imagination—rather than transcriptions of tales from oral performance, stories with religious significance, or writings intended as nonfiction.[3]

Given the established bias of academic cultural critique toward first defining terms and then overcomplicating those definitions, it is hardly surprising that the meaning of "Native American," "American Indian," and related phrases such as "Indigenous American," "First Nations," etc., has long been a source of dispute for the field. The answer is defined through the answers to several overlapping questions. Do these terms refer to a race, an ethnicity, a state of citizenship, a religious affiliation, or a colonial imposition? (Or, rather, "and/or a colonial imposition," since these terms are not exclusive.) Should the power to decide who is or is not Native reside with the individual, the family unit, totemic associations, religious leaders, community leaders, tribal judges, elected governing bodies, unelected tribal genealogists, the tribal community as a whole, or with the U.S. Department of the Interior? Should the decision be based on parentage, upbringing, kinship, appearance of ancestors on Dawes Commission rolls, cultural continuity, cultural belonging, spiritual practice, language competence, community participation, community service, recommendation by recognized tribal members, knowledge of tradition, Certificate Degree of Indian Blood card, or any of the dozens of further possibilities? Should the decider's guiding impetus be expansive, trying to accommodate as many writers as possible under these banners and thus expand both the critic's remit and also the possibilities for an indigenous canon? Or should it be contractive, trying to avoid overmuch cultural dilution in the face of an overwhelming, centuries-long attack on indigenous cultural tropes and values?

No wonder Jace Weaver calls these questions "the delicate gymnastics of authenticity" (*That the People*, 4), a phrase that nicely sums up the endlessness of these debates. And it might further be objected that, anyway, these questions are not properly the concern of literary criticism (a concern framed by David Treuer's phrase "echo not origin" [5]) and that they might be better left to others. Charles Larson, for example, would hold that authenticity is a question "best left to cultural anthropologists" (15), while Gerald Vizenor, noting Larson's granting social scientists the authority to make such decisions, seems to imply that elders' objections to Hyemeyohsts Storm's "pose as a member of the Northern Cheyenne" should be resolved intratribally.[4] And it should not be forgotten that pronouncements of authentic/inauthentic, tribal/nontribal, inheritance/pose, whether made in scholarly book or anonymous Internet forum, cause real hurt to real people every day. For a non-Native literary critic to presume the mantle of tribal judge is surely unjustified.

And yet these questions, despite their complexity and irresolvability, press themselves on anyone working in Native American literatures. I here of necessity take an illustration from personal experience. In 2010, I created what I believe to be the first course in Cherokee Literatures in English taught outside the United States. The tribalcentric focus was designed to aid Cypriot students, most of whom were not cognizant of even many of the stereotyped representations of American Indians, in understanding the relationships between Native-authored texts and tribal histories. Rather than a "greatest hits" approach—the usual Alexie/Erdrich/Harjo/King/Momaday/Silko/Tapahonso/Vizenor/Welch syllabus most commonly followed in European universities—this course outline I hoped would allow my students to appreciate the complexity of one corner of the behemoth of Native American literatures in English, allowing them subsequently to read other Indian authors with an appreciation of the weight of cultural specificity.[5] We considered creative contributions from Marilou Awiakta, Robert Conley, Qwo-Li Driskill, Diane Glancy, Gogisgi, Joy Harjo, Stephen Graham Jones, and Louis Owens, and made use of nonfictional or theoretical texts by Daniel Heath Justice, Jack F. and Anna G. Kilpatrick, N. Scott Momaday,[6] MariJo Moore, Circe Sturm, plus LeAnne Howe's documentary *Spiral of Fire* and Randy Redroad's film *Doe Boy*. I checked this course with a Cherokee academic and a non-Cherokee whose work has often centered on Cherokee writing.[7] And yet at conferences, in private conversations, in email exchanges, I have found my choices repeatedly (and sometimes angrily) challenged on the grounds that some of these writers are either "not Native" or "not Cherokee" or "not Native/Cherokee *enough*." To date, I have been told this about four (out of eight!) of the creative writers and three of the nonfiction writers, by challengers both Native and non-Native. To delete or not to delete these writers from the course—to include or not to include others—either of these decisions involves the gymnastics of authenticity, however tired many critics find these debates to be, and however outside the competence of the literary critic they ultimately are.

Answering such questions at one time meant affiliating with one of two major strands of thought. Though these answers within American Indian communities surely have much longer pedigrees, it will be convenient here to attribute each to one of the two acknowledged progenitors of the Native American Renaissance, N. Scott Momaday and Vine Deloria, Jr. For Momaday, being Native is a condition of blood and imagination. He gives the example of his mother, who in adulthood "imagin[ed] herself Indian" (as summarized by Weaver, *Other Words*, 5) after growing up identifying with the majority non-Indian portion of her heritage: his praise for her (re)claiming is natural to a thinker who imagines his grandmother Ko-Sahn "stepp[ing] out of the language . . . on the page" to tell him that "You see, I have existence, whole being, in your imagination. It is but one kind of being, to be sure, but perhaps it is the best of all kinds" (*Man Made of Words*, 164). In the Momadayan strand of personal identification we might recognize writers such as Diane Glancy, who records that "I know little of my Indian heritage" but that "even that small part has leavened the whole lump" ("Two Dresses," 169); we might also recognize Greg Sarris, who writes powerfully of recognizing his face in a high school yearbook photograph and working his way from that insight back to a sense of identity as Pomo (*Mabel McKay*, 141–42). Deloria, on the other hand, surveying the moment as the "energies of the Indian movement reach out and include people who have not previously considered themselves Indians" ("Popularity of Being Indian," 238), warns that community cohesion will weaken under such conditions. He suggests that "standards of conduct ought to be reestablished" and that "impostors must be driven out" (239); such a standard is natural to a thinker who spent much of his energies on synthesizing Native intellectual traditions to try to define Native worldviews.[8] Deloria's thought is followed by that of Elizabeth Cook-Lynn, who differentiates "those Indian authors who are merely self-serving and those who are in the service of their tribal nations" and recommends that the latter should be the main or sole focus of criticism ("American Indian," 172); indeed, it is also backed by Sarris, whose self-understanding as Pomo is refined through what amounts to an apprenticeship to elder Mabel McKay and whose service to the tribe has now extended to his becoming elected tribal chair.

Although these ideas speak to the seemingly opposed expansive/contractive aims I mentioned previously, they do not necessarily contradict one another. The Momadayan strand primarily considers the ontology of Indianness, which allows for individual imaginative and empathic leaps from limited experience and/or tenuous kinship; the Delorian is epistemological, concerned with the circumstances under which such leaps are made and what effect these affirmations have both on the self and on the wider communities invoked. As American Indian critical theory has advanced in the past two decades, it has in fact become normal to embrace both, allowing for an expansive definition of Native authorship while increasingly insisting on tribal specificity, allowing heterogeneous forms of creative production into consideration while increasingly insisting on the primacy of critical tools drawn from indigenous traditions. A complex understanding has evolved of American Indian identity in text as multiple and processual, with a concomitant insistence on the critic's role in drawing out the ways that authors claiming these identities respond to, continue, and creatively adapt tribal political and cultural understandings in the light of changing circumstances. Thus Gerald Vizenor, in *Fugitive Poses* (1998), describes eight "theaters" of *indian* identity (concession, creation, countenance, genealogies, documents, actual situations, trickster stories, and victimry (88), later making clear in conversation with A. Robert Lee that the first of these would "include anyone as an *indian* who so desires" and adding a ninth theater of "futurity" (*Postindian Conversations*, 153). Thus Craig Womack, in his essay "Theorizing American Indian Experience," destroys any stable, essentialized notion of American Indian identity, pointing out that such claims when made in a pedagogical setting tend toward "all the good stuff" being Indian, a political move that disrespects human experience (359).

However, this refinement, this anti-essentialism, does not mean that we can assume that the boundary between Native/non-Native has simply disappeared.[9] Neither Womack nor Vizenor makes the claim that there is no such thing as *a* tribal perspective, simply that there is no such thing as *the* tribal perspective, let alone *the* Native American perspective. Rather, we should recognize that there is a spectrum between insider and outsider and that both author and critic may occupy multiple points along that spectrum at different times. Penelope Myrtle Kelsey, for example, creates a tribal theory for literary critique from Dakota language and practice, a theory that is applied to and learns from Dakota-authored texts and that, moreover, has been reviewed by all bands of the Dakota Nation in Minnesota. Despite such closeness, she is a Seneca critic, and thus conceptualizes her critical position as that of outsider (Kelsey, 11–12). Therefore, to try to formalize the duty of the non-Native critic is precisely not to replicate old boundaries, but rather to ask how any critic, now defined as "outsider" in all but the most specific of circumstances and thus including even tribal citizens working outside their own historical and cultural context, should go about approaching a Native-authored text.

In four decades of published critique of American Indian literatures, ethical questions have been and remain to the fore. Indeed, in commissioning the essays that form *Reasoning Together* (2008), the editors began by asking their contributors to "Describe an ethical Native literary criticism" (Womack, *Reasoning,* 95). This is natural, given, first, the way that academia has frequently been seen as distorting Native cultures, with cultural critics, historians, ethnologists, and so forth making statements that are not supported by the people they supposedly describe. Vine Deloria, Jr., the most implacable critic of this form of bad-faith academic inquiry, opens *We Talk, You Listen* (1970) with sarcastic riffs on inaccurate perceptions by economists, radical politicians, and anthropologists:

> [A] noted female anthropologist presented a scholarly paper to the effect that Indians drink to gain an identity. Anyone who has ever seen Indians would laugh at the absurdity of the idea. It is unquestionably the other way. Indians first ask what your name is, then what your tribe is. After these preliminaries you are sometimes asked to have a drink. . . . If we acted the way anthropologists describe us, we would get lousy stinking drunk, THEN DECIDE WHAT TRIBE WE WANTED TO BELONG TO, and finally choose a surname for ourselves. [11]

Although Deloria is as always a polished polemicist, the fury of those capital letters must be understood in the context of a book published just one year after the founding, under protest and with little institutional support, of the first Native American studies (NAS) program at the University of California, Berkeley. In other words, there was as yet no effective power base within the academy from which Indians could challenge mistaken perceptions and academic abuses. The published anthropological account would have, for most outsiders, greater force than insiders' lived experience.

This history of bad faith makes itself felt with particular force in literary criticism. Karl Kroeber gives the example of Tristram P. Coffin's introduction to *Indian Tales of North America* (1961), in which Coffin seems blinded by "modernists who pretended to admire 'the primitive' while denying there could be a meaningful primitive 'tradition' of art because there were no individualistically self-conscious primitive artists" (Kroeber *Artistry*, 6). The result—and Kroeber makes it clear that this is typical of the overwhelming majority of such collections—is a description of complex Native storytelling traditions that is patronizing and frequently empirically incorrect, and fails to do its basic job of aiding outsider readers in understanding the complexities of an oral storytelling art that works on principles different from those of English-language poetry and prose. Although Kroeber is discussing ethnopoetics, he makes it clear that the situation is just as bad in other branches of cultural criticism: "I have learned that internalized cultural prejudices often block modern readers' enjoyment of Indian stories' moral, intellectual and emotional richness. Ironically, the most obstructive prejudices have been fostered by recent literary criticism, especially that influenced by European structuralist and poststructuralist ethnological theorizing" (ix). How the outsider critic is to avoid both institutionalized inaccuracy and personal (fostered) prejudices, then, becomes an urgent question, since these actively stand in the way of appreciation.

It is significant that Kroeber chose in 1977 to open the first issue of the *Newsletter of the Association for Studies in American Indian Literatures*—which would become the journal *SAIL*—with Elaine Jahner's "Indian Literature and Critical Responsibility." In this essay, Jahner argues that it is incumbent upon the critic to "recognise personal limitations, fortify himself or herself with every scrap of cultural information available and then inch warily but imaginatively into the area" (3). This ethical stance, in turn taken from Bernth Lindfors, appears frequently in the critical literature and is surely the first baseline for the outsider critic. It is indicative of the disrespect historically shown to indigenous cultures, however, that it should be seen as any kind of special insight that needs stating. After all, what chance would a would-be critic of Edmund Spenser, say, have of being taken seriously if they did not recognize and attempt to compensate for the distorting effect of historical distance? What response would await the outsider critic of Wisława Szymborska who made no effort to understand the high Polish traditions in and against which her work plays, or the political context that inevitably frames even a surreal poem such as "Seen from Above"? Recognizing distance and doing the research should be fundamental duties for all critics.

Jahner's concern, then, is with interpreting the material in as correct a fashion as possible, sensitively probing the writer's relationship with a broadly understood notion of tradition. This seems, as I have indicated, to be an uncontroversial, indeed expected, way of doing literary study.[10] But however natural such an approach might be in pure literary studies, in which the main concern is with avoiding invisibility and getting cultural references right, this is not the only context in which Native literatures are studied. Since the 1960s growth of area studies, in particular the foundation in 1969 (that Renaissance year again) of the first formal NAS programs, it has become increasingly clear that disinterested literary/cultural/historical theory is not the only way to examine these texts. The ethics of interpretation, therefore, become more than just "getting it right," and move toward "doing the right thing."

Though it is surely not originary, Clara Sue Kidwell's 1978 article, "Native American Studies," with its provocative subtitle, "Academic Concerns and Community Service," sums up the anxieties that would become increasingly central in Native American literary theory (to the point that her essay feels contemporary, where Lincoln's *Native American Renaissance* is, as Chadwick Allen observes, "mostly ignored in the current conversation" [121]). Kidwell surveys the foundation and growth of NAS as a discipline, noting its origins in student protest and community activism, and the resistance to its existence by some traditional academic departments and funding bodies. She argues for an interdisciplinary approach that would correct past errors in scholarship and function to explicate the root causes of "the terrible conditions of social breakdown and poverty on . . . reservations" (39). Kidwell's argument is turned toward the necessity of professionalizing NAS, admitting the limited ability of academic study to effect social change. Nonetheless, NAS must always recognize its obligations to community, to the extent of putting its scholarship at the service of the most immediate concerns of tribal nations.

Although Kidwell does not use the term, she seems to be saying that NAS should have decolonization as its fundamental aim. In the context of small communities that (with a few exceptions) could likely never function as truly independent nation-states, and a deep settler society that forms a super- or even hyperpower, this word has to bear a more nuanced meaning than it did in the twentieth century's national independence movements of countries such as Kenya or Cyprus. (As Jace Weaver says, "Only the most winsome dreamer and the most prophetic visionary believe that the colonizers are going anywhere" ["Indigenousness," 233]). Waziyatawin and Michael Yellow Bird offer a succinct recent definition: "Decolonization is the intelligent, calculated and active resistance to the forces of colonialism that perpetuate the subjugation and/or exploitation of our minds, bodies and lands, and it is engaged for the ultimate purpose of overturning the colonial structure and realising Indigenous liberation" ("Beginning Decolonization," 2.)

The language may seem dramatic for outsiders not versed in the basic facts of Native America, which include horrific rates of absolute poverty, health problems, the lowest life expectancy of any American or Canadian ethnic group, alcoholism, corruption in badly structured tribal governments, and low rates of high school graduation. Such outsiders—who are to be found at any Native-oriented conference—might do well to make their first research text the 2007 Amnesty International report, "Maze of Injustice," which concludes that as many as one-third of American Indian women have been raped, in the vast majority of cases by a non-Native man who escaped prosecution. The moral imperative on NAS researchers is therefore surely to expose the underlying structures that enable such abuses and, in full knowledge of the harm done by externally imposed solutions, to aid communities in developing solutions to modern problems, using older traditions as a guide.

In such a context, literary study can seem a poor relation to such immediately useful disciplines as health sciences, law, town planning, or social services. As Renate Eigenbrod observes of her own NAS students: "they . . . feel the pressure . . . to take courses that seem to relate more directly to finding solutions for . . . social problems" ("Necessary Inclusion," 3). It is surely a result of such pressures that there has been such a strong recent move to examining nonfiction texts in literary analysis. For example, Robert Warrior's *The People and the Word: Reading Native Non-Fiction* (2005) discusses, among other things, the Osage constitution (49–93), while Lisa Brooks opens up Northeastern writings, including *awikhiganak* word-maps to a literary examination (*Common Pot*, 246–54), and Scott Lyons considers the implications of "X" signatures signed to early treaty documents (*X-marks*, 1–34). These are surely great examples of interdisciplinary work, bringing the literary critic's relentless focus on language and meaning to bear on texts more usually of interest to historians, geographers, or legal experts.

However, this expansive movement of literary focus is seemingly accompanied by another school of critics who perform the opposite maneuver, subjecting imaginative literary texts to nonliterary constraints that serve to contract the range of available approaches and exclude uncomfortable readings. Sam McKegney, for example, argues that indigenous texts have suffered "decades" of "violence perpetrated . . . [by] literary criticism dominated by non-Native academics wielding analytical strategies developed outside Native communities" ("Stragegies," 56). Making the case that Native critics' voices should be privileged in interpreting Native texts, he argues that this is not so much because they are likely to have superior knowledge or "valid cultural understanding," but because Native critics are of necessity involved in the ongoing lives of the stories that they critique. In other words, stories grow from communal experience, but then affect the community from whence they come. As such, a communal member who will suffer the effects of misplaced, inaccurate, or "violent" criticism will be best placed to avoid creating such harms. McKegney notes that "Although I endeavor to be as sensitive and respectful as I am able, as a non-Native critic I simply do not stand to inherit the adverse social impact my critical work might engender, and this, it seems to me, impacts the way my work functions and is something about which I must remain critically conscious" (58).

McKegney quotes both Jace Weaver and Craig Womack in support of his position that Native texts of necessity have a fundamental relationship with Native communities. For these thinkers, the responsibility on every critic is to bear in mind the putative damage that "violent" criticism can cause, and by implication the beneficial effects that "respectful" criticism can have. The challenge is to navigate a highly complex moral maze. It is necessary to be "ethically appropriate" (McKegney, 58) to ensure that Native critics are privileged in one's work, to have personal interactions with community members and indeed to have "community involvement" (57), while being conscious that getting it wrong can cause actual harm to those communities.

McKegney states that "I reject the reigning strategies for ethical disengagement in order to seek out strategies for ethical engagement" ("Strategies," 63). He goes on to quote Jace Weaver's call for "simpatico and knowledgeable Amer-European critical allies" (Weaver, "Splitting," 11) and argues that the role of ally is the one that the non-Native critic should seek to fill. "An ally, in my understanding," McKegney writes, "is one who acknowledges the limits of her or his knowledge, but neither cowers beneath those limits nor uses them as a crutch" ("Strategies," 64). Specifically, an outsider critic must do the following: gain knowledge of the culture from which a writer comes before offering critique of the work; privilege the work of Native "scholars, writers and community members"; work with Indigenous communities; "act out of a sense of responsibility to Indigenous communities." These join the conditions to avoid disengagement that can be deduced from the earlier sections of his essay: not to examine white representations of indigeneity; not to be overly self-reflexive; not to use social science to explain Native literatures as the deterministic product of historical/economic forces; not to apologize. Facing the would-be critic with this challenge, he finishes by quoting Daniel Heath Justice that "to be a thoughtful participant in the decolonization of Indigenous peoples is to necessarily enter into an ethical relationship that requires respect, attentiveness, intellectual rigor, and no small amount of moral courage" (Justice, "Conjuring," 9).

It seems that in promoting the "critical posture" of ally, McKegney falls into an elephant trap, wherein he simply re-creates the conditions under which the "strategies of ethical disengagement" were first formed. Take, for example, the condition of "knowledge." If the critics should be silent until they have sufficient knowledge of a tribal culture, how will they know when to speak other than by self-reflexive analysis? How to avoid privileging nonliterary sources above literary ones (especially given the paucity of tribalcentric literary studies)?[11] How to avoid putting such analysis on the page if one is to acknowledge the limits of understanding? How to make all these moves without very quickly ending up in the position of the nervous self-castrater? In other words, by insisting on these criteria, McKegney would surely force outsider critics back into the "tremendous anxiety" he has just diagnosed (58). Rob Appleford, writing in response to McKegney, makes a similar point, asking whether McKegney's series of ethical imperatives constitutes an "attractive invitation to strap on the gloves" ("Response," 63). Of course, attractiveness is not necessarily the point: sometimes intellectual labor should be hard or even unpleasant. The question is whether these constraints would allow the critic room to carry out meaningful intellectual work at all.[12]

On the other side, there has been a tendency in recent discussions of American Indian literatures to polarize the debate into nationalists on the one side and cosmopolitans on the other.[13] This discussion has been fuelled by aggressive statements, particularly from cosmopolitan critics who find the NAS-inflected tone of nationalist literary discussion unpleasant. Elvira Pulitano's *Toward a Native American Critical Theory* has probably by now taken enough knocks, but in illustration we can contrast Kenneth Lincoln's statement that Craig Womack promotes an insider-only "purge" through "Red Stick criticism" (*Speak*, 4–6) with Womack's actual defense of critical plurality in the theoretical introduction to *Red on Red*: "[M]y argument is not that this is the *only* way to understand Creek writing" (4); "there are a number of legitimate approaches to analyzing Native literary production" (2).[14] Womack has eloquently described the ways that hybridity theory, potentially a useful tool for discussing the mingling of different traditions, became in thoughtless hands a procrustean assessment that damaged Native agency.

Any overtly ideological approach, with its capacity for becoming either a rigid template or a self-parody, should surely be resisted. The seemingly literal use of terms such as "literary colonizers" and "critical violence" should surely be avoided without demonstration of a specific harm, if only to avoid insulting the dead and disappeared of the very real American genocides, while arrogation to oneself of the title of "ally" is surely a self-important step too far. For a critic to "ally" to the fate of a real-world community is to show a profound ignorance of the complex, shifting, uncertain aesthetic and ethical plays of imaginative fiction. While there is a case to be made for respect of this kind when it comes to traditional stories with spiritual significance, this debate is theological and not literary. Equally, in considering the ways that literary criticism—which deals with, at a fundamental level, a form of crafted untruths—can be guided by Waziyatawin's definition of decolonisation offered above, one must surely privilege "intelligent, calculated and active resistance," and the imagination of a futurity in which "Indigenous liberation" is realized, over the documenting and lamenting of "the subjugation and/or exploitation of our minds, bodies and lands." The *first* duty of a literary critic, surely, is to understand that there is a difference between representation and reality.

Of all the terms to have emerged from the theory wars, perhaps none has proved as evocative as *survivance*, Gerald Vizenor's term of art introduced in *Manifest Manners* (1994) for (among other things) the distinctive quality of Native literatures. The active suffix *-ance*, as Vizenor explains, changes the mere word survival to an active quality ("Aesthetics," 19). This motivates art that is not merely lamentation or documentary reportage, but rather *creative* in the fullest sense of the word, creating new possibilities for Native aesthetics and tribal self-understanding. In the "trickster criticism" promulgated by Vizenor and Louis Owens, which became a significant movement in the 1990s, the disruptive figure of the trickster was used mostly as a signifier for subversion and has been lambasted for its consequent deferral to Euro-Western norms (e.g., Sinclair, "Trickster Reflections," 28). Survivance, on the other hand, is a more grounded term that allows for tribal custom and history to inform indigenous literatures without ever making those literatures represent a grand tribal Tradition.

The idea that American Indian cultures, like any others, can embrace change, even far-reaching change, without losing something essential, is hardly restricted to Vizenor. Craig Womack in his most recent work declares a similar insight, declaring that "I say make excellence, especially originality, the central criterion as to what makes something tribally specific rather than some threshold level of beads and feathers" (*Art*, 75). Nor is the idea of bundling resistance and continuance in with the brute act of survival. Paula Gunn Allen declares that "the American Indian poetry of extinction and regeneration . . . is ultimately the only poetry a contemporary Indian woman can write" ("Answering," 98). Robert Dale Parker quotes Carlos Montezuma's lines:

> Who says the Indian race is vanishing?
> The Indians will not vanish.
> The feathers, paint and moccasin will vanish, but the Indians
>   —never!
> Just as long as there is a drop of human blood in America, the
>   Indians will not vanish.
> His spirit is everywhere; the American Indian will not vanish.
> He has changed externally but he has not vanished. [287]

Parker takes the title of this poem for the title of his anthology, *Changing Is Not Vanishing* (2011), and implicitly takes it for a critical manifesto, too, in celebrating nontraditional verse from early Indian writers.

Survivance as a term of art embodies each of these insights and more. Helmbrecht Breinig, for example, remembers the term's legal properties as a "right to succession" ("Native Survivance," 40), implying the rights and responsibilities that flow to the survivors of genocides and the inheritors of great cultural traditions. Linda Lizut Helstern finds "semantic parallelism" with dominance, suggesting survivance's emphasis on liberation ("Shifting," 163). Alan Velie stresses its essential literariness, given that the performative element of survivance must be reached through storytelling ("War Cry," 147), while Chadwick Allen notes that it has now become such an established "part of how we 'do' our work" that a recognition of survivance must surely serve as a beginning point "for the construction of more focused questions about how literary texts produce meaning and effects within multiple contexts and for multiple audiences," rather than an end in itself (121–23).

I have already gestured to Craig Womack's "spectrum" of literary analysis, in which his particular set of critical practices becomes just one of many options open to the critic. Reflecting the realities of the theory explosion of the last decade and a half, this spectrum should now maybe be conceived rather as a series of interlinked and overlapping axes on which individual acts of criticism can be plotted. One axis might be from tribalcentric work that makes the specific nation the space of critique (e.g., Daniel Heath Justice's *Our Fire Survives the Storm* [2006]), through pan-Indian comparison that places Native work in context of shared histories and political goals (e.g., Sean Kicummah Teuton's *Red Land, Red Power* [2008]), to cosmopolitan or global comparative work (e.g., James Ruppert's *Mediation in Contemporary Native American Fiction* [1995]). Another might be from work that prioritizes traditional story as context (e.g., Christopher Teuton's *Deep Waters* [2010]) to that which places most emphasis on contemporary political realities (e.g., Sam McKegney's *Magic Weapons* [2007]). Yet another might be the axis between criticism based in interdisciplinary NAS and that based primarily in literary study discussed above. An axis might be drawn between work that takes spatial readings as primary (e.g., Helen May Dennis's *Native American Literature* [2007]) and that which is more concerned with chronological periodizing (e.g., Rebecca Tillett's *Contemporary Native American Literature* [2007]), while as in all fields of literary criticism there is a balance to be struck between single-author specificity and broad survey.

Acknowledging the field's richness is to put the lie to a damaging form of zero-sum thinking that surely lies behind the attempts listed above to legislate *one* form of approach or *one* list of approved authors. The underlying idea here is that if a book putting forward the "wrong" approach, if an anthology containing the "wrong" writers, if an essay with an "incorrect" moral stance is published, it crowds out the "right" approaches, writers, stances—as if there was a set quota of books to be published in any subject each year. Lisa Brooks, a thinker for whom I have particularly deep respect, nonetheless promulgates a form of this when she states that "Pulitano's work diminishes my belief in the prospect of real dialogue" ("Afterword," 234). Surely the opposite of dialogue is silence, not writing, however error-full that writing might be perceived to be. And a field full of debate, disagreement, competing methodologies, heterogeneous insights into the way that literary art and imaginative thought play in differing contexts, all in the service of promoting an understanding of Native survivance, is not only a healthy field, but one that is constantly creating new opportunities for publishing ever-better writing on Native literatures.

In this chapter I have problematized the term "non-Native," suggesting that outsiderhood can include American Indian and First Nations critics writing away from home turf. I have also questioned the idea of a single monolithic duty and suggested that an adherence to the shifting, imprecise term "survivance" is of necessity preferable to a narrowly moralistic or exclusionary criticism. And yet I return to the question with which I started: what is the duty of the non-Native critic? It seems to me that the duty, for all the developments of the past thirty years, has not changed one jot since Kenneth Lincoln wrote *Native American Renaissance.* The outsider critic needs to aspire to Lincoln's breadth of knowledge, his commitment to a nonidealized, nonessentialized Native continuance, and the generosity that leaves that book overflowing with material. Yet the outsider critic also needs the courage to make gestures such as declaring a "Native American Renaissance," for all the possible quibbles of inaccuracy, accusations of literary colonization, and interpretive violence. In the end, clear statements of individual understanding do more to advance the field—even if only through being later challenged or dismantled—than coy plays that keep to prechewed theorizations.

NOTES

1. Many thanks to David Stirrup and David J. Carlson for their comments on this essay, and to the volume editors for their comments and patience.

2. Lincoln largely omits literary work by First Nations and Mexican indigenous peoples from his analysis. While this might be problematic in terms of perpetuating a colonial reality, I think it is a decision that can be explained on perfectly practical grounds (such as time and page space available).

3. Neither the fact that the boundaries between these different types of writing can be blurred, nor the fact that tools developed for critiquing one type can be usefully applied to the other, means that there is no meaningful distinction to be made here. There is no suggestion that any of these categories are in rigid binary opposition.

4. Storm's *Seven Arrows,* a publishing sensation in 1972, was fiercely attacked by the Northern Cheyenne tribe to which Storm was nominally attached. See Costo, "*Seven Arrows* Desecrates Cheyenne," pp. 41–42.

5. I do, incidentally, strongly recommend this method of course composition as a way of introducing outsider students to Native American literatures without making the primary focus the reaction to European colonization. There are many indigenous nations whose literary output would bear the weight of an entire semester's scrutiny. David Stirrup, for example, has created a course focusing exclusively on Anishinaabeg writings in English at the University of Kent.

6. Momaday identifies as Kiowa. He was included in the course as a means for discussing his concept of imagination and affiliation in relation to his Cherokee mother (discussed below).

7. I did not check the course with tribal authorities for two reasons: first, this seems too close to inviting censorship (for it would be very difficult to reject their

suggestions); and second, I rather hope that they have more important things to do.

8. "A dedicated and passionate advocate of anti-colonial pro-Indian ultra-tribal-indigenous-nationalism, Vine was an Indian super-patriot" (Echo-Hawk, *Magic Children*, p. 114).

9. Such a boundary is necessary in the real world. Consider, for instance, the case of affirmative action, or the rights uniquely held by tribal citizens. (Thanks to Alan Velie for this insight.)

10. New Critical approaches are sometimes caricatured as avoiding such engagements with history and cultural context. However, even Randall Jarrell's "Texts from Housman," offered in the New Critical anthology *Praising It New* (2008) as "embod[ying] the central New Critical method: 'close reading'" (Davis, 161), considers Housman as working within and commenting on English understanding of classicism (164–65) and Greek history (164). Jarrell places the poet within a broad idea of "English poetry" (167), relates him to the peculiarly English philosophy of John Stuart Mill (168), and finally considers the way that his poetry unconsciously anticipates the twentieth century's "psychological or psychoanalytic commonplaces" (169). The only difference is that Jarrell here is functioning as an insider critic and takes such contexts for granted, rather than overtly theorizing them.

11. Although books such as *Red on Red, Tribal Theory in Native American Literature, Our Fire Survives the Storm*, and so forth are inspiring, they are still few in number. As I wrote in a review of Daniel Heath Justice's *Our Fire Survives the Storm*, "[A] feeling persists that the work is barely started." Until there is a plurality of tribalcentric literary criticism, the outsider critic who wants to situate a text firmly in tribal experience will of necessity have to draw on either pan-Indian theory and/or nonliterary sources.

12. McKegney's theorization springs from his own admirable work on First Nations life-writings by residential school survivors in *Magic Weapons*.

13. For comparison, see Krupat, who divides critics into three: the overlapping camps of nationalists and indigenists, and then the mostly opposed camp of cosmopolitans (*Red Matters*, 1).

14. Even sympathetic critics can misread nationalist writers as overly separatist. Michael Snyder, for example, states that Warrior made a "political decision to cite only indigenous sources" in *Tribal Secrets*, when a quick perusal of that book's bibliography would have shown this to be incorrect (49).

WORKS CITED

Allen, Chadwick. Review of *Survivance: Narratives of Native Presence. Studies in American Indian Literatures*, 2nd ser., 23:4 (2012).

Allen, Paula Gunn. "Answering the Deer." *American Indian Culture and Research Journal* 6:3 (1982). Reprinted in Kenneth Lincoln, ed. *Gathering Native*

Scholars: UCLA's Forty Years of American Indian Culture and Research. Los Angeles: UCLA American Indian Studies Center, 2011, 91–100.

——. "The Sacred Hoop: A Contemporary Indian Perspective on American Indian Literature." In *The Remembered Earth: An Anthology of Contemporary Native American Literature.* Edited by Geary Hobson. Albuquerque: Red Earth, 1979, 222–39.

Amnesty International USA. "Maze of Injustice: The Failure to Protect Indigenous Women from Violence." Amnesty International, April 24, 2007; Web, August 11, 2011.

Appleford, Rob. "A Response to Sam McKegney's 'Strategies for Ethical Engagement: An Open Letter concerning Non-Native Scholars of Native Literatures.'" *Studies in American Indian Literatures,* 2nd ser. 21:3 (2009), 58–65.

Breinig, Helmbrecht. "Native Survivance in the Americas: Resistance and Remembrance in Narratives by Asturias, Tapahonso and Vizenor." In *Survivance: Narratives of Native Presence.* Edited by Gerald Vizenor. Lincoln: University of Nebraska Press, 2008, 39–60.

Brooks, Lisa. "Afterword: At the Gathering Place." In Jace Weaver, Craig Womack, and Robert Warrior, *American Indian Literary Nationalism.* Albuquerque: University of New Mexico Press, 2006, 225–30.

——. *The Common Pot: The Recovery of Native Space in the Northeast.* Minneapolis: University of Minnesota Press, 2008.

Coffin, Tristram Potter. Introduction. *Indian Tales of North America: An Anthology for the Adult Reader.* Ann Arbor, Mich.: American Folklore Society, 1961, i–xvii.

Cook-Lynn, Elizabeth. "American Indian Studies: An Overview. Keynote Address at the Native Studies Conference, Yale University, February 5, 1998." *Anti-Indianism in Modern America: A Voice from Tatekeya's Earth.* Urbana: University of Illinois Press, 2001, 171–82.

Costo, Rupert. "*Seven Arrows* Desecrates Cheyenne." *Indian Historian* 5:2 (1972), 41–42.

Davis, Garrick. "Close Reading." In *Praising It New: The Best of the New Criticism.* Edited by Garrick Davis. Athen, Ohio: Swallow, 2008.

Deloria, Jr., Vine. "The Popularity of Being Indian: A New Trend in Contemporary American Society." *Centerboard* 2:1, 1984. Reprinted in *Spirit & Reason: The Vine Deloria, Jr., Reader.* Edited by Barbara Deloria, Kristen Foehner, and Samuel Scinta. Golden, Colo.: Fulcrum, 1999.

——. *We Talk, You Listen: New Tribes, New Turf.* New York: Macmillan, 1970.

Dennis, Helen May. *Native American Literature: Towards a Spatialized Reading.* Abingdon, Oxford: Routledge, 2007.

The Doe Boy. DVD produced by Randy Redroad; performed by Kevin Anderson and Robert A. Guthrie. Wellspring, 2001.

Echo-Hawk, Roger. *The Magic Children: Racial Identity at the End of the Age of Race.* Walnut Creek, Calif.: Left Coast, 2010.

Eigenbrod, Renate. "A Necessary Inclusion: Native Literature in Native Studies." *Studies in American Indian Literatures,* 2nd ser., 22:1 (2010), 1–19.

Erdrich, Louise. *Love Medicine.* New York: Rinehart and Winston, 1984.

Glancy, Diane. "Two Dresses." In *I Tell You Now: Autobiographical Essays by Native American Writers.* Edited by Brian Swann and Arnold Krupat. Lincoln: University of Nebraska Press, 1987, 167–84.

Helstern, Linda Lizut. "Shifting the Ground: Theories of Survivance in *From Sand Creek* and *Hiroshima Bugi: Atomu 57.*" In *Survivance: Narratives of Native Presence.* Edited by Gerald Vizenor. Lincoln: University of Nebraska Press, 2008, 163–90.

Jahner, Elaine. "Indian Literature and Critical Responsibility." *Newsletter of the Association for Studies in American Indian Literatures,* 1st ser., 1:1 (1977), 3–10.

Jarrell, Randall. "Texts from Housman." *Kenyon Review,* Summer 1939. Reprinted in Garrick Davis, ed. *Praising It New: The Best of the New Criticism.* Edited by Garrick Davis. Athens, Ohio: Swallow, 2008.

Justice, Daniel Heath. "Conjuring Marks: Furthering Indigenous Empowerment through Literature." *American Indian Quarterly* 28.1–2 (2004), 2–11.

———. *Our Fire Survives the Storm: A Cherokee Literary History.* Minneapolis: University of Minnesota Press, 2006.

Kelsey, Penelope Myrtle. *Tribal Theory in Native American Literature: Dakota and Haudenosaunee Writing and Indigenous Worldviews.* Lincoln: University of Nebraska Press, 2008.

Kidwell, Clara Sue. "Native American Studies: Academic Concerns and Community Service. *American Indian Culture and Research Journal* 2:3–4 (1978). Reprinted in Kenneth Lincoln, ed. *Gathering Native Scholars: UCLA's Forty Years of American Indian Culture and Research.* Los Angeles: UCLA American Indian Studies Center, 2011, 33–42.

Kroeber, Karl. *Artistry in Native American Myths.* Lincoln: University of Nebraska Press, 1998.

Krupat, Arnold. *Red Matters: Native American Studies.* Philadelphia: University of Pennsylvania, Press, 2002.

Larson, Charles R. *American Indian Fiction.* Albuquerque: University of New Mexico Press, 1978.

Lincoln, Kenneth. *Native American Renaissance.* Berkeley: University of California Press, 1983.

———. *Speak Like Singing: Classics of Native American Literature.* Albuquerque: University of New Mexico Press, 2007.

Lyons, Scott Richard. *X-marks: Native Signatures of Assent.* Minneapolis: University of Minnesota Press, 2010.

Mackay, James. "Native American Literary Theory." Review essay. *Journal of American Studies* 41 (2007): 675–80.

McKegney, Sam. *Magic Weapons: Aboriginal Writers Remaking Community after Residential School.* Winnipeg: University of Manitoba Press, 2007.

———. "Strategies for Ethical Engagement: An Open Letter concerning Non-Native Scholars of Native Literatures." *Studies in American Indian Literatures,* 2nd ser., 20:4 (2008), 56–67.

Momaday, N. Scott. *The Man Made of Words: Essays, Stories, Passages.* New York: St. Martin's, 1998.

———. "The Man Made of Words." In *The Remembered Earth: An Anthology of Contemporary Native American Literature.* Edited by Geary Hobson. Albuquerque: Red Earth, 1979, 162–73.

Montezuma, Carlos. "Changing Is Not Vanishing." In *Changing Is Not Vanishing: A Collection of Early American Indian Poetry to 1930.* Edited by Robert Dale Parker. Philadelphia: University of Pennsylvania Press, 2011, 287–88.

Ortiz, Simon J. "Towards a National Indian Literature: Cultural Authenticity in Nationalism." *MELUS* 8:2 (Summer 1981), 8–12.

Parker, Robert Dale. *Changing Is Not Vanishing: A Collection of American Indian Poetry to 1930.* Philadelphia: University of Pennsylvania Press, 2011.

Pulitano, Elvira. *Toward a Native American Critical Theory.* Lincoln: University of Nebraska Press, 2003.

Ruppert, James. *Mediation in Contemporary Native American Fiction.* Norman: University of Oklahoma Press, 1995.

Sarris, Greg. *Mabel McKay: Weaving the Dream.* Berkeley: University of California Press, 1997.

Sinclair, Niigonwedom James [now Niigaanwewidam James Sinclair]. "Trickster Reflections Part I." In *Troubling Tricksters: Revisioning Critical Conversations.* Edited by Deanna Reder and Linda M. Morra. Waterloo, Ont.: Wilfred Laurier, 2010, 21–58.

Snyder, Michael. "Gerald's Game: Postindian Subjectivity in Vizenor's Interior Landscapes." In *Gerald Vizenor: Texts and Contexts.* Edited by Deborah L. Madsen and A. Robert Lee. Albuquerque: University of New Mexico Press, 2010, 46–66.

Spiral of Fire. DVD by LeAnne Howe, directed by Dir. Carol Cornsilk. Adanvdo Vision, and Native American Public Telecommunications, 2005.

Storm. Hyemeyohsts. *Seven Arrows.* New York: Ballantine Books, 1972.

Szymborska, Wisława. "Seen from Above." 1976. In *View with a Grain of Sand.* Translated by Stanislaw Barańczak and Clare Cavanagh. London: Faber and Faber, 1995, 103.

Teuton, Christopher B. *Deep Waters: The Textual Continuum in American Indian Literature.* Lincoln: University of Nebraska Press, 2010.

Teuton, Sean Kicummah. *Red Land, Red Power: Grounding Knowledge in the American Indian Novel.* Durham, N.C.: Duke University Press, 2008.

Tillett, Rebecca. *Contemporary Native American Literature.* Edinburgh: Edinburgh University Press, 2007.

Treuer, David. *Native American Fiction: A User's Manual.* Minneapolis: Graywolf, 2006.

Velie, Alan R. *Four American Indian Literary Masters: N. Scott Momaday, James Welch, Leslie Marmon Silko, and Gerald Vizenor*. Norman: University of Oklahoma Press, 1982.

———. "The War Cry of the Trickster: The Concept of Survivance in Gerald Vizenor's *Bear Island: The War at Sugar Point*." In *Survivance: Narratives of Native Presence*. Edited by Gerald Vizenor. Lincoln: University of Nebraska Press, 2008, 147–62.

Vizenor, Gerald. "Aesthetics of Survivance: Literary Theory and Practise." In *Survivance: Narratives of Native Presence*. Edited by Gerald Vizenor. Lincoln: University of Nebraska Press, 2008, 1–24.

———. *Fugitive Poses: Native American Indian Scenes of Absence and Presence*. Lincoln: University of Nebraska Press, 1998.

———. *Manifest Manners: Postindian Warriors of Survivance*. Hanover, N.H.: Wesleyan University Press, 1994.

Vizenor, Gerald, and A. Robert Lee. *Postindian Conversations*. Lincoln: University of Nebraska Press, 1999.

Warrior, Robert. *Tribal Secrets: Recovering American Indian Intellectual Traditions*. Minneapolis: University of Minnesota Press, 2001.

———. *The People and the Word: Reading Native Nonfiction*. Minneapolis: University of Minnesota Press, 2005.

Waziyatawin, and Michael Yellow Bird. "Beginning Decolonization." In *For Indigenous Eyes Only: A Decolonization Handbook*. Edited by Angela Wilson Waziyatawin and Michael Yellow Bird. Santa Fe, N.M.: School of American Research, 2010, 1–8.

Weaver, Jace. "Indigenousness and Indigeneity." In *A Companion to Postcolonial Studies*. Edited by Henry Schwarz. Cambridge, Eng.: Blackwell, 2005, 221–35.

———. *Other Words: American Indian Literature, Law, and Culture*. Norman: University of Oklahoma Press, 2001.

———. "Splitting the Earth: First Utterances and Pluralist Separatism." In *American Indian Literary Nationalism*. Edited by Jace Weaver, Robert Allen Warrior, and Craig S. Womack. Albuquerque: University of New Mexico Press, 2006, 1–90.

Womack, Craig S. *Art as Performance, Story as Criticism: Reflections on Native Literary Aesthetics*. Norman: University of Oklahoma Press, 2009.

———. *Red on Red: Native American Literary Separatism*. Minneapolis: University of Minnesota Press, 2006.

———. "Theorizing American Indian Experience." In *Reasoning Together: The Native Critics Collective*. Edited by Craig S. Womack, Daniel Heath Justice, and Christopher B. Teuton. Norman: University of Oklahoma Press, 2008, 353–410.

3

N. Scott Momaday's *House Made of Dawn* and Myths of the Victim

ALAN R. VELIE

It has long been the consensus of critics of Native American literature that the publication of Scott Momaday's *House Made of Dawn* in 1968 was the impetus for the efflorescence of works of literature now known as the "Native American Renaissance." The success of the novel, both in sales and critical reception—it won the 1969 Pulitzer Prize for literature—greatly encouraged authors like James Welch, Gerald Vizenor, and Louise Erdrich, among many others. As Louis Owens puts it:

> Before 1968 only nine novels by American Indian authors had been published. . . . However, as if Momaday had triggered a long dormant need among Indians writers, the 1970's saw the publication of a stream of novels by Indian writers including Janet Campbell Hale, Nasnaga (Roger Russell), Chief George Pierre, Ted Williams, Dallas Chief Eagle, Hyemeyohsts Storm, Denton F. Bedford, James Welch, Virginia Driving Hawk Sneve, Gerald Vizenor, Charles Penoi, and Leslie Silko. [24]

Owens goes on to add authors who debuted in the eighties and nineties, a list that reached sixty when Owens published his bibliography of Indian novels in 1992.[1] Today the number is in the hundreds.

Native American literature, while not a tight-knit movement launched with a manifesto like Surrealism, nonetheless encompasses a group of writers, related by ethnicity, who read each others' works and are influenced by them. Momaday's success with *House*, the story of a Pueblo man named Abel who suffers from the traumatizing effects of combat in World War II, encouraged James Welch to publish *Winter in the Blood*, a novel in which Welch uses the myth of the wasteland to tell the story of a Blackfeet protagonist who suffers the same sort of anomie and alienation as Abel, though his condition results from familial rather than military trauma. In *Ceremony*, Leslie Silko returns to Momaday's subject of a Pueblo victim of what is now called "post-traumatic stress disorder," but uses Pueblo myths very similar to those of the wasteland: traditional stories of sin causing drought, and ritual tasks that bring the freeing of the waters. Momaday, impressed by Silko's use of tribal myths, and cognizant of Gerald Vizenor's *Darkness in Saint Louis: Bearheart*, in which the hero turns into a bear, tells the story of Kiowa painter Locke Setman in *The Ancient Child*, a novelization of Kiowa myths of a boy who turns into a bear. Louise Erdrich, having read all of the above-mentioned novels, ends *The Bingo Palace* by having Fleur Pillager turn into a bear.

Silko, Vizenor, and Erdrich all began their careers by using tribal myths to undergird their novels; Momaday and Welch began by using Christian myths, before moving in subsequent novels to tribal myths.[2] It is noteworthy that while white critics often viewed these books as bleak or even tragic, the books, sometimes because of the myths they are based on, sometimes despite that, end on a positive note.

Momaday's use of myth and symbol is an important key to understanding his fiction. As a graduate student at Stanford, Momaday, under the tutelage of his mentor Yvor Winters, developed a strong interest in Herman Melville.[3] Matthias Schubnell points out Momaday's debt in *House* to Melville: the sinister whiteness of the albino Juan Reyes Fragua has its genesis in *Moby Dick*, and Abel, the inarticulate victim, owes something to Billy Budd. Schubnell overlooks another source of influence in *House*: Melville's use of the Bible. In *Moby Dick* the name "Ishmael" is an allusion to the illegitimate son of Abraham, the nomadic progenitor of the Arabs.[4] Ahab is named after the evil king of Israel who whored after false gods like Baal, and with his wife, Jezebel, persecuted the saintly prophet Elijah.[5] Even in minor touches, Melville alludes to the Bible: the mother ship that loses its whale boat is the *Rachel*, who, in Matthew's description of Herod's slaughter of the innocents, is "weeping for her children, and would not be comforted."[6]

Momaday bases his protagonist in *House* in part on the Abel of Genesis, the prototypic victim. A crucial question for understanding the novel is: who or what is Abel the victim of? My students for the past forty years, raised on a narrative about the "plight of the Indian," the Indian conceived primarily as victim, have usually identified "white society" as the force that attempts to destroy Abel. Interestingly, this answer both is and isn't true. On the literal level of the novel, Abel, like his biblical counterpart, is the victim of brotherly violence. It is a series of brother Indians, not a group of strangers, who consider him an outsider, who inflict the most damage on Abel. However, on a symbolic level, Abel's attacker is "the white man."[7]

The theme of victims and victimization has been central to Indian literature since John Rollin Ridge's hero, Joaquin Murieta, a Mexican miner in California, is beaten and forced to watch the rape of his wife by white American claim jumpers. During the Native American Renaissance, the writer who has written about victims more than anyone else (because he has written more than anyone else, for one thing), is Gerald Vizenor. Vizenor is, of course, aware of white American mistreatment of Indians, but he objects bitterly to the condescension involved on the part of whites who insist on seeing Indians primarily as objects of pity. In his essay "Wistful Envies" from *Fugitive Poses* (1998), Vizenor deploys a series of neologisms to express his outrage: "The *victime* is the sufferer, the one who bears the experience of evil, torture, and termagancy. The victime, the one who suffers, is not the perpetrator of aesthetic miseries and not the one who owns the name of victimry. . . . The victime is the one who suffers, not the author of aesthetic victimry. The victime is the one who restores a sense of presence and tragic wisdom in the stories of survivance" (96).

Thirty years before Vizenor wrote this, Momaday had embodied similar ideas in his depiction of Abel. Abel is not simply a *victime*, a sorry figure worthy only of the reader's pity. Rather, he is a complex character, damaged by his experiences at the hands of whites and Indians, including those in his own tribe, but capable of healing himself to become the hero in a story of survivance.[8]

To understand Momaday's Abel, it is helpful to start with the Abel of Genesis. The biblical account is, as usual, cryptic. The story is the first recorded instance of the enmity between rancher and farmer, later a common theme of American westerns (e.g., *Shane*, *Oklahoma!*). We learn that Abel is a "keeper of sheep," and Cain a "tiller of the ground" (4:2). The brothers make offerings to the Lord, who "had respect for Abel and to his offering" (4:4), but scorn for Cain and his. Cain, whose "countenance fell" at God's treatment, "rose up against Abel, his brother, and slew him" (4:8).

While it seems clear that Cain acts out of jealousy, it isn't clear why God rejects Cain's sacrifice. Commentators from the second-century rabbis who wrote *midrashim* to postmodern critics like Regina Schwartz (*The Curse of Cain*, 1997) have speculated as to why God despises Cain. However, for the most part, people who read the Bible assume that Cain is simply evil, and God, being all-knowing, recognizes it. The story produces two archetypes, Abel, the victim, and Cain, the bloody criminal marked by God.

What Momaday uses from Genesis is the idea that Abel, the prototypic victim, was attacked viciously by brother Indians. But there is more to it than that. Abel is also a victim of white American racism toward Indians, as well as a being a victim of his own fecklessness. Most important, he refuses to wallow in his misery, but rehabilitates himself, and by the end of the novel is on the road to recovery.

Momaday emphasizes his protagonist's biblical connection by not revealing his last name—he is only identified as "Abel." The first of the Cains to attack Abel is Juan Reyes Fragua, the albino who is Abel's fellow tribesman. Momaday never names the tribe. He calls the pueblo "Walatowa," its old tribal name, and uses the term "Tanoan," the name of a language group, for their language, but we can tell from Momaday's account of his childhood in *The Names*, that the tribe and pueblo he depicts are based on Jemez, New Mexico.

The narrator of *House* usually refers to Fragua as "the white man" and makes it clear that there is something sinister about him. In one scene Fragua lurks mysteriously in the fields worked by Francisco, Abel's grandfather. Francisco senses his presence as "alien," and connected with the "evil [that] had long since found him out and knew who he was" (66). In one of the most dramatic scenes in the novel, depicting the ritualistic game that involves pulling a partially buried rooster out of the ground, Fragua, who accomplishes this feat, uses the rooster to beat Abel, an act of "mute malice" (44).

At the time of his humiliation at the hands of Fragua Abel had been feeling particularly vulnerable, further alienated by his experiences in combat during World War II from the tribe he had never fully been part of anyway because of his illegitimacy. Although Fragua serves as the Cain who ruthlessly attacks Abel, at the same time there is a curious reversal of their archetypal roles. In Genesis, because Cain felt humiliated by Abel at the ritual sacrifice, Cain murders Abel. In *House*, because Fragua humiliates Abel at the rooster ritual, Abel murders Fragua—symbolically, Abel murders Cain.

The murder scene is freighted with symbolic significance. For one thing, the language is intensely sexual:

> They went out into the darkness and the rain. . . . Abel waited. The white man raised his arms as if to embrace him, and came forward. But Abel had already taken hold of the knife, and he drew it. . . . The white man's hands lay on Abel's shoulders. . . . Then he closed his hands upon Abel and drew him close. Abel heard the strange excitement of the white man's breath, and the quick uneven blowing at his ear, and felt the blue shivering lips upon him, felt even the scales of the lips and hot slippery point of the tongue, writhing. He was sick with terror and revulsion, and he tried to fling himself away, but the white man held him close. The white immensity of flesh lay over and smothered him. [82]

On a literal level Abel is knifing Fragua, killing him. However, on a figurative level "the white man"—in the sense of white society—is raping Abel. Momaday, as integrated and assimilated as he was at the time he wrote *House*—he was a professor of English at the University of California at Santa Barbara—he still felt the sting of white prejudice against Indians. In 1964, when he was in the middle of writing *House*, he published a strong indictment of that prejudice, "The Morality of Indian Hating," in *Ramparts*, a radical magazine.[9]

Momaday's description in *House* of the dying Fragua is phallic: "the white man" is clearly a giant prick in every sense of the term: "He seemed just then to wither and grow old. In the instant before the fell, his great white body grew erect and seemed to cast off its age and weight; it grew supple and sank slowly to the ground, as if the bones were dissolving within it" (83).

Abel feels absolutely no guilt at killing Fragua: Fragua is simply an embodiment of evil. "He had killed the white man . . . it was very simple. It was the most natural thing in the world . . . he would kill the white man again if he had a chance. . . . A man kills such an enemy if he can" (103).

Testifying in Abel's defense, Father Olguin, the priest at Jemez, attributes Abel's beliefs to "the psychology of witchcraft" (101). Fragua is part of what Pueblo Indians call "the witchery." Abel, for all his alienation from the tribe, was on the side of the angels. "Evil was" he knew, and it was his duty to confront it and destroy it if he could (104). In short, Momaday's Abel is far less passive than the biblical figure. He is not simply a victim; he launches a deadly attack at his tormentors.

The second Indian to play Cain to Abel is the Right Reverend John Big Bluff Tosamah, a curious figure who is principally a caricature of Momaday himself. Tosamah, the self-styled "Priest of the Sun," is a pastor in the Native American Church, a Christian sect that employs peyote in its chief ritual. To begin with, Tosamah physically resembles Momaday: "[B]ig, lithe as a cat, narrow-eyed . . . he had the voice of a great dog" (91) would serve as an apt description of Momaday during the 1960s.

Both Momaday and Tosomah are Kiowa, and most remarkably, when Tosamah tells his life story to his congregation, it is Momaday's story that he tells. Ostensibly part of a sermon he is delivering, Tosamah's description of the Kiowas' migration southward from Wyoming to Oklahoma, and Tosomah's own voyage repeating their journey, is an account Momaday first published in *The Reporter* in 1967. Later, in 1969, he appended it to *The Way to Rainy Mountain* as an introduction. The piece describes Momaday's experiences. Novels often incorporate and parody other genres—this is what Bakhtin has called "heteroglossia"[10]—but it is remarkable that Momaday would assign a previously published piece of autobiography to a lout like Tosamah, a character who functions as a villain by trying to destroy the protagonist.

Tosomah's hostility stems from the fact that Abel, whom Tosomah thinks of as a "longhair" and "real primitive sunuvabitch" (149), is an embarrassment to Tosamah, who has achieved a degree of respectability and assimilation into mainstream American society. Tosamah is ambivalent in his attitude toward Abel—he recognizes that whites are fundamentally opposed to all "diehards" and "renegades" like him and Abel—but Tosomah feels that Abel's behavior, especially at his trial where it comes out that Abel literally thought of Fragua as a snake, puts all Indians in a bad light (149). Whatever sympathy or solidarity he may occasionally feel towards Abel, Tosamah treats him only with disdain, on one occasion riding him mercilessly until Abel snaps and wants to fight him. Abel is much too drunk to fight effectively, and the ridicule he is subjected to damages him badly. He stays drunk for several days, losing his job, and much of what is left of his self-respect.

Tosamah's hostility toward Abel reflects Momaday's own ambivalence toward Indians, especially "longhairs," traditional unassimilated full-bloods. Momaday's father, Al, a well-known painter, was Kiowa, but Scott's mother,

Natachee, had a more tenuous claim to Indian identity, only through a Cherokee great-grandmother. Natachee's family had no sense of Indian identity, but
despite her flimsy claim to Indian heritage, either genetically or culturally, Natachee made a decision to live as an Indian. After high school she enrolled at
Haskell Institute, the Indian school in Lawrence, Kansas. After they married,
the Momadays lived in Mountain View, Oklahoma, in the heart of traditional
Kiowa country. The Momaday family never accepted Natachee, and so she
and Al were forced to decamp, and after several moves around the Southwest,
settled at Jemez. They made trips back to Mountain View to let Scott meet his
family, but Scott records feeling alien and strange in Oklahoma. In his memoir, *The Names*, he tells of his imaginary childhood enemy the "ugly Indian."
"Well anyway I have this gun this real-looking gun black and brown smooth
and hard a carbine tomorrow I will shoot an Indian down by the creek . . . he
is *ugly* of course he has a knife it is a great big knife and it gleams and flashes in
the sunlight it was stolen . . . the ugly Indian sees me and I am looking right at
him . . . he has of course killed many women and children with the knife and
he is called Knife sometimes Big Knife sometimes Knife Thrower"(75, 76).
    Later in his childhood Scott imagined himself riding with Billy the Kid,
who had a reputation as an Indian killer. On occasion in these reveries Scott
has to rescue helpless white women from hostile Indians. In *My Strange and
True Life with Billy the Kid*, Momaday records these teen-age daydreams:

Riding is an exercise of the mind. I dreamed a good deal on the back of
my horse, going out into the hills alone. Desperadoes were everywhere
in the brush. More than once I came upon roving bands of hostile Indians and had, on the spur of the moment, to put down an uprising. Now
and then I found a wagon train in trouble, and always among the settlers there was a lovely young girl from Charleston or Philadelphia who
needed simply and more than anything else in the world to be saved. I
saved her. [48]

The scene of saving a girl from savages is common in Westerns, of course, but
even if there are historical precedents for it, it has racist implications. That
Momaday should share these feelings that Indians are savages is a clue to his
ambivalence toward his ethnic identity.
    In addition to his mixed feelings toward the Kiowas of Oklahoma, another
source of Momaday's ambivalence toward Indians is probably his experience
growing up among the Jemez. Although the Jemez were Indians like him,
he was not a member of their tribe, and although they liked and respected
the Momadays, the Jemez thought of them as outsiders: "And throughout the
year there were ceremonies of many kinds, and some of these were secret
dances, and on these holiest days guards were posted on the roads and no
one was permitted to enter the village. My parents and I kept to ourselves, to

our reservation of the day school, and in this way, through the tender of our respect and our belief, we earned the respect of the Jemez people and we were at home there" (147).

In short, Momaday makes it clear that although he grew up at Jemez, and even loved it there, he was always aware of being different from the Jemez. Students often naïvely assume that since Momaday is an Indian, his Indian protagonist, Abel, is an alter ego. Abel isn't, but Tosomah, Abel's enemy, is. In another odd reversal, an avatar of the author plays the villain in regard to his protagonist.

The third character to act as Cain to Abel is Martinez, the policeman who beats Abel so severely that he is hospitalized. Momaday never identifies Martinez's ethnic group, but he is most probably Chicano. Many Indians, especially in the Southwest, have Spanish surnames, but Martinez is in Los Angeles, and, given California demographics, it is more likely that the policeman is of Mexican descent. Although in the United States Chicanos and Indians generally consider themselves separate ethnic groups, most Chicanos, of course, have a good deal of Indian "blood," and there are Indians—e.g., Jack Forbes,[11] Leslie Silko[12]—who argue that Chicanos and Indians are essentially the same people.

Martinez's brutal beating brings Abel to his lowest point. He lies on the beach, passing in and out of consciousness, his body throbbing with pain, while nearby the grunion, small silver fish, throw themselves onto the beach to spawn. The grunion flop around on the sand, to "writhe in the light of the moon . . . the most helpless creatures on the face of the earth" (89). Momaday's symbolism is pretty heavy-handed here: as a pueblo Indian in Los Angeles, Abel is a fish out of water. Martinez represents not only Cain, but also illicit violence on the part of official authority. He is a corrupt policeman who shakes down and terrorizes Indians. Among Abel's enemies in *House,* Martinez is the least like a brother, despite his Indian blood.

Momaday's portrayal of Abel calls to mind another archetypal figure, this one from both history and popular culture: Ira Hayes, the Pima Marine who raised the flag at Iwo Jima. Hayes could not adjust to life on the reservation after the war and died of exposure while drunk. He became a symbol of the Indian whose country treated him like a hero during a war, but had no place for him during peacetime. Hayes was the subject of a popular song, Johnny Cash's "The Ballad of Ira Hayes," and a film, *The Outsider,* starring Tony Curtis of the Bronx as Ira. Both film and song couch a message of social protest in highly sentimental rhetoric. Momaday appropriates the figure of the Indian veteran who can't adjust to life in postwar America, but makes important changes to the character and his fate. Most importantly, unlike Ira, Abel doesn't die—he flounders for quite a while, suffers through a jail term, Relocation, and a near-fatal beating—but he survives, and *House Made of Dawn* ends not with his death, but with a victory of sorts.

Abel's problems antedate his relocation to California under the government program that moved Indians from reservations to cities around the

West.[13] They start with his illegitimacy, which alienates him from the Jemez, a tight-knit tribal community: "He did not know who his father was. His father was a Navajo, they said, or a Sia or Isleta, an outsider anyway, which made him and his mother and Vidal somehow foreign and strange" (11).

Abel's experiences in combat during the war—Private Bowker describes his giving an enemy tank the finger, and jumping up and down "doing a goddam war dance"—contribute to his fragile psychological condition, his alienation from his tribe. This alienation deprives him of the power of language. The use of language, how it empowers a person and makes him human, is a repeated theme in Momaday's work. In *House* Momaday has Tosamah express these ideas. As a text for his sermon, Tosamah chooses the Johannine prologue, the opening verses of the Gospel of John, beginning with, "*In principio erat Verbum*" (91). But, Tosamah continues, John, not content to leave things at that, goes on to embellish that truth. Apparently referring to the phrase, "and the Word was with God, and the Word was God" (John 1:1), or perhaps "The Word was made flesh" (John 1:14), Tosamah says, "The Truth was overgrown with fat, and the fat was God." Tosomah continues: "And he said, 'In the beginning was the Word. . . .' And, man, right there and then he should have stopped" (93). Tosomah's statements are apparently a critique of Christian anthropomorphism.

To Tosamah the Word is sacred, and the white man's sin is that he embellishes this truth until he falsifies it: "Now, brothers and sisters, old John was a white man, and the white man has his ways. . . . He talks about the Word. He talks through it and around it. He builds it up with syllables, and prefixes and suffixes and hyphens and accents. He adds divides and multiplies the word, and in all this he subtracts the truth" (94).

That this is a fair description of what Tosamah himself is doing is beside the point here. To Momaday, it is a Kiowa belief, shared by many other Indians, that in what had always been an oral society the spoken word was sacred. And, the chief symptom of Abel's malaise is that he has been rendered speechless:

His [Abel's] return to the town had been a failure. . . . He had tried in days that followed to speak to his grandfather, but he could not say the things he wanted; he had tried to pray, to sing, to enter into the old rhythm of the tongue, but he was no longer attuned to it. . . . Had he been able to say it, anything of his old language—even the commonplace formula of greeting "Where are you going—which had no being beyond sound, no visible substance, would once again have shown him whole to himself; but he was dumb. Not dumb—silence was the older and better part of custom still—but inarticulate. [58]

It isn't just the ability to speak that Abel lacks, but the related abilities of singing and praying. Abel realizes what he needs to do, he just can't do it:

"[H]e wanted to make a song out of the colored canyon, the way the women of Torreon made songs upon their looms out of colored yarn, but he had not got the right words together. It would have been a creation song; he would have sung lowly of the first world, of fire and flood, and of the emergence of dawn from the hills" (59).

The song Abel is looking for is, of course, "House Made of Dawn," the Navajo song that Benally teaches him, the song that is an important part of Abel's recovery. Momaday implies that Abel's absent father was Navajo—or at least that's what Benally believes. "We're related somehow, I think" (153) is the way he puts it, and whether that's true or not, the Navajo song plays an important part in Abel's recovery. "House Made of Dawn" is a prayer song, specifically concerned with physical and mental recovery from illness or injury. It goes in part:

> Restore my feet for me,
> Restore my legs for me,
> Restore my body for me,
> Restore my mind for me . . .
> Happily I recover. [147]

Nursed back to health by Benally and his girlfriend, Milly, Abel completes his recovery, especially the psychological aspect of it, by returning to Jemez and joining in the ritual life of the tribe. Milly, Abel's paramour, grew up a poor white in the rural South. Despite her unhappy childhood, Milly is naïvely idealistic, a believer in "Honor, Industry, the Second Chance, the Brotherhood of Man, the American Dream" (107). Momaday capitalizes the terms to indicate the fatuousness of those who believe in them. Milly is very devoted to Abel, who rewards this by being "brutal with her" (109). Here again, we see Momaday's ambivalence about race relations and his own ethnicity.

Abel's first task in rejoining the ritual life of the Jemez is to prepare his grandfather, Francisco, for burial in the traditional fashion, sprinkling meal in the four directions. Abel leaves the body for Father Olguin to bury—Jemez religion is syncretic, a mixture of Christianity and tribal practices—and sets off to participate in the race for good hunting and harvests that his grandfather had won decades before. As he runs, he sings, "*House made of pollen, house made of dawn*" (212). In participating in a ritualistic race of his mother's people, the Jemez, and singing a song from his father's people, the Navajo, Abel integrates the two aspects of his heritage and is able to express himself the way he wanted to, thus achieving psychological peace.

My experience in teaching *House Made of Dawn* for the past forty-odd years is that white students rarely see anything happy about the ending. Given their expectations, shaped by popular versions of the Ira Hayes saga, or their idea that Indians are tragic figures, "vanishing Americans," they get the idea that Abel is somehow running off into the sunset, never to be seen again. The idea of Indians as the "vanishing Americans" is a product partially of the dramatic modifications of their traditional way of life that occurred with the "winning of the West," and partially their decline in population, which reached its nadir in 1890 at half a million, down from the five to eight million it had been before Columbus.[14] It is also a product of the way Indians were depicted by white artists like photographer Edward Curtis and sculptor James Earle Fraser. Curtis's famous photograph *Vanishing Race—Navajo* was one of a series of photographs of Indians from many tribes that Curtis published in twenty volumes starting in 1908. *The North American Indian* is Curtis's valediction for a doomed people. Visually stunning, the pictures were nonetheless faked to an extent: as Gerald Vizenor points out, Indians were forced to take off wristwatches and replace their cloth pants with britches made of deer hide. Curtis also "retouched tribal images; he, or his darkroom assistants, removed hats, labels, suspenders, parasols, from photographic prints. In one photograph entitled 'In a Peigan Lodge,' the image of an alarm clock was removed from the original negative" (*Crossbloods*, 85).

Curtis saw his photographs as a visual elegy to a people and way of life rapidly going the way of the passenger pigeon. Their sepia color suggests that Curtis was preserving the memories of Indians like flies in amber.

J. P. Morgan funded Curtis's project; Teddy Roosevelt wrote a laudatory foreword to the first volume. When that volume appeared, the *New York Herald* hailed Curtis's undertaking as the most ambitious publishing project since the King James Bible. Curtis not only influenced many people at the time he originally published his works, but also when the American Museum of Natural History issued a one-volume selection in 1971, when the Native American Renaissance was just underway. In an introduction to the 1971 edition, W. D. Coleman claimed, "*The North American Indian* will probably come to be recognized as the most profound document of pure Indian culture ever made" (Curtis, vii).

Some Indians, understandably, take a dimmer view of Curtis and his work. Vizenor complains about the falsification of Indian life, Curtis's refusal to let Indians and Indian culture change and adapt the way all cultures must, and his consignment of Indians to a highly romanticized past—chiefly, in Vizenor's view, for commercial purposes, claiming that "Curtis paid some tribal people to pose for photographs; he sold their images and lectured on their culture to raise cash to continue his travels to tribal communities. He traveled with his camera to capture neo-noble tribes, to preserve metasavages in the ethnographic present as consumable objects of the past" (*Crossbloods*, 85).

Another iteration of the theme of the "Vanishing American" is James Earl Fraser's sculpture, *The End of the Trail*, which depicts an Indian slumped over his horse, the embodiment of defeat. Fraser's brave is alive, if barely, but obviously he is on his way out—out of this life, out of American life. Fraser's large plaster statue (it was supposed to be bronzed but the money ran out) was first displayed at the Panama-Pacific International Exposition in San Francisco in 1915, but fell into disrepair. Eventually the National Cowboy Hall of Fame (now the National Cowboy and Western Heritage Museum) in Oklahoma City acquired and refurbished it, and that is where it is displayed today. Like Curtis, Fraser viewed the Indian as *victime*. Unaware of their condescension the two believed that Indians were on their way out and would soon be gone with the wind like the Old South, the Old West, and the young cowboy in white linen who died on the streets of Laredo.

But Indians aren't gone, and the novelists of the Native American Renaissance refuse to use the elegiac tone of white depictions of Indians like "The Ballad of Ira Hayes," *The Outsider, Vanishing Race,* or *The End of the Trail.* Not only Momaday's *House Made of Dawn* but other Indian novels as well end on an upbeat, though critics often miss this.

For instance, James Welch's *Winter in the Blood,* a novel structured around the myth of the Holy Grail, ends, like the Grail myth itself, on a positive note: the freeing of the waters. Welch never names his hero (we can deduce that his last name is First Raise), a man in his early thirties who still lives with his mother. Montana is a wasteland of "burnt prairie" and "dry, cracked gumbo flats" (3) because, as his mother says, "It never rains anymore" (4). The hero, like the Fisher King, tries his luck as an angler, but there are no fish in the local river. The hero drifts from bar to bar, occasionally picking up a woman. He isn't on much of a quest, although he is trying to find Agnes, a girl who had lived with him briefly. What he does accomplish is finding out something of his identity: he is descended from Yellow Calf, the hunter who supplied the meat that kept the hero's grandmother from starving when the tribe abandoned her. The hero is in a state of emotional paralysis—winter in the blood is the metaphor Welch uses to describe his feelings—brought about by the death of his father and brother, and the callousness of his mother. Just when the reader feels that the hero will never pull himself together and amount to something, he has an epiphany brought about by a sudden rain shower. Grail stories differ in details, but most end with the hero finishing a quest, which brings the "freeing of the waters" and ends the terrible drought. While sitting in the rain, the hero comes to grips with the fact that his father and brother are dead, and his feelings of depression and paralysis lift: "Some people, I thought, will never know how pleasant it is to be distant in a clean rain, the driving rain of a summer storm. It's not like you'd expect, nothing like you'd expect" (172).

The positive ending is muted, certainly, and the epilogue shows that the hero hasn't changed much, but at least the ice in his blood has thawed, and he can feel again.

Leslie Silko's *Ceremony* deals with a similar situation and has a similar ending to *House Made of Dawn* and *Winter in the Blood.* Like Welch, Silko bases her novel on a myth of desolation and restoration, but in her case she adapts Laguna and other Pueblo myths that deal with the subject. She intersperses her versions of the myths into the text. Momaday wrote a blurb for *Ceremony*, calling the work not a novel but "more precisely a telling, the celebration of a tradition and form that are older and more nearly universal than the novel as such."

In *Ceremony*, Tayo, like Abel, is a World War II veteran who suffers from PTSD. In fact, his symptoms are more severe than Abel's: his severe hallucinations make him highly dysfunctional. New Mexico, like Montana, has become a wasteland because of a severe drought. Tayo, who believes he has caused the drought by praying for the torrential rains to stop when he was on the Bataan death march, undertakes a quest as part of a cure prescribed by a Navajo medicine man named Betonie.

With the aid of a mysterious, possibly divine, figure named Ts'eh Montano, Tayo accomplishes the tasks Betonie sets him, and escapes the agents of the witchery, Emo, Pinkie, Leroy, and Harley, to complete his cure, his return to sanity. The return of Tayo's health is linked to the health of his land. When Tayo completes the tasks that constitute his quest, there is a freeing of the waters: it rains and the land blooms again: "He was dreaming of her arms around him strong when the rain on the tin roof woke him up. . . . The valley was green, from the yellow sandstone mesas in the northwest to the black lava hills to the south. . . . The new growth covered the earth lightly, each blade of grass, each leaf and stem with space between as if planted by a thin summer wind. There were no dusty red winds spinning across the flats this year" (219).

On hearing Tayo's account of events, his grandmother says: "It seems like I already heard these stories before . . . only thing is, the names sound different." Silko ends the novel with the refrain from a myth:

It [the witchery] is dead for now.
It is dead for now.
It is dead for now.
It is dead for now.

Like Momaday and Welch, Silko ends her book on a positive note.

Gerald Vizenor's *Darkness in Saint Louis: Bearheart*[15] is a dystopian fantasy about the United States after it has literally run out of gas. The government is commandeering trees from Indian reservations, in particular Red Earth in Minnesota, home of the Anishinaabe (Chippewa). The protagonist, Proude Cedarfair, manages to come into conflict with government agents and his own tribal government, so he sets out on foot on a cross-country odyssey with a ragtag band of clowns and tricksters. The members of the group are victims of all sorts of violence—poisoning, immolation, strangulation, dismemberment—all of which Vizenor describes with a great deal of *schadenfreude*.

Traditional Chippewa cosmology describes a series of stacked worlds. At the end of *Bearheart*, Proude escapes from this world, the third world, to a better world, the fourth, changing into a bear in the process. This may seem like a dubious fate to a white reader, but it is clear that to Vizenor it is happy, even triumphant, ending: "That morning when the old men when inhaling the dawn and laughing during the first winter solstice sunrise, Proude Cedarfair and Iniwa Biwide flew with vision bears ha ha ha haaa from the window on the perfect light into the fourth world" (243).

Momaday's second novel, *The Ancient Child*, also ends with the protagonist turning into a bear. In this case it isn't as clear that it represents a happy ending, but at least it seems to be a matter of the natural and necessary turn of events, and something to be celebrated, not mourned. The book is the novelization of a Kiowa myth of Tsaoi, the boy who turns into a bear and chases his sisters up a tree. The sisters become the stars of the Big Dipper, the tree becomes Devils Tower, a monolithic volcanic rock in Wyoming. The protagonist's name, Locke Setman, portends his fate. Locke was called "Loki" as a child, for the Norse trickster, noted for shape-shifting. *Set* is the Kiowa word for bear.

Locke is Kiowa by birth, but after his parents die he is adopted by whites and grows up in San Francisco with no knowledge of his tribe or its culture. He returns to Oklahoma for the funeral of a distant relative and falls under the thrall of a Kiowa/Navajo woman named Grey who prepares the unwitting Locke for his metamorphosis. In the last scene of the novel, Locke turns from a human into a bear:

> Something was wrong, terribly wrong. His limbs had became very heavy, and his head. He was dizzy. His vision blurred. . . . At the same time there was a terrible dissonance in his ears, a whole jumble of sounds that came like a blow to his head. He was stunned, but in a moment the confusion of sounds subsided, and he heard things he had never heard before, separately, distinctly, with nearly absolute definition. . . . And there came upon him a loneliness like death. He moved on, a shadow receding into shadows. [314]

Momaday's tone is not as triumphant as Vizenor's; in fact, there is a distinct note of anguish in it. However, the metamorphosis is totally appropriate as Locke's fate. It is what happened in myth; it is what must be. Momaday's Kiowa fatalism echoes Alexander Pope's Christian optimism: "Whatever is, is right."

Louise Erdrich shares Vizenor's Chippewa heritage, and one of her heroes undergoes the same transformation as Proude Cedarfair. In *Bingo Palace*, Fleur Pillager, shape-shifting trickster extraordinaire, turns into a bear twice. The first time is when Lipsha Morrissey asks her for a love medicine:

"She does not answer, but continues at her task, and then, unexpectedly, too quickly for an old lady, she whirls around and catches me in the dim light, looks steadily into my eyes until I blink, once, twice. When I open my eyes again she broadens, blurs beyond my reach, beyond belief. Her face spreads out on the bones and goes on darkening and darkening. Her nose tilts up into a black snout and her eyes sink" (137).

Apparently she changes back at some point, but perhaps her transformation was only a matter of Lipsha's superstitious imaginings. Erdrich's brand of magical realism makes either option a possibility. At any rate, at the end of the novel Fleur is in human form when she somehow intuits that Lipsha is about to freeze to death in a blizzard. To save him, she turns into a bear, a form of death that allows Lipsha to live: "Outdoors, into a day of deep cold and brilliance that often succeeds a long disruptive blizzard, she went, thinking of the boy out there. Annoyed, she took his place" (272).

Fleur doesn't go to the fourth or any other world, however. Like Set she remains on this earth, still a presence to her people: "She doesn't tap our panes of glass or leave her claw marks on eaves and doors. She only coughs, low, to make her presence known. You have heard the bear laugh—that is the chuffing noise we hear and it is unmistakable" (274).

The laugh is the "ha ha ha haaa" that Proude made when he left for the fourth world. It is a happy and triumphant sound, not the whine of a *victime*.

There are those who argue that American Indian literature is distinct from American literature, a separate Anglophone literature.[16] I wouldn't go that far—Momaday, Welch, Silko, Erdrich, Vizenor, et al. were born, raised, and educated in the United States, and their works very much reflect that. However, the works of Indian writers do form a distinct corpus within American literature, and the writers are a self-conscious group who read each other's work and react to it. Nowhere is this clearer than in the chain of literary responses that followed the publication of *House Made of Dawn*. One of the distinctive themes Indian writers employ is the concept of the Indian as master or mistress of his or her own fate. He or she may be feckless or self-destructive, but she or he is not a passive *victime*.

NOTES

1. *Other Destinies*, pp. 283–85.

2. The story of Cain and Abel was a Hebrew myth before it was Christian, but Momaday, whose family belonged to the Rainy Mountain Baptist Church, would have encountered it in a Christian context. For a discussion of Welch's use of Blackfeet myth in *the Death of Jim Loney*, see Purdy, "Bha'a and *The Death of Jim Loney*."

3. See Schubnell, *N. Scott Momaday*, pp. 22, 127.

4. Genesis 16.

5. 1 Kings 16:28*ff.*
6. Melville, *Moby Dick,* ch. cxxviii; Matthew, 2:18. *Moby Dick* also has a ship named *Jereboam,* the king who led the newly separate Israel astray (1 Kings 12:16*ff*). The story of the *Jereboam* includes a man who calls himself the archangel Gabriel (chapter lxii). Chapter lxxxii includes a disquisition on the historicity of Jonah.

7. Abel is, in a sense, a victim of whiteness in a Melvillian context. See chapter xlii, "The Whiteness of the Whale."

8. For a full discussion of what Vizenor means by "survivance," see Vizenor (ed.), *Survivance.* For the present, suffice it to say "survivance" means a proactive attitude to survival.

9. This article also owes a debt to Melville. See *Confidence-Man,* chapter xxvi, "Containing the Metaphysics of Indian-Hating."

10. Bakhtin, *Dialogic Imagination,* "Epic and Novel," p. 7*ff.*

11. See nas.ucdavis.edu/forbes/aztlan.pdf.

12. *Almanac of the Dead* is devoted to the proposition that Mexicans and Indians are blood relatives.

13. For a description of Relocation, see Rawls, *Chief Red Fox Is Dead,* pp. 46–50.

14. Figures on Indian population vary widely, depending in large part on the politics of the estimator. I use Cherokee demographer Russell Thornton's *American Indian Holocaust and Survival,* pp. 32*ff.*

15. Originally published in 1978, reissued with minor modifications as *Bearheart* in 1990.

16. See, for instance, Weaver, Warrior, and Womack, *American Indian Literary Nationalism.*

WORKS CITED

Bakhtin, M. M. *The Dialogic Imagination.* Austin: University of Texas Press, 1981.
Curtis, Edward S. *Portraits from North American Indian Life.* New York: Outerbridge and Lazard, 1972.
Erdrich, Louise. *The Bingo Palace.* New York: HarperCollins, 1994.
Melville, Herman. *The Confidence-Man.* Oxford: Oxford Univeristy Press, 1989.
———. *Moby Dick.* Boston: Houghton Mifflin, 1956.
Momaday, Scott. *The Ancient Child.* New York: Doubleday, 1989.
———. *House Made of Dawn.* New York: Harper & Row, 1968.
———. "The Morality of Indian Hating." *Ramparts* 3:1 (1964), 29–40.
———. *The Names.* New York: Harper & Row, 1976.
———. "The Strange and True Story of My Life with Billy the Kid." In N. Scott Momaday, *In the Presence of the Sun: Stories and Poems, 1961–1991.* Albuquerque: University of New Mexico Press, 1992.
———. "The Way to Rainy Mountain." *The Reporter,* January 26, 1967, 41–43.
———. *The Way to Rainy Mountain.* Albuquerque: University of New Mexico Press, 1969.

Owens, Louis. *Other Destinies: Understanding the American Novel.* Norman: University of Oklahoma Press, 1992.

Purdy, John. "Bha'a and *The Death of Jim Loney.*" *SAIL* 11:1 (1987).

Schubnell, Matthias. *N. Scott Momaday: The Cultural and Literary Background.* Norman: University of Oklahoma Press, 1985.

Schwartz, Regina. *The Curse of Cain.* Chicago: University of Chicago Press, 1997.

Silko, Leslie. *Ceremony.* New York: Viking Press, 1977.

Vizenor, Gerald. *Crossbloods.* Minneapolis: University of Minnesota Press, 1990.

———. *Darkness in Saint Louis: Bearheart.* St. Paul: Truck Press, 1978.

———. *Fugitive Poses.* Lincoln: University of Nebraska Press, 1998.

———. *Survivance: Narratives of Native Presence.* Lincoln: University of Nebraska Press, 2008.

Welch, James. *Winter in the Blood.* New York: Harper & Row, 1974.

4
On the Cutting Edge
Leslie Marmon Silko

REBECCA TILLETT

Leslie Marmon Silko's contribution to contemporary Native American literature is inestimable. Along with Simon Ortiz and James Welch, Silko was a key
member of the "first wave" of Native writings to follow N. Scott Momaday's
groundbreaking Pulitzer Prize– winning *House Made of Dawn* (1968). Moreover, her work has also helped to create both a popular interest in, and a market for, a whole range of Native women's writing, including that of Paula Gunn
Allen, Linda Hogan, LeAnne Howe, Luci Tapahonso, and the internationally
acclaimed Louise Erdrich. Significantly, Silko's fictional works are implicitly
and often explicitly political: the semiautobiographical *Storyteller* (1981), with
its familial and communal focus, extends beyond the personal to demonstrate
and politically situate a specifically Laguna worldview;[1] the localized "witchery" of *Ceremony* (1977), which is identified within the text as all forms of
exploitation and oppression, is exploded on a truly global scale in *Almanac of
the Dead* (1991) to address multiple grotesque atrocities of an almost unimaginable magnitude. Finally, Silko's most recent novel, *Gardens in the Dunes*
(1999), filters European and American cultures through the worldview of the
Indian child Indigo, alongside a passionate condemnation of Euro-American
nature-culture separatism that enables and actively encourages environmental abuse and destruction. Given their prescient vision and their continuing
relevance to emerging American and more global political events, Silko's literary works have been, therefore, not only cutting but truly on the cutting edge.

Indeed, what is most cutting-edge about Silko's work is her consistent demand for an active reader who has the potential for activism. Consequently,
her reader is not only expected to *actively listen* to an alternative worldview,
but to *actively participate* as a witness to a wide variety of contemporary forms
of oppression and exploitation directed at Native peoples. *Storyteller* clearly
demonstrates Silko's ongoing political and cultural project to foreground Laguna cultural traditions and worldviews, including the profound power of
the act of storytelling, alongside a formidable critique of contemporary Euro-
American ideologies and policies and their damaging impact upon Native

communities. *Storyteller* is also, importantly, a multivocal text, presenting a range of complementary and dissonant voices and viewpoints. These reveal not only the dynamics of oral storytelling, but also the dynamics of community at Laguna in ways that forcefully reject established Euro-American cultural assumptions. This is most immediately evident within Silko's written deployment of oral storytelling conventions, where the written form emulates the spoken to demand active audience participation, and to provide important cultural information to emphasise the active and interactive process of exchange inherent within the storytelling process:

> *The Laguna people*
> *always begin their stories*
> *with "humma-hah":*
> *that means "long ago."*
> *And the ones who are listening*
> *Say "aaaa-eh."* [1981, 38]

Here, Silko carefully traces the connections between the past ("long ago") and the present (those now listening/reading) to offer political commentaries on a range of historical and contemporary conflicts. Indeed, Silko's inclusion of an audience response demonstrates her ongoing political project: to demand not only an active listener but, more importantly, an active *response*. This, I argue, is the most important aspect of all of Silko's work, which makes profound political demands on its readers, forcing a reading experience that is active and a response that has the potential for activism.

In the context of the activist reader, the most significant idea that runs throughout Silko's fictional work is the concept of "witchery," which encompasses all kinds of destruction, oppression, exploitation, and manipulation directed not only at humans but also at the natural world by the Kunideeyahs, "the Destroyers" (1981, 145). Significantly, witchery also includes the reductive binary thinking that maintains imposed artificial hierarchies and enables and perpetuates all kinds of violence, including racism and environmental destruction, and all historical and contemporary forms of oppression by those unquestioned (and usually unanswerable) institutional bodies such as the federal government, state legislatures, the church, the legal system, the police, the military, capitalist corporations, etc. In this context, David L. Moore identifies a key story that is deployed repeatedly through the first three texts I am discussing here: "Estoy-Eh-Muut and the Kunideeyahs" (Arrowboy and the Witches). Silko's retelling of this traditional Keresan story in *Storyteller* demonstrates both how witchery works and how it impacts on individuals and communities. Arrowboy is adamant that "[s]omething felt out of place" (1981, 140), and follows his wife, Kochininako (Yellow Woman), to discover that she is "a secret member/of the Kunideeyah Clan" (1981, 145), a group of witches intent on causing harm to those around them. Consequently, the Destroyers "cause madness," kill a "lone . . . traveller," "strangl[e] a sleeping baby," and ensure that "the village people would go hungry" (1981, 148). However, what is significant is that destructive magic cannot work if there is a witness:

> "Something is wrong,"
> the leader said.
> "Kochininako, go and see
> if an outsider is spying on us." [1981, 146]

As in *Ceremony*, where "Ck'o'yo magic won't work/if someone is watching us" (1977, 247), Silko's concern is with notions of witnessing and, as Moore argued in his influential essay on the subject, it is the ritual role of the witness that her reader is required to adopt (1999, 150). The term "witness" has profound political implications: to witness is to draw upon established "knowledge." To witness, therefore, is by definition to "take, accept, and assume responsibility." Moreover, as Shoshana Felman and Dori Laub argue, witnessing is "a mode of . . . accessing reality" (1992, xx). As Moore contends, the reader's role as witness creates a dialogue between the reader and the text, whereby the reader attains a "specular power" (1999, 150, 176). This effectively means that the witnessing "gaze" of Silko's reader-witnesses reverberates with the events of the text. The gaze of the witness therefore directly meets, recognizes, and subverts the gaze of the oppressors, and witnessing becomes a moral and ethical practice for the reader.

In terms of Silko's textual politics, the role that is demanded of the reader is highly significant. If, as Moore asserts, both author and reader "witness, elude, and neutralize destruction" (1999, 150), then this can be applied extratextually to the very real contemporary political situations that Silko depicts in her fiction. Significantly, this means that all the institutional bodies that have historically impacted destructively upon Native communities, and—most significantly—those that *continue* to do so, are subject to the witnessing gaze. Reliant upon American society turning a blind eye to localized, and often racialized, instances of oppression and exploitation, such institutional bodies are subject to constraints through those witnessing their actions, even textually at secondhand. The moral and ethical implication is that, as the Kunideeyahs observe in the traditional stories, all oppressive actions are thus neutralized: if someone is watching, the destructive magic simply does not work. While this is evident in the witchery stories embedded within *Storyteller*, it is within the linked thematic concerns of *Ceremony* and *Almanac of the Dead* that witchery is clearly identified as the primary cause of contemporary destruction, and the key obstacle to individual and communal healing and well-being.

Both healing and well-being are therefore the chief concerns of *Ceremony*, not only of the emotionally and psychologically damaged mixed-blood war veteran Tayo, but also of an equally fragile wider Laguna community beset with the external pressures of assimilation that, in some crucial cases, have been internalized and are even more insidious and difficult to address. Tayo's cousin Rocky is taught by the Euro-American education system to abhor and belittle traditional Laguna culture, and to actively question the wisdom and knowledge ("superstition" [1977, 51]) of his elders; while Tayo's Auntie's Christian faith complicates her traditional Laguna notions of relatedness so that her relationship with both Tayo's mother, her own sexually promiscuous sister, and with Tayo himself is clouded by the recognition that the experiences of Tayo's mother do "not happen to her alone" but rather to all of the Laguna community, and Auntie's subsequent actions emerge from desperation: from her "desperat[e]" attempt "to reconcile the family with the people" (1977, 69). Indeed, the ambivalence in Auntie's treatment of the mixed-blood Tayo, who is the physical result of his mother's "interaction" with white society, exposes the complex politics of blood that the Laguna have been forced to negotiate because of the federal imposition of the blood quantum as the definitive legal quantifier of "Indianness." Yet most problematic are the other war veterans who have all been doubly dislocated, first by their unexpected apparent acceptance into Euro-American culture ("Anyone can fight for America . . . [i]n a time of need" [1977, 64]), and then by their equally sudden rejection as soon as the war is over: "The war was over, the uniform was gone. All of a sudden that man at the store waits on you last" (1977, 42). These war veterans are not only self-destructive but also destructive toward all others. Yet, significantly, Silko's analysis of witchery refuses to apportion blame solely to white or Indian groups: as Betonie comments, "the trickery of the witchcraft . . . want[s] us to believe all evil resides with white people" (1977, 132). Rather, Silko's analysis emphasizes individual agency: witchery is both more dangerous and more insidious because it is a demonstration of the human capacity for hatred.

In keeping with the types of oppression that Silko engages with in *Ceremony*, the witchery of the text is revealed as a highly resourceful and manipulative form of destruction. In the most powerful deliberation on hatred in the text, the "witchery poem," Silko outlines how hatred of self and others emerges from the kinds of separatist ideology that has marked western empirical thinking:

> *They fear*
> *They fear the world.*
> *They destroy what they fear.*
> *They fear themselves.* [1977, 135]

Significantly, this separatist thinking is evident in the intense emphasis upon categorization that characterizes not only Enlightenment philosophy but also contemporary science and that has resulted in the legitimization of a range of highly exploitative and oppressive acts of hatred: racial "classification" and hierarchies; the colonization of lands and peoples; historical and contemporary acts of genocide; the "institution" of slavery; and, more recently, atomic and nuclear testing and the policies and practices of environmental racism. As my final emphasis here on the environment suggests, for Silko this separatist thinking is also evident in the kinds of culture-nature separatism that dominates both the Christian worldview that advocates a hierarchy that ranks the natural world much lower on the scale of "importance" than humanity and, more worryingly, also the self-destructive scientific thinking and environmental policies of the early twenty-first century. As Helen Jaskoski argues, the text is an "extended critique[e] of the nuclear age," which demonstrates that "nuclear weapons and nuclear power" are "the logical and inevitable culmination of western empirical thought" (1990, 2) because, for Silko's witches, "[t]he world is a dead thing" (1977, 135). Based in separatist ideology, this oppressive worldview not only refuses to recognize the symbiotic relationship between human groups, or between humanity and the natural world, but also fails to recognize how self-destructive this attitude is: "*They destroy what they fear. / They fear themselves*" (1977, 135).

This self-destructive hatred is embodied in the text by the war vets and by the multiple damages inflicted upon the natural world. Silko's discussion is therefore both local, through the violence of Emo, Pinkie, Harley, and Leroy, and the drought that Tayo believes is the result of his curse upon the rain, as well as national: through acts of aggression such as the atomic bombs unleashed on Hiroshima and Nagasaki and their profound international impacts. In this context, "white warfare" has become not only "monstrous" but also clinical and detached, "killing across great distances without knowing who or how many had died"; and, as Tayo's telling comments on the "dismembered corpses" and the bodies that simply "evaporated" warn, this is something new and "terrible" because "[n]ot even oldtime witches killed like that" (1977, 36–37). Accordingly, Silko's depiction of the war vets shows the local consequences of a national deployment of hatred, emphasising the vets' creative use of highly negative rituals, where they "repea[t] the stories about [the] good times . . . like long medicine chants, the beer bottles pounding on the counter tops like drums" as "part of the ritual where they damn those yellow Jap bastards" (1977, 43). Like the old-time witches who make ritual use of body parts, Emo carries a bag of human teeth, "war souvenirs . . . he had knocked out of the corpse of a Japanese soldier" (1977, 60–61). As a kind of " inverted" medicine bundle, Emo's collection of teeth demonstrates the types of hatred and oppression that Tayo fights against, which grow in power the more hatred, inhumanity, and contempt are shown: "[Emo] pushed . . . [the teeth] into circles and rows like unstrung beads; he scooped them into his hand and shook them like dice. . . . Emo grew from each killing. Emo fed off each man he killed" (1977, 60–61). The effects on Tayo are painfully physically evident, as he spends the early part of text vomiting the poison of witchery from his system and searching for a ceremony that will act as a cure. Indeed, given that Silko's text has been interpreted by many critics as a wider ceremony for her readers, it could be argued that the connections that Silko makes between the local and the national/international actively enable the workings of hatred to be more widely recognized, and Tayo's ceremonial cure to be more widely applied. As Jane Caputi comments, Silko's reader is required to recognize not only that Tayo's illness derives from "the same evil that now threatens the planet with nuclear destruction" but also that his healing is representative "of a much larger ritual" for humanity more widely (1992, 14).

As a result, the climax of the text occurs at the uranium mine[2] where the earth resembles "fresh graves" (1977, 245) and where Tayo makes links not only between the separatist ideology feeding the decision to test the atomic bomb on Indian land and its subsequent deployment in Japan (where "Japanese voices . . . merg[e] with Laguna voices" [1977, 246]), but also the connection of these decisions with the ongoing casual environmental destruction evident in the uranium industry in the Southwest and its unspoken policies of environmental racism toward Native communities. At the mine, Tayo sees that the witches "had taken these beautiful rocks from deep within the earth and they had laid them in a monstrous design, realizing destruction on a scale only *they* could have dreamed" (1977, 246). Silko's analysis bluntly points to the fact that the Destroyers, in the form of contemporary nuclear powers, quite literally have the power to lay their monstrous design "*across the world / and explode everything*" (1977, 137). Most significantly, when denied Tayo as a ritual victim, the forces of hatred in the form of the war vets demonstrate their self-destruction through a "gree[d] for human flesh" (1977, 251) evident in the ceremonial torture and execution of Harley. Silko's textual conclusion makes it clear that the battle against hatred is ongoing: witchery is defeated but only "for now" (1977, 261). The close of Silko's *Ceremony*/ceremony is a reminder to her witnessing reader of the need to be ever-vigilant against the destructive forces of witchery, a reminder that hatred is dangerously enduring.

Silko's own recognition that the political project of storytelling is that "the story must be told as it is" (1981, 31), even when the story is one of enduring hatred, is perhaps most evident in the disturbing and graphically violent *Almanac of the Dead*, where the patterns of *Ceremony* are explored on a truly global scale. Tracing the actions of individuals and groups across the Americas and then more widely, *Almanac* is a searing indictment of the hatred feeding the imperial ideologies that enabled the colonization of the New World (and elsewhere), and of the ideological hatred that has fed—and continues to feed—the policies of five hundred years of American settlement. As Silko's title suggests, the text is crowded with the "furious, bitter spirits" of those who have died as a result of ideological hatred, and who are still "howl[ing] for justice" (1991, 424, 723). Yet Silko's analysis is not simply historical; her assertion that "the Indian wars have never ended in the Americas" (*Almanac* map legend) forces her reader to bear witness to both the historical records of genocide and oppression and to their contemporary legacies. As a result, *Almanac* carefully traces the ideologies of hatred that continue to oppress, and the ways in which ideological hatred is currently deployed through a range of cultural practices, as well as through explicit national and international policies and legislation. Accordingly, the emphasis is on corruption, and the reader witnesses multiple graphic images of the kinds of corruption that emerge from the hatred of witchery. The text is saturated with violence: with gangsters and hit men; with corrupt governmental and military figures and political assassinations; with homicide and genocide; with illegal trafficking of all kinds; with a wide range of sexual abuses; with environmental abuse and destruction; and with the racist histories of genetic science. Above all, Silko explores—and forces her reader-witness to explore—the effects of the oppressive separatist ideologies of "vampire capitalis[m]" (1991, 312), its deployment through power structures such as science, technology, and industry and its widespread exploitation of human misery and environmental destruction for lucrative financial profiteering.

In this context, Silko's own choice of metaphor is at times highly problematic, leading to suggestions that she is embracing a range of ideologies—including homophobia and an antiabortion agenda—that themselves are examples of the kinds of hatred and witchery she is discussing. However, Silko's exploration of all forms of hatred is significant here and, in the wider context of the text, her metaphors should not be interpreted within such simplistic binaries. For example, Silko's highly graphic description of a "late" abortion, where the "tortured tiny babies" are seen to "grimace and twist away" in an attempt to escape their inevitable fate (1991, 102), could easily be interpreted as an antiabortionist statement. However, within the context of the book, Silko makes it is quite clear that what is actually being discussed is the *filming* of that abortion and its subsequent distribution as a form of entertainment. Therefore, the real subject for discussion is the highly profitable *market* for these films. As a result, Silko's analysis is a far more complex assessment of the commodification of human suffering and death, and the example seems carefully chosen for its emotive and contentious nature. The emphasis is, therefore, very much on the *reception*—and so the enjoyment—of these images by a very specific audience: Silko is quite clear that one such audience is "the antiabortionist lobby" itself, "which paid top dollar for the footage" (1991, 102). This is, clearly, one example of the kinds of "vampire capitalism" Silko is exposing. Similarly, Silko's depiction of homosexual characters is also problematic, not least because all except one (Eric, who commits suicide) are utterly ruthless and obsessed with power. Yet any simplistic reading ignores and even erases a much more complex textual analysis, and I concur with Janet St. Clair who suggests that this is not a simple statement of homophobia, but rather an examination of the excesses of male power in a deeply problematic patriarchy that Silko herself defines as a "culture of death." Certainly both Beaufrey and Serlo define themselves in terms of their exclusive social and economic status, primarily by race and gender—and the extreme version of this "exclusivity" is depicted sexually, since both are contemptuous of women as inferior beings who are the carriers of disease. Silko's depiction of homosexuality can, therefore, be read as an extreme example of male power that is attempting to free itself of any connection to women, as is evident in Beaufrey's obsession with the creation of artificial wombs, where women are reduced simply to their reproductive capabilities with the aim of eliminating the need for female reproduction, and indeed women themselves, entirely. (See my more detailed discussion below.) As St. Clair comments, these are not (and are not meant to be) accurate depictions of gay male culture, but rather the representation of "unchecked [patriarchal] egomania" and of the "malevolent and voracious monsters" that such a system encourages (1999, 207).

Identified by Craig Womack as "one of the most important books of . . . [the twentieth] century," *Almanac*'s positioning of its reader-witness is crucial to its rejection of "entropy"—political stasis—in favor of "a redistribution of energy" (1999, 252–53). In Silko's text, this redistribution of energy is profoundly revolutionary, foregrounding the vast army of indigenous peoples from across the Americas and the multiethnic American army of the homeless who, by the close of the text, converge to invade and occupy American national space. Silko's text thus becomes "a radical, stunning manifesto" (Niemann, 1992, 1) for the restoration of well-being and for healing on a scale far exceeding Tayo's own ceremony. Moreover, some decidedly revolutionary futures are testified to by the reader-witness, as are their roots in the damaging and self-destructive separatist ideologies of science, technology, and industrial capitalism. Alongside the lack of regard and respect that oppressive individuals show to human groups deemed "unworthy" is the equal lack of regard and respect shown to the natural world. Indeed, the two identically oppressive attitudes are clearly related in Silko's text, where those who demonstrate the hatred of witchery direct their lack of respect and indifference indiscriminately at the world around them. Such groups include the military (the Mexican General J), the Old World aristocracy (the Euro-American Beaufrey and Columbian Serlo), and the capitalist corporate world (the Euro-Americans Trigg, owner of Bio-Materials Inc., and Leah Blue, owner of Blue Horizons and Blue Water corporations). Accordingly, the reader acts as a witness to an almost overwhelming depiction of hatred and oppression that not only taps into very real political situations but also into the ideologies informing equally real policies directed against oppressed groups throughout the Americas and more widely.

Specifically, Silko traces the role played by inhumanity and casual racism in the deployment of horrendously damaging ideologies, and in scientific, corporate, and governmental policies that actively dehumanize those they wish to exploit. Significantly, the examples in *Almanac* also expose the complex historical and ongoing links between science, capitalism, and the workings of witchery. Thus General J's eminently practical response to the indigenous refugees flooding into Mexico to escape a range of brutal South American military regimes is to advocate "quick annihilation" (1991, 495). The racist origins of this type of response are laid bare: for General J, "'disappearances' and death squads" are clearly "superior" to the kinds of "death factories" employed by the Nazis, not only because they are less "incriminating" (1991: 495) but, more significantly, given Silko's analysis of vampiric capitalism, they are also more *productive*. In this context of vampiric profitability, the business practices of capitalist "entrepreneurs" are also explored, and the links between various forms of exploitation made explicit. Leah Blue pursues profit at any cost, including irreversible damage to the environment, as her new real estate development of "Venice, Arizona" (1991: 652) replaces the desert wastelands of "cactus and scraggly greasewood . . . [and] grey volcanic gravel" with desirable and profitable "Mediterranean villas and canals" (1991: 378). Silko's reader witnesses not only Leah's inability to see the connections between humans and the natural world, but also her failure to see the waste and obscenity of creating a network of waterways in the desert. For Leah, access to water is not a basic human right, rather water is a valuable commodity and a highly profitable industry. But the most extreme example is the Euro-American Trigg, owner of Bio-Materials Inc. that markets human blood, tissues, and organs "sourced" from the dispensable and faceless homeless populations of Tucson. Viewed by Trigg as "human debris" and "refuse" (1991, 444), the homeless exist only as a commodity to be exploited then exterminated. A true vampire capitalist, Trigg quite literally bleeds his inconsequential victims dry, so that he can harvest organs as well as blood. What is clear to the witnessing reader is that, for Trigg, the dispossessed are worth no more than the sum of their available body parts. In terms of the marketability of their blood, tissue, and organs, the dispossessed are merely "produce" that is ripe for "harvesting" (1991, 444).

Perhaps most interesting are the connections Silko makes with science and industry, especially through the (self) interests of the Euro-American Beaufrey and the Columbian Serlo, which take this separatist ideology to its extreme. Here, the hatred of witchery is at full play: both are convinced of their own social and "racial" superiority, and both are equally obsessed with science in the disturbing context of blood "purity," biological warfare, and genetic research, where Silko draws undeniable parallels with the "logic" informing Nazi science. Moving beyond General J's practical and relatively simplistic application of racial extermination, Beaufrey and Serlo represent the kinds of separatist thought that informs a science that has no boundaries, limits, ethics, or morals of any kind. It is, more disturbingly, a science that is intoxicated with its own political power. The dangers are immediately apparent and echo some of the ongoing extratextual moral debates about the power of, and limits to, science. So the racial eradication of the "swarms of brown and yellow human larvae called natives" (1991, 545) is assured through the deployment of "the great biological bomb" in the form of "the first 'designer virus,'" HIV (1991, 548); women, who are identified (as they have been historically by science and medicine) with infection and disease, are removed from the reproductive chain through the creation of "an artificial uterus" that will enable the production of "a superior human being" (1991, 547); and, in response to seemingly unstoppable industrial pollution, "Alternative Earth modules" that will be "loaded with the last of the earth's uncontaminated soil, water, and oxygen" are created to enable the survival of "the select few" in "luxury and ease" (1991, 542). Moreover, Beaufrey explicitly states his own sense of superiority: he can act without remorse because "others did not fully exist," and it is his only own extreme individualism, his "selfishness," that provides "great satisfaction" (1991, 533). Both Beaufrey and Serlo demonstrate extreme versions of the kinds of shortsighted separatist thinking that increasingly informs not only Euro-American science, but also the refusal of industry to address the increasing problems of environmental pollution. While, as Joni Adamson argues, Beaufrey and Serlo are deployed to "explicitly cal[l] attention to the ways in which scientific discourses empower, even mandate, the modern scientist, state, or multinational corporation" (2001, 170), both clearly also represent the growing gulf between scientific and industrial shortsightedness and an increasingly urgent need to develop sustainable global environmental policies. Moreover, in their absolute self-interest and self-promotion, in their active hatred of all other life forms, both Beaufrey and Serlo also represent the very real and ongoing threat of witchery for Silko's reader to witness: the Destroyers are those "who hold political, financial, and military power in the Americas" and who "have in common a taste for violence [and] a disregard for humanity and the earth" (Sol, 1999, 35).

With so much hatred saturating the text, it is clear that, as for Tayo, a ceremony is required. Having borne witness to the chaos caused by extreme separatist thinking, Silko's reader is also required to testify to the healing potential of holistic indigenous epistemologies that actively acknowledge the long-term effects of individual and communal actions and promote balance and cooperation. As a result, the text provides a specific space where therapeutic social and cultural processes can begin to facilitate the healing of wounded individuals and communities, a space where holism triumphs over individualism. The International Holistic Healers Convention is, therefore, home to "cures of all kinds" (1991, 716), where alternative and more respectful worldviews are given the space and the freedom not just to exist but to develop. Although the characters at the Healers Convention have clear individual agendas (the reclamation of elided communal histories and the retaking of stolen lands, the social reintegration of the poor and the homeless, for example), it is also clear that these agendas converge to form clear communal goals, such as universal social enfranchisement and the eradication of poverty and racism. The Convention, therefore, is clearly a ceremonial space, where there is potential for a radical redistribution of cultural, economic, political, and spiritual power. And part of that healing is clearly humor: in a text that is so profoundly horrific, the Convention also marks a space where humor is deployed. Here, Silko satirizes both Anglo and Indian cultures and individuals alike: from the white "Indian lovers" who financially profit from the "New Age" market for "Indian spirituality" (1991, 709), to the satirical representation of the Indian poet lawyer Wilson Weasel Tail, whose personal history (dropping out of law school to become a poet because "[t]he law served the rich" [1991, 713]) has clear and highly humorous connections with Silko's own repeatedly stated background: "I completed three semesters of the American Indian Law School Fellowship Program before I realized that injustice is built into the Anglo-American legal system . . . [and] I decided the only way to seek justice was through the power of stories" (1997, 19–20). Perhaps because of the way that satire works in this textual space, the space of the Convention enables the reader to make connections between dispossessed groups, to witness the hatred associated with the dangerously pervasive worldview of witchery, and to recognize the need for constant vigilance that is identified in *Ceremony*. Above all, the reader-witness is required to recognize and accept the potential of communal action/activism: "This was the last chance the people had against the Destroyers, and they would never prevail if they did not work together as a common force" (1991, 747).

Silko's most recent novel, *Gardens in the Dunes* (1999), continues and elaborates the key concerns evident in her earlier novels: the complex interrelationships of human and natural worlds and the damage caused by the exploitative worldviews that Silko identifies as witchery. By analyzing Euro-American thought systems through the eyes of an Indian child, the worldviews and ideologies that we accept without question are defamiliarized and problematized, forcing the reader to act as a witness to the profound social and political consequences of those worldviews and ideologies. These consequences include the enormity of contemporary environmental damage and its origins in the inability of Euro-American thought systems to address the complex interrelationships between humans and the natural world, plus an examination of holistic alternatives. Silko's deployment of a historical setting (the 1890s) allows her to trace the legacies of a range of contemporary social and political ills in established historical events and socio-political attitudes. As a result, the reader is required to witness a range of social and cultural histories of the land: the physical and spiritual significance of agriculture to the sedentary indigenous populations of the arid American Southwest, and the centrality of agriculture and land cultivation to the economic, religious, and political sensibilities of the Europeans who settled the Americas.

Gardens therefore analyzes relationships with the land that are established and maintained by the diverse cast of characters: the old Sand Lizard gardens in the dunes; the citrus groves and hothouses of California; the horticultural excesses of Long Island; the lush greenery of English gardens near Bath; the formal Italian gardens of Genoa; and the Chemehuevi Reservation gardens in Arizona. As in both *Ceremony* and *Almanac*, the reader witnesses the inability of phallocentric, Christian, capitalist worldviews to adequately address the symbiotic relationship between human life and the natural world, and the damage caused by the imposition of hierarchies that attempt to rank different life forms in terms of their "importance." In particular, *Gardens* engages with the attitudes and motivations of science/technology and capitalism/industry through an analysis of orchid collecting in Brazil; the global rubber market; citron production in Corsica; mining in Arizona; and the construction of a dam on the Colorado River.[3] Science and capitalism are clearly linked in the text: gardens are defined as "research laborator[ies]" (1999, 75), and the Euro-American urge to collect botanic specimens is identified as explicitly imperial. Moreover, the reader witnesses the political role of capitalist forces behind the wanton destruction of the Brazilian rain forest (to break Brazil's "world monopoly" on rubber and ensure no competition from "foreign" orchid collectors [1999, 131, 144]) and of an environment blighted by the construction of a dam on the Colorado, where the redirection of the river transforms a landscape of trees into "exposed piles of white skeletons" (1999, 396). Silko's reader is therefore required to witness "what capitalism makes people do to one another" (Silko, cited in Arnold, 1998, 21), and this includes the rise of a powerful new "throwaway" consumer culture in the early twentieth century, demonstrated by the annual "remodelling" of the gardens of Long Island, where a devotion to "conspicuous consumption" (Silko, cited in Arnold, 1998, 20) ensures the promotion of unsustainable and highly damaging relationships with the environment.

For the witnessing reader, it becomes evident that Silko is drawing connections with the kinds of witchery and hatred identified in both *Ceremony* and *Almanac* that result from specific Euro-American capitalist worldviews. Clearly, therefore, Silko's reader must continue to bear witness to the need for constant vigilance against destruction. In part, the real problem of these highly damaging worldviews is the refusal to consider alternatives. For Silko, the pressing question is how this can be remedied in the context of environmental damage, and *Gardens* is therefore a sustained analysis of *alternatives*. Presenting a range of female perspectives, *Gardens* explores notions of relatedness as a means by which to consider holism and to address questions of cultural and environmental sustainability. In direct contrast to the promotion of the kinds of exploitative, manipulative, and ultimately oppressive relationships with the natural world outlined above, Silko's reader acts as a witness to a discussion of alternative philosophies regarding human-nature interactions, where a range of cultural worldviews (Sand Lizard, American, European) are based on the relationships between sustainable agriculture and cultural sustainability, and on the importance of providing and, most importantly, *sharing*: the requirement that we not be "greedy" (1999, 17). Perhaps most significantly, gardens act within the text as a space within which dialogue and exchange of all kinds can take place, where the reader is required to witness that gardens and horticulture/agriculture are primarily concerned with relationships and power relations: between cultural groups, and between individuals/communities and the land. Indeed, the garden as a metaphor offers the possibility of a space, much like that of the International Holistic Healers Convention in *Almanac,* where cultural difference can be asserted and cross-cultural exchange can take place. Importantly, the exchanges and dialogues of the text do not evade or ignore the imbalances of power, but rather subvert, invert, and transform them through an emphasis upon indigenous philosophies.

While Silko's fiction demands that its readers act as witnesses both to a series of historical political events that are identified as the basis of the excesses and corruption of contemporary European/Euro-American societies, and to the legacy of that heritage in the ongoing, inherently colonial, oppression of contemporary indigenous peoples worldwide, it is significant that her fiction also establishes subversive and otherwise unattainable dialogues with powerful institutional, political, and corporate bodies; emphasizing not just the exchange inherent in dialogue, but the active and reciprocal nature of that exchange. Moreover, the role of the reader as witness is crucial to the dynamics of Silko's texts: as Moore argues, the witnessing reader can attain the power to "effect a different reality" (1999, 151), and this transformative power is profoundly political. While the definition of the recent burgeoning of Native writing as a "renaissance" is highly accurate in its description of the sudden growth in the numbers of Native writers finding publication, it is also profoundly inaccurate in its tendency to obscure the often specifically political histories of Indian oratory and writings upon which many Native writers are drawing. Accordingly, Silko's reader acts as a witness not just to Indian cultural traditions and their very real significance to the kinds of contemporary socio-political and environmental problems that Silko depicts as witchery, but also to an *alternative*: to a contemporary Native reality that is both political and politicized.

NOTES

1. Although the Laguna scholar Paula Gunn Allen vehemently criticized Silko's publication of clan stories that should remain untold, subsequent scholarship has traced the sources of Silko's traditional stories within *Ceremony* to previously published materials that had already been made public and widely circulated. See Paula Gunn Allen, "Special Problems in Teaching Leslie Marmon Silko's *Ceremony*," and Robert Nelson, "Rewriting Ethnography."

2. The mine in Silko's text has been widely identified extratextually as Jackpile mine. See, for one example, Connie Jacobs, "A Toxic Legacy."

3. The Colorado dam is a fictionalized prefiguration of much later dam construction in this region in the 1930s.

WORKS CITED

Adamson, Joni. (2001). *American Indian Literature, Environmental Justice, and Ecocriticism: The Middle Place.* Tucson: University of Arizona Press.

Allen, Paula Gunn. (1990). "Special Problems in Teaching Leslie Marmon Silko's *Ceremony.*" *American Indian Quarterly* 14:4, 379–86.

Arnold, Ellen. (1998). "Listening to the Spirits: An Interview with Leslie Marmon Silko." *Studies in American Indian Literatures* 10:3, 1–33.

Caputi, Jane. (1992). "The Heart of Knowledge: Nuclear Themes in Native American Thought and Literature." *American Indian Culture and Research Journal* 16:4, 1–27.

Felman, Shoshana, and Dori Laub, M.D. (1992). *Testimony: Crises of Witnessing in Literature, Psychoanalysis, and History.* London: Routledge.

Jacobs, Connie A. (2004). "A Toxic Legacy: Stories of Jackpile Mine." *American Indian Culture and Research Journal* 28:1, 41–52.

Jaskoski, Helen (1990). "Thinking Woman's Children and the Bomb." *Explorations in Ethnic Studies* 13:2, 1–22.

Moore, David L. (1999). "Silko's Blood Sacrifice: The Circulating Witness in *Almanac of the Dead.*" In Louise K Barnett and James L Thorson (eds.), *Leslie Marmon Silko: A Collection of Critical Essays.* Albuquerque: University of New Mexico Press, 149–83.

Nelson, Robert M. (2001). "Rewriting Ethnography: The Embedded Texts in Leslie Silko's *Ceremony.*" In Elizabeth Hoffman Nelson and Malcolm Nelson (eds.), *Telling the Stories: Essays on American Indian Literatures and Cultures.* New York: Peter Lang, 47–58.

Niemann, Linda. 1992. "New World Disorder." *The Women's Review of Books* IX:6, 1, 3–4.

Silko, Leslie Marmon. (1977). *Ceremony.* New York: Penguin.

———. (1981). *Storyteller.* New York: Arcade Publishing.

———. (1991). *Almanac of the Dead.* New York: Penguin.

———. (1997). *Yellow Woman and a Beauty of the Spirit: Essays on Native American Life Today.* New York: Simon and Schuster.

———. (1999). *Gardens in the Dunes.* New York: Simon and Schuster.

Sol, Adam. (1999). "The Story as It's Told: Prodigious Revision in Leslie Marmon Silko's *Almanac of the Dead.*" *American Indian Quarterly* 23: ¾, 24–48.

St. Clair, Janet. (1999). "Cannibal Queers: The Problematics of Metaphor in Leslie Marmon Silko's *Almanac of the Dead.*" In Louise K Barnett and James L Thorson (eds.), *Leslie Marmon Silko: A Collection of Critical Essays.* Albuquerque: University of New Mexico Press, 207–22.

Warrior, Robert. (2005). *The People and the Word: Reading Native Non-Fiction.* Minneapolis: University of Minnesota Press.

Womack, Craig S. (1999). *Red on Red: Native American Literary Separatism.* Minneapolis: University of Minnesota Press.

5
The Use of Myth in James Welch's Novels

ALAN R. VELIE

The novelists of the first decades of the Native American Renaissance—among them Momaday, Welch, Vizenor, Silko, Erdrich—took pains to incorporate traditional tribal stories into their works. The trickster archetype may be glimpsed in characters like Abel, Proude Cedarfair, Gerry Nanapush, Jim Loney, and the nameless protagonist of *Winter in the Blood*.[1] Further, Leslie Silko goes as far as to make *Ceremony* a novelization of Laguna and other tribal myths.[2] This inspired Scott Momaday to create a novel, *The Ancient Child*, out of Kiowa legend. In fact, Kenneth Lincoln makes incorporating tribal lore into contemporary Indian fiction a hallmark of the Native American Renaissance: "The Native American renaissance here targeted ... is a written renewal of oral traditions translated into Western literary forms" (8).

Nowhere is that statement truer than in James Welch's major novels, *Winter in the Blood*, *The Death of Jim Loney*, and *Fools Crow*. *Winter*, on the surface a gritty, realistic saga of Montana in the 1970s, has an underlying mythic structure combining Indian, primarily Gros Ventre, but also Blackfeet, legend and ritual with the Grail Myth that figures so prominently in twentieth-century modernism. Louis Owens makes this point in *Other Destinies*, though he misses the point that there is more Gros Ventre material than Blackfeet. Owens says: "[Welch employs] images of a wasteland which ... merge with Blackfoot[3] mythology to become a central metaphor in the novel" (129).

He adds a few pages later: "While Blackfoot mythology plays a major role in *Winter in the Blood*, it would be a mistake to ignore another mythology operating here, that of the Fisher King from the grail romance, the central figure of Eliot's *The Waste Land*, and much subsequent American literature. Welch both incorporates this myth into the fabric of the novel and has great fun parodying it" (132).

To start with Blackfeet influences, Welch's protagonist, and narrator, is nameless. There might be many explanations for this: Welch might be influenced by Ralph Ellison's nameless Invisible Man perhaps, a figure nameless because of his inconsequentiality to whites. But it is important to note that traditionally it was improper for a Blackfeet to reveal his name, and the hero is narrating the story.[4]

Possibly Welch's protagonist is nameless because Blackfeet names are bestowed for significant acts,[5] and when the novel opens he has done very little with his life. At thirty-two he is still living with his mother. Like the calf he berates, though he is long past the age for it, he hasn't been weaned (10). He is ignorant of his past, his tribal heritage (though he learns this in the course of the novel), and oblivious to the future. He has no career, no prospects, no relationships. The deaths of his father and brother have resulted in a state of emotional paralysis, a winter in his blood: he feels no love for his mother, Teresa, his stepfather, Lame Bull, or the Cree girl, Agnes, he brings home under the pretense they're married. When he deserts her to go to town, she steals his gun and electric razor, symbols of his manhood. Although he spends the rest of the novel trying to win her back, he never succeeds.

A cursory look at the action of the book might lead a reader to believe that nothing much happens. The hero drifts from his home on the reservation into town and back, indulging in a few meaningless affairs. At one point he learns who his maternal grandfather is. At the climax of the book, he tries to save a drowning cow and fails. In the epilogue, the family buries his grandmother. Were it not for the mythic substructure, the novel would seem formless. But, there is an Indian myth that underlies the novel, a Gros Ventre story, and the Grail Myth as well, and these serve to give the book its shape.

Welch is mixed-blood, Gros Ventre and Blackfeet, but because of the epiphany at the climax of *Winter,* where the hero finds out that his maternal grandfather is Yellow Calf, a Blackfeet, as well as later novels like *Fools Crow* and *The Indian Lawyer,* which focus solely on Blackfeet characters, it is common to think of Welch as primarily a Blackfeet writer. His second novel, *The Death of Jim Loney,* is about a mixed-blood Gros Ventre, but this seems to be the exception. Welch himself helps further this impression: in *Winter in the Blood* he is cagey about revealing tribal identities, not identifying the Gros Ventre characters, Lame Bull, Ferdinand Horn and his (nameless) wife, or even First Raise, as Gros Ventre. The narrator and other characters use the term "Indians" for the most part, rather than mentioning specific tribes. Welch does identify Yellow Calf as Blackfeet, and Agnes as Cree, but never says that any of the Gros Ventres are Gros Ventres. Although much of the action of the novel takes place on a reservation, Welch never names it. But, we can tell from the location of nearby towns of Montana's Milk River valley, Harlem, Malta, Dodson, and Havre, that the reservation is Fort Belknap, home of the Gros Ventre and Assiniboine tribes. Presumably, First Raise is a Gros Ventre who married Teresa, a Blackfeet who was living on a Gros Ventre reservation because her mother had been ostracized by the Blackfeet.

William W. Thackery discusses Gros Ventre myth and ritual in his article "'Crying for Pity' in *Winter in the Blood.*" Briefly, Thackery contends that what the hero is undertaking in *Winter in the Blood* is a vision quest as practiced by the Gros Ventres. During this quest the hero must reach an emotional nadir, at which point he cries out for pity, and with the help of a spirit guide in the form of an animal he begins to heal. According to Thackery, this animal helper is Amos, the duck that First Raise wins at a fair, and Teresa ends up cooking for Christmas dinner. This is the least plausible part of Thackery's thesis, but one must remember that although Welch employs mythic structures, he also parodies them, so one can't rule Amos out of a role as animal helper. At any rate, the hero and Amos are certainly closely related: the hero dreams that Amos emerges from Teresa's vagina with a hurt knee, the same wound that has disabled the hero since the death of his brother (52).

The next stage of the quest involves "seeking a grandfather"; the quester must select an elder as a guide. In *Winter* the hero chooses Yellow Calf, who, it turns out, is literally his grandfather. Finally there is a sacred task; in *Winter* this involves saving a drowning cow.

Thackery lays out the elements of the Gros Ventre vision quest and their parallels in the novel clearly enough, but he should have mentioned that Welch treats the quest in a parodic manner. This is consistent with Welch's approach to the novel as a whole. Indians love humor—Vine DeLoria has a whole chapter on it in *Custer Died for Your Sins*—and Welch is no exception. He says of *Winter*: "Many people are afraid to laugh with that book, and I can't understand why. They think it's Indian and about alienation and so on and, therefore, there should be no funny moments in the novel. But I intentionally put comic stuff in there just to alleviate that vision of alienation and purposelessness, aimlessness."[6]

The central scene in Welch's depiction of the hero's quest, the point at which the hero's grandfather, Yellow Calf, reveals the secret of the hero's ancestry, is comic:

I thought for a moment,
Bird farted.
And it came to me, as if it were riding one moment of the gusting wind,
as though bird had had it in him all the time and had passed it to me in
that one instant of corruption. [138]

The novel turns on the hero's recognition of Yellow Calf's role in his history, but Welch's use of the flatulent epiphany makes the scene comic rather than moving.

The final stage of the hero's quest is the task, saving a cow that is drowning in a slough. That he fails in is keeping with his general ineptitude.

Although the Gros Ventre quest ritual is important in understanding the structure of *Winter*, even more important is the "Waste Land" portion of the myth of the Holy Grail.[7] The Waste Land has been a major symbol of the decline of the West for modernists since Eliot's poem. Hemingway's *The Sun*

Also Rises and Fitzgerald's *The Great Gatsby* make use of the myth as a symbolic background to universalize the stories of Jake Barnes and Jay Gatsby Bernard Malamud goes even further in making *The Natural* a novelization of the Grail Myth.

In *Winter* the Milk River valley and, in particular, the hero's reservation have become a Waste Land. The hero's malaise, his emotional frigidity, at least in part derive from the condition of his land: "It could have been the country, the burnt prairie beneath a blazing sun, the pale green of the Milk River valley, the milky waters of the river, the sagebrush and cotton woods, the dry, cracked gumbo flats. The country had created a distance as deep as it was empty, and the people accepted and treated each other with distance" (2).

The reason is, as Teresa tells the hero, "It never rains anymore" (3). The reason for that may well be the fate of the hero: like the Fisher King, he has been wounded and spends time fishing, though with no luck. The Fisher King of Arthurian legend is often wounded in the groin—his impotence the cause of his country's lack of fertility. Hemingway's Jake Barnes shares this affliction. Malamud's Pop Fisher, manager of the New York Knights, is afflicted in his hands. Welch's hero has a wounded knee, a suitable injury for an Indian protagonist.

A contemporary version of the Waste Land myth that Welch parodies is Saul Bellow's *Henderson the Rain King*. Louis Owens recognizes this in *Other Destinies*. He cites Welch's account of a *Sports Afield* story in which two hunters, Henderson and McLeod, pose with a lion they have killed in Africa (12). Owens points out that Bellow's Henderson goes to Africa, "fall[ing] into the role of both grail knight and fisher king, riotously 'freeing the waters' for a 'primitive' people whose land—like Welch's narrator's—is suffering from drought. Furthermore, Henderson actually becomes, by befriending a young tribal prince, a sacrificial deity whose responsibility it is to bring rain and restore the wasted land" (133).

Bellow's Henderson turns up in *Winter* as the mysterious "airplane man," a nameless figure who befriends the hero and is later arrested for unexplained crimes. The hero says, when he first sees the airplane man: "He had on one of those khaki outfits that African hunters wear. I thought of McLeod and Henderson in *Sports Afield*" (45).

We never find out what the airplane man is running from or looking for. Not surprisingly he intends to go fishing (45), but that's about all we know. Welch is playing with the reader, and with Bellow's book. As Owens puts it, "Welch is having fun with Saul Bellow's *Henderson the Rain King*, a novel in which Bellow was having fun with Eliot's version of the grail romance" (133).

If there is a sacred task to this Waste Land story, it would be the fatal roundup of First Raises's cattle, which ends in the death of Mose. The roundup starts successfully but ends with disaster when one cow, "the wild-eyed spinster" who is leading the herd, refuses to go through the gate to their land. While the other cows mill around behind her, a calf breaks from the herd, and when the hero and Mose give chase, Mose is killed by a car and the hero thrown from Bird, injuring his knee. The scene of saving the cow drowning in the slough, which according to Thackery had been the task for the Gros Ventre vision quest, is closely related to the roundup scene—what one might call a *Doppelszene*, a scene that reprises an earlier scene in a sort of literary déjà vu. In this case, fiction repeats itself, to borrow a phrase from Marx, occurring first as tragedy, then as farce.

A cow, mother of the calf that won't be weaned, may not be the same actual cow that balked at the gate,[8] but in the hero's mind they are the same: "I had seen her before, the image of catastrophe . . . .the same hateful eye, the long curving horns, the wild-eyed spinster leading the cows down the hill into the valley" (166).

Eventually the hero's efforts to save the cow are in vain. The hero lassos the cow, Bird heroically tries to extricate it from the mud, but the horse slips, and the cow drowns in the mud. As in the first scene, the hero fails to complete his task. Both scenes use elements familiar from horse operas: cowboy, horse, cow. Only in *Winter* the cowboy is an Indian, the horse is out of control, and the mission fails. However, unlike the first tragic scene, the second version is anticlimactic. Although both Bird and the cow die, the hero misses neither. To soften the effect for the reader, the action occurs offstage, and Welch mentions the deaths obliquely: "The cow down in the slough had stopped gurgling" (172); "The red horse down in the corral whinnied. He probably missed old Bird" (176). In fact, the symbolism of the Waste Land myth indicates that this is a triumphant moment: it begins to rain, the "freeing of the waters." The climactic passage of the novel is "Some people, I thought, will never know how pleasant it is to be distant in a clean rain, the driving rain of a summer storm. It's not like you'd expect, nothing like you'd expect" (172).

Welch adds an anticlimactic epilogue to the book, detailing the hero's grandmother's funeral, during which the hero daydreams about going after Agnes again. The scene implies that the hero hasn't learned much from the epiphanic moments of his discovery of his heritage and the peace of mind that descends during the "freeing of the waters." Nonetheless, the mythic structure seems to indicate that perhaps the hero has turned a corner in his life: as Shelley noted, "if winter comes, can spring be far behind?"

Welch's second novel, *The Death of Jim Loney*, seems like a variation on a theme of *Winter in the Blood*. It is as if Welch, having explored a situation in the form of a comic novel, was trying to see if he could work out the same situation in a tragic fashion.[9] Both books center on the theme of a search for identity—the hero tries to discover who he is, and what it means to be an Indian in twentieth-century Montana. Welch was Blackfeet on his father's side, and Gros Ventre on his mother's. The hero of *Winter* has a Blackfeet mother and Gros Ventre father. Jim Loney has a Gros Ventre mother and white father.

The title of Welch's second novel, *The Death of Jim Loney*, is less cryptic that his first. "Death" lets us know in advance the hero is doomed. "Jim" is apparently self-referential; it's the name Welch's friends called him. "Loney" combines "lonely" and "loner."

As in *Winter in the Blood* Welch makes use of the Waste Land story and Gros Ventre myth in *Death*. Louis Owens notes in *Other Destinies*, "Loney's Montana is another Indian-and-white wasteland, a cold and barren landscape populated by displaced persons incapable of commitment to anyone or anything. . . . And in an unmistakable echo of Eliot's *The Waste Land*, Welch causes Loney's sister, Kate, to ask, 'What shall we do today,' and three paragraphs later, 'What shall we do today?'" (149). The difference in the application of the Waste Land myth in the two novels is one of degree and ending. In *Death* Welch employs the myth only in passing, and he doesn't end with the freeing of the waters. While in *Winter* the downpour at the end of the novel represents the end of the drought and the rebirth of hope in the hero, in *Death* the rain that falls on Loney is just precipitation. According to Owens, "The long-awaited rain that ended the psychic drought in *Winter* falls unheeded here, suggesting that for Loney no renewal or rebirth may be possible" (148).

Welch also uses the Bible, particularly the Book of Isaiah, as a source of mythic symbol. *Death* begins with Jim watching a football game. A quote from Isaiah pops into his head. "Turn away from man in whose nostrils is breath, for of what account is he?" This is the *Revised Standard Version* of Isaiah, 2:22. Loney, not much of a Bible reader—he hasn't read the Bible in fifteen years, he tells us (4), and it's the only passage he can think of (1)—can't place the passage in its biblical context. The quote is part of Isaiah's vision for Judah: the day of the Lord is coming, and woe will befall "every one who is proud and lofty, and every one who is lifted up, he shall be brought low" (2:12). Sinners will hide in caves and holes, but to no avail. Isaiah urges those who would be saved to separate themselves from their fellow men, and give themselves to God.

Loney has already turned away from man. He is a loner who holes up in his house, having no regular job, and little contact with friends or family, although he has a sister who loves him, a lover who is devoted to him, and at least one friend who cares about him. Although Loney increasingly turns away from the people who love him as the novel progresses, he does not turn to any heavenly power, neither the God of Isaiah nor the Supreme Being of the Gros Ventre religion, Ixtcibəni:həhat.

According to anthropologist John Cooper, Ixtcibəni:həhat means "The One Above" (2). A second name, Behä:tixtč, means "master, boss, head, leader of all" (2). Other names are translated "the being who has control over everything by thought or will" (4), "our father" (5), and "owner, or master or life" (5).

Cooper's Gros Ventre informants described Ixtcibəni:həhat in this way: "He is entirely in a class by himself. We think so much of him that we dare not try to learn what he looks like. He is the most wonderful and powerful of all beings who have no bodies" (4). The Gros Ventres traditionally believed that Ixtcibəni:həhat communicated to humans through dreams and through his messenger, the crow (Cooper, 7). Loney has two dreams with religious significance. In the first Loney sees his father, Ike, weeping for the family he has abandoned. When Rhea says, "But he is alone," Ike answers, "Alone as that bird he would believe in" (24). The bird is the messenger of Ixtcibəni:həhat, and Loney's problem is that he doesn't believe in it or the being who sends it. Ike's term "would" is apt: Loney wants to believe in the bird, but is so spiritually paralyzed that he cannot summon the will to seek a hierophant who can explain the significance of his vision.

The dream ends with Ike giving Loney a shotgun. At the end of the novel, when Loney tells his father that he has killed Pretty Weasel, Ike gives him a shotgun. The fact that Loney's dream accurately foresees future actions indicates that we should view the dream not in Freudian terms, as a message from Loney's unconscious, but in terms of Gros Ventre belief: the dream is a message from Ixtcibəni:həhat.

Loney's second dream is about the Catholic Church near the Gros Ventre Agency. It is padlocked, a pretty obvious bit of symbolism, and Loney cannot get in. The description is crystal-clear to the reader, if opaque to Loney: "He seemed to be searching for something, but it was not inside the church." The scene shifts to an Indian woman who is weeping and wailing for her son, who is gone. She tells Loney, "I will never find him, because he will not allow himself to be found" (34).

The dream means nothing to Loney at the time, but at the end of the novel, when he is waiting for the lawmen to find and kill him, he realizes that the woman is his mother, and that she is heartbroken because she realizes her mistake in abandoning her family. Loney imagines an afterlife where he and his mother would be reunited:

> And he wondered if he would be found, if he would see her again, if heaven and hell existed. But there had to be a place where people bought one another drinks and talked quietly about their pasts, their mistakes and small triumphs; a place where those pasts merged into one and everything was all right and it was like everything was beginning again without a past. No lost sons, no mothers searching. There had to be a place, but it was not on this earth. [175]

Cooper tells us little about Gros Ventre conceptions of the afterlife, only that they have one, often called the "Big Sand," and that if they die a worthy death, in battle, for instance, they "would be better off than here" (225). Loney's details, like buying drinks, add some touches from contemporary Montana life to a Gros Ventre conception.

To sum up about the dreams, Ixtcibəni:həhat sends Loney messages, but Loney is too alienated from his Indian culture, and too damaged psychologically, to decode the messages and act on them.

In addition to dreams, Ixtcibəni:həhat communicates through his messenger, the crow (Cooper, 7). According to Cooper, "The crow, on account of his relationship to the Supreme Being was sort of a sacred bird" (7). One of Cooper's informants said that the bird was actually a close relative of the crow, the raven, a bird with a call something like the human voice (7). This is apparently the bird that Loney repeatedly sees in visions: "It came every night now. It was a large bird and dark. It was neither graceful nor clumsy, and yet it was both" (20). Loney's bird obviously has some supernatural significance, and it clearly resembles a crow—large, dark, and clumsy when walking, but graceful in flight.

Another black bird important to Gros Ventre religion is Bha'a, the thunderbird, also called "black hawk," "a certain very large, black-feathered hawk known locally as 'bullet hawk'" (Cooper, 10). Bha'a is central in Gros Ventre religion, the supernatural figure Cooper's informants mention more frequently than any other save Ixtcibəni:həhat. Bha'a controls the weather; he is responsible for storms, thunder, and lightning. John Purdy argues at length that Loney is linked to the boy in Gros Ventre myth to whom Bha'a gives the Feather Pipe.[10] Like Loney, the boy is a loner who doesn't play with other boys, but has powers that more than compensate for his loneliness and lack of possessions. Purdy latches on to a flippant remark of Loney's to demonstrate his relationship to Bha'a: When Rhea comments on the severity of the wind, Loney says, "I might have something to do with it" (28).

Purdy pushes the evidence pretty hard, but it is certainly possible that Welch had some combination of the crow and Bha'a in mind when he conceived of Loney's bird.[11]Whatever its exact nature, the bird would seem to be a signal from Ixtcibəni:həhat, but Loney is unable or unwilling to figure it out. Loney's Gros Ventre mother left him when Loney was very young, and Loney has lost all contact with her tribe. Loney is dimly aware that he is being signaled by spiritual powers, both Gros Ventre and Christian, but he can't (or won't) respond to the messages. He tells Rhea about the bird, and the verse from Isaiah, and adds: "I want to make a little sense of my life, and all I get are crazy visions and Bible phrases. They're like puzzles" (105).

They may be puzzles, but Loney doesn't make an effort to solve them. Leah tells him the verse is from Isaiah, but Loney never looks it up to see what it means in context. As for his vision, Loney lives right outside the Gros Ventre Agency, but makes no effort to consult any of the elders about the bird, even though he tells Rhea: "I think it is a vision sent by my mother's people. I must interpret it, but I don't know how" (105).

The reader wants to shout at Loney: "Why don't you ask your mother's people?" but by this point it's obvious that he is psychologically incapable of doing that. Loney is extremely frustrated at being shut off from the Gros Ventre, but he doesn't feel he is entitled to make contact with the tribe. Part of Loney's tragic situation is that although he views the Gros Ventre as a nation, he is a man without a country.

Louis Owens, among others, has argued that Welch's characters suffer from alienation. When David Harvey argues, "We can no longer conceive of the individual alienated in the classical Marxist sense," Owens retorts about the hero of *Winter*: "He is alienated precisely in [that] sense" (131). Owens claims the problem is recovering the hero's "sense of identity as Indian, and specifically Blackfoot" (131). I would apply the same to Loney: his problem is that he cannot define himself ethnically. The cure to his problems would lie in recovering his Gros Ventre identity. His tragedy is that he cannot do it, despite the prodding he gets from supernatural agents.

Early in the novel Rhea tells Jim, "Oh, you're so lucky to have two sets of ancestors. Just think, you can be Indian one day and white the next. Whatever suits you" (14). Having chewed on this for weeks, Loney decides that his mixed-blood heritage is a curse rather than a blessing: "He had no family and he wasn't Indian or white. He remembered the day that he and Rhea had driven out to the Little Rockies. She had said that he was lucky to have two sets of ancestors. In truth he had none" (102).

Jim and Rhea represent two sides of the debate on the nature of ethnicity, whether it is something that fate bestows on us, or something we can choose. To borrow historian David Hollinger's terms, Rhea is a "cosmopolitan," and Jim is a "pluralist." Cosmopolitanism "favors voluntary affiliations . . . promotes multiple identities, emphasizes the dynamic and changing character of many groups," while pluralism "respects inherited boundaries and locates individuals within one or another of a series of ethno-racial groups to be protected and preserved" (3).

Rhea is cosmopolitan in that she thinks Loney ought to be pleased with his options, and exercise his freedom to change ethnicity at will. Loney is a pluralist; he believes ethnic groups are distinct, permanent affiliations, and longs for the security of belonging to one group or another. It is his misfortune that his mixed-blood heritage gives him no clear identity, and he is powerless to choose one on his own. Welch seems skeptical of both positions in *Death*. Rhea's position seems facile. Harlem, Montana, isn't viciously racist—it isn't segregated, for instance—but there is a sort of constant racial tension in the air, which is one reason that Kenny Hart, the Indian bartender, keeps a brick behind the bar. One would guess that had Loney chosen to consider himself white, for instance, it wouldn't have followed that the whites of Harlem would have thought he was one of them. On the other hand, had Loney made the existential choice to reach out to his mother's tribe, they probably would have accepted him. In fact, he has a right to join the tribe. The Gros Ventre demand only 25 percent blood quantum for membership;[12] Loney has 50 percent. But

Loney cannot make the effort to connect with his mother's people. The novel makes it clear that the Gros Ventre god Ixtcibəni:həhat has been sending constant messages to Loney through dreams and through the dark bird, but Loney doesn't have the energy to respond, to reach out to the Gros Ventres.

However, if Loney's life is marked with futility and failure, he manages to achieve a measure of success and dignity with his death as a warrior. Loney's death seems to be a matter of fate, followed by an existential choice. A crucial scene in the book, the place where Loney commits the tragic error that leads to his death, is the one in which he shoots Myron Pretty Weasel. Loney and Pretty Weasel, out hunting deer, think they see a bear, a highly unlikely event in that part of Montana. Pretty Weasel goes to check out the situation, and Loney, blinded by the sun, inadvertently shoots his friend.

What exactly happens is ambiguous, the result of the blurring of two cultural traditions. According to the conventions of realism typical of the contemporary novel, Loney, looking into the sun, must have simply mistaken the backlit Pretty Weasel for a bear, and shot him by mistake. According to Gros Ventre traditions, it is possible that supernatural powers might have been involved, that what Loney saw was a spirit in the form of a bear.

To begin with realistic conventions, Pretty Weasel's decision to change their quarry from pheasant to deer, a seemingly unimportant decision, brings about the premature death of Loney. Had they hunted pheasant as they originally planned, they would have been armed with shotguns full of birdshot, not 30-caliber rifles. Had Loney shot Pretty Weasel with the shotgun, the result would have been much the same as the incident involving Vice President Cheney, who peppered his hunting companion with birdshot—painful for the victim, but not fatal. When Loney shoots Pretty Weasel with the 30-30, he kills him.

But there is another perspective besides the realistic: the traditional Gros Ventre point of view. According to the traditions of the Gros Ventres, like those of many tribes, what appears to be an animal might be a spirit. According to Cooper, the Gros Ventres believed in spirits that took the form of various animals, which, "ranking a little above human beings and possessing certain superhuman powers, were under the leadership and control of the Supreme Being" (21). In fact, Loney thinks that what appeared to be a bear was actually a spirit: "Loney saw the bear in the field, its head bobbing as though it beckoned to them. The image spooked him and he thought of the bear not as a bear but as an agent of evil—how else to explain the fact that there hadn't been a bear in that valley for years and years?—and on Loney's last purposeful day he had succumbed to that evil" (129).

Louis Owens argues that Pretty Weasel became the bear: "Pretty Weasel identifies with the powerful bear spirit as Francisco had in *House Made of Dawn*, and he *becomes* the bear—as a successful hunter must—just before Loney shoots him" (153).

There are examples of men turning into bears in Indian novels both before and after *Jim Loney* (Proude Cedarfair in *Bearheart* before, Locke Setman in *The Ancient Child* and Fleur Pillager in *The Bingo Palace* afterwards), but the matter is ambiguous here. All we know for certain is that Loney believes that he has been tricked by supernatural powers into killing his friend: "That it was an accident did not occur to Loney. That the bear, as rare and inexplicable as its appearance had been, was simply a bear did not occur to him either. And so he was inclined to think that what happened happened because of some quirky and predictable fate" (129).

Loney treats his accidental killing of Pretty Weasel as if it were murder. He doesn't report the killing, and when his father asks him if it was an accident, he says, "I think it was, but I don't know for sure." When his father says, "You mean you might have done it on purpose?" Jim says, "Yes" (147). In a sense they are talking at cross-purposes since Ike thinks "on purpose" means Loney committed premeditated murder, while Loney actually means that he acted as part of a larger design. Loney has decided that fate wants him to die, and so he decides that he will face death stoically, like a warrior. His attitude combines resignation and courage. He feels that he "had lost forever the secret of survival" (155), and so makes sure he brings about death as quickly as possible by telling his father he has killed Pretty Weasel, and then making sure that his father tells the police by shooting out Ike's window, wounding him. Loney finally takes charge of his life, and orchestrates his death. It is as if he interprets the bear incident as a sign. He has been unable to interpret earlier signs—the Isaiah passage and the dark bird—but it seems he believes that killing Pretty Weasel is a sign that he should end his life.

Loney arranges that his death takes place in Mission Canyon. Scenes from Mission Canyon bracket the action in the book. Earlier Loney and Rhea had spent an idyllic afternoon there, eating cheese and drinking wine. Loney returns to Mission Canyon to die, possibly because it is the place where his Gros Ventre ancestors lived: "He thought about the Indians who had used the canyon, the hunting parties, the warriors, the women who had picked chokecherries farther up. . . . These thoughts made him comfortable and he wasn't afraid" (168).

The Gros Ventres, like most other Plains tribes, believed those who died bravely in battle would be rewarded in the afterlife. Loney is dying in the tradition of the warriors who sought glory by dying at the hands of their enemy. Welch's later novel, *Fools Crow*, is about the Blackfeet rather than the Gros Ventres, but the tribal values described there are the same: dying with honor at the hands of one's enemies is a worthy way to end one's life. Welch describes White Man's Dog's emotions on the eve of his first taste of battle: "White Man's Dog sang his war song in a low voice and felt his strength returning. His chest had quit heaving and he felt he could die with honor" (30).

Loney doesn't sing, but his attitude toward death in the final scene is the same. He fires his shotgun toward his pursuers, not with the intention of hitting anyone—a shotgun is useless at that distance—but to show Quentin Doore, the tribal policeman, where he is. He then stands in the open to allow Doore to kill him: "The figure did nothing to hide or run off. It simply stood motionless" (177).

Ironically, Loney's enemy here is a fellow Gros Ventre. Quentin Doore is a sinister misfit with whom Loney had played basketball in high school. Doore, a mediocre player and something of a thug, had been a loner. In an ironic reversal of the most-likely-to-succeed scenario, the lonely, sadistic substitute comes to represent lawful authority, and the popular star athlete turns into the fugitive murderer. But in the value system of the book, lawful authority comes across as sadistic force, and the lawless fugitive is the hero. Welch borrows the tragic pattern Shakespeare often employs; like Titus Andronicus, Romeo, Brutus, and Hamlet, Loney makes a tragic error of killing someone, setting off a train of events that leads to his destruction. In each case, however, the hero remains sympathetic, and seems far nobler than the men that pursue him.

One of Welch's strengths as a writer is his mastery of different genres. *Winter in the Blood* is a splendid example of the comic novel. In *Fools Crow* Welch is able to write a highly successful historical novel, a difficult task, involving developing a plausible language for the Blackfeet to express themselves which is apprehensible to the reader. And *Jim Loney* is a highly successful tragic novel.

A tragic novel, properly speaking, ends with the death of the hero. It is not simply a serious novel with a somber tone like *Moby Dick*, where Ishmael bobs up at the end and lives to tell his tale, or like *The Scarlet Letter*, where Hester survives to win eventually some sort of redemption. Great American tragic novels include *Billy Budd, The Great Gatsby*, and *Light in August*. In these books a flawed but superior hero dies at the hands of lesser men. Loney achieves in his death what he had failed to achieve in his life, a measure of dignity and honor. It can be said of Loney what Malcolm in *Macbeth* says of the Thane of Cawdor, "nothing in his life became him like the leaving it" (I, iv, 6, 7).

Loney's death may seem like a final act of futility in terms of Euro-American values, but it validates his life in Indian terms: he arranges to die bravely at the hands of his enemies. In effect, Loney is behaving like a member of one of the war societies among Plains Indians who wore "no retreat sashes" staking themselves to the ground to fight to the death. Seen in these terms, Loney's death is, as Kay Sands puts it, "not a futile act of annihilation but an appropriate and satisfying conclusion to a painful and solitary detachment from life" (10).

Welch himself has described Loney's death in positive terms. Purdy cites an interview with Bill Bevis in which Welch says of Loney: "He does orchestrate his own death. . . . He creates it . . . he knows how his death will occur. And to me that is a creative act and I think all creative acts are basically positive" (Bevis, 176).

As Loney dies, he imagines he feels a harsh wind, and he sees the dark bird climb into the sky. This too is ambiguous. Even if we assume, with Purdy, that the bird is Bha'a, what does this signify? Purdy assumes that Loney and the bird merge: "The novel ends, as does Loney's life, with a reference to his vision; the sense of complicity lingers, as does the sense that any distinction between Loney's vision and the bird and Loney himself has disappeared (72). This may be the case, but it seems equally likely that the bird is deserting Loney. The ending is tragic; Loney has missed his last chance. He dies with dignity, but he doesn't ascend to heaven. He simply falls to earth.

Welch's next novel, *Fools Crow*, depicts life among the Blackfeet during the nineteenth century while they still retained their traditional culture. Here Welch also uses myth to shape the work, but he uses it in a more overt manner than in the earlier books. Welch draws on figures of Gros Ventre religion like the Ixtcibəni:həhat and Bha'a in writing *The Death of Jim Loney*, but he doesn't mention them by name. In *Fools Crow*, however, the goddess Feather Woman appears as a character, as do other supernatural figures, like talking birds and animals. Gone for the most part in in *Fools Crow* are Western myths and Gros Ventre lore: *Fools Crow* is governed by Blackfeet myth and rituals, some of which Welch learned about from his older relatives, some he read about in the publications of white anthropologists and historians.[13]

To begin with a question from the earlier novels, what's in a name? Unlike the hero of *Winter* who doesn't have one, the hero of *Fools Crow* has three. The tribe replaces his birth name Sinopa (Fox) with White Man's Dog when he is nine because he follows around an old storyteller, Victory Robe White Man (218). He earns his final name, Fools Crow, when he kills the Crow chief Bull Shield. In the fighting that occurs when the Pikunis[14] raid the Crows, White Man's Dog falls and lies stunned at the feet of Bull Shield. Believing White Man's Dog is dead, Bull Shield approaches him. White Man's Dog comes to his senses just in time to shoot Bull Shield. The Pikunis believe that White Man's Dog had been playing possum, deliberately deceiving the Crow chief. After initially protesting, White Man's Dog accepts their version of the story, their accolades, and his new name (151).

Welch uses the paradigm of traditional Blackfeet beliefs in depicting incidents in *Fools Crow*. Dreams are sent by deities, and the Pikunis must do what the dreams tell them to do. Animal helpers, also minor divinities, speak to humans and must be obeyed. But most important, according to Welch, Blackfeet history is determined by the tribe's relationship to its tutelary deity, Feather Woman.

Historical novels, like regular histories, betray distinct historiographical points of view: *Fools Crow* employs what might be called "providential history," history as the working out of the will of divine powers.[15] In short, the Blackfeet are doomed to suffer horrible losses at the hands of the cavalry, and from famine and smallpox, all because the deity charged with protecting them sinned and is being punished by more powerful Above Ones. Most providential histories attribute a people's success or failure to the dutiful nature of the people toward their god(s); e.g., the Deuteronomic histories of the Old Testament (Joshua through 2 Kings) attribute the rise of Israel and its conquest of Canaan to the devotion of the Israelites to Jehovah, and they attribute the fall of Israel and Judah to their apostasy, their "whoring after false gods." In *Fools Crow*, it's the other way around: the Blackfeet don't suffer because they disobey their gods, but rather because their own god has been disobedient.

The Blackfeet story that gives shape to *Fools Crow* is the story of Feather Woman and Star Boy. It is an original-sin story, with obvious similarities to the story of Eve and the apple. Feather Woman, a human, marries Morning Star, one of the Above Ones, and goes to live with his parents, Sun and Moon, in the sky.[16] Feather Woman and Morning Star have a child, Star Boy. In the classic interdiction central to folktale, Feather Woman's mother-in-law forbids her to dig the sacred turnip in the middle of their field. Obsessed with the turnip, Feather Woman cannot resist digging it out. Looking through the hole in the sky, she sees her people, the Blackfeet, becoming homesick. Sun banishes Feather Woman from heaven for her sin, telling her she has brought death and unhappiness into the world. Feather Woman returns to the Blackfeet with Star Boy and dies soon afterwards, in despair. The Blackfeet call Star Boy, who has a facial disfigurement, "Scar Face," and ostracize him. Eventually Star Boy goes on a long journey to the heavenly home of his grandparents, Sun and Moon. He eventually gets there, wins their favor, and learns "great magic and truths of the world." He returns to earth to teach the Blackfeet the Sun Dance, their most important ceremony.

Welch takes this story and puts his own spin on it. Fools Crow shares some of the traits of Star Boy/Scar Face. As a youth the tribe views him with disfavor: "Not so lucky was White Man's Dog. He had little to show for his eighteen winters. His father, Rides-at-the-door, had many horses and three wives. He himself had three horses and no wives. His animals were puny . . . and his animal helper was weak" (3).

Like Star Boy, Fools Crow sets out on a long quest. It takes him to Feather Woman, who isn't dead, as in the myth, but living in exile and disgrace. She shows him "great truths"; she reveals the fate of the Blackfeet. Feather Woman tells Fools Crow that Sun had warned her that her guilt would bring disaster to the Blackfeet, and that this is what is unfolding now: "One dawn, in the long-ago, he [Sun] spoke to me. He said, 'you have brought upon yourself your own misery—and misery to your people.' And it is true. Now you see sickness and hunger, Napikwans and war" (352).

Feather Woman goes on to predict a happier future for the Blackfeet: "One day I will rejoin my husband and son. I will return with them to their lodge and there we will be happy again—and your people will suffer no more" (352).

Judging from Welch's novels of contemporary life among the Blackfeet, *Winter in the Blood* and *The Indian Lawyer*, that time is still to come apparently. The horrors of the late nineteenth century are over, and much contemporary Blackfeet unhappiness is a result of feckless behavior and self-inflicted wounds. Nonetheless, it seems a stretch to say that Blackfeet suffering is "no more."

Feather Woman gives Fools Crow a detailed prediction of what will happen to the Blackfeet, drawing on a magic scroll to depict the disasters of the late nineteenth century—smallpox, massacre, famine—and the sufferings of twentieth, alienation and loss of their traditional culture. The final revelation of the scroll is a scene from the late twentieth century: Blackfeet children are attending public school in what is now the state of Montana. It's recess, and although the Blackfeet are dressed like their classmates, they are not joining in their play. They are standing to one side, watching as outsiders. It is clear that the Blackfeet have survived as a people, but they have lost much of their culture and have become strangers in their own land.

Although Welch gets the story of Feather Woman from Blackfeet mythology, what he does with it is highly original. For one thing, it is not traditional to tie Blackfeet misfortunes to those of the goddess. This is an interesting move, a matter of reclaiming agency in Blackfeet history. Like Gerald Vizenor, Leslie Silko, and Scott Momaday, Welch is fighting against the depiction of Indian history as purely a matter of victimization by whites. Welch certainly depicts the cruelty and hypocrisy of white settlers and soldiers, but as a matter of pride, he asserts that Indian history has been determined by Indian people and Indian gods. Whites play a shameful but ancillary role in the fate of the Blackfeet.

Gerald Vizenor has made it a lifelong project to remove the stigma of being victims from Indians. During an interview, Hartwig Isernhagen, a well-meaning if condescending professor from Switzerland, intimates to Vizenor that he is sympathetic to the Indians because of their dark history and suffering at the hands of other Americans. According to Isernhagen, Vizenor bristles:

> The . . . problem . . . in America and most of the privileged western world . . . of leisure economies [is] the investment in a victim. . . . And communications, literature, popular ideas and culture sell great victims, and "Indians" are the simulated universal victims. Victims have no humor; they offer the world nothing but their victimization, and that makes people who invest in them feel better (85).

Although Isernhagen records Vizenor's words faithfully, there is nothing in the interview to indicate that he has any idea what Vizenor is talking about.

Leslie Silko makes a similar point in *Ceremony* by attributing the invention of white people to Indian witches.[17] As Silko sees it, whites are certainly capable of all sorts of evil, but ultimately they are unwitting agents of Indian witchery.

As for Momaday, as he states in *The Way to Rainy Mountain*, he would rather celebrate the glorious memories of his tribe, the Kiowas, who at the time of his grandmother were "living the last great moment of their history" (6), than he would lament the hard times that follow, what he calls the "mean and ordinary agonies of human history" (3).

Welch is making the same point: Blackfeet have a proud history as lords of the northern plains: they have celebrated victories as well as mourned losses. *Fools Crow* is a record of their great culture while it was still intact. Divine forces brought their glory days of buffalo hunting and horse stealing to an end, but it is the task of their storytellers, including Welch, to keep the memories of their glorious past alive. Their goddess may have let them down, but they're still here. She's adapted, they've adapted, life goes on.

Welch's depiction of Feather Woman is original. Blackfeet tales don't describe gods and goddesses at any length, so Welch is clearly using his own imaginings in depicting Feather Woman as mixed-blood, a woman who seems a hybrid of Napikwan blood and culture as well as Blackfeet. Traditional tales of Feather Woman and her husband Morning Star imply she was wholly Blackfeet. Welch, however, makes Feather Woman a hybrid figure. When Fools Crow first encounters her, she is in the sort of frontier home that a white settler would build: "The small dwelling was made of logs and mud . . . He watched the smoke rise from a long black tube and knew there would be one of the Napikwan woodburners inside. He looked at the small square opening covered with the white man's ice shield" (321).

When Fools Crow finally gets a good look at Feather Woman, he is puzzled because she looks neither white nor Indian. Fools Crow has no frame of reference, but what he sees is a twentieth-century mixed-blood Blackfeet woman, someone like Kate, Jim Loney's sister. "Her skin was a shade lighter than his, yet she did not look like a Napikwan. He looked into her face, and she looked back, smiling. Pikuni women were not that open, nor were the women of other tribes he knew" (333).

It would seem that although Welch believes in the necessity of preserving the memory of traditional Blackfeet culture, he realizes that Blackfeet cannot live in tipis and hunt buffalo in the twentieth century. They should never forget the glories of the old times when they lived by hunting, but in the twentieth century it is appropriate to do what in actuality they are doing: living in Montana among the whites, and living in more or less the same way as the whites. Welch is well aware that whites stole much Indian land in addition to bringing disease and famine to the tribes. Yet he shows that many of the Blackfeet not only survived, they prospered. In *Winter in the Blood* Teresa and Lame Bull are successful ranchers. The hero, their son, may be feckless, but he is heir to 360 acres of irrigated land, a spread that in the 1970s would have been worth hundreds of thousands of dollars. Their circumstances were not typical of Blackfeet of the time—the Native American Renaissance that later brought gaming and business revenue to reservations was just beginning—but Teresa, Lame Bull, and the hero are the characters Welch chooses to portray. Jim Loney falls victim to a paralysis caused in part by difficulty in settling on an identity, but his sister Kate embraces her Indian identity in becoming a successful bureaucrat, a powerful woman very early in the feminist movement.

The jacket copy of the original hardcover edition of *Fools Crow* describes the novel as a tragedy, but the book ends on a positive note. Welch could have ended the novel with the cavalry's massacre of Heavy Runner's band, or with the Blackfeet's decimation by smallpox, both of which he depicts (378, 371). Welch could have concluded *Fools Crow* with an elegiac final chapter like "The End of the Dream" epilogue with which Neihardt ends *Black Elk Speaks*. The final words are "There is no center any longer, and the sacred tree is dead" (276). Instead, Welch chooses to end the novel on a positive note:

> That night there was much feasting in all the Pikuni camps. Winter was over and the men talked of hunting, of moving their camps out of the valleys, of moving on. The women prepared their meager feast and fed their men, their children, their relatives and friends. They knew that soon the meat pots would be full and the hides would be drying in the sun. Outside, the children played in the rain, chasing each other slipping and skidding in the mud. They were Pikunis and they played hard. [390]

This is language of melodrama, not tragedy. Welch sounds a note of defiance: the Blackfeet are no victims. To borrow a phrase from Gerald Vizenor, they are masters of survivance.

The myths that underlie these three Welch novels lead to positive endings. Welch is no Pollyanna: he doesn't shy from showing massacres, starvation, and epidemics, but he has chosen myths that lead to ultimate triumphs. The Grail Myth ends with the freeing of waters, and so does *Winter in the Blood*. Jim Loney is shot down by a ruthless man, but given Gros Ventre religious beliefs, this is a triumphant way to die. And *Fools Crow*, shaped by the story of Feather Woman and Star Boy, ends with neither a bang nor a whimper, but on a note of hope: "They were Pikunis and they played hard."

NOTES

1. See Velie, "Indians in Indian Fiction."

2. The Laguna have criticized Silko for not being faithful to the myths in incorporating them, but despite the fact that she took aesthetic liberties with Laguna stories, and borrowed stories from other tribes when the Laguna didn't have one that fit her purpose, Silko does construct the novel from Native sources.

3. Owens was unaware that in America Blackfeet use "Blackfeet," while in Canada they say "Blackfoot."

4. Owens, *Other Destinies*, p. 130.

5. For example, in *Fools Crow* the hero earns his name when he (presumably) feigns death to kill a Crow warrior.

6. Quoted in Owens, *Other Destinies*, p. 145.

7. The essential element of the Waste Land section of the myth of the search for the Holy Grail, the cup Jesus drank from at the Last Supper, is that a king has been wounded, and as a result his land suffers a terrible drought. A questing knight, Parsifal is one of several, finds the king, who spends his time fishing, and is kept alive by the Grail, which mysteriously descends during dinner. When the knight completes his tasks, the king is cured, and there is a drought-ending rainstorm, the "freeing of the waters."

8. Though this could be the same cow. Wikipedia allows that although twelve years is the average lifespan of a cow, they can live and breed into their early twenties. The hero was twelve at the time of the accident, and is thirty-two now. That means the cow could be twenty-two or so.

9. In *Understanding James Welch*, Ron McFarland calls *Death of Jim Loney* an "anti-type" of *Winter in the Blood* (p. 129).

10. Purdy, "Bha'a and *The Death of Jim Loney*," pp. 17–24.

11. "Rhea" is not only the name of Loney's love, but the name of a large bird, whose grey-brown feathers might qualify as dark. But although at least one critic has linked Rhea to Loney's bird (see Nelson, "Function of the Landscape," www.facultystaff.richmond.edu/~rnelson/PandV/welch.html, p. 8.), it is likely that her name is an arbitrary signifier here. Certainly she conveys no supernatural message to Loney.

12. See http://nativenews.jour.umt.edu1998/choosing.

13. See Gish, "Word Medicine," p. 352.

14. The Blackfeet name for Fools Crow's band.

15. To borrow categories from historiographer Hayden White (though not his obscurantist labels), other philosophies would include history as the deeds of men, as a reflection of the spirit of the age, and as the working out of laws. See White, *Metahistory*, ch.1, passim, and Velie, "Indian Historical Novel," pp. 391*ff*.

16. See *Fools Crow*, pp. 349*ff*. It may be found online at http://www.firstpeople.us/FP-html-Legends/TheStoryofPoia-Balckfeet/html.

17. See *Ceremony*, pp. 132*ff*.

WORKS CITED

Bevis, Bill. "Dialogue with James Welch." *Northwest Review* 20:32–33 (1982), 163–85.

Chanady, Amaryll B. *Magical Realism and the Fantastic.* New York: Garland, 1985.

Cooper, John M., and Regina Flannery. *The Gros Ventres of Montana: Part II Religion and Ritual.* Washington: Catholic University Press, 1956.

Deloria, Vine, Jr.. *Custer Died for Your Sins: An Indian Manifesto.* New York: Macmillan, 1969.

Gish, Robert. "Word Medicine: Storytelling and Magical Realism in James Welch's *Fools Crow. American Indian Quarterly* 14:4 (Fall 1990), 349–54.

Hollinger, David. *Postethnic America: Beyond Multiculturalism.* New York: Basic Books, 1995.

Isernhagen, Hartwig. *Momaday, Vizenor, Armstrong: Conversations on American Indian Writing.* Norman: University of Oklahoma Press, 1999.

Levin, David. *History as Romantic Art: Bancroft, Prescott, Motley, and Parkman.* Palo Alto, Calif.: Stanford University Press, 1959.

Lincoln, Kenneth. *Native American Renaissance.* Berkeley: University of California Press, 1985.

McFarland, Ron. *Understanding James Welch.* Columbia: University of South Carolina Press, 2000.

Momaday, N. Scott. *The Ancient Child.* New York, Doubleday, 1989.

———. *The Way to Rainy Mountain.* New York: Ballantine Books, 1970.

Nabokov, Vladimir, trans. *Eugene Onegin.* Vol. II. Commentary and Index. Princeton: Princeton University Press, 1990.

Neihardt, John G. *Black Elk Speaks.* Lincoln: University of Nebraska Press, 1961.

Nelson, Robert. "The Function of the Landscape in *The Death of Jim Loney*." www .richmond.edu/~rnelson/PandV/welch.html.

———. *The Function of Landscape in Native American Fiction.* New York: Peter Lang, 1993.

Owens, Louis. *Other Destinies: Understanding the American Indian Novel.* Norman: University of Oklahoma Press, 1992.

Purdy, John. "Bha'a and *The Death of Jim Loney*." *SAIL* 11:1 (Winter 1987), 17–24.

Sands, Kathleen Mullen. "*The Death of Jim Loney*: Indian or Not?" *SAIL* 5:3, 4 (Fall, 1981), 5–8.

Thackery, William. "Crying for Pity in *Winter in the Blood. MELUS* 7:1 (1980), 61–78.

———. "*The Death of Jim Loney*." *SAIL* 5:3, 4 (Fall 1981), 1–3.

Todorov, Tzvetan. *The Fantastic.* Translated by Richard Howard. Cleveland: Case Western University Press, 1973.

Velie, Alan. "The Indian Historical Novel." *Genre* XXV (Fall 1992).

———. "Indians in Indian Fiction." *American Indian Quarterly* (Fall 1984).

Welch, James. *The Death of Jim Loney.* New York: Harper & Row, 1979.

———. *Fools Crow.* New York: Viking, 1986.

———. *Winter in the Blood.* New York: Harper and Row, 1974.

White, Hayden. *Metahistory: The Historical Imagination in Nineteenth-Century Europe.* Baltimore, Md.: Johns Hopkins University Press, 1973.

6

"The Event of Distance"

James Welch's Place in Space and Time

KATHRYN W. SHANLEY

> . . . Coyote Man turned and looked
> shocked, and studied the young man's
> step, then declared, "well, it's a
> fancy step all right, but I don't
> think you'll win any girls with
> it," which set the other men to
> laughing, which good mood Coyote
> Man needed to get about his business.[1]
>   Peter Blue Cloud (Mohawk)

In response to questions about his career success, James Welch frequently described himself as "lucky"—as being in the right place at the right time.[2] While it is no doubt true that good things happened to him, "luck" was the least of it.[3] Openhearted and eager to become a writer, he found mentors whom he trusted and who believed in him, and he fell in love with and married Lois Monk, who provided him with support on all levels.[4] Once he realized his life could be the experiential basis for his work, rather than the work being generated from some mysterious thing called "imagination," he set about the "business" of writing—a tricky business at that.[5] His humor, described by critics in various ways, conveys through realistic detail and linguistic play the illusion of existential truth, as though a humble, honest self simply offers up his vision, realistic and raw. The human comes mostly in the form of visually peculiar foibles and ironic found-word objects. Kenneth Lincoln, for example, describes *Winter in the Blood* as "a modest romance based on dark comic promise" (6), while literary critic Louis Owens unequivocally states, "*Winter in the Blood* is no romance, with a 'right' ending. . . . He is 'mixing his sorrow with an account of blows he has received'" (36–37). And in the process Welch creates a coherent, though fluid, narrative of his life through an absurdist humor that works to endear him to readers. Welch's work follows in the tradition of the romance, as opposed to the tragedy, in that his works end with optimism, albeit guarded. Yet what Welch truly offers the world (and offered his readers in the 1970s) is a unique vision in his time, and he did so out of his own experience as one clothed in the word "Indian"[6] and living in a space and time where Indians bore the marks and carried the legacy of a brutal colonial history. Indians were not only marked, they were simultaneously and paradoxically invisible.

The publication of *Winter in the Blood* in 1974 signaled success for Welch, as a review on the front page of the *New York Times Book Review* indicated, and meant that he had further shattered the idea that American Indians had vanished from contemporary America—a change in mainstream thought begun by the publication of the first classics of the Native American Renaissance, Vine Deloria, Jr.'s, *Custer Died for Your Sins* and N. Scott Momaday's *House Made of Dawn*. With the appearance of these classics-in-the-making and with the Occupation of Alcatraz (1969–1971), Indians gained a voice in asserting their rights to representation on all levels, indeed, their right to be "Indian," much as African Americans reclaimed the previously deemed negative term "black." As Scott Lyons remarks, "traditional culture was on the ropes," and activists and writers sought to promote a "cultural revival" (Lyons, 74–75). Later, in 1973 in South Dakota, the seventy-one-day occupation of the town of Wounded Knee, which became known as "Wounded Knee II," provided another stage for protesting lost lands, resources, traditions, and ongoing oppression. Indian voices were beginning to be heard across the nation through political action and leadership as well as through literature. Welch's writing added to the chorus attesting to the fact that Indians hadn't disappeared, as policy and popular American lore would have it.[7]

In his first novel, *Winter in the Blood*, Welch provides a voice from the inside of Indian Country. The narrator speaks as if he is seeing from a neutral space, not only observing how little control he has over his life, but also revealing a sensibility not easily defined or grasped by people from other places. Sidner Larson (A'aninin/Gros Ventre) captures the scenario well when he states: "[I]n a situation where the language that evolved over millenia to fit a certain place has been destroyed, simple acts of naming become near impossible. Add to such destruction the enforced substitution of a foreign language used primarily for deception, and it begins to become understandable why history, reality, and language seem to stand so far apart from one another in the tribal community perceived by the narrator in *Winter in the Blood*" (275).

Hence, the narrator's voice is the primary "trick" Welch employs, his "contrary doubleness" (Larson, 275). Conspicuously nameless, he begins to glimpse his situation, and using Homi Bhabha's terms for the postcolonial, Welch's character "makes graphic a moment of transition, not merely [within] the continuum of history," but through "a strange stillness" that makes his life "uncannily visible."[8] The space and time dynamics introduce a temporality

that intersects geography, geopolitics, and identity with despair, albeit a despair of a contemplative rather than an angry nature, as some might expect
from American Indians in the protest eras of the 1960s and '70s. An elegiac
stillness characterizes Welch's early work, as his characters walk among the
ruins of more sovereign times and spaces, distortions of human potential,
desire, and perception. Others' perceptions of them are equally distorted, as
Sherman Alexie so aptly writes in *Reservation Blues*, "All Indians grow up with
drunks. But most Indians never drink. Nobody notices the sober Indians"
(151). They are marked, but paradoxically invisible.

In *Understanding James Welch*, Ron McFarland links Welch with other
writers of the early days of the Native American Renaissance such as N. Scott
Momaday (Kiowa) in *House Made of Dawn* and Leslie Marmon Silko (Laguna
Pueblo) in *Ceremony*. He also links Welch with events, but sees Welch as having set himself apart in some ways from aspects of the political movements
of the time, while remaining sympathetic to American Indian causes. Mc-
Farland writes, "It has become critical commonplace to contextualize Welch's
early career by way of political events like the takeover of Alcatraz Island in
1969 by 'Indians of All Tribes' and the confrontation at Wounded Knee in 1973
. . . however, Welch seems to distance himself from such an overtly political
agenda" (8). In fact, on many occasions, Welch clearly stated that he was not
a "spokeman" for American Indian people, but at the same time, he wanted
to make certain he spoke truthfully and realistically about American Indian
life. He worked to avoid stereotypical depictions of Indians as noble, tragic, or
politically angry and alienated; he was writing against formulas that diminished Indian subjects and erased the complexity of their lives and struggles.
McFarland also reiterates the fact that few American Indian writers—D'Arcy
McNickle, a Métis Native writer from Montana, for example—had been available to Welch as influence. Instead, Welch drew inspiration from authors such
as Ernest Hemingway and John Steinbeck and during the writing of *Winter*,
Elio Vittorini, the author of *Conversations in Sicily* (McFarland, 11, 57). Saul
Bellow's *Henderson the Rain King*, Louis Owens argues, is being spoofed in
Winter (30–31).[9] Whatever Welch happened to be reading at the time seemed
to figure in as well, but the world of Montana Indians provided his primary
source material.[10] It is important to note, also, that the political and historical
themes in his work become more palpable after the 1970s, beginning with
Fools Crow (1984), which revolves around the Marias Massacre of Blackfeet
people in 1870.

In his early writing—*Riding the Earthboy 40* (1971, 1976), *Winter in the
Blood* (1974), and *The Death of Jim Loney* (1979)—Welch presents a temporality more starkly recognizable as the here and now than do Momaday
and Silko in their early work. Welch's narrators throw off the past "Indian"
of Western movies and the tragic narratives of Manifest Destiny at the same
time as they make an implicit claims for themselves as "multidimensional

and fully sentient human beings," to borrow Alfonso Ortiz's words.[11] *Indian Lawyer* similarly follows a contemporary vision, while *Fools Crow* and *The Heartsong of Charging Elk* fall within the genre of historical fiction. *Indian Lawyer* stands apart from Welch's other novels in that the protagonist succeeds at his quest to achieve manhood with integrity and a role for himself in the world; nonetheless, many of the same issues and themes arise in that text. Like all Welch's protagonists, Sylvester Yellow Calf of *Indian Lawyer* finds the Indianness within himself as well as in Indian Country—in other words, he finds his difference from European American people and mainstream culture. Welch achieved significance in the flourishing of the Native writing of the Native American Renaissance through a situated Indianness in his early work, which coheres through four key tropes: distance, recognition, criminality (or in Welch's term, being a "renegade"), and innocence.

DISTANCE AS A CONFRONTATION WITH THE SUBLIME AND THE SELF

At the heart of clichés regarding Indigenous peoples' connections to the universe and to other species rests a truth about differing epistemologies, which in some instances are more a matter of degree than type. Cultural difference in response to what in Western traditions is called "the sublime" function in *Winter* in profound ways. As Matthew Sharpe notes in "'Ideological Judgment in Eagleton and Zizek," encounters with the sublime frequently lead to self-reflection and a resulting sense of inadequacy:

> In the instance of the sublime, the manifold that bombards subjects confronted by things of great magnitude or power (hurricanes, the infinities of space) arrest the happy and harmonious play of their cognitive faculties. Try as the subject might, s/he cannot "get her/his head around" the sublime object(s). . . . [T]his painful experience of epistemic finitude is only the first "moment" involved in the Kantian analytic of the sublime. In Kant's words, in a second "moment" to this experience, a self-reflexive representation arises "in which we would least of all look for it." This reflexive representation takes as its object exactly the subject's own "first order" failure to comprehend the sensuous manifold of the sublime object. It "lets us see (the imagination's) own inadequacy." [108–109]

Against the backdrop of Montana's vast landscape—big skies, powerful winds, and cleansing rains—*Winter's* narrator confronts his own "epistemic finitude,"and in the end, he says to the reader ("you"): "Some people, I thought, will never know how pleasant it is to be distant in a clean rain, the driving rain of a summer storm. It's not like you'd expect, nothing like you'd expect" (172). From the beginning, he seeks wisdom from the world around him and quickly locates his problem as originating within him. As he ponders his surroundings, he does not express fear, only self-reflexivity and musings about his own personal history and the animals in his realm. In Indigenous worldviews, the world works according to its own rightness and order; he knows that. Humans stand pitiful within it, and his "crying for pity" fits within what humans know and for which they are responsible (Thackeray, passim). Being in a pitiful state, while not a comfortable thing for any human, has been honed within Native ceremonies as a familiar and acceptable state, one that can lead to power, enlightenment, and heightened connectedness. Hence, the narrator's position of alienation carries with it great potential from the beginning of the narrative, and his knowledge comforts him as a person in the world, along with hawk, horse, and fox—as one not entirely alone.

The situated Indianness that the protagonist's circumstances suggest was initially missed by several reviewers. The novel's point of view, for example, prompted Reynolds Price, on the front page of *The New York Times Book Review*, to see it as more "universal" than "Indian"; Price misses the "Indian" part substantially.

> *Winter in the Blood* is by no means an "Indian novel." There is nothing in it—character, incident, language or emotion—which will not be familiar or quickly comprehensible to any middle- or working-class white or black Southerner, Jew, Spanish-speaking American, homosexual, or other minority member, literate country-club social chairman included. What it is is a nearly flawless novel about human life. To say less is to patronize its complex knowledge, the amplitude of its means, and its clear lean voice. [1]

Welch's "trick" worked, apparently, given that it got the literary establishment men dancing, as he went about his business of staying alive, as he writes in his poem "Surviving,"

> That night the moon slipped a notch, hung
> black for just a second, just long enough
> for web black things to sneak away our cache
> of meat. To stay alive this way, it's hard. [*Riding*, 46]

Jim Barnes understood well Welch's dilemma as an American Indian writer, what a "dance" of survival it can be, when he writes in "Postcard to James Welch in Missoula":

> ... when I said dance, damn it all.
> I meant make it work. Isn't it odd how

we think we have the old pump handle
in hand, then find our grip's empty air? [60].

Living is precarious business.

Winter in the Blood rides with ease on the narrator's tricky, solitary voice and through his lens of awe toward the natural world, opening a consciousness to mainstream readers that had seldom been available in literature about Native Americans at that time. And yet it involves human experiences with the universe and the self's place within it. The text works both in and against the tradition of as-told-to Native American autobiography, a subgenre that is predicated on notions of the Vanishing Indian. Such an autobiographical tradition reflects a reading public's desire to hear a "real" Indian speak and to glimpse Native worlds now tragically lost. That said, while solitary, existential moments indeed define a person, what empowers the individual over time to make his or her distinct imprint on the world remains somewhat mysteriously bound by cultural moorings. Culture in *Winter* is far from the exotic yet accessible knowledge sought by readers of Native American autobiography. As Robert Winthrop notes, "The ambitions of ethnographers notwithstanding, 'cultures' are not the type of knowledge system that can be exhaustively codified; they are not comparable in clarity to more specialized bodies of knowledge such as the rules of criminal procedure or contract bridge" (163).

On the individual level, some people are crushed by the pressures of their times and places, while others who seemingly share similar life circumstances, find voices to speak back to their worlds and to expose to view the marked, otherwise invisible self. Inasmuch as the crux of individual identity and achievement necessarily involves moving in and out of encounters with others and in particular, with others who are relatively distinct culturally, Welch depicts encounters with many non-Indians in terms of influence and purposively involves motion. In a 1982 William Bevis interview about his early writing, Welch remarks, "In a poem I could always take the snapshot, but this time I wanted to make a movie. That's why I had my character moving through different situations, through different landscapes so that it would always be changing, and I could always be writing about that change" (65). "Change" stands as a peculiar term to those who would see the sparse population and vast landscape of Montana in contrast to urban experience.

Many critics have sought to analyze the trope of distance in Welch's *Winter*, described by the narrator as not coming "from country or people; it came from within me" (2). In a general way the critics identified *Winter*'s place as bearing the "destructive legacies of Euro-American colonization" (Gone, 374), but judiciously situating Welch's first two novels demands a close examination of how and why healing requires place and a close probing of psychological and social maladies.[12] From a psychological point of view, the narrator presents as depressed (as a psychologist might say) and yet also as possessing a poignant desire for peace. He tells us, "I want to lose myself . . . to stand beneath the clouds and have my shadow erased, myself along with it" (*Winter,* 125). His recognition of the distance within him ties to his need for others to see him and for him to find people who are "easy to be with, even on a rainy day," as were First Raise, his deceased father, and Mose, his deceased brother (172). Upon leaving a visit to Yellow Calf's cabin, where the narrator has just discovered the truth about his heritage, he reflects upon the significance of his newfound knowledge: "Yet I had felt it then, that feeling of event. Perhaps it was the distance, those three new miles, that I felt, or perhaps I felt something of that other distance; but the event of distance was as vivid to me as the cold canvas of First Raise's coat against my cheek" (*Winter,* 161).

Distance, though ultimately inscrutable, rests within him as both exhilarating and comforting, a rebirth and a return to the safety of parental love represented by the feel of his father's coat. While "event of distance" stands as an example of catachresis, blending as it does time and space, indefinite (openness) and definite (event), the feeling in it matters most. In a sense, the narrator's "event" can hardly be expressed in English as one reaches for words such as "epiphany," "realization," "insight," and so forth to describe it. Rather, the landscape figures into memory and his numbness to the implications of other events in a way that suggests that meaning comes together both peacefully and ineffably, yet resides in space.

Because the narrator does not speak a Native language, perhaps he lacks the words necessary to capture the sense of "time, person, and causality" that would have been available to him through different cultural moorings. Boarding schools, as part of a concerted effort on the part of the U.S. government's assimilation policy, sought to erase the Indianness resident in Native languages. "[T]he control of language—discouraging of the use particular languages or dialects; elevating others to the status of official or national languages—offers a powerful tool of statecraft" (Winthrop, 169). Song or chant might be the most poignant and appropriate response to human experience in space, placing the human being in the center of the universe. The novel's only music is honky-tonk, the stuff of vapid sentimentality, and Welch is a master of reworking such clichéd sound imagery.

Vine Deloria, Jr., describes well the dynamics of what inhabiting a place can mean to American Indians:

> The key to understanding Indian knowledge of the world is to remember that the emphasis was on the particular, not on general laws and explanation of how things worked. . . . [P]ower and place are dominant concepts—power being the living energy that inhabits and/or composes the universe, and place being the relationship of things to each other. . . . Power and place produce personality. [qtd. Gone, 369, 2008]

Although the energies shape the individual's sense of place, the stories that generate from that energy do offer their own explanations of "how things work." Reading the world as a multifarious text allows for shaping one's existence. Space means everything to Welch's protagonists in ways not transparent to readers who live elsewhere and who know little about northeast Montana and reservation life in general. During the 1970s, most American Indians lived in rural America, frequenting small towns like the towns in *Winter* and returning to open country from work or diversion elsewhere.

Drawing on the work of Joseph Gone, an A'aninin (Gros Ventre) psychologist who studies people and space, and who interrogates culturally appropriate mental health treatment modalities, we find that *Winter's* protagonist in his time resides on the cusp of awareness needed for reconnection to himself, other people, traditions, kin, and space. That cusp is A'aninin in many ways. Listening to the voices of residents of Fort Belknap Reservation offers insight into the contemporary reality in terms of time and setting for the two Welch novels—*Winter in the Blood* and *The Death of Jim Loney*. In Gone's interview with Traveling Thunder, for example, a resident of the reservation, Traveling Thunder tells his story of the 1970s:

> It was just a social accepted custom to start drinking every weekend after payday . . . to go out with the other people and party. And then it became habit forming, I guess, after a while. And then we looked around and realized that . . . we left something behind, and now the Whiteman is gonna give us our opportunity to reopen our culture. So we started going back to the hills to fast. We started going back to the mountaintops to fast. We started going to the sweat lodges to pray and to sweat. We started going to the elders to learn. Regain . . . what we were missing. We never was happy; you know, living like a Whiteman. [Gone, 370]

The stabbing words, "The Whiteman is gonna give us our opportunity," reveal the depth of oppression Native people suffered under government bureaucracies, in particular, the Bureau of Indian Affairs and the Indian Health Service. A sea change had occurred in Congress following the Civil Rights Movement, and as part of that change the American Indian Religious Freedom Act became Public Law 95-341 on August 11, 1978. The law set out two dicta:

(1) [The] inherent right of freedom to believe, express, and exercise the traditional religions of the American Indian, Eskimo, Aleut, and Native Hawaiians including but not limited to access to sites, use and possession of sacred objects, and the freedom to worship through ceremonials and traditional rites; and,

(2) The President shall direct the various Federal departments, agencies, and other instrumentalities responsible for administering relevant laws to evaluate their policies and procedures in consultation with native traditional religious leaders in order to determine appropriate

changes necessary to protect and preserve Native American religious cultural rights and practices. [Federal Historic Preservation
Laws, 138]

Clearly, traditions had been kept alive—how else could the government
consult with "native traditional religious leaders"? But the law displaced the
missionaries' authority to determine public religious practices as well as the
government's responsibility to assure Native peoples' rights to religious freedom. The government was also required to assess the effectiveness of the act
after twelve months and consider new legislation if it was determined necessary (Federal Historic Preservation Laws, 138). Inhabiting the space of the
Fort Belknap Reservation in traditional ways began a renaissance for A'aninin
people in their own ways of seeing the world and themselves as both pitiful
and potentially powerful within that space.[13]

Gone goes on to say that for Traveling Thunder "'putting up a ceremony'
and 'praying from the heart' for the inflicted individual was . . . a far superior
means of obtaining help than involving such a person in the mental health
service system" (382). Seen in light of Traveling Thunder's epistemology, the
behavior of *Winter's* narrator fits more fully with the distance between the
"natural" world and the individual that can bridge spacialized openhearted-
ness, the "clean rain" he shared with his brother and father. Because he cannot
find a social context anything like the one Traveling Thunder describes, he
fashions his own ceremony, however subconsciously.

POSTCOLONIAL PROCESSES OF RECOGNITION
AND "THE GIFT OF IDENTITY"

Coming to terms with one's place within a social realm among other human
beings may sometimes be more difficult than either living within the experience of the sublime in the universe or interacting with animals. Grasping the
terms through which social relations operate takes a different set of skills, yet
as we define ourselves, our identities, we hope for acceptance and belonging. Scott Lyons captures that idea well in speaking of the perspectives of an
Ojibwe elder whom he knows: "This gift of identity, by which people come to
see themselves as distinct from others, explains why George Goggleye, who
conducts a wide array of Ojibwe ceremonies, once told me, 'When I live my
day-to-day life, I'm just George, a person like anyone else. But when I light my
pipe, I am *only Ojibwe*'" (87). In Mr. Googleye's identity matrix, the humble
self resides among fellows as "just George," but within the realm of universal
powers, he finds safety under a larger umbrella as an Ojibwe. As with Traveling Thunder, one of the ten A'aninin people Gone interviewed, personhood
comes nestled within ceremonial and tribal encounters.

Encounters with Indian and non-Indian people leave *Winter's* narrator
not only exhausted and hungover, but also bone-weary, even confused. Many

critics have remarked on the "winter in the blood" imagery: people gone—
dead or just "out there somewhere"[14]—drought, disappeared fish, and the
dilapidated Earthboy cabin. He moves as if surveying it all. Retreating into
nature after his social encounters in town is part of the depiction of motion
Welch refers to as his goal in writing *Winter in the Blood*. Granted, motion and
change follow identity's rhythms and flows, but identity also requires rooting
in other ways and within social realms, which in turn requires recognition by
and through others. Readers may recognize the universal aspects of human
terrains, but like tourists, they may also lack the insight to see it as something
more than a corrupt vision of the Old West. Sands notes that that part of
the country with "its honky-tonk bars and sentimental songs, drunk Indians,
drought, and summer tourists hurrying to cross the high plains—holds the
reader at arm's length—stock stuff for westerns, that" (76). Existential realities elude gawking passersby, since the scene presents as at once too real and
unreal.

In exploring issues of what being marked by race can mean, both in terms
of invisibility and/or visibility only as Other, Kelly Oliver persuasively argues
vis-à-vis Franz Fanon's philosophy that alienation comes from a lack of meaning making power and psychic space:

> [W]ith Fanon, . . . colonization operates through racism and . . . any
> theory of colonial alienation must account for racist alienation. . . . It is
> precisely the sense of arriving too late to create one's own meaning that
> can make the colonization of psychic space so effective. Fanon describes
> going to films and waiting to see himself, his meaning already predeter-
> mined by racist stereotypes. . . . Debilitating alienation is the result of
> being thrown into a world of preexisting meanings as one incapable of
> meaning making. And the greatest pain of this alienation comes from
> the fact that even the meaning of one's own body has already been de-
> fined. [Oliver, 12, 15]

Psychic space in the world of *Winter's* narrator is dominated and inscribed
with meanings that shut him out, especially as he sees the ubiquitous demands for him to conform to the hierarchal, patriarchal system values in
order to "make something of himself." Who he is as an Indian does not figure
into the equations of worth.

The cardboard, life-sized cutout of Randolph Scott, for example, shoots
the narrator and Mose dead when they leave the Western movies, even
though they are themselves "cowboys" and look to the movies for heroes as
do other boys their age. "Indian Cowboy" does not register in that time and
place, although today things have changed somewhat. Throughout the novel,
the narrator attempts to negotiate his way through a host of encounters with
people who do not respect, accept, or recognize him; his mother Teresa and

stepfather Lame Bull act especially disrespectful and dismissive of him. As many critics have noted, other people continually refer to him as if he were still a child. Shut out from "adult" worlds, he wonders what his mother and the priest can possibly have to say to one another; then, rather than read the priest's letter to his mother, a missive that might reveal something to him, he tears it up as a gesture that suggests his effort to show some dignity and integrity—not having to know the details, being strong enough not to violate her privacy by snooping.

A deep-seated shame often underlies the narrator's choices, shame in part extending from his father's shame, and from a larger perspective, the intergenerational trauma to American Indian manhood of colonial subjugation. Not only does shame figure into the narrator's situation, as will be discussed later, his exploration of his life takes shape around an inchoate emotion that requires a particularly childlike innocence of him as a character, probably developmentally fitted to the narrator's age when his social detachments came. Relative to the work of Thomas Scheff, who proceeds from the idea that "[A] threat to attachment is always inherent in shame," Joseph Adamson and Hilary Clark note, "As the positive affects of interest and enjoyment are particularly instrumental in the establishment of attachments and bonds with others, so shame which brings about a partial reduction of precisely these two positive affects (and thus disturbs without destroying mutuality), is particularly instrumental in the regulation of social interaction" (3).

Understanding and refocusing the narrator's alienation as an indication of shame and a sense of unworthiness moves us away from the discourse of disease and toward the discourse of spiritual and cultural dis-ease, since the alienation ties to the narrator's father, First Raise, and his experience of a generation's position between the old traditional ways and the colonial next stage of American Indian existence. Names like "First Raise" and "Earthboy" carry ties to aboriginal life, primary belonging, and cultural rootedness that go beyond individual life histories. The narrator's distance, when seen as a reduction of interest and enjoyment, ties his state to his father's state. But fortunately, the Plains Indian traditions of his father included vision questing designed to transition men ritualistically through a sense of worthlessness (pitifulness) and aloneness (loss of attachment, desertion) to a peaceful place within community. An important part of the ritual process includes the subjugation of bodily needs, as is reflected by the narrator's state as the novel opens—thirst, hunger, pain—all underpinnings of shame.

The novel's narrator especially needs to understand his life in relation to a gendered universe—that is, a dynamically balancing set of energies—manhood represents one pole in the reciprocal process. The narrator needs to learn from elders, but he can no longer hope to learn from his father in an interactive way. Death creates a gulf that neither "sinners" nor "bad beginners," descriptors from Welch's poems, can readily transverse. For the narrator, living on after the deaths of his older brother and his father means living without guidance or support, without role models. Without Mose and First Raise, the narrator is indeed a bad beginner. Thus, he tries to find guidance through exploring his memories of his father, by recalling the dream his father had had every fall, that of hunting elk in Glacier National Park. Thinking through the details seemed to give him great comfort: "He planned. He figured out the mileage and the time it would take him to reach the park, and the time it would take to kill an elk and drag it back across the boundary to his waiting pickup. He made a list of food and supplies" (7). Despite the enthusiasm and anticipation First Raise's fantasy indicates, he seems to get caught in an ambivalence, trapped by an imagined prospect of being arrested if he succeeds in bagging an elk: "He inquired around, trying to find out what the penalty would be if they caught him. He wasn't crafty like Lame Bull or the white men of Dodson, so he had to know the penalty, almost as though the penalty would be the inevitable result of the hunt. He never got caught because he never made the trip. The dream, the planning and preparation were all part of a ritual" (7). I would add: First Raise's dream stands as a postcolonial ritual to feign the possibility of his being visible, of making his own meanings and naming himself; yet simultaneously, the dream marks his knowing that with visibility comes a new way of being marked—as a criminal or renegade.

THE CRIMINALIZATION OF AMERICAN INDIAN MEN

The theme of criminality creeps into the narrative with First Raise's thwarted dream, which, even though it was his "ritual" of sorts, did not serve to recover agency for him in his world. He died drunk and in despair. In Welch's novels that follow, each protagonist faces an epistemic dilemma similar to that of First Raise's, a dilemma around the price of visibility he must pay as an Indian. Jim Loney (*The Death of Jim Loney*) dies at the hands of a sinister Indian cop; Sylvester Yellow Calf (*Indian Lawyer*), when he's on the brink of running for the U.S. Senate, faces off against criminals who attempt to entrap him through blackmail and to destroy his professional future; White Man's Dog, or Fools Crow as he is eventually named (*Fools Crow*), lives with the threat of being pulled into "renegade justice" represented by Owl Child's gang and his childhood friend, Fast Horse; and Charging Elk (*Heartsong of Charging Elk*) actually ends up in prison after his legal identity is erased through bureaucratic error and ineptitude, and after he kills someone who, he believes through his Lakota cultural lens, must rightly be killed—a man who drugs and sexually violates him. In each instance, the male protagonist becomes a criminal, even though he is innocent of the crime of which he is accused.

Most significant in the description of First Raise's dream of hunting in a place where his ancestors were once free to hunt is the idea that because he is not "crafty" like white men, or Indian men who are like white men, he will be arrested. First Raise sees punishment as inevitable. Just as Archilde in D'Arcy McNickle's *The Surrounded* and Jim Loney in the *Death of Jim Loney* carry a sense of doom about them, so does First Raise—doomed to disappoint, to fail, to die before his time, perhaps even to die drunk. Nevertheless, hunting elk represents a beginning point in self-definition—a way of regaining stature as an Indian man. As Welch says in the poem "Blackfeet, Blood and Piegan Hunters" about the loss of manhood:

> If we raced a century over hills
> that ended years before, people couldn't
> say our run was simply poverty or promise
> for a better end. We ended sometime
> back in recollections of glory, myths
> that meant the hunter meant a lot
> to starving wives and bad painters. [36]

The repetition of "meant" serves to emphasize meaning in a once-ordered world where actions fit within a nexus of relations. To live for others (families) and for the self (bad painters) represented gender balance, albeit glorified by those who now "dance for pennies" (36). Although careful to disclaim the practicality of past mythic glory, the poet's narrator nonetheless ends with a collective "we" that endures.

> Look away, and we are gone.
> Look back. Tracks are there, a little faint,
> our song strong enough for headstrong hunters
> who look ahead to one more kill. [36]

The two pieces of writing together offer complementary views of what is possible. As pathetic as *Winter's* narrator's memory of his father's "song" may be, he carries it forward, and with it the hope to recover his inherent sovereignty as an individual and to live in an Indian way.

Harkening back to a time when honor meant something, the poem offers a vision *Winter's* narrator seeks. Kwame Anthony Appiah refers to such visions as risking being seen as "old-fashioned," then adds, "But systems of honor not only help us to do well by others, they can help sustain us in our pursuit of our own good. If the codes are right, an honorable life will be a life genuinely worthy of respect" (179). The Native American Renaissance centrally grapples with restoring such honor, and with it, hope. The desperately sad and crushingly depressing aspects of Welch's work, like the loss of past glory and the futility of hoping for its return, resonated with readers, Indian and non-Indian alike, in the 1970s when he rose to recognition, first, with *Winter in the Blood*, and then with *The Death of Jim Loney*. The stage was set by *Bury My Heart at*

Wounded Knee by Dee Brown, which was a best-seller in 1971, on the injustices dealt to American Indians. Sacheen Little Feather (Apache/Yaqui) served as a proxy for Marlon Brando at the forty-fifth Academy Awards in 1973, when Brando refused to accept the Oscar for the *Godfather;* he refused the award because of the negative images of American Indians in film and on television. In addition, the U.S. government was at war in Vietnam, and although young people were paying the price for it, that war was not of their making or to their liking. Hence, *Winter in the Blood* and *The Death of Jim Loney* were central among the cultural voices rising from Indian Country precisely because of Welch's powerful aesthetic, which eludes nostalgia, all the while evoking the deeply complex emotions Americans tend to feel toward American Indians.

The mantra of the counterculture of the 1960s linked the alienation youth felt from their own roots (their parents' generation) with the need for recognition on their own terms. Even though *Winter's* narrator certainly does not come across as a "flower child," the spirit of the times was being carried by this young American Indian man to Native and non-Native readers alike who bore cynicism about "the establishment" as boldly as they bore their belief in their own power to remake the world from the environment up. Brother-/sisterhood among Indians in the pan-Indian movements of the day represented resistance that was resonant with the countercultural youth's alignment with American Indian iconography and causes made for times.

THE CEREMONIAL RETURN TO INNOCENCE THROUGH EXPERIENCE

Exposing the stereotypes of Indians created by Hollywood was a long time in coming, as Rita Parks notes in discussing the "mythic analogies" inherent in criticism and "analysis of the Western experience." She describes the ideological pattern well as it ties to Manifest Destiny and the Bible:

> the rancher-nester war as a repetition of the rivalry between Cain and Abel; the prairie schooner plowing through the plains like the ship of Ulysses sailing from Troy; the lonely gunfighter as a suffering god doing the killing for the community and then moving on as an exiled scapegoat, or the knight-errant on an unending quest. And last, but not least certainly, there is the myth of the Edenic Garden and the return to innocence. [18]

Clearly, the genre of the Western lurks within this novel, and no doubt some of *Winter's* appeal comes from the narrator's return to primordial beginnings, but his is a garden of an Indigenous sort. As discussed early on in this essay, the distance reflected in metaphors of nature does not suggest alienation from nature, but from self. The return to innocence, rather than pre-Lapsarian, represents a birthing into connection with other humans and a recognition of the self by oneself and by others—both reversing the Vanishing Savage iconography of the West.

Just as surely as First Raise internally knows his hunting song, he also anticipates his guilt under laws that brand him "renegade" for being who he is. The social conditions formerly colonized peoples suffer (poverty, unemployment, and so forth) result from being denied the inherent right to determine their own cultural identities and destinies. D'Arcy McNickle, writing in *Native American Tribalism* in 1973, delineates the marked yet invisible status of Native people that, I would argue, continued throughout much of the twentieth century:

The anomalous legal situation of Indians at the turn of the century continues into the present, despite the fact that Indians were "granted" citizenship in 1924, and have been recognized as sovereign or quasi-sovereign in recent Supreme Court decisions.[15] The United States Court of Claims, in reviewing an Indian case at the end of the last century, ... found the legal situation anomalous, a situation "unknown to the common law or the civil law or to any system of municipal law. [The Indians] were neither citizens nor aliens; they were neither persons nor slaves; they were wards of the nation, and yet, ... were little else than prisoners of war while war did not exist." [87]

Thus the narrator's dilemma in *Winter* must be seen as more than that of a dysfunctional individual attempting to create a meaningful life for himself in his homeland. His legacy includes the sort of political and cultural erasure implied by the words "neither citizens nor aliens ... neither persons nor slaves ... wards of the nation, and yet ... little else than prisoners of war while war did not exist." Not surprisingly, Welch must be careful in portraying a man such as the narrator, in places such as he travels, if an author hopes both to elude the pathos inherent in the man's situation and to thwart the expectations of readers who think they already know the "plight" of Indian life in the 1960s and '70s.[16] As Gerald Vizenor so cogently remarks in *Postindian Conversations*, "Native American literature is much more than a challenge to the social sciences, as you know; it is liberation, and a visionary sovereignty" (90). Welch captures the peculiarity of '70s' Indian identity well.

As the narrator's namelessness suggests, and as he says of himself, he is "nothing to anybody"—a typically Welchian play on words, which reflects an uneducated person's awkward attempt to use perfect grammar so as to avoid a double negative, that is, to sound educated. Those words can be taken to mean that he'll play the part of "nothing" for anybody who desires that he do so—in this case, the airplane man (57). He risks visible criminality by doing so, but he innocently goes along with the unfolding events simply because the airplane man offers him a modicum of recognition. Once he had a chance "to become something," working at a rehabilitation clinic in Washington, but he rejected the opportunity because he discovered that the institution only wanted to hire him in order to qualify for grant money. He nevertheless needs a definition of himself and a dream of a future. In search of both, he looks for meaning in the lives of Indian people he knows and has known. The contestation at the core of it all is his very being.

In l970, in his book aptly titled *The Right to Be Indian*, Ernest L. Schusky describes the more dismal aspects of reservation life at that time: from 74 percent of the water being contaminated to 81 percent of families having to haul their own water. An even greater number of people have no suitable way to dispose of excreta. "The average size of Indian houses is less than two rooms, with an average household of more than 5.4 occupants. On the other hand, the nonIndian house has an average nationally of only 2.9 occupants and more than four rooms" (v).

As the Kennedy and Johnson administrations began waging their "War on Poverty," images of the mean aspects of Indian life (as described above) began entering middle-class homes across America via television. As graphically real as such images are, they did not adequately portray the complexity of Indian responses to their own life circumstances, nor did they inform the viewer of the unique historical factors which have perpetuated poverty among Indians.[17]

For one thing, the "right to be Indian" can best be realized on reservations, or in Indian communities, as legally anomalous as Indian "citizenship" continues to be there. To those Indians who attempted to relocate to cities (or actually stayed) during the years of the termination policy, "[u]rban life proved a difficult challenge." Not only were Indian people plunged into the sort of culture shock any rural people would be when economically forced to move to the city, they were also "[i]nsulated from the mainstream culture by strong aboriginal traditions," and "ill-prepared for city life, especially fullbloods, illiterates, and non-veterans. The anonymity of the city contrasted sharply with the personalisms so characteristic of the reservation," and the relocated people's collective identity was "at odds with the materialism of city life."[18] Most faced severe economic struggles.

Back on the reservation, a century of cultural oppression made life in "traditional" Indian terms less than fully realizable as well. Policies like allotment had turned many reservations lands into checkerboards of white, mixed-blood, and full-blood ownership; missionization and governmental educational systems had taken their toll on the continuing practice of Indian religions, on kinship structures, as well as on tribal leadership. In 1970, Indian men made barely more than $3,500, compared to an average for European Americans of nearly $9,000. On reservations it was even worse, with an annual per capita income for Native Americans averaging less than $1,000 in 1980.[19]

Economic control continues to rest in the hands of the BIA, and more often than not that means Indians do not control their own funds and resources, do not have full autonomy to plan their own futures, and do not have full juris-dictional power in their own systems of tribal justice.

All of these things provide the backdrop for *Winter,* but for the author to foreground those facts would have doomed the novel to the realm of social tract or political polemic. The aesthetic requires the narrator's innocence, a space from which he can contemplate his life "out loud," as it were, without numbing details of real life. In many respects, to write or speak about such things is, on the one hand, to tell an old story, one which every American more or less thinks s/he knows. On the other hand, how does one characterize any Indian person's life in fiction without in some sense accounting for that person's status as a member of a "domestic dependent nation"?[20] The tragedy of the losses strikes a chord in the American mind, no matter what.

However important it may have been for Welch to avoid both nostalgia and polemic, *Winter's* narrator could not be innocent in unreal ways either, naïve but not innocent. The scene where he slaps Marlene for asking him to have oral sex with her gives the character's portrayal anti-sympathetic depth and shows how off balance he truly is. She asks him to meet her need and asks in a manner that suggests she would like more genuine intimacy and personal interaction, rather than just drunk, anonymous sex. In fact, Marlene and the airplane man seek something from him, his involvement in their lives. Paradoxically, his experience with his own insignificance via his grasp of the geographic magnitude of the space he inhabits signals a desire to make con-nections with others, particularly with his wayward girlfriend.

The "event of distance" that *Winter's* narrator experiences thus provides a taproot for him into self-recognition, something beyond internalized co-lonialism and postcolonial erasure and toward the acquisition of meaning-making power. The "tricks" Welch employs in the writing of *Winter* involve teasing out the agonistic, existential side of being Coyote, the appetite-driven wanderer, in addition to the political situatedness of persons caught in the cat-egory "Indian." Through complexly rich humor, Welch thwarts easy appropri-ation of the man's experience. Neither noble nor entirely pathetic, he "wakes" to find himself in a place and time where the larger society's objectification of the "Indian" individual has almost erased his own ability to step out into his beingness and voice. In the 1970s, simply removing the "mask" (to borrow Franz Fanon's term) was a radical act in self-representation. James Welch's portrayal of this nameless character opened a landscape of Indigenous exis-tence and experience into the realm of recognition.

NOTES

1. Blue Cloud, "Coyote Man and Saucy Duckfeathers," p. 43.

2. Whenever Welch attributed his success to luck, I always read it two ways: as a way of skirting grand claims to talent—in other words, a modest gesture—and

as an opening or portal to the "other" world, to spiritual knowledge much as a traditional vision seeker waits for such an opening. I seriously doubt Welch would have characterized himself that way, but I do, because his humility, sincerity, and vision provide the requisite grounds for "crying for a vision," as William Thackery notes in his article, "'Crying for Pity' in *Winter in the Blood.*"

3. "Luck" recurs as a term in Plains Indian autobiography to refer to ritual connections to the great powers of the universe wherein the supplicant does all that he can do to seek power, but is not guaranteed connection. When connection occurs, the merit of the supplicant is not the cause. While Welch's usage of the term may not have been intended to link with the nineteenth-century usage, he may have acquired the term throughout his life from his experiences as an American Indian.

4. The title for this essay was inspired by a piece Lois Welch did on *Reflections West*, a radio program on literature that airs on KUFM; the series is produced by Lisa Simon and David L. Moore (www.reflectionswest.org). In episode 26, which aired on March 15, 2011, Dr. Welch spoke about a passage in James Welch's *Winter in the Blood* that inspired me to think about the epistemological space of the West in new ways.

5. Richard Hugo told Welch that he could and should write about what he knew, and such knowledge gave him the encouragement he needed to develop his own voice. Contained in the Beinecke Library archives at Yale University, his short fiction of the 1960s consists entirely of stories unrelated to his experiences as a Native American.

6. The title of *Winter in Blood* was originally *The Only Good Indian*, taken from the phrase "the only good Indian is a dead Indian." I prefer to use the term Native American to refer to indigenous peoples of the current United States—American Indians, Alaska Natives, and Native Hawaiians—but recognize that among indigenous people of the lower forty-eight states, "Indian" is the term most used and perhaps preferred.

7. Volume II of *The Native American Renaissance* will include an essay on the Red Power movement.

8. The language of this paragraph is taken from Homi Bhabha, *The Location of Culture*, p. 224.

9. Interestingly, *Henderson the Rain King* (1959) is thought to be influenced by Camara Laye's *Radiance of the King* (1954); both are set in Africa with white protagonists who are seeking affirmation of self, even heroism in their mid-life crises. Although each proceeds differently, these two novels set in Africa with white protagonists seek to create and be part of peaceful, racially harmonious worlds.

10. Although McFarland is correct in stating, "Welch had lived away from Indian communities for most of his life," I would add that because Welch grew up in Native American communities as wide-ranging as Alaska, Fort Belknap, and Minnesota, he developed within American Indian cultures and among American Indian peoples; moreover, his Blackfeet father was a native language speaker. As a

writer, he set himself apart to write, but frequently worked with youth groups and in other settings where he could serve as a role model.

11. For a fuller discussion of this idea, see Shanley, "Writing Indian," p. 134.

12. For example, see Kunz, "Lost in the Distance of Winter," and Reedy, "*Winter in the Blood*," p. 306. See also the special edition on the novel of the *American Indian Quarterly* 4:2 (1978).

13. The revival of traditional Indian religions is part of the Native American Renaissance and will be covered in Volume II of this series.

14. The title of Simon Ortiz's 2002 collection of poems, *Out There Somewhere,* is a translation of *hauchaw tyah haati,* which serves "as a reply to a query by someone who is looking for another person, perhaps a parent looking for a child or a friend looking for his or her friend" (preface). Ortiz is careful to point out that the person, though seemingly lost, will "continue to be absolutely connected socially and culturally to our Native identity. We insist that we as human cultural beings must always have this connection because it is the way we maintain a Native sense of Existence" (preface). Ortiz's words strike me as hauntingly true of the protagonists of Welch's first two novels; they seem lost at the same time as they are themselves searching for something lost, something or someone "out there somewhere."

15. In 1996, Elouise Cobell filed a class-action lawsuit on behalf of individual Indian landowners whose resources the Bureau of Indian Affairs holds in trust. In the suit, the lawyers for Cobell, et al., argued for an accounting of the income and expenditures for trust lands and resources. Although Judge Lambert ruled in the plaintiffs' favor and has held three successive Secretaries of Interior in contempt of court for failing to produce the records demanded by the court—indeed, for destroying records—full accounting never occurred and no one went to jail for thievery or fraud. Congress has now settled the claim for a mere fraction of what was initially sought. See www.indiantrust.org for an in-depth report on the settlement details. According to the website for the *Salazar v. Cobell* settlement, "On December 11, 2012, the Court approved the commencement of payments to Historical Accounting Class Members. Distribution of checks began the week of December 17, 2012 to all living Class Members" (accessed February 23, 2013). For an overview of the three sovereignties (state, federal, and tribal) under U.S. federalism, see Vine Deloria, Jr., and Clifford M. Lytle, *The Nations Within.*

16. Because American Indians control significant resources in the United States and because the fiduciary responsibility of the government requires particular services be rendered to Indians in perpetuity, they continue to be subject to control that resembles colonialism. The difference involves the right to self-determination, also guaranteed by law. See Echo-Hawk, *In the Court of the Conquerer.*

17. As tools of social science, poverty indicators function to set norms, and customarily overlook other quality-of-life factors related to cultural identity; in other words, being poor by white middle-class standards may not mean the same thing as being poor means for other cultural groups. For example, in Plains tribal

societies, high value is placed on sharing and on noninterference in other people's affairs; hence, while a low average income and close living quarters no doubt reflect certain deprivations and inequalities, traditional tribal values, which can lead to a sense of belonging and importance, may somewhat compensate for not having more money and more "room." Of course, the pitfall in saying so is that of romanticizing poverty. I certainly do not mean to do that; for one thing, the wants and "needs" created by media compromise traditional values in complicated ways. Romanticizing poor peoples, who are in fact deprived of opportunities to prosper economically, often denotes privilege on the part of the spectator.

18. Olson and Wilson, *Native Americans in the Twentieth Century*, pp. 152–53.

19. Ibid., p. 186. The toll of such statistics on a people's health and welfare becomes graphically clear in the authors' fuller accounting of diseases: Poor nutrition and housing generated a tuberculosis rate more than six times the national average in 1980, and frequently contaminated water supplies made Native Americans seventy times more likely than European Americans to suffer dysentery. Their influenza and pneumonia rates are three times the national average; and they are ten times more likely than European Americans to fall ill to strep throat, eight times more likely to get hepatitis, and three to four times more likely to catch mumps, chicken pox, and whooping cough. The Native American suicide rate in the early 1980s was six times greater than for any other ethnic group in the United States" (186–87). Also see Steinberg, "The Ignominious Origins," pp. 5–43. In speaking of the reservation system, Steinberg writes, "With the political and economic affairs of the reservation empowered by the Bureau of Indian Affairs, the Indian had effectively been reduced to colonial status, as is suggested by the following description of the reservation system [by Robert Berkhofer, Jr.]: 'Ultimately, white officials determined who would live upon a reserve, where, and how. Depending upon the time, they also decided upon the sale and leasing of tribal lands and other resources, the overall economic development of the reserves, the nature of educational facilities, and even at times the churches and religions, as well as whether or not to recognize tribal governments. The line of command stretched from officials and politicians in Washington to the BIA agents on the reservations who were expected to put these policies into effect and so were given power to call out the military to enforce their powers, to exercise judicial authority at times, to control rations and trust funds, to lease and sell lands, water rights, minerals, and forests, to remove children from their parents in order to send them to school, and to recognize or to sidestep traditional tribal political systems—all to further decisions made in the capital. Thus Indians became at best clients patronized by the agents sent to rule over them. So complete was the agents' authority that some analysts have likened the reservation to a colony; others have gone so far as to depict the reserves as the equivalent of concentration camps'" (19, 20).

20. A trilogy of U.S. Supreme Court decisions in the first decades of the nineteenth century established in law the concept that carried the right to colonize, the Doctrine of Discovery. See Miller, *Native America, Discovered and Conquered*.

WORKS CITED

Adamson, Joseph, and Hilary Clark. *Scenes of Shame: Psychoanalysis, Shame, and Writing*. Albany: SUNY Press, 1999.

Alexie, Sherman. *Reservation Blues*. New York: Atlantic Monthly Press, 1995.

Appiah, Kwame Anthony. *The Honor Code: How Moral Revolutions Happen*. New York: Norton, 2010.

Barnes, Jim. "Postcard to James Welch in Missoula." *Chicago Review* 28:4 (Spring 1977), 60.

Bastien, Betty. *Blackfeet Ways of Knowing: The Worldview of the Siksikaitsitapi*. Calgary, Alb.: University of Calgary Press, 2004.

Bevis, William. "Dialogue with James Welch." *Northwest Review*, 20:2, 3 (1982), 163–85.

Bhabha, Homi. *The Location of Culture*. New York: Routledge, 1994.

Blue Cloud, Peter. "Coyote Man and Saucy Duckfeathers." *Elderberry Flute Song: Contemporary Coyote Tales*. Trumansburg, N.Y.: Crossing Press, 1982.

Deloria, Jr., Vine, and Clifford M. Lytle, *The Nations Within: The Past and Future of American Indian Sovereignty*. New York: Pantheon Books, 1984.

Echo-Hawk, Walter R. *In the Court of the Conquerer: The Ten Worst Indian Law Cases Ever Decided*. Golden, Colo.: Fulcrum, 2010.

Federal Historic Preservation Laws. http://www.nps.gov/history/locallaw/fhpl.htm.

Gone, Joseph. "'So I Can Be Like a Whiteman': The Cultural Psychology of Space and Place in American Indian Mental Health." *Cultural Psychology* 14:3, 369–99.

Jahner, Elaine. "Quick Paces and a Space of Mind." *Denver Quarterly* 14:4 (1980), 34–47.

Kunz, Don. "Lost in the Distance of Winter: James Welch's *Winter in the Blood*." *Critique* 20:1 (1978), 93–99.

Larson, Sidner. "Colonization as Subtext in James Welch's *Winter in the Blood*." *American Indian Quarterly* 29 (Winter-Spring, 2005), 274–80.

Lincoln, Kenneth. "Winter Naming: James Welch." *American Indian Culture and Research Journal* 29:3 (2005), 1–23.

Lyons, Scott. *x-marks: Native Signatures of Assent*. Minneapolis: University of Minnesota Press, 2010.

McFarland, Ron. *Understanding James Welch*. Columbia: University of South Carolina, 2000.

McNickle, D'Arcy. *Native American Tribalism: Indian Survivals and Renewals*. London: Oxford University Press, 1973.

Miller, Robert J. *Native America, Discovered and Conquered*. Lincoln: University of Nebraska Press, 2008.

Momaday, N. Scott. *House Made of Dawn*. New York: Harper & Row, 1968.

Oliver, Kelly. *Witnessing: Beyond Recognition*. Minneapolis: University of Minnesota Press, 2001.

Olson, James S., and Raymond Wilson. *Native Americans in the Twentieth Century*. Urbana: University of Illinois Press, 1984, 152–53.

Ortiz, Alfonso. "Indian/White Relations: View from the Other Side of the 'Frontier.'" *Indians in American History, An Introduction*. Edited by Frederick E. Hoxie. Arlington Heights, Ill.: Harland Davidson, Inc., 1988, 1–16.

Ortiz, Simon. *Out There Somewhere*. Tucson: University of Arizona Press, 2002.

Owens, Louis. "Earthboy's Return—James Welch's Act of Recovery in *Winter in the Blood*." *Wicazo Sa Review* 6:2 (Autumn 1990), 27–37.

Parks, Rita. *The Western Hero in Film and Television*. Ann Arbor, Mich.: UMI Research Press, 1982.

Price, Reynolds. "When Is an Indian Novel Not an Indian Novel?" *New York Times Book Review*, November 10, l974, sec. 7, l.

Purdy, John Loyd. *Writing Indian, Native Conversations*. Lincoln: University of Nebraska Press, 2009.

Reedy, Gerard. "*Winter in the Blood*." *America* 132 (April l9, l975), 306.

Sands, Kathleen Mullen. "Closing the Distance: Critic, Reader and the Works of James Welch." *MELUS* 14:2 (1987), 73–85.

Schusky, Ernest L. *The Right to Be Indian*. San Francisco: Indian Historian Press, 1970.

Shanley, Kathryn. "'Writing Indian': American Literature and the Future of Native American Studies." In *Studying Native America: Problems and Prospects*. Edited by Russell Thornton, pp. 130–51. Madison: University of Wisconsin Press, 1998.

Sharpe, Matthew. "'Ideological Judgment' in Eagleton and Zizek." *Political Theory* 34:1 (February 2006), 95–120.

Silko, Leslie Marmon. *Ceremony*. New York, Viking, 1977.

Steinberg, Stephen. "The Ignominious Origins of Ethnic Pluralism in America." In *The Ethnic Myth: Race, Ethnicity, and Class in America*. Boston: Beacon Press, 1981, 1989, 5–43

Thackeray, William. "Animal Allies and Transformers of *Winter in the Blood*." *MELUS* 12:1 (Spring l985), 37–64.

———. "'Crying for Pity' in *Winter in the Blood*." *MELUS* 7:1 (Spring, l980), 61–78.

Vizenor, Gerald, and A. Robert Lee. *Postindian Conversations*. Lincoln: Universtiy of Nebraska Press, 1999.

Welch, James. *The Death of Jim Loney*. New York: Harper and Row, 1974.

———. *Heartsong of Charging Elk*. New York: Doubleday, 2000.

———. *Riding the Earthboy 40*. New York: Harper & Row, 1971, 1976.

———. *Winter in the Blood*. New York: Viking, 1974.

Winthrop, Robert. "Defining the Right to Culture and Some Alternatives." *Cultural Dynamics* 14 (2002), 161–83.

7

Gerald Vizenor on Imagination

KATHRYN HUME

Gerald Vizenor writes so frequently about imagination that his comments now seem too familiar to arouse notice. He praises imagination for rewriting history and unpleasant experience and for contributing to tribal "survivance," a state that rejects victimization narratives. He upholds imagination as necessary to avoiding "terminal creeds," by which he means limiting self-definitions of all sorts. Imagination also helps the individual choose options that provide the most liberty.[1] As he says of his experiences in China, "I *imagined* my own liberation as play." On this same note, he has explained, "You can't have liberation if you're confined to discourses based on the real. Once you're confined to the real you're trapped; your stories lose all their magical power, you're limited by all sorts of restrictions that trickster discourse wants to explode, deny."[2] His take on the ways and purposes of imaginative power, and their embedding in his writings, has been central to his role as a mainstay in the Native American Renaissance.

The emphasis on interior mental life shares similarities with attitudes found in a variety of religions: the condition of one's consciousness (or conscience) matters, while what happens in the outside world does not. In Vizenor's case, this means developing an imaginative and creative approach to the external world. The extreme inward orientation of this philosophy may seem irresponsible or a counsel of despair if you consider the world itself to be endangered. My trying to tease anything consistent out of Vizenor may be a foolish and very academic thing to try, but I shall analyze the claims he makes for the functions of the imagination. The imagination is his answer to what other writers see as the dead ends of the postmodern condition.[3] He does recognize the problems of weighing the individual against the community and the world. The building blocks of his argument are sufficiently unusual that he provides answers that are less banal than the turns to family and religion in other recent postmodernist novels that question the nature and function of the individual. Given that he both seeks and offers values, he might qualify as post-postmodern, and a Native postmodern at that.

One very important function that Vizenor attributes to imagination is rewriting one's experience. Rewriting involves assuming responsibility for one's own outlook and refusing to accept any sense of victimization. He applies the term, "rewriting" in two ways, one of them likely to seem valuable to many readers, and the other likely at first to seem of dubious worth. While a purist's view of "Truth" might reject both, rewriting one's own traumatic memories gets a rather different response from fancifully rewriting "history."

Survivance is Vizenor's term for not just surviving but for coming through with a positive outlook at having survived and for taking some pride in one's trickster escapes. "Survivance is an active resistance and repudiation of dominance, obtrusive themes of tragedy, nihilism, and victimry."[4] Whether the individual was truly responsible for escaping or not, thinking in those terms helps one deal with trauma and encourages one to maintain a trickster outlook. Given that some trauma therapies—Group Therapy, Traumatic Incident Reduction, and Exposure Therapy—involve re-envisioning the catastrophe but reducing one's panic, startle response, adrenaline rush, and other negatives until the image no longer rouses those reactions, Vizenor's argument seems psychologically plausible. Where Western therapies tend to stress reducing the negative, Vizenor's emphasizes the positive: one escaped in part because of one's responses and so can take some credit for the escape. As he puts the point in the McCaffery-Marshall interview, one must take grim experiences and play "this material back in a way so that it seems to be a different song" (294). He wants us to internalize a positive sense of agency and resist the helplessness of victimry. This is not a popular attitude: as Vizenor notes sardonically in *Chancers*, "the director of native studies on the campus" antagonized "every romantic native student on campus. [He] would not stand for even the slightest pout of victimry."[5]

By implication, this concept of the imagination also implies that we are responsible for how happy we feel overall. How we feel about our experience depends on how we let our selves feel about it. This may seem to demand that you deny reality. Why force yourself to feel good if someone has done something horrible to you? Then again, are you better off feeling good or bad? Vizenor upholds feeling good. Another writer who has explored this issue recently is Richard Powers. In *Generosity*, Powers creates a character who, having survived massacre and cultural transplantation, explains that all of life is the proverbial, nonexistent free lunch.[6] The laws of thermodynamics say life shouldn't exist; the laws of probability say that any particular individual should not exist. Had a different sperm out of several millions made connection with the egg, after all, one would never have been born, so any life one gets is truly a free lunch. Vizenor seems at least partly to be thinking in these terms, but he puts more emphasis on creating that happy outlook through conscious mental manipulation rather than achieving it through the genetic good fortune that Powers explores.

Rewriting history to make it more palatable will cause many readers uneasiness.[7] Holocaust deniers as rewriters of history are not exactly respectable, so why should rewriting Columbus in wildly and deliberately unhistorical ways be useful or desirable? All my instincts rise against what seems like frivoling with history, but one must remember just how dishonest history written by the victors can be. Given the atrocious skew to official histories from any minority viewpoint, writing the Native American holocaust into history makes sense, but that is clearly not Vizenor's aim. He produces a fantasia on the idea of the explorer in *The Heirs of Columbus*, and talks about Columbus's Native American descendants by a healer-shaman. All "Indians" are, in a sense, the heirs of Columbus, since he invented the notion of their shared identity and these specific heirs have a genetic inheritance of healing from that shaman. As heirs, they can enjoy the chance to play around with the idea of Columbus, and they postulate a Columbus descended from Mayas who made it to Europe in prehistoric times. Vizenor tries to "co-opt or colonize Columbus . . . make Columbus serve the revolution and to be responsible for healing the victims and the mutants of the first five hundred years of the Chemical Civilization." His characters see Columbus as "just this mythic figure that they can transform in their storytelling into anything they want to" (McCaffrey and Marshall, 297). The heirs want healing stories, so that is how Columbus is used. The heirs also exercise their abilities to view official accounts with extreme skepticism, an outlook Vizenor upholds as necessary to sanity in our world. By implication, of course, the larger culture is insane, or the sanity of individuals would not be so imperiled by contact with it. This point is important for his overall vision.

Another function of the imagination is to guard us against a fatal attraction to terminal creeds. Vizenor has Belladonna Darwin-Winter Catcher poisoned in *Bearheart: The Heirship Chronicles*; her audience considers that fit punishment for her drippy, stereotyped descriptions of what makes Indians culturally different from whites.[8] His own utter refusal to define what being Native American might mean may irritate Euro-American readers, but is in keeping with his avoidance of terminal creeds: "native identities are personal creations of the real, not the decorative lace of metaphysics or the false memories of citatory dominance."[9] The point of life is to be flexible, ever-developing, and ever open to change and chance. He calls those who leave their lives open to chance rather than trying to control everything "Chancers," and applies the term to the Amerindians whose skeletons are displayed in the anthropology museum in his novel of that name. This differentiates their culture radically from the control-culture of Western civilization. One of his objections to a creed is that you block off change and chance.

I suggest that total refusal to define limits or beliefs is not completely possible, even for Vizenor. His saying that lives should be open to chance identifies an important belief. He obviously believes that Euro-Americans have behaved criminally over the last three or more centuries toward natives of the land, and I doubt he would consider that belief trivial or easily changed. I think he differentiates the claims of beliefs and terminal creeds by applying them to the individual. If you try to define *yourself,* you limit *yourself.* You may feel that you should guide your actions by some belief—that killing other humans is bad, say—but he would probably deny that any rule should be absolute. While the murders he inserts in his novels are not realistic and his form of writing not representational, he does seem to consider death an appropriate punishment at times—for sexual abuse by a priest of his altar boys in *Father Meme* for instance, or for several characters in *Bearheart.*[10] He ostentatiously refuses to define Native American or even tribal, but he does not refuse to identify beliefs; he tries, though, to keep them from being absolutes that will limit the individual. He believes that acting on your beliefs is far more important than defining them.[11]

Refusing creeds forces one to narrow one's attention to the present. To be responsive to change and not impose rules that turn decisions into formulas, one must focus on the here and now and not plan for the future. Vizenor's characters do seem present-oriented. One never sees them thinking about how they will pay for a child's education or finance their retirement. Those are admittedly middle-class mainstream-society concerns. Some of the Browne family members in *Hotline Healers* and *Trickster of Liberty* live in cities and pursue ordinary jobs, but their concerns are short-term and they appear not to have families of their own. This focus does demand an intensity of engagement with the moment that does not encourage daydreaming or slacking off, and in that sense it encourages them to lead their lives fully. Furthermore, one is not likely to enjoy the kind of cheerful consciousness he approves of without working on it, working all the time to keep the right balance between the self and the world. Alternatively, one focuses on very short-term projects: killing irritating university administrators and substituting their bones for the liberated bones of Amerindians in the anthropology museum, for instance (*Chancers*); striking a dishonest but lucrative trade deal with China on ginseng roots ("Trickster of Liberty"); or working one's way through the wanaki cards day by day (*Dead Voices*) so as to experience life from the point of view of each animal on the cards.

Vizenor's emphasis on the individual's mental state does resemble some religious understandings of life. If you maintain the right openness to God or to the present moment, or enter the right prayerful state, or keep repeating the right mantra, you can achieve everything from indifference toward worldly temptations on up to ecstasy. In a religious context, the individual is usually concerned with his or her own spiritual state, and takes responsibility for that and not for the surrounding civilization. This is fine in an era when civilizations can rise or fall without harming the earth, but more worrisomely self-centered if the earth itself may be seriously damaged. How does Vizenor relate the individual to the local community or to the world at large?

His essay "The Aesthetics of Survivance" gives the clearest answer that I have found in his writing. In his *Native Liberty,* he quotes Dorothy Lee's

Freedom and Culture about Dakota beliefs: "Dakota were responsible for all things, because they were at one with all things. In one way, this meant that all behavior had to be responsible, since its effects always went beyond the individual. In another way, it meant that an individual had to, was responsible to, increase, intensify, spread, recognize, experience this relationship."[12] Vizenor further quotes Lee, who goes on to distinguish between responsibility and accountability, saying no "Dakota was accountable to any one or for any one." A Dakota would not speak for others or answer questions about someone else, and felt no obligation to disclose information about himself either. In *Native Liberty* Vizenor sums this up as "Original, communal responsibility, greater than the individual, greater than original sin, but not accountability," and he feels that it "animates the practice and consciousness of survivance" (99), which I take to be in agreement with Lee. In practice, this seems to mean that one's actions should take the community into account, but if one feels the need to pursue some goal separate from the community, then one is free to do so.

One low-key, realistic form of community responsibility that we note occasionally in his novels is that children whose parents have died or abandoned them usually get taken on by some other members of the community.[13] That seems characteristic of Vizenor's sense of community, and in the cases of the characters he describes, clan affiliation does not seem to interfere. Mixed-bloods are not less likely to be adopted, problems that do keep children from being recognized or welcomed in some other tribal cultures, as Leslie Marmon Silko shows in *Ceremony*. Accepting dogs and bears as members of the tribal community is another way in which he defines the group. Sometimes an individual contributes to the community. Gesture Browne is a "denturist," an untrained dentist who fixes bad teeth and supplies dentures for free (*Hotline Healers*, 17). Slyboots Browne hires inhabitants of the reservation to work in his microlight airplane factory (*Trickster of Liberty*, 129–32). Other signs of community activity are more difficult to discern. Storytelling evidently counts as major community involvement, and so does healing. We see, though, few other possible kinds of community interaction in reservation scenes. While Vizenor's emphasis on individual imagination is central, he does not set the individual up against the community in ways that American individualism has, but neither does he develop any detailed image of a happily functional community. That would create a kind of terminal creed, and would be theorizing rather than doing and experiencing.

The chief description of someone organizing a community into action is Almost Browne's persuading the Transethnic Situations Department to hold a *debwe* festival dance, and the community in question is an academic department, not a tribal group (*Hotline Healers*, 49–77). In the original *debwe* ceremony, monks at the headwaters of the Mississippi supposedly masturbated with animals, a celebration that Vizenor describes in some detail in *Hotline Healers* (159–72).[14] "Academics could do much better if they only 'learned how to masturbate more often with an animal rather than with models and paradigms in mind'" (*Hotline Healers*, 58). The dance seems not to have figured much physical masturbation, and any animals present were shamans in their human form. The carnivalesque spirit shows in faculty teasing each other and in some of them arguing and acting in ways opposite to their usual scholarly stances. Ishmael Reed, for instance, appeared in a Gloria Steinem mask and carried a copy of *The Color Purple* (69). While this almost surreal-seeming celebration does illustrate organizing a community action with trickster aims, it does not offer much of a model for organizing communities. Vizenor, in other words, does not give us blueprints for community activities; we will have to imagine those for ourselves.

Vizenor's insistence on masturbation as a community activity may seem odd, but it reflects his larger view of sexuality. He mentions masturbation fairly frequently, evidently because pleasure rather than austerity is good for the individual and for community relations.[15] His seeing it as an activity with animal partners emphasizes his point that animals are equal members of any community he respects, and he has insisted (regarding Lilith Mae's sexual relationship with her boxer dogs) that he finds "nothing wrong in the love of an animal."[16] In some instances, one might question what the animal gets from such a relationship, but in Lilith Mae's case, her boxers are eager for the treat. Such human and animal interchanges, which in the *debwe* festivals are indeed masturbatory rather than penetrative, the outcome seems less destructive than his vision of the magic trickster crystal that can make unwitting girls pregnant if they touch it (*Hotline Healers*, 65, 151–58). Vizenor's unwillingness to take careers seriously as a means of organizing life for anyone does increase the emphasis on women's role as child bearer and reduce women's social and professional options in his visionary world. In *Griever: An American Monkey King in China*, the trickster protagonist's impregnating a Chinese woman causes her death at the hands of her angry father. The only sorrow Griever seems to feel is for the unborn mixed-blood child. Vizenor subordinates women to community needs for future generations far more than he does men; in this regard his sexual material is a lot more liberatory for men than for women.

Healing is another community endeavor shown in some detail. Individual shamans—human, dog, bear—practice their art, often by touching or licking the spot and making it well. The claims made for such healing are extreme. In *The Heirs of Columbus*, a deformed tribal child is given a "genetic implant" from the heirs. Although she had been born without hands, and with a crooked spine and chin, shamans touch her and she is told stories (164–65). She grows hands and her body straightens. We are told that scientists contribute only one part of the healing. The heirs do more "with stories and humor, and what they say becomes, in some way, the energy that heals. This story energy somehow influences the genetic codes and the children are mended in one way or another" (164). As if to keep us from nodding in complacent

disbelief, Vizenor says that the stories are told by heirs but also by clinic robots. I am not sure whether this is just inconsistency concerning the importance of face-to-face interaction with storytelling, or whether robots, at least
at times, are to be recognized as part of the community. If nothing else, Vizenor is jarring us into wakefulness by refusing to give us what we expect.

Storytelling is probably the chief community-building enterprise that Vizenor describes. He seems to value it for the heartening effect it can have
and its ability to persuade people not to feel victimized. Beyond that, it is an
activity that brings people in contact with each other and builds sympathy
and interaction. Storytelling often involves a large audience. Those heirs of
Columbus who come to the stone tavern in the evening tell each other stories.
In *Hiroshima Bugi*, a Japanese woman comes to the reservation, and tries to
tell how she believes Ronin to have died. An old woman who loved Ronin
shouts her down. Miko shouts back, and their flyting draws an enthusiastic
audience. But Miko is still denied her chance to tell the death story. Since
Ronin disappeared into the sky, he may not be dead and that tale may be premature. Thus, refusing to let someone tell a story may have justification that is
not obvious amid Vizenor's usual effusive praise of storytelling, but even the
act of preventing its telling creates a community get-together.[17]

Insofar as the stories reflect tribal beliefs and social patterns, they also encourage cultural survivance. Vizenor insists that his stories and many other
Native stories are trickster tales, so they emphasize liberty, agency, overcoming odds, and irritating the powers that be.[18] The stories in *The Trickster of Liberty* are all about members of the Browne family, each of whom is a trickster.
The story "The Trickster of Liberty" tells of how Ginseng Browne manages to
survive a lawsuit in white courts over selling ginseng to China; this involves
issues of endangered species (endangered not by Native use but by white destruction of hardwood forests), sowing domesticated ginseng seed and selling
that to the Chinese instead of wild ginseng they think they are getting, trick-
ing immigration officials, and striking a lucrative deal. The story about Slyboots Browne tells of a man who got his education at Dartmouth. He wrote a
proposal for building microlight airplanes on the reservation, but was turned
down by the government because the project was "un-Indian." Therefore, he
proposed constructing ATVs and got the start-up funds. Then the government imported a cheap foreign ATV and destroyed the Native industry. Was
Slyboots downcast? No, being a trickster, he may have had this in mind from
the start. He used his leftover ATV motors and built very successful micro-
lights. He also recognized the importance of having a good lawyer. Being a
trickster sometimes means being practical.

Where does this leave Vizenor, then, in terms of the primary importance of
the individual's imaginative life versus the claims of community and broader
culture? Saying that he believes in community and feels that individuals are
responsible to community is too easy an out.[19] Four of his novels may just be
refusing closure by having the main character disappear, but this also suggests

that he finds no way of achieving an ongoing relationship between these in-dividuals and society.[20] Making the individual disappear mysteriously even suggests a kind of despair, at least about the larger world. *Bearheart's* Proude Cedarfair is primarily inward-oriented, and transcends to a fourth level of creation, leaving others, including his somewhat neglected wife, behind. If Vizenor sees him as "responsible" to the community, that responsibility does not hold Proude if he wishes to abandon its members. In *Bearheart*, spiritual transcendence seems to trump community commitment. *Hiroshima Bugi* also ends with the main character, Ronin, disappearing into the sky. Symbolically, he may be ascending to his Crane-clan ancestry, but in practical terms, he seems to be giving up on this life. In *Griever*, the trickster escapes from China in a microlight airplane and is never heard from again. He takes with him his rooster and a new sexual partner, his previous one having been murdered by her own father because of her pregnancy. Realistically, his trickster be-havior will not change the People's Republic, so his leaving makes sense, but he does not bring this experience back to his tribal community. *Griever* sug-gests that the individual may enjoy stirring up a bit of chaos and symbolically that chaos may be salutary for the community, but in practical terms, noth-ing improves, and the individual can only hope to transcend the grim reality through imagination.

Dead Voices ends with a similar narrative move, but it functions some-what differently. The bear shaman Bagese disappears into a world visible in a special mirror. She is old enough that this may just betoken her death more than her giving up on this world, and she earlier makes interesting comments on how the real life of tribal people is now found in cities and on more bears (probably bear shamans) being in cities than on the reservation. She insists that her stories not be published, but her pupil in shamanic exercises of the imagination decides to publish them anyway, so we end on a dissonance, not sure what to make of his going against her wishes. If stories no longer pass from one person to another in the physical presence of each other, can they do much to encourage community or survivance? Does publishing them mark a step away from tribal community, or does it acknowledge that more Native Americans live in cities and they need stories too, however purveyed?

The other way in which Vizenor's focus on the individual and imagination seems at odds with community erupts in some of the violence he describes. Granted, these unrealistic murders produce no horror, but the function of such murders in his stories needs to be considered. Perhaps the most straight-forward is that in the most recent novel, *Father Meme*, which concerns a priest who abuses tribal boys sexually. At the end, they beat him up and push him under the ice in the lake. His death is described in considerably more detail than his predations, which seem to have amounted to genital fondling and possibly fellatio—no doubt psychologically very damaging for embarrassed boys who could not tell anyone of what was happening to them, but not as physically damaging as his raping them would have been. Vizenor's altar boys impose fourteen torments on the priest that correspond to the fourteen Stations of the Cross; several of these involved careful sniping at Father Meme that left him scared but unharmed. The narrator, one of the boys now in suave, sociable middle age, keeps speaking of the murder as a sacrifice, though it does not fit usual meanings of that word. Despite the Via Dolorosa image of the Stations, this is no crucifixion, just murder by execution. The narrator makes much of the boys' refusal to feel victimized, in part through their dreaming up and imposing the fourteen torments. That being so, why then go on to murder? Perhaps, his point is that they sacrifice their future peace of mind (as he claims to have done) in order to rid the community of a criminal. Doubtless Vizenor would say that the story is supposed to make us think, not hand us a prepackaged moral.

Murder in *Chancers* seems less directly justifiable. Yes, most academics occasionally enjoy the thought of killing university administrators, but murder seems an extreme reaction to stupidity or to differences over policy. The Solar Dancers, who carry out these murders, are very mixed-blood indeed, including as they do Russian, Hindustani, and Chinese cross-bloods with Native Americans. Furthermore, Vizenor shows them spouting various terminal creeds and calls them "natives of resentments and malice" (28). He does not give us much evidence that the bones in the museum really matter to these people, so what is the point to their several murders? My best guess is that Vizenor enjoys messing with readers' minds. Yes, bones and bone courts are serious issues to some people, but he is not going to give us the expected pious argument, since that would be redolent of terminal creeds. Instead, Anglo characters and readers are given a taste of random-seeming killings carried out by malignant but not very rationally motivated people, much as tribal people experienced such slaughters by demonic-seeming soldiers and white settlers.

Violent solutions to a clash between individual and community do not seem to bother Vizenor unduly, at least for the characters he portrays. I believe he would agree that many motives for killing are not licit. His own father was murdered, and Vizenor does not shrug this off as the act of someone killing for what he considered good reasons or for the community's best interests. Presumably money or drunken bad temper or racist rage would not be acceptable reasons. Within the bounds of what Vizenor insists are all trickster stories, however, he permits violence. Since so much violence has been perpetrated by those in power, part of his concept of liberty evidently demands at least the pleasurable contemplation of visiting such violence from the subordinate position on those who abuse their power. Perhaps that feeds the sense of survivance.

As for how Vizenor weighs the survivance of the individual against the demands of the whole culture (be it Chinese culture in *Griever* or American in his other novels), the answer seems pretty clearly to be that he accounts the individual more important and more deserving of respect. *Bearheart* shows this very clearly. Vizenor seems to revel in the catastrophic collapse of energy-addicted American civilization, and seems unmoved by the millions who will starve or those who are murdered in the chaos that follows. He considers that society insane, so the violence that would follow its destruction is a fair price to pay. The level at which he feels good about organization is the relatively small tribal community; anything else is suspect or worse. The impossibility of an individual changing a monstrous country is such that he is forced to settle for trickster gestures, attempts to create temporary pockets of liberty. They probably do the trickster himself most good, and incidentally enlighten observers, but only briefly. Part of the imagination's importance may lie in precisely this problem: the individual can do little, other than set an example. If the individual is not to be destroyed by despair or corrupted, then the imagination must create a mental world in which that individual wishes to live. But that world has little effect on the outside world and bears little relationship to it.[21]

Vizenor is not alone in considering American culture insane. Thomas Pynchon, Richard Powers, Kathy Acker, and David Foster Wallace, to name a few authors, would agree with that sentiment. Given that Vizenor says that "Native American storytellers were the first postmodernists" because their work emerges from "postmodern *conditions*,"[22] I want briefly to compare his conclusions to those of other major postmodern figures who are struggling with some of the same issues. Wallace analyzes the addictive patterns of consumption. Acker simply screams in response to oppression[23]—her fiction serves as her panic holes. Pynchon's paranoid vision leaves relatively little agency or room for individual action. His answer in *Vineland*, *Against the Day*, and *Inherent Vice* to the military-industrial-government complex is to put emphasis on the family. Democracy may have become a hollow mockery, but adults must care for and protect their children. He does not offer much to live for, but is certain that life is much worse without such a bedrock belief in protecting children. Powers does offer a sense of the visionary beauty inherent in mathematics, biology, even in human creations, and wants us to learn to feel wonder rather than seek to control and consume what we explore. Although one of his characters says that the whole race is clinically psychotic, Powers does allow for a beauty in interconnectedness and complexity that stands outside the individual. The individual gains by learning to harmonize with that complexity.

Vizenor gives us bits and snippets of beauty: when his tricksters scream into panic holes, the region's flowers receive psychic nourishment and bloom more profusely and beautifully (*Trickster of Liberty*, 10; *Hotline Healers*, 17–18). Most of these moments of beauty are experienced on the reservation, which suggests that his sense of such beauty is to some degree place-oriented and tribal.[24] He does not deny beauty to be elsewhere, but shows his tribal people mostly enjoying such insight on their own land. His haiku obviously testify that he can feel such piercing insights anywhere, but insofar as he theorizes this aspect of his cosmos, he seems to feel that a special relationship exists *or should exist* between people and their communal "proper" place. Vizenor sums this up in an early interview: "I believe my particular presentation of the mythic experience and the energy I go after, and the imagery in poetry, I celebrate from tribal sources. It's universal, too, but I celebrate from tribal sources" (Bowers and Silet, 47). This sense of oneness with local nature is not Powers's scientific sense of beautiful architectonic complexity, but both writers reach beyond the blunt and insensitive assumptions of the majority culture about landscape and nature.

Vizenor does not advance any naïve argument that the individual can change the nature of the larger culture, but in a sense he reverses the terms. What is wrong is inside us and subject to imaginative manipulation; it is not just external. "Things go wrong, and there is exploitation, dishonesty, evil acts; all of these are contradictory and within us, not outside. Evil games are imagination, not objectivism. That, I think, is a principal distinction, a primal distinction in worldview and philosophy between Western and Native American."[25] He feels that "concentration, meditation, a thoughtful attention to the peaceful healing interests of a good story, the poetic ecstatic moment, an instance of inspiration, careful and thoughtful poetic attention to a condition of life, can transform it."[26]

Exercising the imagination properly also demands courage. As Simona Fojtová sums up Vizenor's *Manifest Manners*, "Rather, when we create we let our imagination run loose; in effect, we make sense of words with sacrifice. Our mind and imagination have to step into a seemingly empty territory between ourselves and the other, which requires giving up the previous place, position, or structure and risks losing the familiar for the sake of the unknown. The fear of this risk is the fear of difference."[27]

Vizenor emphasizes not just courage but responsibility when he focuses on the individual imagination. Most of what matters about life has to do with how we process our experience and how we let it affect us. This seems to me noticeably different from the answers found in other contemporary writers. What with postmodernism having deconstructed all the old rules and deterritorialized everything, the next wave of writers is having to try to construct meaning and ways of achieving a sense of meaning afresh. They may turn back to religion (as Pynchon does in *Against the Day*) or family (*Vineland*). They may argue for small communities of elected affinities, as Douglas Coupland does in *Microserfs*. They may try to invoke a sense of obligation to local community or to a cause like organic farming, as Ruth Ozeki does.

Vizenor's insistence that we should live within our imaginations suggests a narcissistic inward turn, but he tries to balance that with community orientation. Whereas Pynchon offers family as an answer to postmodern failure of meaning, Vizenor's focus on the tribal group and its location within a specific landscape can be seen as an improvement on Euro-American fetishizing of the vulnerable and unstable nuclear unit. The tribal group offers a wider array of contacts and supports and models of behavior than any small family can. Shared stories within this group also produce an imaginative world that is partly shared. This reduces what might otherwise seem a solipsistic element in Vizenor's philosophy. Vizenor's emphasis on place puts him at odds with the Western notion of a career that makes you live where the work is, separated from family and earlier friends. Beyond kin and locus, however, he values exercising the imagination in ways that lets the individual survive life with minimal damage. Such creative activity involves treating all experience as interior, and taking responsibility for inventing one's own mental and emotional structures. Postmodern theory undercuts the philosophical possibility of personal agency, so Euro-American authors flounder when trying to imagine conscious action, but Vizenor can and does imagine that agency.[28] Perhaps because of his experience in tribal philosophy and worldview as well as Western, he does not suffer this problem of separating the individual from the larger culture, and from Vizenor's perspective, the individual is indeed capable of creating a balanced inner world.[29] In this respect, as in any number of others, his contribution to the Native American Renaissance has been at once contestatory but always resourceful, a genuinely distinctive voice.

NOTES

1. For an analysis of Vizenor's overall philosophy and world vision, see Hume, "Gerald Vizenor's Metaphysics."

2. McCaffery and Marshall, "On Thin Ice, You Might as Well Dance," both quotations on p. 303.

3. For analysis of Vizenor's relationship to postmodernism, see Jahner, "Trickster Discourse."

4. Vizenor, "Aesthetics of Survivance," p. 88.

5. Vizenor, *Chancers*, p. 7.

6. Powers, *Generosity*, p. 51.

7. Stuart Christie takes Vizenor to task for playing too fast and loose with history, arguing that *Heirs of Columbus*, by creating a fantastic story about Point Roberts, overlooks and buries a real story relating to Indian struggles to protect their land there. See his "Trickster gone golfing."

8. Vizenor, *Bearheart*, pp. 194–204.

9. Vizenor, *Fugitive Poses*, p. 73.

10. Vizenor defends the varied and imaginative array of grotesque violence in *Bearheart* by comparing it with that seen in the news and entertainment. Because we are ashamed of the violence, we leave out many details, and we hide from death. Without absorbing some of that raw violence into our lives, we "are denied the tragic wisdom of the violence." *Bearheart* supposedly rights that balance. See his interview with Hartwig Isernhagen in *Momaday, Vizenor, Armstrong*, p. 132.

11. Preference for action over theorizing in Native American philosophies is discussed by Hester in "On Philosophical Discourse," pp. 263–67, especially p. 264.

12. Vizenor, *Native Liberty*, p. 98.

13. See the case of Cozie Browne in *Hotline Healers*, p. 151.

14. The provenance of the manuscript detailing this ceremony is discussed in Vizenor, *Heirs of Columbus*, pp. 112–13.

15. Vizenor tells of a trick played on him as a teen-aged innocent in the army when he was sent from one officer to another to get his "Masturbation papers" in *Interior Landscapes*, pp. 80–83.

16. Vizenor and Lee, *Postindian Conversations*, p. 101. As we are dealing with a trickster, every reader has to make his or her own decision as to whether to believe such statements or not. Consider the erotic attractions of the opossum; not only did the monks find the hairless tail attractive and useful for wrapping prehensilely about their penises, "opossum have no hair on their ears either, a feature the monks raved about in their carnal trades at the heart dance" (*Hotline Healers*, p. 168).

17. Vizenor, *Hiroshima Bugi*, pp. 206–208.

18. Louis Owens attaches the term "Ecstatic Strategies" to Vizenor's trickster narratives. See chapter 8 in his book *Other Destinies*. For discussion of many Native American novels as trickster tales, see Velie, "Trickster Novel," pp. 121–39.

19. Vizenor himself has attempted to muster community action, both through his journalism to get Thomas White Hawk's sentence commuted, for example, and in terms of social welfare work. See Bowers and Silet, "Interview with Gerald Vizenor," p. 45. In a different vein, he works to protect all communities from fraud, which is how he saw the antics of AIM at Wounded Knee. See A. Robert Lee, "The Only Good Indian Is a Postindian?" pp. 263–78.

20. Hochbruck analyzes this pattern of escaping, not just in the novels, but in Vizenor's whole endeavor, in "Breaking Away." And LaLonde analyzes such transcending escapes and crossing of thresholds in "'The Ceded Landscape of Gerald Vizenor's Fiction."

21. In an interview with Kimberly Blaeser, Vizenor talks of our being prisoners in our bodies, but sees trickster stories as capable of liberating our minds. This suggests the value of such stories for the individual at least, as well as suggesting the negative nature of life within the larger culture. See Blaeser, *Gerald Vizenor*, p. 162.

22. McCaffery and Marshall, "On Thin Ice," p. 293.

23. See Hume, "Voice in Kathy Acker's Fiction," pp. 485–513.

24. For a discussion of Vizenor's connection to landscapes, see Monsma, "Liminal Landscapes," pp. 60–72.

25. Breinig and Lösch, "Gerald Vizenor," p. 148.

26. Coltelli, "Gerald Vizenor," p. 102.

27. Fojtová, "Forging the Discursive Presence," p. 95.

28. Such issues of agency are taken up by Linton in "The 'Person' in Postmodern Fiction," pp. 3–11.

29. My thanks to Jeffrey Gonzalez and Sean Moiles for suggestions and criticism.

WORKS CITED

Blaeser, Kimberly M. *Gerald Vizenor: Writing in the Oral Tradition*. Norman: University of Oklahoma Press, 1996.

Bowers, Neal, and Charles L. P. Silet. "An Interview with Gerald Vizenor." *MELUS* 8:1 (1981), 41–49.

Breinig, Helmbrecht, and Klaus Lösch. "Gerald Vizenor." Interview in *American Contradictions: Interviews with Nine American Writers*. Edited by Wolfgang Binder and Helmbrecht Breinig (Hanover, N.H.: University Press of New England, 1995), 143–66.

Christie, Stuart. "Trickster gone golfing: Vizenor's *Heirs of Columbus* and the Chelh-ten-em Development Controversy." *American Indian Quarterly* 21:3 (1997), 359–83.

Coltelli, Laura. "The Trickster Heir of Columbus: An Interview." In *Native American Literatures: Forum* (Pisa) 2:3 (1990–1991), 101–16.

Fojtová, Simona. "Forging the Discursive Presence in Gerald Vizenor's *Manifest Manners: Postindian Warriors of Survivance*." *Para-doxa: Studies in World Literary Genres* 15 (2001), 86–97.

Hester, Jr., Thurman Lee. "On Philosophical Discourse: Some Intercultural Musings." *American Indian Thought*. Edited by Anne Waters. Malden, Mass.: Blackwell Publishing, 2004, 263–67.

Hochbruck, Wolfgang. "Breaking Away: The Novels of Gerald Vizenor." *World Literature Today* 66:2 (1992), 274–78.

Hume, Kathryn. "Gerald Vizenor's Metaphysics." *Contemporary Literature* 48:4 (2007), 580–612.

———. "Voice in Kathy Acker's Fiction." *Contemporary Literature* 42:3 (2001), 485–513.

Isernhagen, Hartwig. "Gerald Vizenor." Interview in *Momaday, Vizenor, Armstrong: Conversations on American Indian Writing*. Norman: University of Oklahoma Press, 1999, 77–134.

Jahner, Elaine A., "Trickster Discourse and Postmodern Strategies." *Loosening the Seams: Interpretations of Gerald Vizenor*. Edited by A. Robert Lee. Bowling Green, Ohio: Bowling Green State University Popular Press, 2000, 38–58.

LaLonde, Chris. "The Ceded Landscape of Gerald Vizenor's Fiction." *Studies in American Indian Literatures* 9:1 (1997), 16–32.

Lee, A. Robert. "The Only Good Indian Is a Postindian? Controversialist Vizenor and *Manifest Manners*." *Loosening the Seams: Interpretations of Gerald Vizenor*. Edited by A. Robert Lee. Bowling Green, Ohio: Bowling Green State University Popular Press, 2000, 263–78.

Lee, Dorothy. *Freedom and Culture*. Prospect Heights, Ill.: Waveland Press, 1959, 1987.

Linton, Patricia. "The 'Person' in Postmodern Fiction: Gibson, Le Guin, and Vizenor." *Studies in American Indian Literatures* 5:3 (1993), 3–11.

McCaffery, Larry, and Tom Marshall. "On Thin Ice, You Might as Well Dance: An Interview with Gerald Vizenor." In *Some Other Frequency: Interviews with Innovative American Authors.* Edited by Larry McCaffery. Philadelphia: University of Pennsylvania Press, 1996, 287–309.

Monsma, Bradley John. "Liminal Landscapes: Motion, Perspective, and Place in Gerald Vizenor's Fiction." *Studies in American Indian Literature* 9:1 (1997), 60–72.

Owens, Louis. *Other Destinies: Understanding the American Indian Novel.* Norman: University of Oklahoma Press, 1992.

Powers, Richard. *Generosity: An Enhancement.* New York: Farrar Straus and Giroux, 2009.

Velie, Alan. "The Trickster Novel." *Narrative Chance: Postmodern Discourse on Native American Indian Literatures.* Edited by Gerald Vizenor. Albuquerque: University of New Mexico Press, 1989, 121–39.

Vizenor, Gerald. "The Aesthetics of Survivance." In *Native Liberty: Natural Reason and Cultural Survivance.* Lincoln: University of Nebraska Press, 2009, 85–103.

———. *Bearheart: The Heirship Chronicles,* first published as *Darkness in Saint Louis: Bearheart* in 1978. Minneapolis: University of Minnesota Press, 1990.

———. *Chancers: A Novel.* Norman: University of Oklahoma Press, 2000.

———. *Dead Voices: Natural Agonies in the New World.* Norman: University of Oklahoma Press, 1992.

———. *Father Meme.* Albuquerque: University of New Mexico Press, 2008.

———. *Fugitive Poses: Native American Indian Scenes of Absence and Presence.* Lincoln: University of Nebraska Press, 1998.

———. *Griever: An American Monkey King in China.* Minneapolis: University of Minnesota Press, 1987.

———. *The Heirs of Columbus.* Hanover, N.H.:University Press of New England, 1991.

———. *Hiroshima Bugi: Atomu 57.* Lincoln: University of Nebraska Press, 2003.

———. *Hotline Healers: An Almost Browne Novel,* Middletown, Conn.: Wesleyan University Press/University Press of New England, 1997.

———. *Interior Landscapes: Autobiographical Myths and Metaphors.* Minneapolis: University of Minnesota Press, 1990.

———. *Native Liberty: Natural Reason and Cultural Survivance.* Lincoln: University of Nebraska Press, 2009.

———. "The Trickster of Liberty." In *The Trickster of Liberty: Tribal Heirs to a Wild Baronage.* Minneapolis: University of Minnesota Press, 1988, pp. 140–54.

Vizenor, Gerald, and A. Robert Lee. *Postindian Conversations.* Lincoln: University of Nebraska Press, 1999.

8

"One Story Hinging into the Next"

The Singular Achievement of Louise Erdrich's Interrelated Novels

CONNIE A. JACOBS

In 1985, Kenneth Lincoln, after reading Louise Erdrich's first novel, *Love Medicine*, predicted that she could be ranked among the great American writers, with the likes of Eudora Welty, Flannery O'Connor, F. Scott Fitzgerald, and Ernest Hemingway (*Native American Renaissance*, xv–xvi). Today, twenty-eight books later—thirteen novels, seven children/young adult books, three poetry collections, a short story collection, two nonfiction works, and two books coauthored with Michael Dorris—Erdrich is not only a best-selling novelist, but she also is one of the best-known and most popular contemporary writers.[1] The fact that she is an enrolled member of the Turtle Mountain Chippewa Band of Indians certainly contributes to her popularity, a legacy of America's love-hate relationship with American Indians. But it is her craft—her lyrical language, absorbing characters, abundant humor, innovative narrative techniques, steadfast compassion for humans with all of their weaknesses, abiding theme of the power of love, and compelling stories—that has helped secure her legions of fans and won her dozens of prestigious awards.[2] The sheer volume of scholarly work devoted to Erdrich attests to her popularity.

Lincoln's original assessment of Erdrich's potential to be a great writer has certainly been borne out. Scholars name N. Scott Momaday, James Welch, Leslie Marmon Silko, and Louise Erdrich as "founders" of the Native American Renaissance,[3] which, it must be noted, yet again, is not so much a rebirth as it is a concourse that gathered momentum originating from a long tradition of oral narratives, as-told-to autobiographies, speeches, and fiction. What these four writers brought to the literary scene in the late 1960s through the 1980s was a creative blast of talent that burst onto the existing literary landscape. After Momaday was awarded the Pulitzer Prize for *House Made of Dawn* in 1969,[4] awareness grew of the talents of American Indian writers of fiction, poetry, plays, essays, and criticism. The irony is, of course, that talented American Indian writers have been writing since the eighteenth century, but now they were much more visible and numerous, and they kept appearing, one after the other, until their critical mass could no longer be denied. It was into this newly expanded and enlarged literary world that the work of Louise Erdrich emerged.

What distinguishes Erdrich among other participants in the ongoing renaissance of American Indian writers is the way in which all of her fiction is connected, is woven together into one long story. Hers is not a series of books with the same protagonist, supporting characters, and setting that you find in popular young adult books,[5] mysteries,[6] science fiction,[7] and fiction.[8] Rather, the narrative pattern established in *Love Medicine* is distinctive: linked stories, linked lives, and linked landscape. Lincoln wrote of *Love Medicine*, "All the stories finally collate. . . . From first to last . . . parts and people all relate. . . . These are voices of clan lineage gathering the ghosts of an extended Indian family, tattered in the unraveling warp and woof of American history (xiii). The many ways in which Erdrich's novels connect as one long story are the focus of this essay.

THE STORIES

All people, all cultures need and have stories. Leslie Marmon Silko, herself a powerful storyteller, contends, "You don't have anything if you don't have the stories" (*Ceremony*, 2). Stories sustain, guide, nourish, and protect, and for American Indian peoples traditionally, stories are more than entertainment; stories are alive, and they have power. Gerald Vizenor insists, "You can't understand the world without telling a story. There isn't any center to the world but a story" (Coltelli, 156). We need good stories, to laugh and to understand ourselves and others a little better. We need stories to make sense of our lives. Thomas King in his important book, *The Truth about Stories*, declares, "The truth about stories is that's all we are" (2). We are all made of stories; our life is a story; and our living is a story. Stories have always played an important role in Erdrich's life, and she was raised in a family who loved to tell them. Relates Erdrich, "I suppose that when you grow up constantly hearing the stories rise, break, and fall, it gets into you somehow" (Schumacher, 175). She is, by her own admission, "hooked on narrative" (Schumacher, 175). In an interview with Katie Bacon from the *Atlantic*, Erdrich talks about her writing:

> Primarily I am just a storyteller, and I take [stories] where I find them. I love stories whether they function to reclaim old narratives or occur spontaneously. Often, to my surprise, they do both. I'll follow an inner thread of a plot and find that I am actually retelling a very old story, often in a contemporary setting. I usually can't recall whether it is something I heard, or something I dreamed, or read, or imagined on the spot. It all becomes confused and then the characters take over, anyway, and make the piece their own.

In another interview with Mark Rolo, Erdrich shares, "My stories are tucked far away in my thoughts. I never am actively seeing them worked out." Erdrich's remarkable gifts as a storyteller have been the focus of numerous critical articles.[9] Scholars describe her novels as a collection of short stories, situate her writing as emanating from Ojibwe[10] oral tradition, describe her stories as a quest, as reminiscent of traditional Ojibwe stories, and analyze her use of traditional symbols, narrative techniques, humor, and trickster characters. These analyses are significant and valuable contributions. This article, however, will differ from traditional scholarship by considering the whole of her work and not just the specifics of individual novels. Approaching Erdrich's work holistically shows that her many books are, in fact, just one long novel, connected stories of a particular group of people occupying a specific landscape. Her books tell the story of the Anishinaabe people in the last 175 years, how and why they journeyed from the islands of Lake Superior into Minnesota and then onto the plains of North Dakoka; their interactions with immigrant settlers who claimed a right to the land of the Anishinaabeg and with the U.S. government and the soldiers who brought disease, alcohol, and broken treaties; of relocation into Minneapolis; and of the defeats and triumphs of both traditional and contemporary Anishinaabeg as well as the settlers who live side by side with them on a particular piece of land. Erdrich's singular and distinctive approach to her fiction of has been one of her major contributions to the Native American Renaissance.

THE CHARACTERS

Erdrich's thirteen novels and four young adult books connect in notable ways: by characters, "touchstone" stories, place, and theme. What is noteworthy is that Erdrich by her own account did not intend to write a continuous story. The events she depicts do, however, constitute one. Erdrich offers that the characters in *Love Medicine* "have the kind of family connection which has always been the core of the tribe" (Coltelli, 45). And it is the stories of those various tribal/family members from *Love Medicine* that begin the story and become the seven Little No Horse novels.[11] In *Love Medicine*, readers meet major characters whose stories continue to be told, retold, revised, and expanded in other novels. There are three characters at the center of the reservation novels; the novels are their stories, and all that happens revolves around them. These pivotal characters turn out to be a very disparate group of women: June Morrissey Kashpaw, Fleur Pillager, and Pauline Puyat/Sister Leopolda.

June Morrissey Kashpaw's life and death haunt her sons King Kashpaw and Lipsha Morrissey, lover Gerry Pillager, husbands Gordie Kashpaw and Jack Mauser, and family, especially Marie Lazarre Kashpaw, Eli Kashpaw, and Albertine Johnson. Erdrich tells June's story in *Love Medicine, Beet Queen, Bingo Palace,* and *Tales of Burning Love. Love Medicine* is the story of her life, death, and resurrection in the form of a deer. The novel opens with June in Williston,

North Dakota, waiting to take a bus back to the reservation, a scene that is repeated, even using some of the wording from *Love Medicine* in the opening chapter of *Tales of Burning Love*. June's memory permeates *Bingo Palace* and *Burning Love*. June lived hard and fast, forever the victim of a disastrous childhood before Marie took her in. Marie recalls, "There was a sadness I couldn't touch there" (*Love Medicine*, 91). Her "presence" as a helpful ghost in *Bingo Palace* and *Tales of Burning Love* is unique among Erdrich's characters.

Fleur Pillager provides another important link among the North Dakota novels. Readers follow her story in *Tracks, Four Souls, Love Medicine, Beet Queen*, and *Bingo Palace* from the time she was a young girl and the only family member to survive tuberculosis to her fight to keep her land by meting out vengeance on those who would take it from her. She is inheritor of the Pillager magic, and while she uses it to heal, she also misuses it. Nanapush believes that "In her mind she was huge, she was endless. There was no room for the failures of others. At the same time, she was the funnel of our history . . . as the lone survivor of the Pillagers" (*Tracks*, 178). She is complicated, proud, stubborn, canny, alluring to men, devoted to Nanapush and her family but willing to send her daughter Lulu away to boarding school to keep her safe while she seeks revenge on those reservation families trying to steal her land. Her magic harms many but heals more. She appears, additionally, in three off-reservations novels, *The Beet Queen, The Antelope Wife* and *The Painted Drum*. In *Beet Queen*, Fleur has left the reservation and comes upon and treats the injured Karl Adare in Argus. In *Antelope Wife*, Fleur is the niece of Blue Prairie Woman, and in *Painted Drum* Fleur's half-sister Niibin'aage goes east to attend Carlisle Indian School and in time becomes the grandmother of Faye Travers, one of the main narrators in *Painted Drum*. Erdrich tells Fleur's story in seven of her thirteen novels, making Fleur a principal link in the books.

Pauline Puyat/Sister Leopolda is the character readers love to hate. She has few redeeming qualities, yet she is a continuous nagging presence in the Little No Horse novels, *Beet Queen*, and *Tales of Burning Love*. Her crow-like presence hovers over the novels. In *Tracks* she is a major narrator who, for the first time, encounters Fleur and thereafter attempts to rival Fleur's traditional powers. When Pauline becomes a nun, she practices extreme forms of renunciation: "I was hollow unless pain filled me" (*Tracks*, 192). She is responsible for many deaths by carrying disease from one house to another. She strangles Napoleon Morrissey, the father of her child. By *Tales of Burning Love*, Eleanor Schlick Mauser is researching Sister Leopolda's "saintly" life, and the *Last Report* finds Father Jude wanting to propose Leopolda's name for sainthood over the strenuous objections of those who know her best: Maria Lazarre Kashpaw, her daughter, and Father Damien, her priest. Pauline internalizes colonization, renounces her tribal affiliation, and, using her position in the Catholic Church, inflicts emotional harm on reservation children and adults.

Several other key characters link the Little No Horse novels. Marie, Pauline/Leopolda's daughter and wife of Nector Kashpaw, is transformed from a skinny young girl raised by a no-account family to become a respected, beloved, and powerful presence on the reservation (*Love Medicine, Tracks, Bingo Palace, Last Report*). Lulu Nanapush Lamartine Morrissey, Fleur's daughter, is a complex and influential character: a flirt, political activist, tribal leader, and devoted mother of eight sons and one daughter, all from different fathers. Just like her mother Fleur, she knows "no fear" (*Love Medicine*, 108). When she elects to live at the Senior Citizens Home, at age sixty-five, she becomes even more powerful and determined. She rekindles an affair with Nector Kashpaw, works to restore traditional lands, and manages to have a much younger priest, Father Jude, fall madly in love with her. All the Little No Horse novels to some degree revolve around her and her sons, especially Gerry Nanapush, Lyman Lamartine, Henry Lamartine, and her grandson Lipsha Morrissey (*Love Medicine, Tracks, Bingo Palace, Last Report*).

Nanapush is an elder, a storyteller, and the last of the old-time traditionalists. He is the tribal historian and has served as tribal chairman, the one who cautions reservation families not to sell their land to the timber companies. He acts as father to both Fleur Pillager and her daughter Lulu, husband to Margaret Kashpaw (as well as three previous wives), and friend of Father Damien/Agnes. Nanapush is also a lewd rascal and a modern embodiment of Nanabozho, the traditional Anishinaabe trickster figure. His stories and his influence on tribal affairs are told in *Tracks, Love Medicine, Bingo Palace, Four Souls, Last Report,* and *Round House.*

Other supporting characters act as significant links in the North Dakota novels: Albertine Johnson (*Love Medicine, Bingo Palace*), Margaret (Rushes Bear) Kashpaw (*Tracks, Love Medicine, Four Souls, Last Report*), and Father Damien, Modeste/Sister Agnes DeWitt (*Tracks, Love Medicine, Last Report, Round House*). What is fascinating is how Erdrich additionally has minor characters popping up in the Little No Horse novels, another reason to read Erdrich's novels as a linked series of stories "hooked from one side to the other, mouth to tail" (*Tracks,* 46). Jewett Parker Tatro, the Indian agent on the Little No Horse Reservation and the person largely responsible for the loss of reservation land, has minor but important roles in *Love Medicine, Bingo Palace,* and *Four Souls.* All of the many valuable tribal objects he "collected," especially a sacred drum, drive the story of *The Painted Drum.* Father Jude Miller, the baby abandoned in *Beet Queen,* ends up a priest in *Tales of Burning Love* and *Last Report on the Miracles at Little No Horse,* an admirer of both Sister Leopolda and Lulu Nanapush Morrissey Lamartine.

THE TOUCHSTONE STORIES

Connecting Erdrich's characters are "touchstone" stories, the shared memories of various family members. Cally in *Antelope Wife* tries to describe them: "Family stories repeat themselves in patterns and waves generation to generation, across blood and time. Once the pattern is set we go on replicating it. . . . From way back our destinies form. I am trying to see the old patterns in myself and the people I love" (200). Touchstone stories are born from events that have impacted the lives of many of the characters in the Little No Horse novels: hanging June (*Love Medicine*), June dying in the Easter blizzard (*Love Medicine, Tales of Burning Love*), Lipsha being thrown into the slough (*Love Medicine, Bingo Palace*), Henry Lamartine's drowning (*Love Medicine, Bingo Palace*), Lulu's house burning down (*Love Medicine, Bingo Palace*), Fleur's drowning three times but always living (*Tracks, Love Medicine, Bingo Palace*), Misshepeshu haunting the waters of Lake Matchimanito (*Tracks, Love Medicine, Bingo Palace, Antelope Wife*), Marie going to the convent to become a nun (*Love Medicine, Tales of Burning Love, Last Report*), the tornado hitting Argus (*Tracks, Beet Queen, Last Report*), and Lulu finding Napoleon Morrissey's body in the woods (*Tracks, Love Medicine, Bingo Palace*). *The Round House* continues characters and events from *Plague of Doves* with the Coutts and Milk families. At the center of these two novels is the 1911 brutal hanging of three innocent Indian men by an Anglo vigilante posse. These stories connect families, their history, and their memories, as well as influence current tribal events and relationships among tribal members, and it is noteworthy the degree to which they keep reappearing throughout the novels.

THE LAND

Place and the relationship between land and people also provide a common thread in Erdrich's novels, for "her narratives are nourished by the land" (Barker). Erdrich reflects: "Through the close study of a place, its people and character, its crops, products, paranoias, dialect, and failures, we come closer to our own reality. It is difficult to impose a story and plot on a place. But truly knowing a place provides the link between details and meaning. Location, whether it is to abandon it or draw it sharply, is where we start" ("Where I Ought to Be," 49).

The Birchbark Books (*The Birchbark House, The Game of Silence, The Porcupine Year*, and *Chickadee*) are young adult books that tell the story of Omakayas and her family who live on Madeline Island, "Moningwanaykaning," the place of origin.[12] These books begin Erdrich's long saga of the Ojibwe, chronologically starting with stories of the Ojibwe in the 1840s when they lived on the islands of Lake Superior to their journey to a new life on the Great Plains. These novels describe traditional Anishinaabe culture: they depict Omakayas and her family living in cabins in the winter and building birchbark homes in the summer, making moccasins, tanning moose hides, gathering maple syrup, harvesting wild rice, storing food for the winter, building canoes, and hunting and fishing. There are similarities to stories of characters in other Erdrich novels, especially Fleur Pillager: the *Birchbark* saga opens with the sole survivor of smallpox being a young girl (like Fleur in *Tracks*); there is a powerful and mysterious medicine woman, Old Tallow (like Fleur in *Love Medicine, Bingo Palace*) as well as Windigo stories, the loss of traditional lands, and the resilience of the people despite displacement by settlers and disease, an underlying theme in all of the North Dakota novels.

Historically, encroaching settlers drove the Anishinaabeg bands from their Great Lakes home into Wisconsin and Minnesota, where many groups settled.[13] The band that eventually established a home in North Dakota was driven out of Minnesota by the Lakota and migrated to the Red River valley near Pembina to be near a large trading post. This group was hunting in the Turtle Mountains as early as 1800 and lived and hunted in an area that covered about 20 percent of the present state of North Dakota (Horr, 328). The lands on which this band eventually settled continued to be eroded by treaties.[14] After 1887 and the passage of the Dawes Act, the U.S. government stripped the tribe of more lands, dividing communally owned land into individual plots and taking that which they didn't assign to individual Indians and giving it to settlers.[15]

Erdrich's work is predominately the story of these North Dakota Anishinaabe people. In *Four Souls*, Nanapush movingly describes the importance of the land where he and his tribe eventually settle: "This reservation came about in a time of desperation and upon it we will see things occur more desperate yet. When I look at the scope and drift of our history, I see that we have come out of it with something at least. This scrap of earth. This ishkonigan. This leftover. We've got this and as long as we can hold on to it we will be some sort of people" (210).

The Little No Horse novels are set in northern North Dakota, where the Turtle Mountain Chippewa Reservation is presently located, and in the surrounding Anglo towns: Argus, Hoopdance, and Pluto. The shared piece of land links all of the reservation novels as well as *Beet Queen, Master Butcher's Singing Club*, and *Tales of Burning Love*.[16] These novels narrate a 175-year-old history of the people who settled the lands in northern North Dakota.

Erdrich relates the settlement of Argus in *Tracks, Beet Queen*, and *Master Butcher*. When Fleur goes to Argus in 1913, there are six streets bordering the railroad depot. Soon churches, grain elevators, schools, shops, taverns spring up, more settlers arrive, and the newly prosperous Argus becomes the county seat. In *Beet Queen*, people from the reservation mingle with and are related to the townspeople of Argus, while *Master Butcher's Singing Club* is primarily a novel about Fidelis Waldvogel, a German master butcher, and Delphine Watka, daughter of the town drunk, Roy Watka. The name "Argus" is an interesting one, for in Greek mythology, Argus is the monster with a hundred eyes whom Zeus uses to keep watch on the nymph Io, one of Zeus's many loves. Argus, North Dakota has many eyes observing the townspeople, a familiar vigilance found so often in small towns. Argus is very dependent upon the railroad and beet crops, while being subject to extremes of weather: drought, tornadoes, and blizzards. Argus is watchful, alert to change, and mindful of the complicated relationships among the townspeople and people from the nearby reservation.

Argus, settled by immigrants mostly from Germany and Norway, grows, thrives, and survives. Not so the nearby town of Pluto, another name from mythology, that of the god of the underworld. Pluto, North Dakota, also founded by the railroad, grows and prospers until the railroad is replaced by an interstate that bypasses the town. Like the underworld, Pluto, North Dakota, becomes a place of abandoned hopes (*Plague of Doves*) as the once-thriving town depopulates and is abandoned. Yet the people on the nearby reservation endure as stewards of the land and survivors of colonization.

The third setting for Erdrich's novels is Minneapolis, "*Gakaabikaang*. Place of the falls" (*Four Souls,* 5). Minneapolis became one of the cities where American Indians were relocated during the 1950s, the result of the federal government's misguided attempt to ease poverty on reservations and to provide more educational and job opportunities for reservation Indians. Although the program was unsuccessful and many Indians returned to their reservations, Relocation reshaped Indian Country. According to *Indian Country Diaries: Assimilation, Relocation, Genocide,* "In 1940, only around 8 percent of Indians were living in cities. . . . In the 2000 Census . . . for American Indians, the urban population had risen to 64 percent." Minneapolis, with its close proximity to Ojibwe reservations, became a new migration destination. However, what many American Indians found after leaving the reservation was that they were leaving community, relatives, culture, and homeland for promises of a better life that rarely materialized. American Indians encountered racism and lack of job opportunities other than low-paying menial work like factory and construction jobs. For those who stayed in the cities, "urban reservations" were formed as people created new communities. This is the background for *Antelope Wife,* a novel in which some American Indians did prosper. Chippewas own a bakery, the Kung Fu Studio, and a waste-disposal company and gather as a community to celebrate holidays and marriages and to mourn deaths. However, their home reservation still is a part of their lives, especially in times of troubles, and traditional culture is not eradicated, but rather redesigned for a new environment.

Four Souls, which takes up the story Erdrich began in *Tracks,* is set in Minneapolis as well as on the reservation. Fleur follows the trees that have been cut down on her land and used to build John James Mauser's mansion, located high on a ridge in Minneapolis, in a place that historically was a favorite campsite for the Anishinaabeg. In Minneapolis, Fleur marries Mauser and transforms into a wealthy society lady, but the revenge that brings her to this place also takes Fleur from her community and life on the land from which she gains her powers. During a difficult pregnancy, a doctor prescribes alcohol, and Fleur becomes addicted. Once she enacts her revenge on Mauser and returns to the reservation, she carries the vices of the city with her, along with her child who is probably a victim of fetal alcohol syndrome. Only Margaret's purification ceremony saves Fleur, whose need for revenge has resulted in an estranged daughter and a damaged son.

Shadow Tag is the third novel set in Minneapolis. The story does not treat characters from Little No Horse or the Minneapolis urban reservation. The major characters, Irene and Gil, are both part Ojibwe and assimilated. Irene America's mother was an AIM activist, and Irene grew up reading Shakespeare in a comfortable middle-class home. Irene is working on her doctorate on George Catlin and is, in turn, the subject of her famous artist husband's portraits, the "America Portraits," which show Irene in poses both loving and humiliating. She acts as the muse for his creative genius but, in doing so, sells her image to the world. Through these portraits, Irene "releases a double into the world. It was impossible, now, to withdraw that reflection. Gil owned it. He had stepped on her shadow" (40). This is the novel of a disintegrating marriage, not unlike the marriage of Rozin and Richard Whiteheart Beads in *Antelope Wife*. But it is also the story of great love, for when Gil tries to drown himself, Irene tries to save him, and they both die. What is notable is the location of the drowning, Madeline Island, the place of origin of the Anishinaabeg. Erdrich's story has come full circle.

One novel is set outside of North Dakota and Minneapolis. *Painted Drum* takes place in New Hampshire but is closely connected to the reservation novels in several important ways. First of all, Faye Travers and her mother, Elsie, are Pillagers, the descendents of Fleur's half-sister whom the Indian agent Jewett Parker Tatro "recruited" for Carlisle Indian School. Tatro originates from the same small town in New Hampshire where Faye and her mother live. When Tatro's descendants call on Faye and her mother, who handle estate sales, Faye finds a rare cedar-and-moose-skin sacred drum and traces it back to its rightful owners on the North Dakota reservation located north of Hoopdance. While the novel opens and closes with Faye's story in New Hampshire, the alternating story is told by Bernard Shaawano, a traditionalist, a link among community members, and the one who knows the story of the drum and its importance to the tribe.

THE THEMES

Two major themes run throughout the novels and serve as yet another way of connecting all of the individual stories into one big story.[17] In ways both large and small, Erdrich's novels revolve around the power of love and of political injustice. Love in its many manifestations—between lovers, husbands and wives, parents and children—drives all of the novels. "What is the whole of our existence but the sound of an appalling love," asks Father Damien in *Last*

Report (355). And in *Tales of Burning Love*, the omniscient narrator observes, "We are conjured voiceless out of nothing and must return to an unknowing state. What happens in between is an uncontrolled dance, and what we ask for in love is not more than a momentary chance to get the steps right, to move in harmony until the music stops" (452).

There are numerous examples of parents whose love for their children knows no limits. The communal voice in *Bingo Palace* describes such a love, "The red rope between the mother and her baby is the hope of our nation. It pulls, it sings, it snags, it feeds and holds. How it holds" (6).

This parental love finds many expressions in the novels: Lulu for her sons and daughter (*Love Medicine, Bingo Palace, Last Report*); Marie for her children, especially Gordie when life has beaten him down (*Love Medicine*); Eli for June (*Love Medicine*); Nanapush for Fleur and Lulu (*Love Medicine, Tracks*); Celestine for Dot (*Beet Queen*); Shawnee for Redford (*Bingo Palace*); Blue Prairie Woman for her lost child (*Antelope Wife*); Fidelis for his sons (*Master Butcher*); Marne for her two children (*Plague of Doves*); Irene and Gil for their three children (*Shadow Tag*); and Judge Coutts for his son Joe (*Round House*).

Love between couples is another kind of love that resonates throughout the novels. In *Tales of Burning Love*, Dot Adare describes [this feeling and] her love for Gerry Nanapush: "Some people meet the way the sky meets earth, inevitably, and there is no stopping or holding back their love. It exists in a finished world, beyond the reach of common sense" (417).

Demonstrations of this kind of love are found throughout the novels: Nector for Lulu (*Love Medicine*); Marie for Nector (*Love Medicine*); Gerry for June (*Love Medicine, Bingo Palace, Tales of Burning Love*); Wallace for Karl (*Beet Queen*); Zelda for Xavier (*Bingo Palace*); Lipsha for Shawnee (*Bingo Palace*); Eleanor for Jack (*Tales of Burning Love*); Candice for Marlis (*Tales of Burning Love*); Frank for Rozin (*Antelope Wife*); Klaus for Antelope Woman (*Antelope Wife*); Agnes for Father Wekke (*Last Report*); Fidelis for Eva (*Master Butcher*); Fidelis for Delphine (*Master Butcher*); Elsie for her lover (*Painted Drum*); Faye for Kurt (*Painted Drum*); Morris for Ida (*Painted Drum*); and Brazil for Geraldine (*Round House*). Erdrich writes, "Love—which the young expect, the middle-aged fear or wrestle with or find unbearable or clutch to death—those content in their age, finally, cherish with pained gratitude" (*Tales of Burning Love*, 448). It is additionally worth noting that two of Erdrich's titles contain the word "love": *Love Medicine* and *Tales of Burning Love*.

To some degree, all of Erdrich's novels are inherently political. Thomas King writes of Erdrich's novels, "she explores the shadow land of resistance" (*Green Grass, Running Water*, 111), and Erdrich acknowledged in a 1991 interview with Michael Schmuacher, "There's no way to talk about Indian history without it being a political statement" (174). *Tracks* is an overtly political novel, telling about the Chippewas' loss of their land. Nanapush warns his people, "I've seen too much go by—unturned grass below my feet, and overhead, the great white cranes flung south forever. . . . Land is the only thing that lasts life to life. Money burns like tinder, flows off like water. As for the government promises, the wind is steadier" (33). *Four Souls*, the prequel to *Tracks*, is the story of Fleur's revenge on the man who stole her land and the means she uses to get it restored to her. In *Plague of Doves*, Evelina, who is eager to know the old stories, observes of her grandfather Mooshum and his brother Shamengwa, "I saw the loss of the land was lodged inside of them forever. This loss would enter me, too" (84). And Mooshum sitting with Neve Harp, Pluto's Anglo town historian, demands of her, "How has this great thievery become acceptable? How do we live right here beside you, knowing what we lost and how you took it?" (84). As Father Damien painfully finds out in *Last Report*, "He was determined to restore that land, but once it was gone, it was gone forever from Anishinaabeg hands" (186).

The Dawes Act set up the allotment system, which the U.S. government used as a "legal" means to seize land from American Indians. The narrator in *Last Report* explains:

> As with most other reservations, the government policy of attempting to excite pride in private ownership by doling parcels of land to individual Ojibwe flopped miserably and provided a feast of acquisition for hopeful farmers and surrounding entrepreneurs. So the boundaries came and went, drawn to accommodate local ventures—sawmills, farms, feed stores, the traplines of various families. [74]

The loss of land through the allotment system is told in *Tracks*, *Love Medicine*, *Last Report*, and *Four Souls*.

Other political issues help shape the novels. Erdrich references relocation in *Love Medicine* and *Antelope Wife*. She brings up AIM in reference to Gerry Nanapush in *Love Medicine* and to Irene's mother in *Shadow Tag*. The narrator of *Bingo Palace* describes what prison had done to Gerry (24, 25), and Gerry describes prison in *Love Medicine* as "a hate factory" (201). Gerry's friends did not testify for him to save him from a prison sentence since they "had no confidence in the United States Judicial System" (*Love Medicine*, 202). In *Love Medicine*, Lyman Lamartine describes the many ways in which the U.S. government has assaulted the lives of American Indians: "They gave you worthless land to start with and then they chopped it out from under your feet. They took your kids away and stuffed the English language in their mouth. They send your brother to hell [Viet Nam], they shipped him back fried. They sold you booze for furs and then told you not to drink" (326).

The great Métis leader, Louis Riel, is admired by Joseph Milk in *Plague of Doves* and by Nanapush in *Round House*, and in *Shadow Tag* not only is Irene studying Riel for her doctorate, she and Gil also name their daughter Riel. Of all of the grim injustices suffered by American Indians, the "frontier justice" of the West where American Indians could be strung up without benefit of a hearing or a trial was among the worst. The story at the heart of *Plague of Doves* concerns such a gruesome event and its lasting repercussions on the survivor and on the descendants of both the men who died and the men who hanged them. *The Round House* confronts the issue of the high percentage of Indian women who are raped. The staggering statistics reveal the enormity of the problem: one in three "Indian women will be raped in her lifetime" (*Round House*, 319). How can there be justice when federal and state laws supersede tribal codes, sovereignty rights are disregarded, and justice for Indian victims is elusive? Why hasn't there been more justice and advancements for American Indians, Gil wonders in *Shadow Tag*. His conclusion: "Blacks can be postracial. But Indians are stuck in 1892" (37). Erdrich's sober assessment of the many wrongs suffered by American Indians is a strong undercurrent running throughout her novels.

"ONE LONG NOVEL"

In a 2001 interview with Alden Mudge, Erdrich responded to his question about the degree to which each new novel adds more context and meaning to the previous novels: "I've finally figured out that I'm just working on one long novel. . . . I think it is useful to have read the other books. But I try very hard to make each book its own book. It is its own book. But they all connect in some way."

Perhaps the most obvious of all the connections between Erdrich's novels is the extent to which particular events in one novel play out or are explained in another. Lipsha and the unnamed baby being lost in the blizzard at the end of *Bingo Palace* but being found and rescued in *Tales of Burning Love* is a prime example of such a story resolution between novels.

There are other examples. In the chapter "Lyman's Luck" in *Love Medicine*, Lyman Lamartine conceives the idea of building a casino on the reservation. *The Bingo Palace* is story of this casino. In *Four Souls*, Fleur follows her trees to Minneapolis and ends up marrying the man who stole them, Jack Mauser. Nanapush recounts details of Fleur's life in Minneapolis in *Last Report*. *Tracks* tells the reasons for Lulu's estrangement from her mother, Fleur. In *Last Report*, Father Damien and Nanapush together try to promote a reconciliation between the mother and daughter. In *Love Medicine*, Pauline strangles Napoleon. In *Last Report*, she confesses the killing to Father Damien. In the "Saint Marie" and "Wild Geese" chapters of *Love Medicine*, Marie goes up the hill to the convent where Sister Leopolda ends up stabbing her with a fork. Marie gets out of the convent, literally runs into Nector who ends up having sex with her. She is fourteen. In *Last Report*, readers learn what Marie did after this incident to support herself and until she marries Nector. In *Bingo Palace*, Gerry's plane crashes as he is being transferred from a prison in Illinois to one in

Minnesota. In *Tales of Burning Love*, readers learn that he survives the crash. In the "Fleur's Luck" chapter of *Bingo Palace*, readers learn she has returned to the reservation from Minneapolis with a Pierce-Arrow and a strange white boy. Her return, the car, and the boy are explained in *Four Souls*; in *Bingo Palace*, Fleur is called "a four-souled woman" (140). The reason for this name is detailed in the novel *Four Souls*. And the opening chapter of *Love Medicine* is June's story of her last day spent in Williston before she attempted to walk home to the reservation. *Tales of Burning Love* expands the story, giving the name of the man she is with that night, Jack Mauser.

These stories, which Erdrich continues and expands throughout the novels, are one of the reasons she has so many readers. Reading an Erdrich novel feels familiar in some way. You recognize a character, an event, a place, or a family, and you read on, and on. Erdrich teaches us how to read literature, and she teaches us that there is no definitive version of the truth. Her changing stories are proof of that. As Thomas King reminds readers in *Green Grass, Running Water*, "There are no truths. . . . Only stories" (326). Stories, like life, are never fully known, and they are always influenced by who is telling the story, and why. Motive counts. Erdrich's stories evolve, her characters continue to exhibit various facets of their personality, and the stories take new directions with different storytellers. What a reader can take away from reading Erdrich's novels is the awareness that stories are alive, always growing, and capable being told from multiple perspectives. No one owns a story.

Another reason for Erdrich's popularity, and an additional contribution of hers to the Native American Renaissance, is that Erdrich's novels, her "one long story," bring readers into the intimate world of American Indians. Most of her characters are just like her readers, ordinary people. Her characters are not mythic heroes, noble savages, or bloodthirsty warriors. They are housewives, students, government employees, successful businessmen, artists, judges, lawyers, and teachers, parents, grandparents, and lovers. This is noteworthy, since the majority of Erdrich's characters are American Indians. Dee Horne suggests, "In seeing American Indians as individuals, rather than constructed 'Indians,' settler readers collaborate in the decolonizing process and learn other ways of seeing" (48). What these "other ways of seeing" can lead to then is a revisioning of American Indians and American history. Horne continues, "American Indian stories/histories now infiltrate settler ones so that readers can no longer read these settler narratives without remembering how King [or Erdrich] has re-contextualized them" (48, 49). In other words, American Indians through literature and the arts are now talking back, telling their stories and their histories, and are reclaiming both their place in American history and their voice in the once monolithic settler narrative of the American story.

Through her novels, Erdrich gives American Indian people voices, faces, histories, and interesting lives. Thirty years after the Native American Renaissance was noted and named, Erdrich remains one of the most productive and popular of Native authors because of the beauty of her language and the power of her interrelated novels to describe a shared piece of land, the people inhabiting that land, their common history, and their shared story.

NOTES

I wish to thank Debra K. S. Barker for her suggestions and valuable assistance with this essay.

1. The title phrase is taken from *The Bingo Palace* (48).

2. Some of Erdrich's many awards include the Nelson Algren Award for fiction for 1982; the Pushcart Prize, 1983; National Magazine Fiction awards, 1983 and 1987; the Virginia McCormack Scully Prize for best book of the year dealing with Indians or Chicanos, 1984; the National Book Critics Circle Award for fiction, 1984; the Sue Kaufman Prize for Best First Novel, 1984; a Guggenheim Fellowship, 1985–86; First Prize, O. Henry Awards, 1987; National Book Club finalist for fiction, 2001, 2003; Associate Poet Laureate for North Dakota, 2005; a Pulitzer Prize in Fiction nomination, 2009; an honorary doctorate, Dartmouth College, 2009; and the National Book Award for *The Round House*, 2012.

3. Another author who was major voice in the Native American Renaissance is the wildly popular (or wild and popular) Sherman Alexie. However, his first book, *The Lone Ranger and Tonto Fistfight in Heaven* was not published until 1993, fourteen years after Momaday's *House Made of Dawn* was awarded the Pulitzer Prize for fiction. Therefore, I am not including Alexie in the first wave of the renaissance writers.

4. To date, no other American Indian writer has won the Pulitzer Prize for fiction.

5. Examples of young adult series books are the Nancy Drew novels by Carolyn Keene; the Little House on the Prairie novels by Laura Ingalls Wilder; the Anne of Green Gables books by L. M. Montgomery; All-of-a-Kind Family books by Sydney Taylor; Winnie the Pooh books by A. A. Milne; and Madeleine L'Engle's Time Quartet.

6. Many mystery series exist: Agatha Christie's Miss Marple and Hercule Peroit; Sue Grafton's Kinsey Milhone; Alexander McCall Smith's No. 1 Ladies Detective Agency; James Patterson's Alex Cross; Janet Evanovich's Stephanie Plum; Ian Fleming's James Bond; and Eric Stanley Gardener's Perry Mason.

7. Science fiction series books include Isaac Asimov's Foundation series; Orson Scott Card's Ender Game series; and Frank Herbert's Dune series.

8. Fiction series include Jean Auel's Earth's Children books; Edgar Rice Burrough's Tarzan series; Lucy Agnes Hancock's Harlequin romances; Laura Hamilton's Anita Blake, Vampire Hunter series; Stephanie Meyer's Twilight series; and Sigrid Unset's Kristin Lavransdatter trio.

9. Critical work on Erdrich as a storyteller includes Joni Adamson Clarke's "Why Bears Are Good to Think and Theory Does Have to Be Murder"; Connie A. Jacobs's *The Novels of Louise Erdrich*; Shelley E. Reid's "The Stories We Tell"; James

Ruppert's "Mediation and Multiple Narratives in *Love Medicine*"; and Jennifer Sergi's "Storytelling."

10. The terms "Chippewa," "Anishinaabe," and "Ojibway" or "Ojibwe," all refer to the same tribe.

11. The Little No Horse novels include *Love Medicine, Tracks, Bingo Palace, Last Report on the Miracles at Little No Horse, Four Souls, Plague of Doves* and *The Round House*. Additionally, *The Painted Drum* takes place both in New Hampshire as well as on the reservation. What are often referred to as the North Dakota novels encompass these novels along with *Beet Queen, Tales of Burning Love,* and *Master Butcher's Singing Club. The Antelope Wife* and *Shadow Tag* are both set in Minneapolis.

12. In the preface to the Birchbark Books, Erdrich writes how these books are inspired by her efforts to retrace her family history and their origins on Madeline Island.

13. There are six federally recognized reservations in Wisconsin: Bad River, Lac Courte Oreilles, Lac du Flambeau, Mole Lake, Red Cliffe, and St. Croix. There are seven federally recognized reservations in Minnesota: Bois Fort, Fond du Lac, Grand Portage, Leech Lake, Mille Lacs, Red Lake, and White Earth.

14. The McCumber Agreement of 1892 saw ten thousand acres of the Turtle Mountain Band's tribal lands being given to settler farmers.

15. The 1887 Dawes Act, or General Allotment Act, "gave" American Indians the right to own their own piece of land, 160 acres for the head of the household. However, once the land was divided up among tribal members, the "surplus" land became available for settlers and the railroads. Historians estimate that nearly two-thirds of the lands American Indians occupied were lost because of the Dawes Act.

16. *Beet Queen, Master Butcher,* and *Tales of Burning Love* are often referred to as the "Argus Novels."

17. Other themes help connect the many stories. In her interview with Allan Mudge, Erdrich acknowledges the degree to which revenge runs through her novels as seen especially in Fleur's revenge on those who take her land (*Love Medicine, Tracks, Four Souls, Last Report*). The importance of animals is another significant theme: Fleur's bear power; *Antelope Wife*'s dogs Almost Soup, Sorrow, and Windigo Dog; the Antelope people in *Antelope Wife*; the Devil Dog in both *Antelope Wife* and *Last Report*; the "concierge" dogs in *Shadow Tag* (19); Eva's love for her German shepherd in *Master Butcher*; Omakayas' close relationship with the bears, a crow, and a porcupine, and also in the Birchbark Books, Old Tallow's dogs to whom she is devoted, as they are to her; and in *Round House*, the Coutts' dog, Pearl, who protects the family.

WORKS CITED

Alexie, Sherman. *The Lone Ranger and Tonto Fistfight in Heaven*. New York: HarperCollins, 1994.

Barker, Debra K. S. Phone conversation. January 10, 2011.

Bacon, Katie. "An Emissary of the Between-World": A Conversation with Louise Erdrich." *Atlantic Unbound,* January 17, 2001. http://www.theatlantic.com/past/docs/unbounc/interviews/int2001-01-17.htm.

Chavkin, Allan, and Nancy Feyl, eds. *Conversations with Louise Erdrich & Michael Dorris.* Jackson: University of Mississippi Press, 1994.

Clarke, Joni Adamson. "Why Bears Are Good to Think and Theory Doesn't Have to Be Murder: Transformation and Oral Tradition in Louise Erdrich's *Tracks.*" *SAIL* 4:1 (1992), 28–48.

Coltelli, Laura, ed. "Louise Erdrich and Michael Dorris." In *Winged Words: American Indian Writers Speak.* Lincoln: University of Nebraska Press, 1990, 40–52.

Erdrich, Louise. *The Antelope Wife.* New York: HarperFlamingo, 1998, 2012.

———. *The Beet Queen.* New York: Henry Holt, 1986.

———. *The Bingo Palace.* New York: HarperCollins, 1994.

———. *The Birchbark House.* New York: Hyperion Books for Children, 1999.

———. *Chickadee.* New York: Harper, 2012.

———. *Four Souls.* New York: HarperCollins, 2004.

———. *The Game of Silence.* New York: HarperCollins, 2005.

———. *The Last Report on the Miracles at Little No Horse.* New York: HarperCollins, 2001.

———. *Love Medicine.* New York: Holt, 1984, 1993.

———. *The Master Butcher's Singing Club.* New York: HarperCollins, 2003.

———. *The Painted Drum.* New York: HarperCollins, 2005.

———. *The Plague of Doves.* New York: HarperCollins, 2008.

———. *The Porcupine Year.* New York: HarperCollins, 2008.

———. *The Round House.* New York: Harper, 2012.

———. *Shadow Tag.* New York: HarperCollins, 2010.

———. *Tales of Burning Love.* New York: HarperCollins, 1996.

———. *Tracks.* New York: HarperCollins, 1988.

———. "Where I Ought to Be: A Writer's Sense of Place." *New York Times Book Review,* July 18, 1985, sec. 7:1ff.

Horne, Dee. *Contemporary American Indian Writing: Unsettling Literature.* New York: Peter Lang, 1999.

Horr, David A., comp. and ed. *Chippewa Indians VII: Commission Findings on the Chippewa Nation.* New York: Garland Publishing, 1974.

"Indian Country Diaries." September 2006. Web, March 11, 2011. <http://www.pbs.org/indiancountry/history/relocate.html>.

Jacobs, Connie A. *The Novels of Louise Erdrich: Stories of Her People.* New York. Peter Lang, 2001.

King, Thomas. *Green Grass, Running Water.* Toronto: HarperCollins, 1993.

———. *The Truth about Stories: A Native Narrative.* Minneapolis: University of Minnesota Press, 2003.

Lincoln, Kenneth. *Native American Renaissance.* Berkeley: University of California Press, 1983.

"Louise Erdrich." *World Biography*. 2005. Web, February 23, 2011. <http://www
.notablebiographies.com/newsmakers2/2005-A-Fi/Erdrich.html>.

Mudge, Alden. "Louise Erdrich Explores Mysteries and Miracles on the Reservation." 2001. Web, February 28, 2011. <http://www.bookpage.com/1004bp
/louise_erdrich.html>.

Reid, Shelley. "The Stories We Tell: Louise Erdrich's Identity Narratives." *MELUS*
25:3/4 (2000), 65–87.

Rolo, Mark Anthony. "Louise Erdrich—The Progressive Interview." April 2002.
Web, March 4, 2011. http://findarticles.com/p/articles/mi_m1295/is_4_66
/ai_84866888/?tag=content;col1.htmp.

Ruppert, James. "Mediation and Multiple Narrators in Love Medicine." *North Dakota Quarterly* 59:4 (1991), 229–42.

Schumacher, Michael. "Louise Erdrich and Michael Dorris: A Marriage of Minds."
In Chavkin and Chavkin, eds. *Conversations with Louise Erdrich & Michael
Dorris*, 173–83.

Sergi, Jennifer. "Storytelling: Tradition and Preservation in Louise Erdrich's
Tracks." *World Literature Today* 66:2 (1992), 279–82.

Silko, Leslie Marmon. *Ceremony*. New York: Viking Press, 1977.

Vizenor, Gerald. *Winged Words: American Indian Writers Speak*. Edited by Laura
Coltelli. Lincoln: University of Nebraska Press, 1990, 154–182.

9
Thomas King

Shifting Shapes to Tell Another Story

CAROL MILLER

For eons, within the oral traditions of Native people all over the continent, Coyote or one of his alter egos has been "going along"—as frequently as not, introducing chaos in his role as cautionary exemplar of what constitutes proper (and improper) behavior. The trickster has also been pressed into service as a ubiquitous figure in much of the writing of contemporary Native storytellers. Such has certainly been the case for the mixed-blood Cherokee writer Thomas King, whose fiction has been most frequently situated by a cottage industry of critics within a frame of "trickster discourse."[1] It has been one of the features, if by no means the only one, in his standing as a main player in the emergence of the Native American Renaissance.

Tricksters certainly do have a prominent presence in King's work, centrally so, for example, in his children's books, all of which focus on the exploits of a feckless Coyote whose interventions into human and animal worlds are a recipe for catastrophes of one kind or another. The trickster is perhaps most effectively deployed in what many consider King's masterwork, *Green Grass, Running Water*, in which Coyote unleashes an out-of-control "dog dream" that conjures up a very problematic version of the biblical creation saga. As might be evidenced by the taxidermied furry creature that used to, and may still, grace his living room or a nearby closet, King has himself seemed to acknowledge and encourage the trickster associations that so naturally express the humorous turn mediating even his most serious themes and plot lines.

Over two decades or so, King's artistic career has expanded to include not only literary novels and short stories but children's literature; detective fiction; the popular *Dead Dog Café Comedy Hour* radio program; the distinguished Massey Lecture series, later published as the essay collection *The Truth about Stories;* his foray into spoken-word video, *I'm Not the Indian You Had in Mind;* his multiply exhibited photography series; and a recently published history, *The Inconvenient Indian* (2012). My argument here is that both the theoretical ethos that illuminates almost everything he produces and the creative ambition that drives him as an artist may be more fully appreciated and understood in relation to an even more potent archetype to be found within the traditional oral narratives of many indigenous nations. That archetypal figure is the shape-shifter, a presence in many ways more complex and mysterious in its manifestations than that of the trickster. Shape-shifters, after all, are not, in either ancestral or contemporary narrative, customarily cast as mere exemplars of either effectual or ineffectual "goings along." Rather, they are mysterious beings of agency and force, possessing powers potentially both greatly destructive and/or greatly benevolent to the human communities with which they interact. This intrinsic and often enigmatic agency at the heart of the trope of shifting shapes drives not only the plots and characterizations of some of King's most influential writing but the theory that binds that writing into a coherent and evolving whole. King stands in a line of Native tellers whose work insists upon the shifting nature of story's power to both heal and injure. Perhaps even more ambitiously than most of his peers, however, King should be credited for deliberately translating indigenous storytelling into ever more diverse and contemporary "platforms" of relevance and outreach that advance this fundamental idea.

The presence of shape-shifters is, of course, not exclusive to indigenous narrative—a list of comic-strip superheroes and recent movie franchises evidences their ubiquitousness in contemporary venues of non-Native popular culture. They may certainly be traced in other, more serious intellectual spheres as well.[2] But a brief examination—first, of the functions of the shape-shifters who appear in Cherokee ancestral story; next, in some of their manifestations in the fiction of other contemporary Native writers; and finally, in King's varied narrative forms—illuminates a convergence of meaning and consequence greater than the sum of the parts.

One venerable and centralized source of Cherokee oral traditions is James Mooney's collected *Myths of the Cherokees*. In the section of Mooney's collection labeled under the culturally tin-eared heading of "Wonder Stories," evil beings use their abilities as shape-shifters to exploit or actually destroy the human beings with whom they come into contact. The elaborate "Gambler" story, for example, recounts how a half-human son of Thunder uses his father's powers to overcome a character familiar within many tribal oral traditions—the Gambler, or "Brass," who cheats his human opponents, never losing because he "knew how to take on different shapes, so that he always got away" (311). This character is vanquished and contained when Thunder, aided by the brass-divining Beetle, is able to see through his disguises.

More menacing is another set of stories involving cannibal beings such as Spearfinger, who "could take on any shape or appearance to suit her purpose, but in her right form she looked very much like an old woman" (316–17). In this guise, protected by rock-hard skin and armed with a long, stony forefinger with which she stabs her victims, she can entice children to come near before she impales them and consumes their livers. Or taking on the appearance of a family member, she can enter human homes to prey upon her victims. Only after another instance in which human and animal worlds engage in cooperative effort is Spearfinger ultimately destroyed when she is lured into a pit and finally killed after Chickadee, who knows the location of her heart, directs the hunters to shoot her in her hand.

A more direct example of how the destructive powers of the shape-shifter may be transformed into benevolent outcomes is the story of the Stone Man, another "wicked cannibal monster" (319) who, dressed in stone, is thus almost impossible to kill. When this creature attempts to enter a village that has been alerted to his approach, he is made vulnerable by the "medicine" of seven menstruating women stationed along his path. In an implicit acknowledgement of gendered power, Stone Man is so weakened that he can be pinned to the ground and burned. The significant conclusion of this story has Stone Man attempting to save himself by passing on to his human auditors the formulas of medicines for all kinds of illnesses and the songs that will call up the animals upon which the people depend for sustenance. The destructive power of the shape-shifter, therefore, is countered by human agency and turned to positive good for the human community.

Although, as in these stories, the shape-shifter uses his or her power to evil purpose, the shifting of shapes may in other stories be deployed more benignly as a medium by which an "intercourse" of human and animal beings establishes a foundation of kinship, reciprocity, and interdependence that helps to secure the well-being of the many cohabitants of the indigenous natural world. This is certainly so in the traditional Yellow Woman stories of several Southwestern cultures, in which a human woman meets a "handsome stranger" and follows him away to become eventually a member of his own bear or buffalo clan, in effect bringing about a kin relationship that ultimately benefits rather than betrays her human community.[3]

In Cherokee oral traditions, this function is served by the series of "Bear Song" stories. In the first of these, a Cherokee boy leaves his family to spend time each day in the mountains. After a while, the boy refuses to eat with his family and begins to grow brown hair all over his body. The parents beseech him to stay with them, but the boy wishes to go live with his new family, saying that "it is better there than here, and you see that I am beginning to be different already, so that I cannot live here any longer" (326). The family ultimately decides to follow the boy into the mountains, and when their neighbors attempt to persuade them not to leave, they refuse, declaring, "We are going where there is always plenty to eat. Hereafter we shall be called *yanu* (bear) and when you yourselves are hungry come into the woods and call us and we shall come to give you our own flesh. You need not be afraid to kill us, for we shall live always" (326). As in the Yellow Woman stories, what appears at first to be a defection from one's own kind establishes instead, by means of a shifting of shapes, a kinship relation among human and nonhumans based on security, sacrifice, and reciprocity—features of a natural world in harmonious balance.

As evidenced by now more than forty years of extraordinary literary production by contemporary Native writers, the mysteriousness and potency of shape-shifting as a narrative trope linking traditional orality to print-language "tellings" have certainly been effectually deployed. N. Scott Momaday's Pulitzer Prize–winning novel, *House Made of Dawn,* for example, first published in 1968, turns in part upon the protagonist Abel's killing of the "albino," a demonic, human-but-not-human figure associated with ageless evil. Convicted of murder, Abel feels no guilt for acting upon his recognition of the nature of such a being, "for he would know what the white man was, and he would kill him if he could. A man kills such an enemy if he can" (103).

In Silko's now-canonized novel *Ceremony,* the complexity—and centrality—of the shifting of shapes as a driver of the narrative is even more obviously on display and intrinsic to the novel's most profound meanings. Among these is the seminal idea, also critical to King's work, that stories themselves have life-preserving agency. This is expressed in one of the framing poems that begins the novel: "They are all we have, you see, all we have to fight off illness and death" (2). Silko's cosmology features a "world made of stories, the long ago, time immemorial stories" (95). From stories ceremonies grow, and from ceremonies come the cures of the body, mind, and spirit—healing to thwart the violence, fear, and madness wielded by "destroyers" who threaten the harmony necessary to the very existence of human and natural worlds.

The plot of the novel follows Silko's vulnerable hero as he slowly and painfully comes to understand his place in this post–World War II cosmos after a long process of healing. Ultimately, he must assume his role in a pattern in which "his sickness was only part of something larger, and his cure would be found in something great and inclusive of everything" (125–26). Silko devotes the early portions of the novel to laying out the violence, greed, and guilt that have brought Tayo, his Pueblo relations—and the entire human community— to this point of crisis. But the story's resolution depends upon ceremonial interactions in which shape-shifting becomes a medium of protection, enlightenment, and restoration.

One of the earliest of these interactions occurs when the medicine man Betonie involves Tayo in a ceremony intended to enlist the ancient powers of the bear people to strengthen and clarify Tayo's mind and spirit. This ritual is facilitated by Betonie's young helper "Shush, which means Bear" (128). This boy is apparently in a transitional state recollecting that of the youth in the Cherokee Bear Songs. Betonie cautions Tayo, "You don't have to be afraid of him. . . . Don't be so quick to call something good or bad. There are balances and harmonies always *shifting* [emphasis added], always necessary to maintain. It is very peaceful with the bears; the people say that's the reason human beings seldom return" (130). This is a point our Cherokee ancestors would certainly understand, and it is one among many of the novel's narrative moments in which strategically inserted affirmations of the necessity of maintaining the shifting balances and harmonies of a whole lifeworld signal the thematic importance of this idea.[4] Betonie is one of a lineage of those who have set themselves against the "witchery" of the destroyers. (Another is the Night Swan, the mysterious "dancer" who has earlier initiated Tayo by means of an episode in which physical intercourse has facilitated his first glimpse of his place in a larger pattern: "[R]emember this day," she tells him enigmatically. "You will recognize it later. You are part of it now" (100).

Betonie, realizing Tayo's potential role in this pattern, sets him a series of tasks—finding Tayo's Uncle Josiah's lost speckled cattle, seeking out a portentous pattern of stars in the night sky—as next steps to the completion of the ceremony that will restore Tayo to himself and his community and, temporarily at least, thwart the Destroyers' destructive intentions for human kind. But it is Tayo's relationship with the mountain spirit, Ts'eh, who has taken the form of a human woman, that will bring to culmination Tayo's—and his community's—salvation. When, in the course of his quests, he encounters the strange woman and her dwelling in an arroyo, it is from her porch that he sees Betonie's stars. That night, they make love, and intercourse is again a metaphor for illumination and connection. The critical relationship between Tayo and Ts'eh will deepen and be clarified over the course of the subsequent summer, as they move through the surrounding desert hills and valleys, Ts'eh teaching Tayo how to aid her in her role as a kind of ecological caretaker, gathering and relocating medicinal plants that nurture the spirit as well as the body.

But who is this mysterious figure? Silko has laid out a trail of bread-crumb clues to her identity throughout the story, but the clearest come in her hints to Tayo that "I'm a Montano. . . . You can call me Ts'eh" (223)—a shortened reference to Tse-pi'na, one of the Pueblo people's sacred mountains. Tayo wants to know more about her, but Ts'eh, looking into the distance toward the Black Mountains, merely affirms that she and her brothers and sisters are "a very close family." Finally, Tayo must be content with Ts'eh's refusal to provide more prosaic details about her identity: "Up here, we don't have to worry about those things" (223).

The novel's climax involves Tayo's rejection of the internalized guilt and consequent violence that make victims of both himself and his community and simultaneously reinforce white hegemony. Silko writes, "He had arrived at a convergence of patterns; he could see them clearly now" (254). It is a moment of epiphany through which Tayo comes to understand his place within the love and protection of this avatar representing the potency of the natural world. At story's end, Tayo leaves Emo the Destroyer to his just deserts and returns to the pueblo to tell his story to the elders of the kiva and to carry on Ts'eh's work, affirmed in his certainty that "she had always loved him, she had never left him; she had always been there" (255), with that "she" representing

far more than the human form of Ts'eh's shifted shape. The optimistic resolution of Silko's novel rests upon the idea that human beings exist within a world
that is itself a living entity, an entity whose nature may be understood as an
ongoing story, at once contemporary and "immemorial," in which harmony
and well-being are secured by the interactions of various actors, some of
which—but not all—are human beings. In *Ceremony* then, the shape-shifting
powers of the natural world have, at least for a time, contributed to the preservation not only of Tayo and his Pueblo community, but to all of creation, il-
lustrating Silko's beginning point that stories are "all we have to hold off illness
and death," and animating the primal link between ancient and contemporary
Native storytelling.

Thomas King is a much funnier writer than is Leslie Silko—and in fact
he has insisted in many places that comedy is simply the basic strategy of his
storytelling—but he is also a more deeply pessimistic one, sharing perhaps
the tendency of many Native people to use humor as a cover for pain and
disillusionment. In *The Truth about Stories*, the published "native narrative"
version of his contribution to the Massey Lecture series, King offers a series
of essays, each constructed upon a repeating frame, that adds further dimensions to Silko's claim about storytelling. In King's cosmology, stories are not
all we have: the truth about stories is that they are all we are (32). It is a subtle
but significant distinction, doubling down on the interwoven strands of the
contemporary and personal and the ancient and collective to empower story
even more inexorably as imagination transformed into language transformed
into actions always accompanied by ethical consequences.

For King as an artist, the truth about stories—that they determine who we
are—requires an unflinching exploration of ethical consequences. Thus, in
the first of the *Truth* essays, as King lays out the contrasts between the indigenous creation story concerning the Woman Who Fell from the Sky with the
Genesis story in order to show their differing values, he is really interested in
getting to the ethical consequences involved in selecting one, rather than the
other, to be "true." Summarizing the differences between these "sacred texts,"
King writes, "So here are our choices: a world in which creation is a solitary,
individual act or a world in which creation is a shared activity; a world that
begins in harmony and slides toward chaos or a world that begins in chaos
and moves toward harmony; a world marked by competition or a world determined by co-operation" (24–25). What kind of a world might we have created with that latter kind of a story, he asks—because to privilege one story
as sacred is to devalue the other and thus position it as less powerful and less
determinate of what the resulting world is like.

At the end of each of the Massey lectures, the closing parenthesis of King's
repeating structure asks his readers to take responsibility for the stories
they've chosen to live by—and the ones they've now heard through his telling.
Do whatever you want with these stories, King says, "But don't say in the years

to come that you would have lived your life differently if only you had heard this story. You've heard it now" (29).

In *The Truth about Stories*, King labels himself a "hopeful pessimist" (92), one who, like his friend Louis Owens,[5] writes knowing that "none of the stories we told would change the world. But we wrote in the hope that they would. We both knew that stories were medicine, that a story told one way could cure, that the same story told another way could injure" (92). This idea—that stories may result in benign or malevolent outcomes, that the shapes they take influence the values and behaviors of those who believe and act upon them— would have sounded familiar to those old Cherokee storytellers and comes as close to an articulation of literary theory as may be found in King's own voice.

The Massey lectures amass many different kinds of stories—ones grounded in culture, like ancestral creation stories; personal ones about King's father's desertion; his adult ambitions, successes, and failures; stories of friends and acquaintances, of events of indigenous history and colonial exploitation—all symmetrically arranged to demonstrate this theory of stories as consequential—and to make the listener/reader complicit in those consequences. Stories can kill, and stories can save. "Want a different ethic? Tell a different story" (164) is King's valediction in this collection, elaborated by his personal experience that saving stories are most often grounded in laughter.

It is in King's 1993 masterwork, *Green Grass, Running Water,* that these theoretical ideas are given their most explicit imaginative expression. *Green Grass* employs an extraordinarily complicated and intertextual organization to bring together an indigenous interlocutor (the "I says" whose apparent role is to narrate, repeatedly, the beginning of the world where, with nothing but water everywhere, "here's how it happened"); a Coyote trickster (whose contrary dog dream sets off chaos by declaring himself an unfortunately egocentric biblical "God"); and a timeless set of shape-shifting spirit helpers (a fluidly peripatetic group with the often imperfectly realized goal of "fixing the world")—all of whom eventually interact with each other and with contending creation stories and with increasingly conflated figures of myth, history, popular culture, and with the contemporary, mostly Blackfoot, residents of Blossom, Alberta.

To bring off this narrative sleight of hand, King requires his necessarily agile readers to follow multiple frames of action, chronological jumps, and shifting identities. At the top of a terraced landscape of these narrative frames is that "I" narrator, a sort of master of ceremonies whose qualified omniscience is complicated by the anarchy of Coyote's foolishness. At the next level, four ancients whom some see as old men, others as old women, assume the shapes of the Lone Ranger, Ishmael, Robinson Crusoe, and Hawkeye— those friends-of-the-Indian icons of literary and popular culture—escaping as they periodically do from their "confinement" in the mental hospital overseen by Dr. Joseph Hovaugh (Jehovah). Setting out to fix the world, their modus operandi is to intervene in real-world events by both retelling and re-enacting commingled and revisionist versions of creation stories that upend Euro-American colonialist religion and history. In the time-present of the novel's fictional community of Blossom, they are on a quest to "fix" the particular quadrant of the world inhabited by hapless Lionel Stands Alone and his extended Blackfoot family.

"Want a different ethic? Tell a different story." And so Thomas King does in *Green Grass:* tell story after story, or at least let his slippery tellers tell them—stories within stories; stories highjacking stories; stories that shift the genders of their characters (Moby Dick becomes the lesbian black whale Moby Jane); stories that change their endings (the cavalry doesn't arrive in time to save John Wayne)—all constructing an alternative reality that might be if, say, the triumphalist stories of the Bible, of American history, of Western literature, of Hollywood cinema had not become the sacred texts of our time and place. What if, instead, those were somehow mediated by older, pan-indigenous creation stories featuring First Woman, Changing Woman, Thought Woman, and Old Woman, "fixing up" a spiritual and historical legacy of violence and exploitation to privilege tolerance, community, and stewardship of natural and human resources?

Within this complex matrix, Coyote certainly plays a significant and familiar role as a figure of chaos and, in King's deft handling, comic relief. Coyote is, for example, the instigator of the "dog dream" whose ill-mannered insistence that he is actually God (with a capital G) in turn is responsible for the biblical stories of Ahdamn and the Garden of Eden, Noah and the Ark, Jesus's walk on water, all, it turns out, featuring equally contrary, self-absorbed, and high-handed patriarchal figures. Coyote's singing and dancing are also responsible for the earthquake that destroys the dam whose operation Eli Stands Alone has been resisting by taking his turn residing in the family cabin that stands below it. And Coyote is also apparently responsible for at least two virgin births! (That the second will be the result of Lionel's friend Alberta's pregnancy but the first might be that of the Virgin Mary is a sly example of King's deflection of received ideas about conventional religious doctrine and the agency ascribed to it.)

But King's most original creative imagining in this novel is his setting into motion the many versions of the trope of shape-shifting as the strategic mechanism that allows him to cross-fertilize his narrative frames and bring his multiple stories to satisfying conclusion. Thus, the four old "Indians"—old men to befuddled hospital supervisor Dr. Hovaugh, old women to their shrewdly allusive friend Babo, conceived as the clued-in hospital custodian/cum barber—exist within a dimension that defies mortal boundaries of time and space as they shift and reshift their mysterious personae. As, variously, the Lone Ranger/First Woman, Ishmael/Changing Woman, Robinson Crusoe/Thought Woman, and Hawkeye/Old Woman, they take turns recounting, but also taking parts within, the indigenous creation stories that seek to alter the "ethics" of, in King's cosmology, the more injurious Western creation stories that have spawned colonialism and capitalism.

Here is just one example of King's virtuosity as story spinner. In the first version, "this according to the Lone Ranger" (8), First Woman falls out of the sky; lands on the back of Turtle; makes a garden out of newly formed earth; lives there with Ahdamn until she leaves to avoid the bad-mannered "Christian rules" of the dog/GOD who has also appeared in the Garden; heads west; temporarily assumes the persona of the Masked Man (Ahdamn is Tonto) to avoid Indian-hunting Texas Rangers; is eventually identified as an Indian anyway and sent off to prison in Florida; disguises herself once more as the Lone Ranger and walks out of the gates with the other shape-shifter "Indians," Ishmael, Robinson Crusoe, and Hawkeye; and reappears on the road into Blossom, thumbing a ride with Lionel and his Aunt Norma as the first step in "fixing up" the world by straightening out the life of one person at a time (in this case, the befuddled, underachieving Lionel).

As can be seen by even this brief summary, King's success in adapting shape-shifting to the complicated work of plot and character development depends upon a number of strategies, including, of course, his deployment of the rich resources of Native oral traditions. Another of these strategies derives from the novel's extraordinary profusion of allusions. These work as signifiers of multiple meaning in shorthand references drawn from shrewdly relevant sources such as, for example, Melville's anticolonialist novella *Benito Cereno* (hence the insertion of Babo who, in King's female incarnation, shares an identity with Melville's character as one who is very much more than she/he seems to be). King inundates the novel with allusions major and minor: in one brief scene, Alberta's history class is peopled by avatars of particular resonance for students of Native history: Mary Rowlandson, Helen Mooney, Henry Dawes, et al. More important characters serve as echoing foils, as in the case of Lionel's sister Latisha's abusive husband, George Morningstar, who shares more with General George Armstrong Custer than Custer's time-traveling jacket. (King is plugging in a particularly subtle allusion here, as Custer was associated bitterly by some Native people with the morning star since his preferred method of attack was to strike before dawn when his victims were still sleeping.) Even that jacket must, over the course of the novel, adapt its shape to the forms of various wearers—Custer at the Battle of Greasy Grass, John Wayne in the movie altered by the old men/spirit helpers so that the Indians win (hence the new bullet holes), George who wears it as an affectation, and finally Lionel, to whom it is given as a birthday present by the Old Indians as a sort of Dumbo's feather in a failed attempt to prop up his self-esteem.

Toward the novel's end, what does at least temporarily "fix" Lionel occurs when he takes his rightful place beside his Uncle Eli and other family members in their confrontation with George Morningstar as he surreptitiously tries to take photographs of the Sundance gathering to sell for personal profit. But as earthquakes and floods approach, Coyote, the Lone Ranger, Ishmael, Robinson Crusoe, and Hawkeye must admit that fixing up the world is indeed a lot of work, and they may have to start all over again (435). Coyote's singing and dancing will bring on more calamitous consequences, as King's most broadly comic allusion plays out. Just as their Columbian precursors, the Nina, Pinta, and Santa Maria, appeared on a long-ago horizon, King contrives a shape-shifted ironic reversal of indigenous fortune as the elusive automobiles, the Nissan, the Pinto, and the Karmann-Ghia, float purposefully into sight to break the dam that represents a threat to Native homeland and traditional life.

The novel's converging plot lines here once again make King's point about the power of narrative to injure and heal. Even as the vessels approach, as the earth begins to shake, it's going to be a good day, according to the Lone Ranger. Eli will not survive the quake and flood, but after his death, his sister Norma confirms, "Eli's fine. He came home" (461). Norma and the other family members will rebuild their mother's cabin, and Norma will take her turn living in it, securing its claim to place and custom. (Eventually, even Lionel may get a turn.) Alberta will have her baby. Babo will welcome the old Indians back to the hospital—and they'll begin thinking about a new project to fix up the world. Open-ended, within time and out of it, the stories will need to be told again.

Green Grass, Running Water may certainly be the most imaginative of King's artistic projects and the one derived most fully from his command of an array of oral traditions. These qualities make the novel a natural site for the substantial presence of the trope of shape-shifting as a means of dramatizing his theories about the power of stories to cure or injure and to determine the ethics we live by. The figure may be most directly discernible here, but King returns to it in many other instances. Not surprisingly, for example, all three of King's children's stories center on a trickster coyote, but in the first and most original of these, *A Coyote Columbus Story* (1992), Coyote is a gender-shifted, baseball-crazy creation figure who thinks up the whole Columbian expedition, with all its subsequent "New World" devastation, just to satisfy her desire for new players in her rigged baseball games.

And in *Truth and Bright Water* (1999), the darkest and most elegiac of King's novels and perhaps the one closest to his heart, the fates of the lost boy Lum and his cousin Tecumseh are entwined with the mystery of the woman they may have seen throwing herself into the river that runs between the towns of Truth and Bright Water. The identities of that baffling figure and of the "famous Indian artist," Monroe Swimmer, are connected by a quite prosaic act of shape-shifting that explains what the boys actually witnessed. But the resolution of the novel's secrets and disguises is not enough to preserve Lum from his embittered longing for one parent and the punishing brutality of the other.

It is not only in print-language media that the motif of shifting shapes has been a chosen mechanism for King's artistic energies. In his years-long photographic project shooting scores of pictures of Native artists from all over the United States and Canada, he has amassed one set of straightforward portraits. But in another accompanying group, he has also assumed the tongue-in-cheek persona of a Cherokee Edward Curtis by offering his subjects a variety of props to complicate their photographic identities, the most frequently chosen of these being a slyly suggestive, anticolonial opportunity to don a Lone Ranger mask and strike a literal and figurative new "pose."

King stretches his creative identity in another direction in the award-nominated 2008 spoken-word video, *I'm Not the Indian You Had in Mind.* In this five-minute film, the visual dimension of the form allows King as narrator to wheel out a life-sized wooden Indian as the quintessential stereotype of the Indian you did have in mind, an image quickly augmented by cartoon Indians, Indians in Buster Keaton silent movies, the TV version of Tonto, and other pop-culture references to received versions of the "Native" identity frozen in the aspic of historical stereotype. The work of the video is twofold: to deconstruct those stereotypes by presenting instead a barrage of contemporary, real-world Native identities (including a still frame with King holding up a "pompous Indian author" placard) and to recall King's theoretical anchors linking the stories we tell to the ethics we live by. The capitalist/colonialist exploitation of the resources of the natural world has consumed the earth, leaving a bleak future for coming generations. And yet what if another story had taken hold? What might have happened "had you followed, had we led?" No easy answers result. In fact, "It's not easy," says King as narrator, and "I can't" is his final evaluation of the unlikely possibility that any real fixing up of the world can result from simply telling another story grounded in the values of an indigenous ethos. Retreating from this grim note, the video ultimately returns to the more addressable topic of deconstructing stereotypes, having two of its attractive young actor/speakers go off together for lattes. Overall, though, the motif of shifting shapes has had ample play here, in the movement from wooden-imaged, pop-culture stereotypical images to the diversity of contemporary real-world Native lives—and in the reinforced theme of a diminished present and a threatened future, governed by the triumphalist ascension of the "truth" of one story over another.

These examples and others, including the very popular *Dead Dog Café Comedy Hour,* a fifteen-minute radio show that ran from 1997 to 2000 and then returned for an additional twenty-six episodes in 2006, point to a final dimension of how the shifter of shapes is an apt signifier of Thomas King's prolific career. That show featured King, actually the savvy scripter, as the urban Indian straight man to the gently condescending "traditionals," Jasper Friendly Bear and Gracie Heavy Hand. *Dead Dog,* of course, builds upon a fairly minor plot element in *Green Grass, Running Water,* but the creative energies it takes to transform a witty plot point in a novel into fully imagined, sustained, and successful seasons of radio plays is itself an example of King's uncommon abilities and aspirations as a shifter of genres. In fact, all of these ambitious undertakings—*Dead Dog;* the photography series; the video; the screenplay for the television-movie version of King's early novel, *Medicine River;* the mystery series written under the pseudonym Hartley Goodweather; the children's books; the essays; the recent history text; even King's brief foray into national politics; and of course the "serious" novels and short stories— these compose a metaperspective about what is artistically possible and confirm King's tenacious productivity as a hopeful pessimist. Want a different ethic? Tell a different story. And be audacious in shifting the shapes of those stories to reach as wide an audience as possible. Maybe those stories won't actually change the world, but for Thomas King, it won't be for want of trying.

NOTES

1. For specific examples, see Linton, "And Here's How It Happened," p. 221; or Fleischmann, "Thomas King's Use of Trickster Figures and Trickster Discourse"; or note the more than thirty pages of "Thomas King trickster" citations listed on the Google search engine.

2. Think of archetypal superheroes such as Clark Kent/Superman, Peter Parker/ Spider Man, Tony Stark/Iron Man—and even the various aspects of the Christian trinity of Father, Son, Holy Ghost might be perceived as a form of divine shape-shifting.

3. See Paula Gunn Allen's discussion of Yellow Woman figures—and their culturally informed significance—in the "Kochinnenako in Academe" chapter of *The Sacred Hoop*, pp. 222–44). And, of course, Leslie Marmon Silko demonstrates the fluidity of this figure in her many versions of Yellow Woman stories, for example, in her collection, *Storyteller.*

4. In fact, the novel's fundamental narrative structure results from Silko's juxtaposition of echoing contemporary and "time immemorial" tellings in which parallel droughts are caused by the errant actions of Tayo and Corn Woman, which must be set right before harmony and balance are restored.

5. Owens was a Choctaw/Cherokee/Irish critic and novelist who committed suicide in 2002.

WORKS CITED

Allen, Paula Gunn. *The Sacred Hoop: Recovering the Feminine in American Indian Traditions.* Boston: Beacon Press, 1986.
Fleischmann, Aloys. "Thomas King's Use of Trickster Figures and Trickster Discourse." In a forthcoming volume on Thomas King in the European Studies in North American Literature and Culture Series. Rochester, N.Y.: Camden House.

King, Thomas. *Dead Dog Café Comedy Hour.* Toronto: Canadian Broadcasting Company, 1997–2000, 2007.

———. *Green Grass, Running Water.* New York: Bantam Books, 1994.

———. *I'm Not the Indian You Had in Mind.* Toronto: Big Soul Productions, Spoken Word Video, 2008.

———. *Medicine River.* Toronto: Viking Canada, 1989.

———. *The Truth about Stories.* Toronto: Anansi Press, 2003.

———. *Truth and Bright Water.* Toronto: Harper Flamingo Canada, 1999.

King, Thomas, and William Kent Monkman. *A Coyote Columbus Story.* Toronto: Groundwood Books, 1992.

Linton, Patricia. "'And Here's How It Happened': Trickster Discourse in Thomas King's *Green Grass, Running Water.*" *Modern Fiction Studies* 45:1 (Spring 1999).

Momaday, N. Scott. *House Made of Dawn.* New York: Harper and Row, 1968.

Mooney, James. *Myths of the Cherokees and Sacred Formulas of the Cherokees.* Nashville: Charles Elder, 1972.

Silko, Leslie Marmon. *Ceremony.* New York: Penguin. 1977.

———. *Storyteller.* New York: Little, Brown, 1981.

10

Thriller Survivance

The Subversive Resistance of Louis Owens

LINDA LIZUT HELSTERN

In 1993 Louis Owens was awarded the Josephine Miles PEN Oakland Award for a pair of books published in the Columbus quincentennial year, 1992: *The Sharpest Sight* and *Other Destinies: Understanding the American Indian Novel*. The former was Owens's second novel, a murder mystery and contemporary enactment of the founding myth of Choctaw tribal identity; the latter, a critical monograph tracing the history of the American Indian novel from its inception in 1854, one of the first book-length monographs on Native literature published by a Native mixed-blood writer. Before his untimely death in 2002, Owens published five more books to critical acclaim, three novels—*Bone Game* (1994), *Nightland* (1996), and *Dark River* (1999)—and two multigenre collections that blend life-writing, fiction, and literary/cultural critique—*Mixedblood Messages: Literature, Film, Family, Place* (1998) and *I Hear the Train: Reflections, Inventions, Refractions* (2001). Thematically intertwined, this work grew out of a critical matrix that since the 1970s had focused on ethnic representation, identity politics, and, in the case of Native writers, authenticity, generally understood by the academic critical establishment through an explicit connection to Native oral tradition or ritual.

Owens entered this conversation not so much to change the subject as to change the slant of the discourse with respect to Native peoples, many of them mixed-bloods like himself. In his fiction, attuned to the danger of representations that trap tribal peoples in their past with no opportunity for change, he adopted a strategy to interrogate and alter the construction of Indian identity on the very ground where Indian stereotypes have been created and perpetuated for some three hundred years—in the discourse of popular culture. Determined to "defiantly, even subversively, seize the low ground of American literature"—to borrow a phrase from his admiring essay on Michael Dorris and Louise Erdrich's *The Crown of Columbus*, Owens turned the mass-market thriller to his own uses, creating an avowedly American Indian literature from what is arguably the dominant form of Euro-American cultural production.[1]

Each thriller subgenre in turn—murder mystery, supernatural horror story, Western, and war story—became the basis for a subsequent Owens novel. In plot-centered stories that have surprising affinity with traditional orature, Owens succeeds not only in decentering the thriller's Western cultural foundations—moral, metaphysical, and epistemological—but in privileging such values as communitism and reciprocity, values central to traditional Native culture and contemporary Native lives. "Part whodunit, part spiritual quest" is the way the *Washington Post* described *The Sharpest Sight*, ultimately advising readers, "For a good murder story that responsibly handles the interplay between Native American and white cultures, stick to Tony Hillerman." The problem remained, as Owens later noted, that "for Native Americans, the term 'Indian' is a deeply contested space, where authenticity must somehow be forged out of resistance to the 'authentic' representation." *The Sharpest Sight* was reviewed as an American Indian novel in the *New York Times Book Review,* but his next novel, *Bone Game*, was featured in its "Crime" column.[2]

No one makes Owens's rationale for appropriating familiar thriller plots clearer than Uncle Luther, dream sender and elder humorist of *The Sharpest Sight*. When his confidante and companion, Onatima, asserts that except for her college education, Luther might still "be reading shoot-'em-ups instead of stories that count," Luther explains, with serious humor, that these stories do count, every bit as much as the classic fiction Onatima prefers. Their heroes are the real heroes of the dominant culture—irresponsible Kids like Billy the Kid and the Comanche Kid with no homes and no families, in whose image Indian identity has been configured by Euro-Americans. "That's why they made up all the great-white-father stuff," Uncle Luther insists, "to turn us into kids so's we couldn't know who we really was."[3]

Mrs. John Edwards, the Black Mountain Apache dream sender of *Dark River* who once married a white preacher, also has a passion for thrillers. Her compatriots, Shorty Luke and anthropologist Avrum Goldberg, are at a loss to understand her love of detective novels. Avrum is simply bored by the plot repetition. That's not the problem for Shorty, who frankly admits, "We tell the same stories all the time. My grandmother told me, and I tell my kids and grandkids. Always the same stories from the creation and the way things used to be. But nobody ever gets tired of hearing them. It's always like you're hearing the story for the first time." For Shorty, the problem with detective stories may well be their epistemological grounding. He candidly admits to Avrum, "I tried to read one of those, but I didn't get it."[4]

Owens's strategic appropriation of the thriller is perhaps best characterized as an act of survivance, to use Gerald Vizenor's term: "more than survival, more than endurance or mere response; the stories of survivance are an active presence . . . an active repudiation of dominance, tragedy, and victimry."[5] Surrounded by the greed, lust, and need for revenge that drive the plots of most thrillers and guided by elders with a quick wit and a bawdy sense of humor, Owens's characters live full, contemporary lives in a multicultural society where they (and everyone else) are exposed to a heavy dose of popular culture. In *Nightland,* for example, Billy Keene proves to be an avid reader of personal classifieds though he is promptly shot down by his old buddy, Will Striker, when he tries to share his interest. The scene is revealing because it positions Native people in an evolving present while showcasing personal difference. It stands as a denial of monolithic as well as static identities. No one in this novel is trapped in the past, not even Grampa Siquani, who, at the age or three- or four-hundred years, finally learns to drive.

Owens was certainly not the first Native writer to write in the tradition of genre fiction. He was working in a tradition pioneered by John Rollin Ridge in the first American Indian novel, *The Life and Adventures of Joaquin Murieta, the Celebrated California Bandit,* with its bandit hero hell-bent on revenge against the Americans who have stolen his land, raped his lady, and killed his brother. Three-quarters of a century later, Mourning Dove set out to rehabilitate the stereotype of the notoriously mistrusted half-breed in *Cogwea, the Half-Blood: A Depiction of the Great Montana Cattle Range,* adapting the Western romance and giving the lead role to a young woman. Owens paid tribute to both writers, not only in *Other Destinies* but also in *Mixedblood Messages* and *I Hear the Train.* Their appropriations exemplify for him one way that Native novelists have shaped the English language to make it bear the burden of Native experience.

The strategy is as subversive in Owens's hands as it was in the hands of his predecessors, for it facilitates critique both of contemporary cultural values and of the Native stereotypes being created anew in American popular culture for yet another generation, whether in the best-selling "Navajo" mysteries of Tony Hillerman or the cinematic warrior heroics of the mixed-blood Apache Rambo. The dominant culture is always popular culture, as Owens and his characters are keenly aware. Stereotypes, however, are but the tip of an ideological iceberg. Effecting real change depends upon altering the underlying ideology, and this is not accomplished by shooting your television, a tactic that *Nightland*'s small-time Cherokee rancher Will Striker tries. It is accomplished through repeated exposure to alternative ideologies. Using the familiar lens of the thriller genre, Owens gives readers repeated opportunities to interrogate cultural difference and, potentially, a reading experience that has much in common with traditional Native storytelling.

Owens, indeed, frequently grounds his plots in tribal stories. As Cole McCurtain carries his brother's bones east to Mississippi from the far west in *The Sharpest Sight,* he enacts the migration that grounds Choctaw tribal identity. In *Nightland,* Owens's Cherokee New Mexicans simultaneously enact their roles as marginal ranchers and the Thunder Boys, whose story gives ethical dimension to Cherokee life and identity. In *Dark River,* Mrs. Edwards, Avrum Goldberg, Shorty Luke, and Domingo Perez are more than simply Apache elders. They are the four persons without parents of Apache story—Black Metal

Old Man, Big Black Spider, Black Whirlwind, and Mirage. Alternatively, or simultaneously, Mrs. Edwards, Avrum, and Shorty can be read as the three First Persons, for the number of original people varies from band to band among the Apaches.[6]

It is the experience of the familiar, however, that connects thriller readers and Native listeners. Both genre fiction and Native story incorporate such a high degree of predictability that great significance inheres in slight variation. Because they know the traditional stories already, Karl Kroeber postulates that tribal listeners derive new meaning from the subtle or not-so-subtle differences in the telling. In much the same way, experienced readers of formula fiction come to appreciate the new twists in the handling of formulaic plots, developing, as John Cawelti suggests, an increased "capacity for understanding and enjoying the details of a work."[7] Intimate knowledge of a thriller subgenre also engages readers in its unspoken cultural dimensions.

While Native oral tradition seems at the opposite end of any spectrum from American popular fiction, some important similarities between them should be noted. First, the defining aesthetic of both the thriller and the traditional Native story is their focus on action. As Cawelti notes, "It is almost a cliche that formulaic works stress action and plot, particularly of a violent and exciting sort, i.e., actions involving danger or sex or both." What happens to move the story along is, indeed, far more important than any subtleties of character psychology. In *Artistry in Native American Myths*, Kroeber notes that in the case of Native oral story, the singular focus on plot excludes not only description but "motive analysis, philosophizing, and figures of speech."[8]

Beyond this, both thriller fiction and traditional Native story are grounded in a moral vision. Like the ironic, laughter-provoking trickster story, the thriller seems to emphasize the reverse of culturally accepted moral norms through its glorification of immorality and violence. Allowing the reader to explore "the boundary between the permitted and the forbidden and to experience in a carefully controlled way the possibility of stepping across this boundary" is the preeminent function of the thriller villain, according to Cawelti.[9] His acts, however, are ultimately contained by the moral code that motivates the hero to action. Trickster, on the other hand, much given to sex and violence, often suffers the natural consequences of his own actions, which retain their ability to teach by negative example because of a tribal community's shared moral perspective.

The use of formulaic plots by hundreds of writers, moreover, gives them a communal quality more akin to Native oral story than the original plots of literary fiction. Owens deeply admired the communal quality of the "'authorless' text" in Leslie Silko's *Ceremony* and sought to develop it in his own work.[10] While one dimension of his fictional technique involves balancing genre plot and traditional tribal story, in the spirit delineated by Alan Velie in an earlier essay in this text (see chapter 5), Owens also enhanced the communal nature of his work by weaving in stories by Euro-American and Native writers—notably Silko, Erdrich, Vizenor, and Welch—until his last novel, *Dark River,* truly approaches the condition of authorlessness.

Despite the distinctions that can be drawn between the murder mystery, the tale of supernatural horror, the Western, and the war story, the four permutations of the thriller have much in common. Lust, greed, and anger, often manifesting itself through revenge, almost always set the thriller plot in motion, while the story finds moral resolution in the actions of a chaste (or, at the very least, sexually reticent) hero, traditionally male, whose chastity signals his high moral purpose and who often acts alone, beyond the fears, foolishness, and immorality of his fellow mortals. Thrillers thus enhance the twin ideological foundations of the modern Western world, individualism and private property rights. Jay Gurian, indeed, explicitly describes the hero of the Western as "a commercial extension of the drive for private property." When all is said and done, what the thriller hero ultimately quests for is restoration of the status quo. His task demands a tone of high seriousness, for justice must be served and offenders duly punished.[11]

While making the theft or appropriation of Native lands a central feature of his evolving oeuvre, and one closely tied to the thriller's ideological grounding, Owens inscribes Native difference in his thriller novels in four key ways. First, he refuses to privilege individual heroism. In *The Sharpest Sight* and the three novels that follow it, individual, self-motivated acts are often villainous, while heroic moral actions are typically cooperative ventures. Second, he offers an alternative vision of justice and often a negative view of the American justice system at odds with the dominant culture norm. Third, Owens makes the wannabe Indian a principal villain in his texts. Finally, taking a cue from the Native elders who make their moral points through trickster irony, he uses the ironic humor of elder characters to underscore the most important lessons of the text, lessons in community responsibility and reciprocal relationship.

Subverting the popular thriller to make it bear the burden of Native experience is necessarily a two-part process. It first requires deconstruction of the familiar gendered stereotypes that render young Native men either the white man's sworn enemy or his faithful helper, that make young women both desirable and sexually available to white heroes, that make old men the exclusive source of tribal wisdom, old women earth mothers, and half-breeds (and by extension, all mixed-bloods) eternally distrusted. Then, simultaneously, it requires that the writer convey for a readership both Indian and white a sense of "who we really was," to quote Uncle Luther—and still are, it might be added.[12]

In his novels, Owens does not simply substitute racial others for white heroes. He reconceptualizes the iconic thriller protagonist, the rugged individualist perennially marked, John Cawelti suggests, by his "unsullied isolation" with no one but himself to depend upon, physically and emotionally. Beginning in *The Sharpest Sight,* Owens's heroes work together. *Nightland,* created for the mass market, stands out as the exception. Here Will Striker, somewhat estranged from his best buddy, looks reassuringly familiar as the loner hero who manages to kill everyone who is trying to kill him, even though Grampa Siquani, recalling an old Cherokee story, insists, "A man by himself gets into trouble, like old Kanati."[13] Will's status as a loner is, in fact, cured in the end by his wife's return home and Grampa's decision to move in with them. In *The Sharpest Sight, Bone Game,* and *Dark River,* however, Owens often pairs characters, sometimes brothers or good friends as in many Native origin stories, sometimes uncle and nephew. Almost any combination is possible, and often there are multiple pairings within the same text. These pairs effectively displace the lone hero from center stage.

Simultaneously, Owens features what might be termed a group hero, suggesting the human interdependence that sustains tribal communities. In *The Sharpest Sight,* three elders, Uncle Luther, Onatima, and El Viejo, provide the will to action, while the younger characters, including Cole and Hoey McCurtain, deputy sheriff Mundo Morales, and his nemesis, Jessard Deal, act. It takes all of them, indeed, to enact the many variants of justice depicted in this novel, ranging from vigilante justice to justice tempered with mercy. Perhaps the most important feature of Owens's group hero is that the group always extends beyond ties of blood and tribe. Mundo, El Viejo, and Jessard are every bit as important to the resolution of the plot as the Choctaw mixed-bloods. Their inclusion enables Owens, even as he showcases clear cultural similarities, to explore issues of difference, which must realistically be accounted for in the world as it has come to be. Onatima, a powerful dream sender in her own right with broad experience in the nontribal world, points out to Uncle Luther that a single worldview is not sufficient to the task at hand and that El Viejo's belief that Diana Nemi is a witch, contrary to Luther's belief, will have significant impact on the outcome of the story.

While it is easy to think of *The Sharpest Sight* as Cole McCurtain's story, as his personal quest for his brother's bones and the meaning of his Choctaw identity, a close look reveals just how little action Cole is responsible for. Punching FBI agent and Indian "authority" Lee Scott for telling Indian jokes is the sole action Cole initiates in the entire novel. While perhaps forgivable under the circumstances, this lone act is uncharacteristic. More characteristically throughout this novel, Cole simply obeys his elders, which is perfectly appropriate for a young Indian man. Cole's flight to Mississippi as a draft resister is his father's idea. He returns to California in FBI custody to begin the search for his brother's bones at the behest of Uncle Luther and Onatima.

While he is part of a Native family, Cole is also paired with Mundo Morales, Cole's mirror image in discovering his own mixed heritage. To the readers of traditional detective fiction, Mundo, the independent lawman with a mind of his own, is the obvious candidate for hero, but he, too, breaks the mold. The deputy sheriff declares his stake in solving his best friend's murder, but when he speaks the much-used line about bringing the killer to justice, it rings false even to his own ears. Like Cole, what Mundo really wants is to find Attis's body. His values make him part of the McCurtain family, and when he goes after Jessard Deal for the rape of Diana Nemi, he is saved in a barroom brawl by Cole's father. Here Hoey McCurtain comes closer to traditional heroics than either Cole or Mundo, but his prayers over Diana in the sweat, wordless though they are, have already set Hoey apart from violent heroes or lawmen who privilege retribution over compassion. It takes every man in this novel, and two women as well, to enact justice in its many permutations.

In *Bone Game*, Owens creates an intertribal group hero while focusing on two among the many heroic pairs. Even as the cross-dressing Navajo anthropologist Alex Yazzie and Cole McCurtain's daughter confront the serial murderers in Santa Cruz, Uncle Luther and Hoey provide reciprocal service in the Navajo community, rescuing Katherine Begay from sexual enslavement in California. This pair reverses not only the route across New Mexico but the trajectory that took *Ceremony*'s Helen Jean deeper and deeper into assimilationist degradation. Unlike the lone Tayo, Luther and Hoey take full responsibility for enacting justice. Kate's three kidnappers are punished, but not by Gallup law enforcement—Uncle Luther sees no reason to trust them—and not until after they have been made the butt of Uncle Luther's wickedly male elder humor, held captive by a piss-hex at the urinal in a local bar. Readers are clearly invited to remember the graffito found by the confused protagonist of *Winter in the Blood* in the bathroom of another bar: "Why are you looking up here? The joke's in your hand." Real men, this story hints, do not victimize women. Luther advocates shooting the kidnappers on the spot, telling Hoey, "You shoot those witches, and they ain't going to do this kind of stuff anymore. Others will, there's so many, but these particular ones won't."[14] In the end, Hoey reminds Uncle Luther that trying to kill evil is the white man's way, and they leave the naked perps stuck in the middle of nowhere. The story of their shame will be punishment enough.

Justice in Santa Cruz, however, where Hoey and Uncle Luther are headed and where two serial murderers are operating independently, depends upon every member of the close-knit community surrounding a much older Cole McCurtain, including one of the murderers and Cole himself. Over beers, Alex Yazzie, in a black knit dress, articulates for Cole what might be seen as the fundamental premise of the group hero, a principle contrary to the very notion of the heroic individual: "We all need help."[15] Indeed, Alex's one attempt at lone heroics nearly gets him killed despite his black belt in karate. Independent action is always dangerous in this novel. Cole takes a huge risk when he steps in to save his daughter, endangered by her own independent nature. Abby has already killed her kidnapper, saving herself from rape, but no gun can save her from her kidnapper's spirit double, still consumed by rage and a fierce desire for revenge against the land theft and the physical and sexual abuse perpetrated by the Spanish mission enterprise. Speaking his name—Venancio Assisara—and breaking tribal prohibition, Cole tells the story of his life in its most abbreviated form, bringing a long-forgotten injustice to light.

The premier example of the group hero in Owens's fiction, however, comes in his last novel, *Dark River*, where Owens counterpoints a contemporary casino-owning tribe against a mixed-blood hero of the traditional thriller mold. Jake Nashoba, the lone Choctaw mixed-blood on the fictional Black Mountain Apache reservation, is *The Searchers*' Ethan Edwards and Rambo rolled into one. Jake is a Vietnam vet of unstinting courage whose psychic wounds remain unhealed a quarter century after the war's end. The locals, who have a long history of accepting outsiders into the tribe—their most traditional current member, indeed, a Jewish anthropologist from New York— call him Lone Ranger and send him off to patrol the Dark River canyon to protect themselves both from his ghost sickness and his extreme individualism. A challenge to Jake's heroic stature, orchestrated by a maverick militia ideologue, ultimately reveals to Jake that he is far from alone. The fight for his life, first of all, affirms his relationship with the young granddaughter he has set out to rescue. "Just remember," Jake tells Alison, now an acknowledged warrior in the tradition of Geronimo's sister Lozen, "that these men are the enemy, mine and yours because you're related to me."[16]

This threat to Jake's life also constellates a collective effort that brings together key members of the Black Mountain community and outsiders, including a French woman named Sandrine Le Bris who has bought a very untraditional Apache vision quest from a young Black Mountain entrepreneur, and the archvillain himself. This group hero, however, never quite rises to its heroic task, at least not in any straightforward traditional sense. Despite the courageous acts of Sandrine and her protégé Alison and the elder pair enacting the traditional heroics of Monster Slayer and Child of Water, no one can save Jake Nashoba. Such an ending contradicts the expectations of veteran thriller readers for whom victory over death is "[p]erhaps the basic moral fantasy implicit in this type of story."[17] Discovering that he does, indeed, have relatives makes Jake's death especially poignant, yet justice for his killer remains an uncertain proposition. In the depths of a canyon reminiscent of those where many Apaches were slaughtered by white invaders, the group tries out old thriller endings, rejecting each in turn, and imagines new ones to end the holocaust that has claimed eight lives. They cannot reach consensus, however, and ultimately cannot better the ending typical of contemporary American Indian novels, what William Bevis has called "homing in." This ending akin to a beginning quite simply deconstructs the thriller's focus on endings. Individuals may die, but the community connected by story continues in spite of the tragedies it endures. This is the comedy of survivance. The Black Mountain group heads home, villain in tow, for without the villain, indeed, there is no story, no survivance.

If the expectation of genre fiction readers is that justice will be served, the good guys winning with all loose ends neatly tied up in the process, justice for Owens is largely accidental, and there are always loose ends. Further, Owens insists that readers consider what justice means for Native peoples, present and past. Never in his fiction is justice the consequence of law. As Uncle Luther tells Hoey in *Bone Game*, "The police don't care about Indians."[18] If the Native community benefits when Hoey and Luther design a nonlethal punishment to fit the crime of sexual predation, in a Santa Cruz terrorized by serial murders, justice is the result of unpremeditated impulse. One serial killer kills the second when his own plans are threatened, Abby McCurtain shoots this rapist/killer in self-defense, and Cole speaks the unspeakable to save his beloved daughter from the evil gambler, revealing in the process the sordid history of injustice to indigenous Californians.

In this encounter with dream sender Venancio Asisara, Owens offers for the second time in this novel a lesson distinctly at odds with the traditional expectations of genre fiction readers—that evil itself cannot be killed. The necessary inaction that Cole McCurtain teaches Abby at the moment she is about to play the gambler's game is critical to understanding the world from a tribal perspective. Owens also offers another lesson at odds with the traditional expectations of genre fiction readers—that words may have greater power than violence. Words bring the indigenous world into being. When Cole breaks the Ohlone taboo and speaks the gambler's name, Asisara responds with his own brief words, *"Eran muy crueles,"* thereby revealing the truth of the colonial enterprise.[19] He retires from the scene but may return at any time should his story ever again be forgotten.

Evil cannot ultimately be killed in *Dark River* either. Here we look close up at the creaky machinery of representation and the illusory realism of fictions, not the stuff of traditional thriller endings, where maintaining illusion is considered paramount. With expert help from retired Hollywood actor Shorty Luke, Owens's characters experiment with the magical realism of cinematography. They debate, try out, and discard several alternative endings, including the killing of militia archvillain Lee Jensen by the second villain of the piece, the wheeler-dealer tribal chairman with a Harvard M.B.A. Jensen, who even calls himself "the bad guy," is an active and vitally self-interested participant in the debate. He naturally advocates for villain-kill-all and go free. However, two women, warriors in the tradition of Lozen, Maxine Hong Kingston, and the fictional Vivian Twostar, heteroglot karate expert of *The Crown of Columbus,* give the fictional Black Mountain tribe a degree of control by capturing the evil gambler in his militia ideologue guise. New plots for Natives become possible, Owens suggests, but only when loner heroes like Jake Nashoba discover that death is not the end of the story, just the end of one particular chapter.

Owens also complicates the dominant culture's notion of justice by weaving traditional, tribally specific notions of justice into his plots. From the perspective of the thriller justice, the conclusion of *The Sharpest Sight* is highly problematic, as young Diana Nemi, who has masterminded the murder of Attis McCurtain, heads off to the University of California, Berkeley, instead of to jail. Femme fatale that she is in the best *noir* tradition, she will never be called to face charges in court, all knowledge of her guilt forever buried with barkeeper Jessard Deal. Considered from the traditional Choctaw perspective, however, justice is served, though in an unusually roundabout way. Old-style Choctaw justice demanded an eye for an eye: for murder, the death of either the murderer or a member of his family exacted by a member of the victim's family. Attis's death, then, masterminded by Diana, would atone for Jenna's. However, Diana has also committed another crime in sexually betraying her sister with Attis. Among the Choctaw, according to John Reed Swanton, fornication was traditionally punishable by a notoriously brutal public gang rape.[20] Diana's punishment for her transgression is rape by Jessard Deal. Deal, however, believes he is avenging his friend's murder, but this may be only an excuse, for Jessard glories in unending violence, the kind of violence that contemporary Choctaw Hoey McCurtain shuns when he heals Diana in the sweat lodge and sends Cole to Mississippi as a draft resister. Revenge to the death of the last man is a white plotline, and Jessard Deal is no Indian but a wannabe with clear links to revenge. His horse, like archavenger Joaquin Murieta's, is named Bucephalus.

In Owens's novels, the relationship between good and evil is also far more complex than in the typical genre thriller. No one is without guilt. Even in *Nightland,* written for the mass market, where the obvious bad guys, including the Pueblo crime family, their wannabe-Indian enforcer, and the Apache *femme fatale,* all die, the good guys who survive are, without exception, morally flawed. Despite his compunctions about taking the money that has fallen out of the sky, Will Striker does not hesitate to hide evidence to protect himself when he kills the man sent to recover it. His crime, committed in self-defense, remains hidden only through the complicity of the local sheriff. Even Grampa Siquani, the moral center of the novel, could be arraigned on charges of concealing a body. Moreover, Paco Ortega has no interest in the profits from his illicit drug operation. He lives no differently from any other member of his modest Pueblo community. His sole motivation is revenge for the theft of Indian land. The evil of Duane Scales, the gang's Cajun-black Irish hit man, is tempered by a recognizably benevolent commitment to the environment. He has no kind words for ongoing experiments to fill empty niches in the western New Mexico ecosystem with species native to other continents, for ranchers who graze their cattle on public lands, for wolf extermination, or for the prospect of an Apache nuclear waste disposal site.

Scales is but one of a series of wannabe Indians that populate Owens's thrillers, always in the bad-guy role. Their inclusion offers readers a morally inflected mirror for interrogating both themselves and a range of Indian stereotypes, first and foremost perhaps, the brutal savage. Jessard Deal and Duane Scales are prime examples of the wannabe villain, their violence beyond the pale. *The Sharpest Sight*'s FBI agent Lee Scott, *Bone Game*'s earth protector Robert Malin, and *Dark River*'s militia ideologue Lee Jensen are more complex. Scott, in a parody of the federal-local conflict showcased in Tony

Hillerman's mysteries, has already been precast as the bad guy outsider. It is his pompous confidence in his knowledge about Indians, based on personal experience with one or two, that makes him really insidious, however, and a prime candidate for Uncle Luther's trickery. When all is said and done, Scott cannot even get himself out of the woods, a clear warning to white readers who think they know their way around Indian Country.

Malin, a non-Native sun dancer and true believer, has committed himself to the study and practice of Native spirituality, specifically Lakota spirituality, yet he knows only half the story. He has no understanding of its inherent dangers and remains convinced that his brutal murders are justified, sacrifices necessary to stave off a disastrous earthquake. Malin's discussion with Cole about which version of Black Elk's story to teach first underscores his own blind spot for readers who know how John Neihardt's editorial hand shaped *Black Elk Speaks*. The story recovered by Raymond DeMallie in *The Sixth Grandfather*, Black Elk's conscious rejection of Lakota spirituality in favor of Catholicism, calls the very notion of authentic traditionalism into question. In *Dark River*, privileging a Native insider perspective, Owens conceptualizes both the wannabe and the stereotype in an even more complex way. Jake Nashoba denies his own tribal identity outright, even though he continues to make his home in a reservation community rather than the white world. The Lone Ranger insists to Mrs. Edwards, "Look, Grandmother, I'm no Indian."[21] The tribal elder in question knows better, but Jake has a long learning curve. Like the German-Apache Rambo, Jake slips neatly into a warrior identity without a tribal affiliation, and it is this identity that his nemesis, Lee Jensen, seeks to emulate. Beating Jake at his own game, of course, makes Jensen, the de facto wannabe, a better Indian than the Indians.

Perhaps Owens's most important contribution to reshaping thriller fiction as a vehicle of Native survivance comes in the creation of Native elders who are simultaneously sources of wisdom and humor. Unlike the ultraserious stereotypical sage elder, Uncle Luther, Grampa Siquani, and Shorty Luke are often downright bawdy in precisely the way Keith Basso remembers the elder Western Apache mentor who teased him mercilessly in public about his sex life. This is the kind of tradition almost altogether absent in non-Native writing about Indians. Even Onatima is wryly humorous on the subject of men's private lives. "Indian male menopause is a terrible thing," she admonishes Cole in *Bone Game*. She also insists that he quit drinking alcohol, calling it "the worst Indian cliché of all."[22]

It is a cliché that Tony Hillerman certainly exploits. When he introduces Navajo criminals into his mysteries for the first time in *Coyote Waits* and *Sacred Clowns*, their sole criminal motivation is alcohol. Indeed, in Hillerman's oeuvre, no Indian drinks who is not a criminal. It would be difficult to find another detective novel that ties criminal motivation to alcohol. Greed and revenge are more typical motivations, and these are the motivations of all

Owens's Indian criminals, at least those who are not engaged in acts of civil disobedience. Most of Owens's Indian characters do, in fact, drink, though others like Uncle Luther do not. The traditional wisdom that Onatima conveys about alcohol lies in knowing when to stop.

Tribal wisdom is always serious business in Hillerman's novels, where sex never enters the scene and which always contain a textbook definition of the Navajo concept of *hohzho,* in a word, balance. Owens revels in Hillerman parodies. In one scene in *Nightland,* Billy Keene turns up at Will Striker's house with a copy of the personals from an Albuquerque tabloid and waxes enthusiastic about an ad from a "nice girl" seeking "to explore sexual fantasies such as two men at once." Billy, reframing Grampa Siquani's principal argument in favor of marriage, is careful to explain why he finds this ad so interesting: "See, I've been thinking about you out here all alone, Will. It's not natural. A man needs balance."[23]

The elders' lessons become more complex as Owens's oeuvre develops. In *Dark River,* the Black Mountain elders strive to convey the lesson at the very heart of the tribal worldview and directly contrary to profit-driven capitalist exploitation. Their immediate goal is to stop both the tribally sponsored, guided trophy-elk hunts that carry a fee of $10,500 and the under-the-table sale of permits lining the pockets of the tribal chairman and his head game warden. Concerned about the ethical relationship between humans and animals, the elders begin poaching trophy elk. Leaving the high-value trophy heads behind and distributing the meat to those in need through what Shorty calls "our own little food bank," they bypass the modern cash economy altogether while extending a network of loyalties and reciprocal obligations. Their "poaching" carries no small lesson in traditional ethics and trickster compassion for anyone with the slightest inkling of what is going on. Not only is their redistribution of food resources traditional, but so is the story that grounds their actions. The elders enact an updated version of the Jicarilla Apache origin story. That elk and deer agree to give their meat to assure Apache survival is an act of reciprocal responsibility that grows out of the story of the elk monster whose looks could kill.[24]

Owens's elders are also traditional in their close connection to the spirit world. Owens reminds us in *Other Destinies* that for Native people, contrary to Western logical positivism, the dream world and the waking world are one. In his novels, though, even a lesson in comparative metaphysics can make us laugh, a prime example of forging authenticity "out of resistance to the 'authentic' representation."[25] Uncle Luther cannot effectively intervene in the events being played out in California in *The Sharpest Sight* until, with Onatima's help, he puzzles his way through the Christian understanding of the spirit world. This is as much a mystery as the murder of Attis McCurtain. It is finally Onatima who points out that the Catholic worldview and the Native worldview are at loggerheads and that Uncle Luther is going to have to take this fact into account if he is to help Cole. In a slapstick moment in *Nightland*, the material and spiritual worlds collide like the car and the garage door Grampa Siquani backs through as he learns to drive under the tutelage of the ghost of Arturo Cruz. Here, even the serious matter of returning Arturo's bones to the earth becomes an act of survivance at odds with stereotyped notions of shamanic power and Indian nobility.

Appealing to America's preference for branding, Hillerman frequently uses the term "traditional" to stamp his texts with an aura of authentic Indianness. Alternatively, he may provide an academic frame for a discussion of Indian traditionalism, as he does in *Coyote Waits*, where linguists, historians, and a comparative mythologist all have ties to his chief suspect, a shaman named Ashie Pinto. This old man never has the opportunity to speak for himself. Even his murder confession is lost in translation. Readers hear only his academically authentic tape-recorded voice kept in the archives of an academic library. Real Indians do not need to explain themselves to anyone, Owens suggests in *Bone Game*. When Alex asks if Cole wants to know any more about seven arrows he is making, Cole declines. "No?" Alex responds, "I guess you might really be an Indian. White people always want to know all the mystical secrets. All the Indian hocus-pocus."[26] What the very premise of this thriller ultimately makes clear is that the spiritual world beyond material reality is not necessarily benign. Furthermore, in Owens's work, traditionalism is no guarantee of high moral purpose. The patriarch of *Nightland*'s Pueblo crime family couldn't look more traditional.

In *Dark River*, Owens is not even afraid to poke fun at one of the traditional taboos of thriller writing, pointing a finger directly in Tony Hillerman's direction. Whether in reviews or on *Nightland*'s jacket blurb, Owens was unable to escape comparison with his fellow New Mexican—"[t]he most successful 'Indian' writer of all," Owens once suggested—with no small irony. Hillerman has provided the armchair tour of Indian Country that Owens explicitly resisted. "Don't make any facile jokes," orders the hovering spirit of Jessie James, Sandrine Le Bris's spirit guide, upon the capture of archvillain Lee Jensen in the Dark River canyon. "Violent scenes shouldn't be tempered with wit or jokes, or they lose their force, right, Uncle Luke?" By infusing the thriller with a spirit of comedy, Owens creates a community of readers carried by their laughter across cultural boundaries, tricked simultaneously into self-awareness and an awareness of normally hidden ideological inscriptions. As Owens himself once noted, "Literary terrorism is preferable to literary tourism."[27]

NOTES

1. Owens, "Story of a Talk," in *I Hear the Train*, p. 250.
2. Howard, "Novel Reading," p. 1; Owens, *Mixedblood Messages*, p. 13; Kincaid, "Who Gets to Tell Their Stories?" pp. 1, 24–29; Stasio, "Crime," p. 24.

3. Owens, *Sharpest Sight*, p. 109.

4. Owens, *Dark River*, p. 257.

5. Vizenor, *Fugitive Poses*, p. 15.

6. For an elaborated discussion of this dimension of Owens's fiction, see Dwyer, "Syncretic Impulse," pp. 48–49, and Helstern, "*Nightland* and the Mythic West," pp. 61–66. See also Goddard, *Myths and Tales*, pp. 7–26.

7. Kroeber, *Artistry in Native American Myths*, p. 69; Cawelti, *Adventure, Mystery, and Romance*, p. 9.

8. Cawelti, *Adventure, Mystery, and Romance*, p. 14; Kroeber, *Artistry in Native American Myths*, p. 70.

9. Cawelti, *Adventure, Mystery, ad Romance*, p. 35.

10. Owens, *Other Destinies*, p. 169.

11. Gurian, *Western American Writing*, p. 7; Cawelti, *Adventure, Mystery, and Romance*, p. 35.

12. Owens, *Sharpest Sight*, p. 109.

13. Cawelti, *Adventure, Mystery, and Romance*, p. 151; Owens, *Nightland*, p. 48.

14. Welch, *Winter in the Blood*, p. 92; Owens, *Bone Game*, p. 125.

15. Owens, *Bone Game*, p. 50.

16. Owens, *Dark River*, p. 196.

17. Cawelti, *Adventure, Mystery, and Romance*, p. 40.

18. Owens, *Bone Game*, p. 117.

19. Ibid., p. 241.

20. Swanton, *Source Materials*, pp. 104–110.

21. Owens, *Dark River*, p. 42.

22. Basso, *Wisdom Sits in Places*, p. 41; Owens, *Bone Game*, p.145.

23. Owens, *Nightland*, p. 66.

24. Owens, *Dark River*, p. 67; Opler, *Myths and Tales of the Jicarilla Apache Indians*, p. 61.

25. Owens, *Other Destinies*, p. 248; *Mixedblood Messages*, p. 13.

26. Owens, *Bone Game*, p. 30.

27. Owens, *Mixedblood Messages*, p. 16; *Dark River*, p. 281; *Mixedblood Messages*, p. 46.

WORKS CITED

Basso, Keith. *Wisdom Sits in Places: Landscape and Language among the Western Apache*. Albuquerque: University of New Mexico Press, 1996.

Bevis, William. "Native American Novels: Homing In." In *Recovering the Word: Essays on Native American Literature*. Edited by Brian Swann and Arnold Krupat. Berkeley: University of California Press, 1987, 580–620.

Cawelti, John. *Adventure, Mystery, and Romance: Formula Stories as Art and Popular Culture*. Chicago: University of Chicago Press, 1976.

DeMallie, Raymond J., ed. *The Sixth Grandfather: Black Elk's Teachings Given to John G. Neihardt*. Lincoln: University of Nebraska Press, 1984.

Dwyer, Margeret. "The Syncretic Impulse: Louis Owens' Use of Autobiography, Ethnology, and Blended Mythologies in *The Sharpest Sight*." *Studies in American Indian Literatures* 10:2 (Summer 1998), 43–60.

Goddard, Pliny Earle. *Myths and Tales from the San Carlos Apache*. Anthropological Papers of the American Museum of Natural History. 24, Part 1. New York: American Museum of Natural History, 1920, 7–26.

Gurian, Jay. *Western American Writing: Tradition and Promise*. Deland, Fla.: Everett/Edwards, 1975.

Helstern, Linda. "*Nightland* and the Mythic West." *Studies in American Indian Literatures* 10:2 (Summer 1998), 61–78.

Hillerman, Tony. *Coyote Waits*. New York: Harper, 1990.

———. *Sacred Clowns*. New York: Harper, 1993.

Howard, Jennifer, "Novel Reading." Review of *The Sharpest Sight*, by Louis Owens. *Washington Post Book World*, April 5, 1992, 11.

Kincaid, James R. "Who Gets to Tell Their Stories?" Review of *Winged Words: American Indian Writers Speak* by Laura Coltelli (among other books reviewed in same piece). *New York Times Book Review*, May 3, 1992, 1, 24-29.

Kroeber, Karl. *Artistry in Native American Myths*. Lincoln: University of Nebraska Press, 1998.

Opler, Morris Edward. *Myths and Tales of the Jicarilla Apache Indians*. 1938. New York: Dover, 1994.

Owens, Louis. *Bone Game*. Norman: University of Oklahoma Press, 1994.

———. *Dark River*. Norman: University of Oklahoma Press, 1999.

———. *I Hear the Train: Reflections, Inventions, Refractions*. Norman: University of Oklahoma Press, 2001.

———. *Mixedblood Messages: Literature, Film, Family, Place*. Norman: University of Oklahoma, 1998.

———. *Nightland*. New York: Dutton, 1996.

———. *Other Destinies: Understanding the American Indian Novel*. Norman: University of Oklahoma Press, 1992.

———. *The Sharpest Sight*. Norman: University of Oklahoma Press, 1992.

Silko, Leslie Marmon. *Ceremony*. New York: Viking, 1977.

Stasio, Marilyn. "Crime." Review of *Bone Game* by Louis Owens. *New York Times Book Review*, October 23, 1994, 24.

Swanton, John Reed. *Source Material for the Social and Ceremonial Life of the Choctaw Indians*. Smithsonian Institution Bureau of American Ethnology, Bulletin 103. Washington: U.S. Government Printing Office, 1931.

Vizenor, Gerald. *Fugitive Poses: Native American Indian Scenes of Absence and Presence*. Lincoln: University of Nebraska Press, 1998.

Welch, James. *Winter in the Blood*. 1974. New York: Penguin, 1986.

11

"We've been stuck in place since *House Made of Dawn*"

Sherman Alexie and the Native American Renaissance

JOHN GAMBER

I draw my title from a quote that Sherman Alexie gave in an interview published in *Studies in American Indian Literatures*'s 1997 special issue devoted to the Spokane/Coeur d'Alene novelist, essayist, screenwriter, and poet (Purdy, 9). In that interview, Alexie laments the lack of literary innovation in Native American literature since N. Scott Momaday's field-changing novel was published and received the Pulitzer Prize in 1969. I read Sherman Alexie's work as a new phase of the Native American Renaissance (NAR), particularly in terms of his popular success. Alexie observes, "I'm always going to sell 50–75,000 copies of my books" (Peterson, 108), and of his primary readership: "College-educated, middle-class white women is the largest group by far" (124). Alexie has consciously parted with some of the classic elements of the literature of the NAR, particularly the devotion to a sacred landscape, the tragedy of the homing plot, and the privileging of the mixed-blood protagonist. Joshua B. Nelson calls this Alexie's "stark refusal to write again what Momaday, Silko, or anyone else has already written" (44).

Alexie works against these replications in part because of the tropes of tragedy he reads in much of Native American literature. "We write about being humiliated a lot. And that takes physical forms, emotional forms, and mental forms. I think Native literature is the literature of humiliation and shame" (Peterson, 146). However, Alexie's texts also focus on many of the same themes that NAR novels treat, including the definition of Indian identities, intercultural connections, and relocation. Moreover, while his earlier texts are often read as being particularly focused on the tragic (especially in terms of his portrayals of Native alcoholism, anger, and violence), and his later texts as being overly optimistic and assimilationist, I would like to argue that the themes of tragedy and despair, coupled with those of redemption and hope, exist throughout the entire body of his work.

In a review of Alexie's *Reservation Blues*—a review that might just as easily be termed an article—Gloria Bird asserts that elements of the novel "contribute to an exaggerated version of reservation life, one that perpetuates many of the stereotypes of native people and presents problems for native and nonnative readers alike" (47). Bird lists these problems, which range from misrepresenting the "core of native community" by portraying a cast of "misfits: social and cultural anomalies" (49),[1] to a troubling portrayal of opinions about interracial dating, to a shallow relationship between characters and their landscapes (unlike those in Native American Renaissance foundations *House Made of Dawn* and *Ceremony*), pan-Indianism, and the "stereotypical image of the 'drunken Indian'" (51). Bird posits that Alexie's text lacks "a sense of responsibility to the culture [it is] attempting to represent" (52). As the most successful and popular Native author of our time, Alexie has always faced considerable scrutiny. Where his earlier texts are criticized for their anger and negative portrayals of Indian people and communities, his later works are maligned for their assimilation and tidiness.[2]

Kenneth Lincoln defines the NAR in the following terms: "The Native American renaissance here targeted, less than two decades of published Indian literature, is a written renewal of oral traditions translated into Western literary forms. Contemporary Indian literature is not so much new, then, as regenerate: transitional continuities emerging from the old" (8). Lincoln saw this two-decades-old movement not as some spontaneous generation of literature, but a part or extension of the traditional. The literary developments have been ongoing, but have been ignored by literary scholars who did not know of, or chose to ignore, the texts and literary discourses that have been present in Indian communities forever. "Our failures to hear," Lincoln said, "partly stem from the tragedies of tribal dislocation and mistranslation, partly from misconceptions about literature, partly from cultural indifference" (3). Alexie recognizes some truth to Lincoln's temporal description of the NAR: "I think we're young in terms of writing—I mean, I'm the second generation that ever put pen to paper—so we're still catching up" (Peterson, 165). Alexie is not literally the second generation of literate Natives, but a member of the second generation of the NAR, born of the authors Lincoln discusses in his text.

There are moments when Alexie's work responds to texts of the heavy hitters of the NAR. In response to *Ceremony*, for example, in particular its introductory note, where Silko writes: "I will tell you something about stories, / [he said] / They aren't just entertainment. / Don't be fooled. / They are all we have, you see, / all we have to fight off / illness and death" (2), Alexie's mouthpiece, Thomas Builds-the-Fire, realizes about himself, "More than anything, he wanted a story to heal the wounds, but he knew that his stories never healed anything" (*Reservation Blues*, 6).[3] Nonetheless, Alexie has on several occasions, in interviews and in his creative work, cited Native authors who have positively influenced him or whose work he appreciates. He dedicates *The Lone Ranger and Tonto Fistfight in Heaven* to "Adrian, Joy, Leslie, Simon, and all those Native writers whose words and music have made mine possible" (np). We can safely assume these refer to Louis, Harjo, Silko, and Ortiz, respectively. In *Indian Killer*, a white professor of anthropology teaching a Native American literature course includes only one putatively Native author on his syllabus, the fictional Jack Wilson, who claims to be from a tribe that no longer exists. Marie, the only Native student in the class, suggests the professor include Simon Ortiz, Roberta Whiteman, Luci Tapahonso, Elizabeth Woody, Ed Edmo, and Jeanette Armstrong (67, 68). In "The Search Engine" in *Ten Little Indians* another college student, Corliss, trying to track down a Spokane writer, emails Ortiz, Harjo, Silko and Louis (20).[4]

Alexie further refers to Louise Erdrich's influence on his style as one "of the models I had in writing . . . whose characters reappear in her books over and over again" (Peterson, 159). Erdrich stands as the most successful Native author apart from Alexie. In what I read as an homage, Alexie sets a section of *Flight* on the fictional Nannapush Indian Reservation—an allusion to Erdrich's recurring character, Nanapush. Nonetheless, Alexie differentiates his work from Erdrich's, noting, "Louise Erdrich's Indians are vastly different than my Indians. In fact, as I write, I think William Faulkner's white folks and my Indians are more alike than one would suspect" (Peterson, 190).

Alexie cites certain authors as particularly influential on his writing. In *Flight*, he grants Zits "three paperback novels (*Grapes of Wrath, Winter in the Blood*, and the *Dead Zone*)," by John Steinbeck, James Welch, and Stephen King, respectively, though the authors are not given in Alexie's novel (7). Alexie has frequently noted that reading *Winter in the Blood* changed his life, that he saw Indian characters who resembled Indian people he knew in that text for the first time in literature. "In terms of novels and fiction writing, James Welch is who I looked towards: works like the *Death of Jim Loney*, which is a great book, and *Winter in the Blood*. That was the first Indian novel I read where I recognized the characters" (Peterson, 56). We can see this affinity between Welch and Alexie in Lincoln's description of one of Welch's novels. According to Lincoln, "*The Death of Jim Loney* is more self-consciously interior than *Winter in the Blood*, less historically Blackfeet or Gros Ventre. There is little, if any, older ethnology" (168). This refusal to set a text in the distant past as well as to engage with ethnology in order to explain Native ceremonies or cultures runs throughout Alexie's work. Finally, in *Indian Killer*, in one of the most rewarding scenes for a Native literature devotee, Daniel Smith, the protagonist John Smith's adoptive father, encounters homeless Indian men who direct him toward "that Blackfeet guy, Loney," "that Laguna guy, what's his name? Tayo?" and "Abel, that Kiowa" (220). These characters represent the protagonists of NAR texts *The Death of Jim Loney, Ceremony, and House Made of Dawn*, respectively.[5]

Alexie is similarly interested in, if mostly seemingly annoyed by, Native American literary criticism and critics. Zits explains that the "rich and educated Indians" say things like "*The drunken Indian is just a racist cartoon*," and

"The lonely Indian is just a ghost in a ghost story" (*Flight*, 7). I am not able to find these quotes, though they sound rather like something Gerald Vizenor might say. In "War Dances," the narrator discusses a literary critic's talk he had attended. "Last year, I had gone to a lecture at the University of Washington. An elderly woman, a Sioux writer and scholar and charlatan, had come to orate on Indian sovereignty and literature. She kept arguing for some kind of separate indigenous literary identity, which was ironic considering that she was speaking English to a room full of white professors" (*War Dances*, 37). This unnamed Sioux critic, who sounds a bit like Elizabeth Cook-Lynn, speaks out for tribal literary nationalism, one of the strongest discourses in Native American literary studies in the contemporary moment. Alexie turns nationalism on its ear, claiming it makes no sense in a world in which influences on all writers are far too complex to be so narrowly defined. This is not to say he is utterly opposed to some of the key facets of nationalism. He has asserted that the greatest challenges facing Native American communities are the "challenges to our sovereignty—artistically, politically, socially, economically. We are and always have been nations within this nation and any threats to that are dangerous" (Peterson, 69). In "War Dances," the narrator goes on to explain:, "I wasn't angry with the woman, or even bored. No, I felt sorry for her. I realized that she was dying of nostalgia. She had taken nostalgia as her false idol—her thin blanket—and it was murdering her" (*War Dances*, 37). For Alexie, rigid nationalisms are comfortable fantasies of a past that never was. These modalities of exclusivity run deeply contrary to Alexie's later work, as we will see. In "What Ever Happened to Frank Snake Church," one character warns another on the dangers of nostalgia: "[N]ostalgia is a cancer. Nostalgia will fill your heart up with tumors. Yeah, yeah, yeah, that's what you are. You're just an old fart dying of terminal nostalgia" (*Ten Little Indians*, 228).[6]

As we can see by his inclusion of John Steinbeck and Stephen King in his list of influences, Alexie is not informed exclusively by other Native authors. He repeats those names when he cites his greatest artistic inspirations as his father "for his nontraditional Indian stories"; his grandmother, "for her traditional Indian stories; Stephen King, John Steinbeck, and *The Brady Bunch*" (Peterson, 69). Alexie is the product of Native storiers telling "traditional" and "nontraditional" stories, but also of canonized literary authors like Steinbeck (as well as Kurt Vonnegut in *Flight* as well as other texts),[7] popular fiction writers like King, and popular culture creations like television sitcoms. Similarly, he avers, "Hank [Williams] was our Jesus, Patsy Cline was our Virgin Mary" (*Toughest Indian*, 23). He explains this background influence as a key to his success, "I have a huge Native audience in a way that other Native writers don't because my subject matter is very pop culture oriented and sort of middle-class, lower-class based. So I think that's probably the appeal" (Peterson, 158). While some authors—we can think of the high-modernist tendencies of Momaday, the postmodern fragmentation of Silko, the high theory of Vizenor—might prove off-putting to readers of work like Stephen King's, Alexie creates an approachable world that blends philosophy with pop culture. To that end, Susan Bernardin declares, "As a gateway Native author, Alexie might pull in a wider range of readers to the pleasures and perils of the many indigenous literary texts published by university and independent presses. If he does, it won't be because he lets his readers off easy" (53). Alexie's work is certainly not all fluff; it is both accessible and challenging. Alexie has also declared, "I think I'm pop-culture obsessed because I hope it's an antidote for the disease of nostalgia" (Peterson, 137).

One of the methods by which Alexie differentiates his work from that of the earlier NAR writers is through his portrayal of the land. Alexie's novels especially tend to avoid the prosaic musings on landscape that other writers' texts employ. Lincoln notes of Momaday's work, for example, "Across plains history, Momaday's influence from Black Elk recovers an impressionist reverence for the land, the elders, the traditions, and the spirits alive in all these" (95). This reverence for the land exists in some places in Alexie's work, especially that from earlier in his career. But we see much less of it than in others. Alexie has asserted, "You'll notice there's not much landscape in my stories, not much physical description of anybody or anything. I suppose I'm more interested in interior landscapes" (Peterson, 4). Not only is Alexie not interested in portraying the land in his work, he sees doing so as playing into stereotypes of Indian people. He states elsewhere, "I think most native literature is concerned with place because they tell us to be. That's the myth. I think it's detrimental" (Peterson, 88). *House Made of Dawn* and *Ceremony* are but two examples of the fixation on the nonhuman in representations of Indian place; authors including Gerald Vizenor, Louise Erdrich, Louis Owens, Linda Hogan, as well as more recent novelists like Craig Womack and LeAnne Howe, place a heavy value in the specifics of the nonhuman in their texts. But, Alexie's descriptions of place, even in early works like *Reservation Blues*, echo more James Welch, with a vaguery of description, a refusal to render the land as sacred in a way that outsiders would be able to understand.

While Alexie's earlier work shows far more emphasis on the reservation than his later work, early texts still include possibilities for Native mobility, movement, and motion. Daniel Grassian observes, "In *The Business of Fancydancing*, Alexie exhibits a love/hate relationship with the reservation" (20). We can observe this ambivalence throughout Alexie's work, however. It is true, of course, that *Reservation Blues*'s Chess, perhaps the most culturally conservative of the characters in Alexie's novels, thinks of urban Indians, "those old Indians were a long way from home, trapped by this city and its freeway entrances and exits" (150). Likewise, in "The Lone Ranger and Tonto Fistfight in Heaven," the eponymous story of Alexie's most celebrated collection, the narrator explains, "There's an old Indian poet who said that Indians can reside in the city, but they can never live there. That's as close to the truth as any of us can get" (187). However, later in *Reservation Blues*, Thomas tells Chess, "'I'll go wherever you want to go,' Thomas had said but still knew that every part of him was Spokane Indian" (256). Thomas is perfectly willing to leave the Spokane Reservation with Chess, who had already left the Flathead Reservation. Leaving does not make him any less Spokane or her any less Flathead. Even in this early text, one that centers itself primarily on the reservation, Alexie allows for a multitude of Indian ways of being. Some stay put; others roam. Moreover, as we have seen, the ills of isolation, alcoholism, and poverty exist within both urban and reservation communities. As such, Alexie denies the reservation the idealized position it occupies in the homing plots central to the NAR. Instead, his emphasis is on what he terms "reservation realism" (*Lone Ranger*, xxi). Nelson notes, "As Alexie's poetry and prose uncompromisingly demonstrate, communities are far from uncomplicated and are frequently themselves destructive, as with communities of substance abusers" (46). To counter these destructive elements of community, "Time and again Alexie offers metaphorical escapes, as from patterns of substance abuse, cycles of violence, and other received and unexamined ways of understanding the world" (46). Alexie does not mean to show a fantasy of Indian people, be it a fantasy held by Native or non-Native people. The odds, Alexie shows, are stacked against Indian people wherever they are. Some find positive existences on the reservation; others find them off the reservation; others still find them in the movements back and forth between, while others can't find them at all. This, then, is not the prescriptive mentality that the homing plot espouses, but one open to freedom and agency, one that recognizes the myriad possibilities of modern life. It is important to remember that at the end of *Reservation Blues* the entire community takes up a collection (in a fabulously ironic cowboy hat) to send Thomas, Checkers, and Chess off the reservation. "Some Indians gave money out of spite; some gave out of guilt; a few gave out of kindness" (304). That some of the Indian people can give money "out of kindness" for Thomas to leave marks his departure as something good, something positive (either for him or for the community).

This theme of movement continues throughout Alexie's later work. In *Diary*, Rowdy reminds Junior, "old-time Indians used to be nomadic. . . . Hardly anybody on this rez is nomadic. Except for you. You're the nomadic one" (229). Rowdy's need to couch Arnold's movement in pre-Contact tradition troubles cultural change, but works to justify Arnold nonetheless. Movement is both potentially positive and a Native practice that stretches back throughout history. Arnold is also told by Mr. P., his math teacher, "you have to leave the rez *forever*" because "The only thing you kids are being taught is how to give up" (42).[8] But, while it might be tempting to read *Diary* as an assimilationist narrative, we must remember the guilt with which Arnold is utterly wracked. He reflects, "I had killed my sister. / Well, I didn't kill her. / But she only got married so quickly and left the rez because I had left the rez first. She was only living in Montana in a cheap trailer house because I had gone to school in Reardan. She had burned to death because I had decided that I wanted to spend my life with white people. / It was all my fault" (211). At the same time, shortly after this passage, Arnold reminds the reader and himself, "Reservations were meant to be prisons, you know? Indians were supposed to move onto reservations and die. We were supposed to disappear. / But somehow or another, Indians have forgotten that reservations were meant to be death camps" (217). Such is the ambivalence that Alexie places in the reservation both as a physical space and as an interior construct. Finally, we note the fact that Alexie's recent story collections in particular place financially and personally successful Native people in urban settings, another contrast to much of the work of the NAR (though this is less true of the work of Vizenor and Wendy Rose). Grassian observes that, particularly with *The Toughest Indian in the World* and *One Stick Song*, Alexie begins an increasing focus on homosexuality and urban Indians (151).

Like the other writers of the Native American Renaissance, Alexie spends a considerable amount of time treating Indian identities, musing on what exactly "Indian identity" means. In his earlier work, he seemed far more rigid about this, and, quite unlike other novelists of the NAR, far more dismissive of mixed-bloods. Jane Hafen comments on the body of work prior to texts like *Flight* and *Diary*, "In the world of Indian identity politics, Alexie is uncomfortably essentialist. He raises significant questions, but his answers are uncompromising and not always consistent" (77). While Alexie eschews narratives of the tragic mixed-blood trapped between two worlds, Grassian observes that Alexie's later characters, "Indian though they may be, exist in a kind of limbo, suspended between mainstream American and Indian conceptions of identity" (191). In *Reservation Blues*, Chess again stands as the voice of cultural conservatism. Seeing a blonde woman and her child fathered by a Native man, "Chess wanted to tell the white woman that her child was always going to be halfway. He's always going to be half Indian, she'd say, and that will make him half crazy. Half of him will always want to tear the other half apart. It's war" (283). Chess's first concern here is for the child's sanity; she fears the child will develop psychological trauma. But soon she moves to external fears. "*Your son will be beaten because he's a half-breed,* Chess said. *No matter what he does, he'll never be Indian enough. Other Indians won't accept him. Indians are like that*" (283). Chess's concern moves to external forces, a world that can't accept mixed-race people. However, she immediately moves on, changing the object of her worry, "Chess wanted to save Indians from the pain that the white woman and her half-Indian son would cause" (283). Chess, in fact, worries for both the child and the community, especially in that the half-white child will "*get all the Indian jobs, all the Indian chances, because they look white. Because they're safer*" (283). So, according to Chess's miscegenation discourse, intermarriage, and especially interbreeding, damages everyone. As Grassian notes of this novel, "Alexie suggests that the greatest threat to the reservation may be 'Indians' of mixed ethnicity" (102). We note in this the contrast to what Lincoln observes in the NAR generally: "All peoples stand accountable to all other peoples, the old ways hold; the mixed breed is living testimony to the transitions, the changes, the old ways evolving constantly into new variables" (248). While other writers, from Momaday and Silko to Vizenor, Owens, Hogan, and Erdrich, all celebrate the mixed-blood in the manner Lincoln describes—as "the future" in Owens's words—as proof of Indian survival, as a counter to the tragedy of discourses of purity, Alexie's earliest work seems to run counter to this. (*Mixedblood*, n.p.).

But Alexie's attitudes, as well as what defines "real Indians," are not simple, even in *Reservation Blues*. When Chess continues her pontification, Thomas wonders as to her accuracy. Chess asserts, "as traditional as it sounds, I think Indian men need Indian women" (81). "Thomas agreed with Chess, but he also knew about the shortage of love in the world. He wondered if people should celebrate love wherever it's found, since it is so rare" (82). In Alexie's later work, similar critiques remain, but include explanations for quests of purity and authenticity, if not justifications for them. In "The Search Engine," Corliss knows "Indians were obsessed with authenticity. Colonized, genocided, exiled, Indians formed their identities by questioning the identities of other Indians. Self-hating, self-doubting, Indians turned their tribes into nationalistic sects. But who could blame us our madness? . . . We are people exiled by other exiles, by Puritans, Pilgrims, Protestants, and all of those other crazy white people thrown out of a crazier Europe" (40). In this same story, Harlan Atwater explains that he stopped writing in part because of issues of authenticity both from Native and white people. "No matter what I write, a bunch of other Indians will hate it because it isn't Indian enough, and a bunch of white people will like it because it's Indian" (*Ten Little Indians*, 41). These images of authentic Indianness pervade U.S. culture broadly, and infiltrate everyone's minds.

Alexie also examines out-group definitions of Indian identity. Dr. Mathers, an "adopted Lakota" (reminiscent of Kenneth Lincoln), feels that Marie, because she is "rude and arrogant" (though "intelligent and physically attractive") "hardly [possesses] the qualities of a true Spokane" (*Indian Killer*, 135). Mathers surmises that because these traits "ran in the family like some disease," Reggie Potlatkin had also failed to behave like a true Spokane" (135). Mathers is acquainted with two Spokane Indian people we are aware of, and neither one of them fits his highly romanticized and subservient model of a "true" Spokane. Mathers is one of many characters in *Indian Killer* in particular who claim to understand Indians more than Indian people do and who claim a right to Native cultures, art, and identities. Wilson, a former police officer turned writer of "Indian" mystery novels is another, and we can liken him to Tony Hillerman, the Anglo writer who writes mysteries featuring

Navajo characters. Alexie has decried such activities. "All that appropriation, not just writing, but New Age culture, the men's movement and stuff, take all the good of native culture or native images or native spirituality without accepting any of the bad. The good has to be earned. Tony Hillerman is taking shortcuts, as are any dozens of others you could name" (Peterson, 6). In a final scene of *Indian Killer*, John pleads that Wilson should cease this artistic endeavor. "Please," John asks/demands of Wilson, "Let me, let us have our own pain" (411).

However, this focus on cultural sovereignty does not preclude Alexie from expanding Native American literature beyond the exclusively Native American. Rather, his work recognizes that all people are informed by multiple influences and are members of multiple communities. "Ever since 9/11, I have worked hard to be very public about my multi-tribal identity. I think fundamentalism is the mistaken belief that one belongs to only one tribe; I am the opposite of that" (Peterson, 190). Alexie's move away from exclusive tribal identification has been underway for quite some time. For years he has been crafting characters whose relationship to their tribe or reservation has been tenuous. Even in *Reservation Blues* and *The Lone Ranger and Tonto Fistfight in Heaven*, he fashions Thomas Builds-the-Fire as an outsider in his tribal community. At one moment in *Reservation Blues*, the narrator explains of a crying Thomas, "He just wanted his tears to be individual, not tribal" (100). This is not to say that Thomas, who will ultimately leave the reservation, does not also see himself as Spokane.

Of course, *Indian Killer* revolves around a character who has no connection to his Native ancestry, as does *Flight* with its protagonist, Zits. Both John and Zits know they are of Indian descent, but neither knows from what nation. "When John imagines his birth, his mother is sometimes Navajo. Other times she is Lakota. Often, she is from the same tribe as the last Indian woman he has seen on television" (4). "John's mother is Navajo or Lakota. She is Apache or Seminole. She is Yakama or Spokane" (4). Zits similarly explains, "My father was an Indian. From this or that tribe. From this or that reservation" (4). He continues, "I am Irish and Indian, which would be the coolest blend in the world if my parents were around to teach me how to be Irish and Indian. But they're not here and haven't been for years, so I'm not really Irish *or* Indian. I'm a blank sky, a human solar eclipse" (5). Alexie considers racial belonging as ethnic knowledge. Zits and John, lacking that ethnic knowledge both become heavily disassociative; Zits is a teenage foster child constantly acting out, while John is schizophrenic. The reader can easily conflate their emotional and psychic issues with their tribelessness.

But not all of Alexie's characters are lost in a haze of identity confusion. As Patrice Hollrah notes of another of the main characters in *Indian Killer*, "Marie's intellectual sovereignty resides in the contexts of her Spokane and urban tribal connections, her academic involvement, and her political and social activism" (24). While John and Zits lack any tribal ties, Marie has many. Likewise, Arnold, the protagonist of *Diary*, comes to see himself an immigrant in an immigrant nation. "There were millions of other Americans who had left their birthplaces in search of a dream" (217). However, this does not mean he denies, let alone denounces, his tribal community. Instead, he expands it and recognizes other communities of which he is a member. He sees that he is part of the Spokane tribe, the "tribe of American immigrants," but also belongs to those of basketball players, bookworms, cartoonists, chronic masturbators, teenage boys, small-town kids, Pacific Northwestern-ers, tortilla-chips-and-salsa lovers, poverty, funeral-goers, beloved sons, and boys who really missed their best friends. "It was a huge realization," Arnold reflects (217). Alexie explains through Arnold the myriad connections that define all people. Indian people, like all others, are tied to multiple communi-ties of birth, culture, religion, language, but also those of personal affiliation and affection, including lovers of certain sports, foods, and regions.

Indeed, one could argue that Alexie has moved to overtly questioning the value of tribal identifications. In *Flight*, Justice cites Nietzshe's *Beyond Good and Evil*, telling Zits, "The individual has always had to work hard to avoid being overwhelmed by the tribe. If you try it, you will be lonely often and sometimes frightened. But no price is too high for the privilege of owning yourself" (25). Likewise, Gordy, the narrative voice of wisdom in *Diary* ex-plains, "life is a constant struggle between being an individual and being a member of the community" (132). Alexie's understanding of community has in many ways expanded. Zits discusses the broad spectrum of people who have been involved in making him who he is, the community of voices he car-ries, as we all do, inside of him, and claims them all. "I think about my mother and father. I think about the people I loved. I think about the people I hated. I think about the people I betrayed. I think about the people who have betrayed me. / We're all the same people. And we are all falling" (*Flight*, 130). All of us—those who have supported, abandoned, or ever betrayed us—are in it together. In "The Search Engine," Corliss makes a far less serious assertion, though it is one that echoes a sentiment similar to Zits's. "She knew there would come a day when white folks finally understood that Indians are every bit as relent-lessly boring, selfish, and smelly as they are, and that would be a wonderful day for human rights but a terrible day for Corliss" (*Ten Little Indians*, 11). Corliss trades on her exoticized Indian identity when she can, an understand-able move by a woman from a colonized community. But, she understands perfectly well that Native people are not unlike everyone else. Alexie's move here flirts with a universal humanism, or perhaps he is working to merely humanize people, to get people to identify with one another as members of a global community. He asserts elsewhere, "Hate happens when we romanticize and vilify. As soon as we humanize people, it's really hard to go to war against them" (Peterson, 133). Atwater continues this refusal to draw boundaries be-tween Indian and white people when he later explains to Corliss, "the two best, the two most honorable and loyal people in my life are my white mother and my white father. So, you tell me, kid, what kind of Indian does that make me?" (*Ten Little Indians,* 52). As in much of Alexie's more recent work, we see here a refusal to vilify or valorize people based merely on their race. Instead, he aims for empathy as a counter to totalizing forces or totalitarianism.

All of these humanist leanings do not mean that Alexie is attempting to participate in a postracial ideology. We can recognize that he is expanding his work beyond Indian people, but he is certainly not abandoning them. He remains involved artistically, personally, politically, and financially with Indian causes. But he has also expanded to writing about characters who are white, African and Arab immigrants, as well as the African American and Latino characters he has always included in his writings. In one narrative, a white character, married to an Indian woman with whom he has had four children, confronts postracial discourse. "Now there were plenty of white people who wanted to eliminate the idea of race, to cast it aside as an unwanted invention, but it was too late for that. If white people are the mad scientists who created race, thought Jeremiah, then we created race so we could enslave black people and kill Indians, and now race has become the Frankenstein monster that has grown beyond our control" (*Toughest Indian,* 14). The idea that we can move away from racialized issues is a fantasy adopted particularly by those who have benefited from racist social and political structures and whose cultural predecessors, if not ancestors, *created* those structures. They would now like to ignore them, to pretend they only matter because people (especially people of color) continue to talk and write about them. They would like to ignore these realities because they are unpleasant and underscore their privilege, but the monster is out in the world. Pretending it is not there does nothing to prevent it from smashing through the village.

Perhaps more than anything, critics have noticed a change in Alexie's work in terms of the role of anger and vilification in his more recent texts. Many have always read a tension in Alexie's oeuvre between hope/redemption and despair, especially remarking on his early equation "Survival = Anger × Imagination. Imagination is the only weapon on the reservation" (*Lone Ranger,* 150). Scott Andrews avers that *Reservation Blues* "resorts to a puzzling sense of despair and settles for survival rather than imagining success for its protagonists" (137). Others have criticized the violence of *Indian Killer,* with Arnold Krupat asserting that the novel "encourages [the] expression" of "*murderous rage*" (103). Indeed, even Alexie's motivation to write this novel stemmed from frustration and anger:

> *Indian Killer.* I wrote this first and foremost because people—critics and audiences—kept talking about *The Lone Ranger and Tonto Fistfight in Heaven* and *Reservation Blues* as if they were dark, depressing, Kafkaish, cockroach-nightmare-crawling-across-the-floor kind of books. Actually they're very funny. I think they have happy endings. I thought, 'Okay, you want dark and depressing? Here you go. Here's *Indian Killer*.

You're going to look back with fondness at the whimsical *Reservation Blues*, the lighthearted *The Lone Ranger and Tonto Fistfight in Heaven*." I abandoned my trademark humor and went for the full thriller, murder mystery. [Peterson, 28]

Janet Dean, however, counters Krupat's comment in asserting, "'*murderous rage*' describes the white men in the novel who beat homeless Native Americans with baseball bats as aptly as it describes the attacks of Native American aggressors. Underplaying the universality of racial violence in the novel misses the point" (31). Similarly, Peterson notes, "some reviewers of Alexie's early work were not always even-handed in their assessment of his reservation realism, and many times the negative aspects of reservation life are emphasized without much understanding of the context for his depictions or without acknowledging the love and hope that can be found in the stories and poems as well" (xi). Likewise, Grassian avers, "Alexie . . . uses poetry precisely to transform rage or anger into something productive or constructive" (48), though I would contend that Alexie's work, and not just his earlier work, sees rage and/or anger as itself potentially productive. As Alexie puts it, "Anger itself can be positive or destructive. That's why you need to use imagination to make it positive. . . . Anger without hope, anger without love, or anger without compassion are all-consuming. That's not my kind of anger. Mine is very specific and directed" (Peterson, 10). In short, while *Indian Killer* is a disturbing and violent novel, the agents of violence are not exclusively Native. Many white characters seek out Indian people to assault because of the quite possibly mistaken belief that the serial killer in the text is Native. And, as Marie reasonably asserts, "if some Indian is killing white guys, then it's a credit to us that it took over five hundred years for it to happen" (*Indian Killer*, 418).[9]

In his more recent texts, Alexie has continued to demonstrate the fact that no community has a monopoly on morally abhorrent or redemptive behavior. In *Flight*, Alexie portrays a range of people—homeless children, law enforcement officers, political activists, foster parents, the Cheyenne, Arapaho, and Lakota confederation who defeated Custer's 7th Cavalry Regiment at the Battle of the Little Bighorn, one homeless Indian, and one white pilot—to show that all are in some ways kind and caring people, and in other ways, traitors and villains. While a white police officer, Officer Dave, serves as perhaps the hero of the novella, we see a pair of FBI agents, Hank and Art, who participate in the murder of an Indian activist, Junior. Likewise, Elk and Horse, the two Indian activists who betray and torture Junior and turn him over to the feds, nonetheless take care and time to ensure that Junior's body is properly prepared according to their religion. The white pilot, himself betrayed by a friend and former flight student who turns out to be a terrorist, cheats on his wife. The victorious soldiers and civilians at Little Bighorn desecrate bodies and torture survivors. Nobody comes off looking very good.

In many ways, Alexie's focus in later texts comes in the form of a reexamination of divisions that arise and are reinforced by a discourse of war, one that is present in all elements, including those of peacetime, in the United States. We are reminded of Foucault's work on the correlation between war and social structures of power. Foucault asks rhetorically, "If we look beneath peace, order, wealth, and authority, beneath the calm order of subordinations, beneath the State and State apparatuses, beneath the laws, and so on, will we hear and discover a sort of primitive and permanent war?" (47). For Foucault, all administrative structures of power rely on a mentality of war (for Foucault, a war that is ultimately about race) that undergirds and reinforces dichotomous and hierarchical divisions between the administrative "us" and the outlying, polluting, and dangerous "them."

To that end, one FBI agent, Art, says to the other, Hank, "We don't need to talk about it anymore. We're at war. We're soldiers. . . . And some of the things we have to do, they hurt us, you know? They hurt us inside" (*Flight*, 56). We note in Art's statement that he feels tremendous guilt for his actions. His partner, Hank, although a killer, is likewise portrayed as a loving family man. For these representatives of the federal government, the activists of the AIM-like "IRON" are enemies of the state. Their very presence is tantamount to war. Zits reflects on his archetypally named friend, Justice, who encouraged him to open fire on a crowd in a bank, "Justice made killing make sense. But it doesn't make sense, does it?" (*Flight*, 53). He continues, likening these figures to one another, "Art and Justice fight on opposite sides of the war but they sound exactly like each other. How can you tell the difference between the good guys and the bad guys when they say the same things?" (56). Killing is the product of people becoming convinced that their side of the war, their position either within or outside of the administrative role, is absolutely righteous. Again, Foucault notes that both these positions are created by and reinforce governmental structures of power, both participate in the agonistic modality the administration demands. Zits goes on to implicate even those members of organizations and societies who don't participate in killing, mirroring Arendt's banality of evil. Zits realizes, "I don't kill anybody. But I ride with killers, so that makes me a killer" (90).

But Alexie's all-inclusive worldview has been criticized for being overly simplistic and/or schmaltzy. A review by J. T. Townley in *The Harvard Review* sums up widespread reaction to *Flight*. Townley opines, "Like novels written and marketed to middle-schoolers, the book's font is large, its pages thick, and its ending saccharine" (174). Townley continues, *Flight* offers merely "the pat lesson that all life is sacred" (174). Specifically, Zits opines, "Maybe it's so simple it makes me feel stupid to say it. / Maybe you're not supposed to kill. No matter who tells you to do it. No matter how good or bad the reason. Maybe you're supposed to believe that all life is sacred" (*Flight*, 162–63). Certainly, and Alexie would be among the first to admit this, the lesson Townley points out is not original to *Flight*. But, as a response to the attacks on the United States of 9/11 and the United States's typically violent reaction, including wars in Afghanistan and the uninvolved Iraq, it seems a lesson we need to keep hearing. "Anger is never added to anger," Alexie reminds us, "It multiplies" (*Flight*, 136). Elsewhere he asserts, "[D]eath is never added to death; it multiplies" (*Diary*, 212).

While Alexie might appear to be buying into a facile post-9/11 faith in peace and love, he is far from uncritical toward the United States's extolling of every victim of those attacks. In perhaps the most controversial of his texts, the short story, "Can I Get a Witness," a survivor of a terrorist attack ponders the coverage and victims of the 9/11 attacks. Of the news broadcasts, the repetition of the video of the planes striking the towers, the buildings crumbling, the aftermath, she observes, "It was awful and obscene, all of it, it was grief porn" (*Ten Little Indians*, 91). There was something that many found disturbingly titillating about those images of death (it is all too easy for viewers to watch a building being destroyed whether in New York City or Baghdad without remembering the people who are dying in that destruction). She continues, challenging the ideal of the dead as heroes or innocent victims, not for being the little Eichmanns of Ward Churchill's discourse, but for being very normal, bad people. She wonders, "How many of those guys were cheating on their wives? A few hundred, probably. How many of them were beating their kids? One hundred more, right? Don't you think one of those bastards was raping his kids? Don't you think, somewhere in the towers, there was an evil bastard who sneaked into his daughter's bedroom at night and raped her in the ass?" (89). She continues, "Nobody wants to hear these things, but I'm thinking them, and I have to say them" (90). Alexie's refusal to pull punches continues in his recent work; he is far from the happy-go-lucky sellout that some would claim him to be.

With all these representations of government agents, officials, and employees, it would be easy to think that civil servants would be universally maligned in Alexie's work as they often are (and understandably so) throughout Native American literature. We can think of Indian agents, BIA officials, the justice system generally, government-sponsored and -supported boarding schools and many more destructive individuals and elements for Indian communities. We can also note Alexie's own commentary on police officers who racially profile Indian people or, as Zits describes, "plenty of cops just like to be assholes, and having a badge means you get to be a professional asshole" (*Flight*, 19). Zits is ultimately adopted by a white firefighter, the brother of Officer Dave who befriends the troubled young man and about whom Zits notes, "Good cops are lifeguards on the shores of Lake Fucked" (18). The firefighter, moreover, is married to a nurse, leading Zits to exclaim, "You guys are like the civil servant hall of fame or something" (174). Many readers are troubled by the ending of *Flight* specifically because white government employees serve as the saviors for an Indian teen. One wonders why Alexie would choose such an ending, though he has admitted to having struggled to come to a suitable conclusion. But Alexie has commented that this ending is meant as a "small celebration of civil servants." He concludes, "I believe in civil servants" (Peterson, 182). I argue that we can read Alexie's celebration as being a nod toward those who dedicate their lives, often with long hours, high danger, and mediocre pay, to being those lifeguards on the shores of Lake Fucked. It is less a valuation of the government they represent than a statement in favor of service as a way of life. More generally, Alexie writes in perhaps his most famous single short story "What You Pawn I Will Redeem," "Do you know how many good men live in this world? Too many to count!" (*Ten Little Indians*, 194).

Alexie's work counters many of the conventions of the NAR, pushing its boundaries and questioning some of its central tenets. Alexie writes in a number of places about the state of Native literature and Native writers. He has commented, "I think a lot of Native writers are pretending, writing about the kind of Indians they wish they were, not the kind of Indians they are" (Peterson, 58). These authors are often urban professors, but writing about the reservation. Alexie wants writers to create narratives that reflect their lives. It makes sense, then, that as he lives longer in cities he would write more about them. His lifestyle may be different, but he is staying true to his artistic vision and his vision of artists. He further states, "[M]y entrance into the mainstream has changed the mainstream—forgive the immodesty—but I think my career has totally altered many people's ideas of what an Indian can do and can be. Especially other Indians" (Peterson, 127). In pushing these ideas, Alexie has also paved the way for future writers. As just one example, I see Alexie's stories "The Sin Eaters" in *The Toughest Indian in the World* and "Distances" from *The Lone Ranger and Tonto Fistfight in Heaven* as deeply influential on Stephen Graham Jones's novel *The Bird is Gone*. Alexie stands on the shoulders of the early writers of the Native American Renaissance; he can write about the topics he does because readers have been made familiar with Native issues via the authors who have come before him. Still, he has moved, and continues to move, Native literature in new directions, making use of some of the practices of the NAR while rejecting others. His work has changed, evolved from its prior incantations, and will continue to do so because Alexie is not interested in being stuck in the same place any more.

NOTES

1. Alexie counters Bird's portrayal when he asserts, "Indian writers, all writers in general, but Indian writers, too, were the weird kids, the bizarre kids. The ones who question institutions, the ones who were not all that popular. The ones who people looked at weird" (Purdy, 11).

2. Of course, Alexie is most known for his signature use of humor. He is not the first Native author to make use of humor, of course, but of Native authors and novelists, his work is the most consistently funny, and the most consistent in making the attempt to be so. Alexie has commented that he uses humor particularly in his readings to enable him to access his audience. He explains, "I think humor is the most effective political tool out there, because people will listen to anything if they're laughing" (Peterson, 70). Lincoln recognizes the importance of humor in respect to making the important accessible. He has commented on James Welch's work, "Such realistic humor grounds the narrative visions and illusion in honesty and awareness" (162). But Alexie gives further reasons for the importance of comedy. In *Reservation Blues*, Father Arnold, the Spokane Reservation's Catholic priest "was impressed by the Spokane's ability to laugh. He'd never thought of Indians as funny. What did they have to laugh about? Poverty, suicide, alcoholism? Father Arnold learned to laugh at most everything, which strangely made him feel closer to God" (36). Father Arnold mirrors the view of Indian humor that so many Native authors see in whitestream views of Indian people. As I have shown elsewhere, authors and scholars, including Charles Eastman, Vine Deloria, Jr., Gerald Vizenor, and Kenneth Lincoln, all work against stereotypes of stone-faced, humorless Indian people. But Father Arnold comes to see an element of the sacred in humor, which serves not only as a bridge between people as it is in many of these examples, but between the human and the spiritual. To that end, the narrator explains, "A prayer and a joke often sound alike on the reservation" (*Reservation Blues*, 101). Alexie asserts that humor is less a coping mechanism that a "reflection of strength" (Peterson, 183).

3. Alexie draws on literary and popular representations of Native alcoholism, what NAR author Gerald Vizenor has termed "the firewater myth" (*Manifest*, 171). Alexie has addressed this particular criticism head on: "Some people say I always write about drunks. Well, no, I don't, but if you look at the books you can see a progression, actually. The alcohol is dropping out of the books, because the alcohol is dropping farther and farther out of my life, as I've been sober for more and more years. (Purdy, 12). Similarly, *Reservation Blues*'s narrator explains, "most Indians never drink. Nobody notices the sober Indians. On television, the drunk Indians emote. In books, the drunk Indians philosophize" (151).

4. Alexie has also noted that "Susan Power's *The Grass Dancer* was very subtle" (Peterson, 125).

5. In a subtle moment, a narrator in "The First Annual All-Indian Horseshoe Pitch and Barbeque" in *Lone Ranger* explains, "All the Indians were running; they were running. There was no fear, no pain" (148), a phrase echoing *House Made of Dawn*'s Hemingway-like repetition of "Abel was running."

6. We note, with Alexie's emphasis on the dangers of nostalgia for Native people and his use of the word "terminal," an increasing correlation between Alexie's philosophy and that of Gerald Vizenor, despite the former's earlier criticisms of the latter's work (Peterson, 42).

7. In one story, Alexie mirrors the opening of Vonnegut's *Cat's Cradle*, as well as *Moby Dick*: "Jonah, you can call me Ishmael" (*Toughest Indian*, 102). In "A Train Is an Order of Occurrence Designed to Lead to Some Result," he narrates another phrase from *Cat's Cradle* with one character thinking, "busy busy busy" (*Lone Ranger*, 131).

8. The theme of giving up recurs throughout Alexie's later work, but is not confined to Indian people or the reservation. Arnold explains of running laps at basketball practice that "quitting is contagious" (*Diary*, 138). However, this kind of giving up is not unique to reservations. In "What Ever Happened to Frank Snake Church" Alexie writes of a young woman working her way through community college, "She came from a place, from a town and street, from a block and house, where all of the men had quit, had surrendered, had simply stopped and lay down in the street to die before they were fifteen years old" (*Ten Little Indians*, 235).

9. These assaults are provoked by the Rush Limbaugh-esque radio host, Truck Schultz. (Elsewhere Alexie wonders, "If God were great, why would he create Rush Limbaugh?" (*Reservation Blues*, 166.) "Listen, folks, I admit that what was done to the Indians was wrong. But that was hundreds of years ago, and you and I were not the people who did it. We have offered our hands in friendship to the Indians, but they insist on their separation from normal society" (118). Truck denies the ongoing crime of settler colonialism, opting for a colonial time that creates a distinction between the distant past and the present. Kevin Bruyneel notes that this distinction advances the settler-colonial enterprise by acquitting the present beneficiaries of structures of power established in the past from any moral wrongdoing. In "A Drug Called Tradition," Alexie offers an alternative to this binary construction of time: "That's what Indian time is. The past, the future, all of it is wrapped up in the now" (*Lone Ranger*, 22).

WORKS CITED

Alexie, Sherman. *The Absolutely True Diary of a Part-Time Indian*. New York: Little, Brown, 2009.
———. *Flight*. New York: Black Cat, 2007.
———. *Indian Killer*. New York: Warner, 1996.
———. *The Lone Ranger and Tonto Fistfight in Heaven*. New York: Grove, 2005.
———. *Reservation Blues*. New York: Warner, 1995.
———. *The Stick Song*. Brooklyn: Hanging Loose, 2000.
———. *Ten Little Indians*. New York: Grove, 2003.
———. *The Toughest Indian in the World*. New York: Atlantic Monthly, 2000.
———. *War Dances*. New York: Grove, 2009.
Andrews, Scott. "A New Road and a Dead End in Sherman Alexie's *Reservation Blues*." *Arizona Quarterly* 63:2 (2007), 137–54.
Bernardin, Susan. "Alexie-Vision: Getting the Picture." *World Literature Today* 84:4 (2010), 52–55.

Bird, Gloria. "The Exaggeration of Despair in Sherman Alexie's *Reservation Blues*." *Wicazo Sa Review* 11: 2 (1995), 47–52.

Bruyneel, Kevin. *The Third Space of Sovereignty: The Postcolonial Politics of U.S.-Indigenous Relations*. Minneapolis: University of Minnesota Press, 2007.

Churchill, Ward. *On the Justice of Roosting Chickens: Reflections on the Consequences of U.S. Imperial Arrogance and Criminality*. Oakland, Calif.: AK Press, 2003.

Dean, Janet. "The Violence of Collection: Indian Killer's Archives." *Studies in American Indian Literatures* 20:3 (2008), 29–51.

Foucault, Michel. *Society Must Be Defended: Lectures at the Collège de France*. New York: Picador, 2005.

Grassian, Daniel. *Understanding Sherman Alexie*. Columbia: University of South Carolina Press, 2005.

Hafen, P. Jane. "Rock and Roll, Redskins, and Blues in Sherman Alexie's Work." *Studies in American Indian Literatures* 9:4 (1997), 71–78.

Hollrah, Patrice. "Sherman Alexie's Challenge to the Academy's Teaching of Native American Literature, Non-Native Writers, and Critics." *Studies in American Indian Literatures* 13: 2–3 (2001), 23–35.

Jones, Stephen Graham. *The Bird Is Gone: A Manifesto*. Tuscaloosa, Ala: Fiction Collective 2, 2003.

Krupat, Arnold. *Red Matters: Native American Studies*. Philadelphia: University of Pennsylvania Press, 2002.

Lincoln, Kenneth. *Native American Renaissance*. Berkeley: University of California Press, 1983.

Nelson, Joshua B. "Fight as Flight: The Traditional Reclamation of Exploration." *World Literature Today* 84:4 (2010), 44–47

Owens, Louis. *Mixedblood Messages: Literature, Film, Family, Place*. Norman: University of Oklahoma Press, 1998.

Peterson, Nancy J., ed. *Conversations with Sherman Alexie*. Jackson: University Press of Mississippi, 2009.

Purdy, John. "Crossroads: A Conversation with Sherman Alexie." *Studies in Native American Literatures* 9:4 (1997), 1–18.

Townley, J. T. Review of *Flight*. *Harvard Review* 33 (2007), 172–73.

Vizenor, Gerald. *Manifest Manners: Narratives on Postindian Survivance*. Lincoln: University of Nebraska Press, 1999.

12

A Postmodern Turn

CHRIS LALONDE

Isn't it about time, stranger,
for us to meet face to face in the same age,
both of us strangers to the same land,

Both of us strangers to the same land,
meeting at the tip of an abyss?
Notre Musique

In *Notre Musique* (2004), Jean-Luc Godard quotes these lines from a poem
by the Palestinian poet Mahmoud Darwish to the *indians* who appear periodically in Godard's cinematic meditation on Sarajevo, humankind, war, the
Other, and film itself.[1] The three *indians* haunt *Notre Musique*, at once both
present and absent within the film. For instance, in the scene in the bombed-
out shell of Vijecnica, the building housing the city hall and library, when one
of the three asks the question I have taken for my epigraph and another of the
trio repeats parts of it, a woman is clearly aware of the presence of the *indians*, who are wrestling with her over a book, while another character seems
oblivious to their presence, even as they pose their question to him. That man
simply attends to his ledger, recording the books that have been brought to
the library from patrons; those books end up not in the stacks but on a pile of
texts that we see as the shot widens. The holdings, then, mirror the building
after the latter was targeted as part of the warchitecture campaign designed to
eradicate not just a people but a history and a culture.[2]

Although at once there and not there for the other characters in the frame,
the *indians* are before the whole of the film's audience whenever they are on
screen. Tellingly, they enter the frame in the scene sketched above. Such a
move positions them as supplement: the figure that arrives and in doing so
recontextualizes the shot, the scene, and the film. We need to move carefully
here, to be sure, for *Notre Musique*'s *indians* are precisely that: representations
of the construction of the *indian* created and perpetuated by the dominant
culture. The *indian* and tribal cultures, to quote White Earth Anishinaabe

cross-blood writer and scholar Gerald Vizenor, "have been invented as 'absolute fakes' and consumed in social science monologues" ("A Postmodern Introduction," 5), and Godard's film seems conscious of the identification. While the *indian* is present for some in the frame, absent for others, the existence of the *indian* effectively consigns the Native to absence. A simulation brought into being by Columbus, the *indian* marks the absence of Natives (Vizenor, *Fugitive Poses*, 15). Moreover, Vizenor recognizes that the *indian* constitutes an archive where is deposited "the simulations, discoveries, treaties, documents of ancestry, traditions in translation, museum remains, and the aesthetics of victimry" (*Fugitive Poses*, 50). Fittingly taking place in Vijecnica then, the scene from *Notre Musique* is instructive for our purposes, for the mise-en-scène of a library in ruins, its system of classification effectively annihilated with the incendiary shells that torched Vijecnica, and the image of the *indian* standing before authority and making a claim for recognition—a claim that makes clear that each is a stranger to place and to the other insofar as the *indian* blankets any hope of seeing the Native, and the non-Native does not know him or herself—resonates with both the genesis of this volume and the particulars of an essay whose subject is a postmodern turn to Native American literatures. In a word, the abyss that beckons appeared with the recognition that "the grand narrative has lost its credibility, regardless of whether it is a speculative narrative or a narrative of emancipation" (Lyotard, 17). What is called for, then, is, in Vizenor's words, the *postindian* [that] must waver over the aesthetic ruins of *Indian* simulations" (*Fugitive Poses*, 15).

Yes, we say, rhetorically, circa 1983 and the publication of Kenneth Lincoln's *Native American Renaissance*, isn't it about time that the literature offered by Native writers of North America is recognized and read? Yes, we say, again rhetorically, circa 1969 and the awarding of a Pulitzer Prize to N. Scott Momaday's *House Made of Dawn*, isn't it about time that Native literature is accorded its due, high time that Native representations were circulated and studied? Literary scholars and prize jurors were right then, don't get me wrong, but here, too, we must move carefully, needing to recognize that back then, at roughly the same time as poststructuralism came to the United States (1966) and as Jean-Francois Lyotard set about "Answering the Question: What is Postmodernism?" (1983), what was recognized and what resonated with an audience had, at least in part, a certain modernist strain.[3] This is not to find fault with *House Made of Dawn* or *Native American Renaissance*, to be sure, but rather to recognize that back in the day a certain postmodern turn went wanting. Six years after the publication of *Native American Renaissance*, however, both Native and non-Native scholars were offering readings of Native texts informed by poststructuralism in a volume edited by Vizenor entitled *Narrative Chance: Postmodern Discourse on Native American Indian Literature* (1989). Taking a cue from Vizenor's introduction to that collection and from the quotation from *Notre Musique*, I want to give the postmodern its turn, if you will, by suggesting certain links between it; essays in *Narrative Chance* by Vizenor, White Earth Anishinaabe Kimberly Blaeser, and Choctaw-Cherokee-Irish Louis Owens; Vizenor's *Hiroshima Bugi*; and texts by White Earth Anishinaabe Gordon Henry Jr. and Choctaw D. L. Birchfield.

It may seem doubly odd to give postmodernism its turn when it comes to Native texts, if not wrong-minded. Advocates of Native American and First Nations literary nationalism(s)—Robert Warrior, Jace Weaver, and Craig Womack come immediately to mind—would have one recognize the need for a Native nation-based, tribally centered criticism. To approach Native literary texts with the tools of contemporary theory, especially theory rooted in continental Europe, and of cultural studies, to bring to bear what has been learned thanks to the twin beyonds of poststructuralism and postcolonialism, is to run the risk of relegating the texts, their authors, and the tribal histories and cultures from which they spring to the all-too-typical status of object, subject to the agents and agency of the dominant culture. The position staked out by Weaver, Womack, Warrior, and others is not without merit, of course, but it does not necessarily follow that a turn to the postmodern means either continued colonization or recolonization. Indeed, if we recognize that the beyond of postmodernism articulates "a new space for negotiating both identity and difference" (Hutcheon, 8), then a postmodern turn expresses one possible way to articulate Native identities and, in so doing, make a claim for sovereignty.

Linda Hutcheon is invoking the work of Homi Bhabha, in particular work given over to yoking the insights of postmodernism and postcolonialism. Bhabha reads postmodernism's characteristic indeterminacy and contingency as salutary, for it allows a space to be opened up for critique and the articulation of difference.[4] In his words, "it is as if the arbitrariness of the sign, the indeterminacy of writing, the splitting of the subject of enunciation, these theoretical concepts, produce the most useful descriptions of the formation 'postmodern' cultural subjects" (Bhabha, 176) even as those subjects deploy the "new space" made available to them by postmodernism "to return, in a spirit of revision and reconstruction, to the political *conditions* of the present" (3). Thinking beyond sequentiality, Bhabha would have us see that the critical insight and opportunity afforded us by postmodernism "lies in the awareness that the epistemological 'limits' of those ethnocentric ideas [exploded by postmodernism] are also the enunciative boundaries of a range of other dissonant, even dissident histories and voices" (4–5).

Bhabha's provocative claims for the relationship between postmodernism and alterity notwithstanding, it remains doubly odd to turn to postmodernism, given that both advocates for and critics of it have for no little time now proclaimed that postmodernism's day is done. Indeed, in the same year that both *Narrative Chance* and what would become the lead essay in Bhabha's *The Location of Culture*, tellingly entitled "The Commitment to Theory," were published, 1989, the Stuttgart Seminar in Cultural Studies, entitled "The End of Postmodernism: New Directions," was held. A year later, John Frow asked, "What was Postmodernism?" and Ihab Hassan repeats the question a decade later at century's turn. In 2002, Linda Hutcheon offered some "Postmodern Afterthoughts," and 2010 saw the publication of Josh Toth's *The Passing of Postmodernism*. Declaring that "The postmodern moment has passed," Hutcheon stated that "Post-postmodernism needs its own label" (11) and then, in a move rooted in postmodernism, turned the matter "Over to YOU." Hassan and, after him, Toth are not so willing to give up the ghost, for Hassan considers postmodernism a revenant that keeps coming back ("From Postmodernism to Postmodernity," 1) and Toth, invoking and following Derrida, reads postmodernism as a specter that is itself haunted by the messianic and emancipatory impulse, "a certain teleological aporia, a promise of the end represented by a type of humanism, a certain faith in historical progress, a sense of justice and/or meaning" (4).

Toth's recognition of the end and a promise of its arrival is fitting, for postmodernism has been concerned with, and concerned over, the end of something from day one. Whether it is in Arnold Toynbee's *Study of History* (1934–1954), where the "post-Modern" is marshaled as part of a critique of the West's desire to proclaim history's end, or in Charles Olson's midcentury linking of the postmodern and aesthetics, to cite two examples, we see, as both Hassan and Toth make clear, that the postmodern attempts to name that which signals a break from the modern, and from the Enlightenment, and in so doing tacitly proclaims that what came before it has ended. Later, Lyotard effectively invokes an end when he defines postmodernism as "incredulity toward metanarratives" (*The Postmodern Condition*, xxiv); the decline of the grand narrative brings with it the rise of "little narratives [petit recit]" (*The Postmodern Condition*, 60) that neither lead to nor are governed by any totalizing final answer or end.

Although postmodernism's relationship to what it purports to signal the end of is part of its difficulty—that is, is postmodernism continuous with or a break from the modern, modernism, modernity—an attention to ends and ending certainly resonates with Native people and Native studies, at least insofar as the dominant culture has labored to write the final word on them. That word is "end." Desiring to be done with the indigene once and for all, Europeans and then Euro-Americans and Euro-Canadians first designated the Native as *indian*, which is to say as "other," and then worked to write them off. Vizenor has long held that such acts of damning inscription are both rooted in the "narrow teleologies" ("Postmodern Introduction," 5) of the social sciences and rendered in the tragic mode: "the tribes and the wilderness vanish in tragic narratives" ("Postmodern Introduction," 13).

Essays in *Narrative Chance* by White Earth Anishinaabe writer and scholar Kimberly Blaeser, by Choctaw-Cherokee-Irish writer and scholar Louis

Owens, and by Vizenor are part of the volume's efforts to move beyond ways of seeing and knowing that inscribe the Native to absence. In *"The Way to Rainy Mountain*: Momaday's Work in Motion," Blaeser focuses on the form of N. Scott Momaday's multigenre work of creative nonfiction and the necessity of the reader to adopt an active position toward it while reading. Building on insights offered by reader-response theory, particularly those articulated by Wolfgang Iser, Blaeser points out how the various parts of each section of *The Way to Rainy Mountain,* and in turn the various sections themselves, contribute to the text's openness. For Blaeser, this openness is to be found in the very textuality of the work as well as in the particulars of what Momaday labels "the mythical, the historical and the immediate" (*Way to Rainy Mountain,* 41) strands or voices that are present in his work. The combination of poetry, prose, drawings, typeface, and white space are, Blaeser notes, linked to "the open intention of the work" ("*Way,*" 41), a work with and in which "Momaday presents the reader with unusual juxtapositions, contradictions, intentional gaps, and ambiguity" ("*Way,*" 41).

Blaeser would have us see that the formal and thematic characteristics of *The Way to Rainy Mountain* serve to question boundaries and to dissolve distinctions. For example, she points to the second section of "'The Setting Out" portion of the text, where the story in the mythic strand of a group that is splitting as a result of a quarrel is followed in the historical strand by "reports" that suggest that what we consider myth can be history, what we imagine to be fiction can be fact, and the personal and the immediate can be both. ("*Way,*" 45). As what constitutes the mythic, the historical, and the personal are called into question by the text and the reader's active engagement with it, then "the boundaries of traditional disciplines begin to dissolve for the reader [and] divisions are called into question" (Blaeser, "*Way,*" 45) in order, finally, that Momaday and the reader can recognize "the imagination's power to transcend time, to transport us through history" (Blaeser, "*Way,*" 52), and to create a polyphonic text that leads to new ways of seeing and, I would argue, being in the world (Blaeser, "*Way,*" 47). As such, the text is at home in Hassan's sense of postmodernism, at least as he articulated it in 2001, for he considers "a polychronic sense of time (linear, cyclical, sidereal, cybernetic, nostalgic, eschatological, visionary)" one of the hallmarks of what is, as he put it, "an essentially contested category" ("From Postmodernism to Postmodernity," 6, 1).

Louis Owens recognizes in Vizenor's *Darkness in Saint Louis: Bearheart* elements of structural linguistics and semiotics that are critical to any understanding of Vizenor's controversial novel, and indeed to the whole of his body of work. Throughout his life as a writer, scholar, and community advocate, Vizenor has been concerned with, and concerned over, what he labels "terminal creeds": any position and way of seeing the world, self, and others that locks one in to an inflexible position. Driven to reveal and, in revealing, to undo terminal creeds and their dangerous power, Vizenor, Owens argues in "Ecstatic Strategies," labors in and with his early novel to "free us from romantic entrapments, to liberate the imagination. The principal target of this fiction is the sign 'Indian,' with its predetermined and well worn path between signifier and signified" (144). That well-worn path is ideologically motivated, of course, and in bringing it to light and questioning its veracity, efficacy, and motivation, Vizenor is producing a critique of representation and the politics that lie behind and govern it. Such a focus and critique is in keeping with the postmodern concern with representation and politics (Hutcheon, 6).

It makes perfect sense that a critique of stasis and static definitions of self and world is found in a postapocalyptic road novel. In Owens's reading, a critical spot on the road Vizenor's circus of pilgrims take from northern Minnesota to Jemez Pueblo, New Mexico, is Bioavaricious, Kansas, and the Bioavaricious Regional Word Hospital. The research and development conducted there would lead to language that closes down possibility and play. *Darkness in Saint Louis: Bearheart* reveals that far from serving as a foundation upon which to rebuild the ruined nation, such language, and the desire motivating it, is what has brought nation and world to disaster. Owens likens the efforts at the Regional Word Hospital to Foucault's sense of the ideologically driven attempts to impose identities with and in language, and with and in institutions (149), and then points out that the claims made in *Darkness in Saint Louis: Bearheart* concerning the oral tradition, a tradition that Owens argues stands in telling contradistinction to what the researchers at the word hospital would produce and disseminate, echo Lacan's ideas concerning the relationship between signifier and signified to which Vizenor refers in his essay, "Trickster Discourse" (Owens, 150).

In the preface to *Narrative Chance*, Vizenor writes that "Modernism is a disguise, a pretense of individualism and historicism" (x). Owens argues that the sign "Indian" is critical to modernism, for that recognizable "deracinated, powerless, and pathetic figure" captures the modernist predicament (Vizenor, *Narrative Chance*, 147). Vizenor will have none of it, either in *Darkness in Saint Louis: Bearheart* or elsewhere, and Owens points out that it is with the figure of trickster that Vizenor challenges, and would have his readers challenge, "definitions of the self and, concomitantly, the world defined in relation to that self" (*Narrative Chance*, 142). Trickster, Vizenor proclaims in the volume's introduction, is postmodern (*Narrative Chance*, 9), is "agonistic imagination and aggressive liberation, a 'doing' in narrative points of views and outside the imposed structures" (*Narrative Chance*, 13) that would contain it. Later, in his essay contribution to *Narrative Chance* entitled "Trickster Discourse: Comic Holotropes and Language Games," Vizenor fleshes out the figure of trickster. Making explicit there the link between trickster and postmodernism, Vizenor argues that the former is a "comic sign" but not a "trope to power"; as a sign, moreover, trickster "denies presence and completion"

(192) and, because it is communal, stands in contradistinction to isolation and separation.

The social sciences in general and anthropology in particular are taken to task by Vizenor in "Trickster Discourse." While trickster discourse is associated with play, chance, contingency, and the comic, the social sciences produce a monologue that exists in isolation and is directed toward, and driven by, the tragic mode. For Vizenor, the social sciences are limiting at best, damning at worst, because they isolate elements from Native narratives, structures, and worldview and then press those elements into service in order to get at the truth, which is to say to get at what the disciplines' models hold about the *indian* (*Narrative Chance*, 11). Arriving at its destination thanks to "predacious research" (*Narrative Chance*, 192), the social sciences and its practitioners miss trickster, which is to say they fail to apprehend it as "a chance, a comic holotrope in a postmodern language game that uncovers the distinctions and ironies between narrative voices; [the trickster is] a semiotic sign for 'social antagonism' and 'aesthetic activism'" (192).

In the penultimate section of his essay, Vizenor considers trickster as healer. There he asks us to imagine that, "rather than a trace element, suppose the tribal trickster is atavistic, a revenant holotrope in new and recurrent narratives" (*Narrative Chance*, 205). Like the postmodern revenant conjured by both Hassan and Toth, Vizenor's trickster comes back to haunt us. Glossing and following Derrida, Toth reminds us that a revenant is linked to both the past and the future (19). He stresses, however, that although the specter may herald an end to ghosts, to a moment when all those haunting figures are laid to rest once and for all, such a promise must always be deferred if the promise of postmodernism, a promise to openness, to possibility, and to action is to be realized. Returning to remind us, against our will and wishes, of that which needs to be recognized, addressed, and considered, the revenant that is postmodernism and a postmodern turn in and to Native American literatures can lead to healing. It is about time.

Vizenor's 2003 novel, *Hiroshima Bugi,* is about time. Or rather, in the spirit of the postmodern Derridean supplement that is an addition that upsets, undoes the original formulation, Vizenor's *Hiroshima Bugi: Atomu 57* text is about time. The subtitle makes clear that we are dealing with a different way of telling time, one not linked to any of the various calendars tied to and governed by religion, nor even one linked to geologic time, but rather to a calendar that recognizes and takes as point of origin and reckoning the detonation of an atomic bomb, dropped by the United States in the air above Hiroshima, Japan, obliterating the city and thousands of its inhabitants below. In the spirit of the subtitle, *Hiroshima Bugi* is at once an articulation and critique both of the moment that initiates the Atomu calendar and of the age that came into being with the flash as the device known as Little Boy exploded and the mushroom cloud rose.

A two-stranded narrative, *Hiroshima Bugi: Atomu 57* tells the story of Ronin Ainoko Browne, the mixed-blood son of White Earth Anishinaabe Orion "Nightbreaker" Browne and a Japanese boogie dancer. Conceived during the early days of the U.S. occupation of Japan, Ronin never met his father. He hears stories of Nightbreaker at the Hotel Manidoo in Nogales, Arizona, to which he goes as a grown man to find his father. Arriving a week after Nightbreaker's death, Ronin, Nightbreaker's friend and narrator of the "Manidoo Envoy" sections of the text, and the other wounded veterans at the hotel tell stories over the course of a month, stories that are linked to *survivance* (*Hiroshima Bugi*, 9). The stories that Ronin told at the hotel make up the "Ronin of" sections of the text.

An important word in Vizenor's lexicon, "survivance" is an active stance taken in light of and against the will to power and dominance. It captures the critical quality of resistance to domination, a resistance that is rooted in "active presence" (*Fugitive Poses*, 15). With the manidoo envoy, Vizenor elaborates what Ronin and he mean with the term. Survivance is "a vision and vital condition to endure, to outwit evil and dominance, and to deny victimry" (*Hiroshima Bugi*, 36). Because survivance is also linked to "perfect memory," a phrase that "evokes the comparative ideas of collective memory and 'exact imagination,'" "communal wit," natural reason, and trickster stories (36), it is more than solely an individual response or stance. In Vizenor's case, the centrality of vision, the importance of the natural world in and to the text, the awareness and appreciation of trickster stories, and the invocation of community are all in keeping with Anishinaabe worldview and culture. In the creation story, after all, the process that leads to the creation of the world begins with a vision had by Kitche Manitou.[5] As Vizenor and others have noted, the language of the Anishinaabe, Anishinaabemowin, is rooted in the natural world; is organic; and, rich in verbs, is active.[6] The Anishinaabe trickster Naanabozho is a culture hero for the People, and the stories that feature the trickster help them make sense of the world and human and other-than-human behavior. Those stories are shared, of course, and in and through their sharing community is formed and reenforced.

The form and composition of *Hiroshima Bugi* are indicative of a postmodern turn.[7] Beyond the fact that Ronin and the mandioo envoy take turns narrating the text, Ronin's sections are composed of bits of narrative originally written on scraps of paper, napkins, the backs of tickets, on any piece of paper Ronin can get his hands on. He writes on remnants in honor of *hibakusha* Ota Yoko, who wrote *City of Corpses* on whatever paper she could find in Hiroshima in the first months following the bombing. Ronin's notes and scenes—called shards, scraps, remnants in the text—are sent, organized only by size of the pieces of paper, to the Hotel Manidoo. There, the Native veterans "with great respect and humor" (*Hiroshima Bugi*, 118) unravel the pieces, connect the stories and scenes, and so construct his narrative. The text, then, is characterized by hybridity, a fragmentary nature, a certain indeterminacy and fluidity, and humor. The variable margins of the "Ronin of" strand, moreover, highlight how the bomb's detonation serves to call all borders and boundaries into question.

As "a true measure and touchstone of *hibakusha* survivance in the nuclear world" (*Hiroshima Bugi*, 103), the Atomu calendar is linked to stories and writing, and how both are sites of resistance to domination. In signaling year one of Ronin's new calendar with the atomic bomb's detonation, *Hiroshima Bugi* also makes a point about both postmodernism and politics. If dropping the bomb puts an end, once and for all, to the grand narratives of emancipation and speculation, then that end can mark a new beginning, one in which our incredulity toward totalizing metanarratives opens up a position from which to critique them and posit other ways to apprehend and be in the world. For Vizenor, the critique is rooted in the tease of good humor, of play. The commentary of Nightbreaker's friend and roommate from the hotel, himself an Anishinaabe veteran from the Leech Lake Reservation to the south and east of White Earth, reveals that the particular tease that is the calendar is linked to the modern Japanese practice of linking calendars to the emperor, telling us that, given the "'marriage of calendar to sovereign is not a traditional way of counting time in Japan, but rather a highly modern way of engaging in symbolic politics,'" Ronin's calendar "mocked the imperial reign of the emperors, Showa for Hirohito, Heisei for Akihito" (*Hiroshima Bugi*, 22).

With his narrative at the Yasukuni Jinja, shrine to millions of Japanese warriors slain in conflicts foreign and domestic, Ronin reveals that the emperors misused the shrine, founded in 1868, in order to justify colonial aggression (*Hiroshima Bugi*, 143). When Ronin "invades" the Shinto shrine (143), he does so in the spirit of his calendar: this the narrative makes clear by framing his initial explication of the shrine and his entrance to it with the dates Atomu One and August 15, Atomu Fifty-seven. Ronin would have us see that, while the shrine honors the warriors, it makes nary a mention of "the thousands of children who were incinerated in the service of the emperor" (148) at Hiroshima. Moreover, Ronin holds, "the promises of peace [at the shrine] are undermined by the war criminals that are venerated as kami spirits in the sanctuary. Tojo and the remains of other war criminals are protected by the shrine priests and the rant of nationalism" (150). The new beginning and reckoning announced by the Atomu calendar serve to call attention to the problematic nature of the shrine, and indeed of the Peace Park, its museum, and monuments. Monuments arrest our vision and draw us to them. Hailings in stone, they memorialize person(s) and the past and establish for us a link between past and present. Such links, though, are not ideologically innocent; nor do they necessarily tell the whole story. In the case of the Peace Park and its monuments, what is offered to visitors is at once a remembering of those who perished from the bomb and a forgetting of "the causes and conditions of total war" (Giamo, 705), including the role played by both Japanese and Western imperialism. (Giamo, 704). Benedict Giamo lists all that the Park elides, actions by both the United States and Japan, and in leaving out makes "manifest a dissociated state" (708) where the monuments call to mind and have us keep in mind only a partial picture, only part of the story. One of the first monuments constructed in the Park, the cenotaph for the victims of the bomb, echoes the architecture of Shinto shrines (705–706), which is fitting, given that Shinto shrines are devoted to "'continuity, stability, and the management of uncertainty'" (*Hiroshima Bugi*, 63).

Conversely, Ronin, the manidoo envoy tells us, "is a master of uncertainties and survivance" (*Hiroshima Bugi*, 63). As such, Ronin is rooted in Anishinaabe culture, tradition, and worldview, for the people do not manage uncertainty so much as recognize and live with and in it. Indeed, given the fluid category of person, which includes both human and other-than-human beings, to the equally fluid identity of those beings, for the same object in the life-world may be animate one moment and inanimate the next, to the blurry boundaries of the layered cosmos of the Anishinaabe, uncertainty, possibility, and contingency are the order of the day. A "visionary, an aesthetic warrior of eternal survivance, a *hafu* samarai, but never a fanatical romancer of nationalism or the emperor" (71), Ronin rails against the "simulated peace" he finds, a peace "fake, sentimental [and] passive" (49). His postmodern calendar, and Vizenor's, is a call to action that marks not a reign but a rain—the black rain of "atomu poison" (119) that rained down, survivors recount, within an hour after Little Boy's detonation.

It is worth noting the difference between the A-bomb, imaginatively deployed by Vizenor, the weapon that produced the self-induced rainout laden with radioactive debris, and the tank that rumbles into view for Abel and the reader in *House Made of Dawn*. Traumatized by his experience in World War II, Abel returns home unable to make sense of what happened to him after he left home to join the war effort. The fact that he "could not put together in his mind" (Momaday, 23) what happened stands as an indication of his fragmented state and of the need for him to get the pieces to cohere if he is to have any hope of being well. Amidst the confusion and jumble of the recent past and his memory of it one moment stands out, "one sharp fragment of recall, recurrent and distinct" (23): the enemy combat tank that arrived on the battleground to "clean up" any of the survivors.

Momaday's narrative stresses both the tank's nature and its effect. It is called, over and over, "the machine" as it rumbles toward the hill where Abel initially lies unconscious. It stands in striking contradistinction to the "human force far away and out of sight" (24) that stopped firing mortar rounds as the tank approached the battlefield. If, as Momaday has said, silence is the sanctuary of sound, then the sound of the enemy tank that "moved into the wide wake of silence, taking hold of the silence and swelling inside it" (24) consumes the very silence from which it is born. What is born is deafening, the tank itself "black and massive" (25) when it finally comes into sight. A figure of modern warfare, and of modernism, the tank is a machine that terrifies. It fractures the world and the individual psyche. From its initial deployment in World War I, the tank has been representative of industrial warfare. As Trudi Tate shows in her study of the tank, modernism, and the Great War, the tank accentuates humankind's vulnerability before the machine, even as it offers new combat possibilities. For Tate, "the tank seems to promise new kinds of agency—enabling the human body to enter zones which were previously impenetrable—at the same time as it negates agency and displaces the human subject from the narratives of war" (145).

House Made of Dawn makes clear that the tank and what it represents lead to madness when the moment of its arrival on the battlefield is repeated later in the narrative, this time recounted from the perspective of one of the two other U.S. soldiers to survive the battle. We know that Abel is present as Bowker testifies to an unnamed authority, and he grows angry and confused as he listens to "this white man . . . talk about him, account for him, as if he were not there" (Momaday, 16). Bowker and Corporal Rate witness Abel's actions after the tank crashes past him without those inside it recognizing that he is still alive: he goes "crazy," jumping up and yelling at the tank, "whooping it up and doing a goddamn war dance" (117) until the tank bounces to a stop and opens fire on him. Positioned by the narrative as both eyewitness to the event and audience to its retelling, the reader sees with Bowker and the unnamed "sir" that the tank has driven Abel at least temporarily insane.

The A-bomb is something else entirely, as Peter Sloterdijk makes clear in *Terror from the Air*. More than a difference by order of magnitude, which is of course painfully obvious, Little Boy and Fat Man constitute an attack on the life-world as well as its inhabitants. In the tradition of chemical warfare and fire bombing, the atomic bomb targets not an individual body or military-industrial site "but the enemy's environment" (Sloterdijk, 6), postulating as it were, in Sloterdijk's words, that "if an enemy's body can no longer be liquidated with direct hits, then the attacker is forced to make his continued existence impossible by his direct immersion in an unlivable milieu for a sufficiently long period of time" (16).

Natives have long known and suffered from the dominant society's disregard for both them and the environment. In *All Our Relations*, for instance, White Earth Anishinaabe writer, scholar, and activist Winona LaDuke chronicles the history and effects of persistent organic pollutants' (POPs) and PCB contamination of Akwasasne Mohawk land; highlights the story of the contamination of Native lands throughout the West by mining operations, nuclear testing, and the nuclear industry, with the accompanying effects on the people; and reveals how mining and hydroelectric concerns have been detrimental to the health of the land and the First Peoples of Canada. In short, all too often, as White Earth Anishinaabe poet Kimberly Blaeser writes, Native people have been "designated downwinders" (Blaeser, *Trailing You,* 54), made to try to live in a world where, their land taken, they reside on remnants that are themselves

> later drained dry of water and oil,
> ripped open in searches for its gold heart,
> its copper bosom,
> its coal black eyes,
> remnants chosen for test sites, weapons plants, nuclear burial
> *Trailing You,* 55

The lack of terminal punctuation in Blaeser's poem tacitly proclaims what LaDuke and Blaeser both know: that there is no end to the attempts to harm the land, the environment, and the Natives living there.

Sloterdijk sees explication, or the "revealing-inclusion of the background givens underlying manifest operations," as a central, determining feature of the twentieth century and the rise of terrorism, product design as a concept, and environmental thinking over its course. Individually and together, those three "singular and incomparable features" contribute to "an acceleration in 'explication'" as they compel us ever more and ever faster to recognize and take into account our being in the world (Sloterdijk, 9). Sloterdijk stresses that the bomb and the practice of thermoterrorism that it inaugurates bring to light the hitherto unknown, concealed, and imperceptible (58), and in doing so, everything changes as our understanding of the life-world now includes unseen waves and radiation that can harm. Small wonder, then, that *Hiroshima Bugi* opens in the rain. Ronin addresses the reader, asking her/him to come out of the rain and into the ruins, literal and figurative, produced by the bomb. He knows that we are all in this rain, affected by it, for it is "a reminder of that bright and vicious light that poisoned the marrow and forever burned the heart of our memories. Rain, rain, and the ominous stories of the black rain. No one can ever be sure of the rain" (1).

Small wonder, too, that Ronin's tattoos are invisible until his skin is exposed to extreme heat, be it from sauna, hot baths, or passion. Mirroring the heat produced by the bomb's detonation and what appears after it—both the blisters and sores that come with radiation poisoning and the loss of any totalizing and comforting grand narrative—the tattoos on Ronin's chest, reminiscent of Japanese *irebokuro,* announce a promise: Atomu One, Eight Fifteen (103, 153). Rather than a romantic or sentimental commemoration of the bomb's detonation, however, Ronin's chest tattoo is rendered in Derrida's spirit of, as Toth puts it, a "promise of a future that is forever 'to come'" (19). Rather than being paralyzing, the promise of what is always to come, what is deferred, compels one to move and to act (Toth, 20). Ronin, and *Hiroshima Bugi*, moves and acts in the name of ghosts.

Ronin is haunted by the ghosts of the dead children of Hiroshima parading in the Peace Park every morning at 8:15 (*Hiroshima Bugi*, 65). Caught by the blast and the conflagration that followed, thousands of children perished. Tellingly, after the reference to rain that opens the text, the next remnant we read proclaims, "Listen, the shadows of dead children arise from the stone and shout back at the ravens" (*Hiroshima Bugi*, 1). For Ronin, and for the text, those ghosts constitute a far different hailing in stone from that of the monuments in the Peace Park. They return because the Peace Park relegates them to the passivity of aesthetic victimry (135), a position, Giamo argues, that reinforces the victim consciousness of postwar Japan and a "Japanese narrative of nationalism that views a pacifist people emerging from the very act of atomic victimage" (705). Such a narrative, again, elides much that Vizenor's text would have the reader see and occludes much that Vizenor's postmodern turn is dedicated to keeping open.

As is the case with the Yasukuni Jinja and the Peace Park and its monuments, White Earth was appropriated by a nation, in this case the United States, and its national narrative. Founded in 1868, the White Earth Reservation was part of the nation's efforts to locate in one place the Anishinaabe within the borders of Minnesota, and in doing so make the land beyond the borders of the reservation easier for whites to settle. Because the space within the reservation's borders was already open to the Anishinaabe prior to the formulation of White Earth, the location in the Parkland belt of north-central Minnesota utilized by both Anishinaabes and Dakotas, efforts by the Government constituted an appropriation of the place in the name of a national narrative that defines the *indian* as other and relegates them to a designated remnant of their homeland so that progress can be maintained and Manifest Destiny can be realized. The Anishinaabe of Minnesota turned the tables on the state and the nation, at least initially, by choosing not to relocate to the newly created reservation. Some went so far as to claim the land set aside for them there while staying with band members at locales throughout northern Minnesota.[8]

Vizenor makes clear his awareness that both shrine and reservation were subject to appropriation, writing that "The Shinto Yasukuni Jinja, or shine, was founded in 1868, the same year that the United States government established the White Earth Reservation in Minnesota" (*Hiroshima Bugi*, 117), and he appropriates both in *Hiroshima Bugi* in the name of critique and, critically, healing. Laying bare the dangers of pre- and postwar Japanese nationalism, articulating the connections between the national narratives of Japan and the United States through the linking of the Ainu of Hokkaido and the Anishinaabe of Minnesota, and with the daily ghost parade of the dead children making clear the, at best, limited efficacy of the pose of peace and memorialization of victimry, *Hiroshima Bugi* would have us adopt an active and open stance that is predicated on and produces presence rather than absence. Such a stance, such a way of being in the world, is rooted in White Earth and in stories. While it is through "peace moves" such as setting alight the Peace Pond, renaming the Peace Museum "Hiroshima Mon Amour," and mocking the "vacuous shibboleths" (*Hiroshima Bugi*, 17) worn by tourists to Hiroshima with a T-shirt asking "Is it big enough?" that Ronin makes his presence known in Japan, "on the reservation his presence was animated more by stories" (*Hiroshima Bugi*, 113). In the recognizable postmodern both/and move, the animation cuts both ways. The stories both make Ronin present on the reservation even as he is physically absent, and they animate him more than do other things when he is on White Earth. In particular, trickster stories move Ronin and breathe life into his stories. On the reservation, Ronin experiences the dual nature of trickster stories: they torment and enrich. The torment comes from having one's comforting positions called into question in and through the stories; the trickster stories torment, too, because those that show the audience the ways in which Naanabozho is a culture hero for the Anishinaabe can well lead to one questioning one's own actions and what he or she has or has not done for others. At the same time, the trickster stories enrich Ronin, as they enrich all members of the audience, insofar as they are telling tales of "liberation and survivance" (*Hiroshima Bugi*, 138). As the manidoo envoy tells us, "No terminal believer, monotheist, causation native, or otherwise, could endure the tease of trickster stories without the pleasure and humor of natural irony" (138).

In Japan, Ronin takes comfort in the creation and bear stories told by Ainu elders (126), in no small measure because he is a member of the Makwa, or bear, clan. In the traditional totemic system and social structure of the Anishinaabe, the bear clan is associated with defense. A "*makwa* adventurer" (*Hiroshima Bugi*, 138), Ronin defends the Anishinaabe, the spirits of the children killed at Hiroshima, and, indeed, the world with shouts and teases, actions he learned at White Earth. That "visionary practice" (134) is motivated by the desire that one move from a passive to an active stance—without adopting and being driven by a terminal creed. With shouts and teases, with humor, then, with a postmodern turn rooted in Anishinaabe worldview and Anishinaabe stories, Ronin and Vizenor start us on the path to healing. They offer us survivance stories.

Writers such as fellow White Earth Anishinaabe Gordon Henry Jr. and Choctaw D. L. Birchfield echo in and with their texts elements of the postmodern turn articulated by Vizenor. Henry's *The Light People* (1994), for instance, highlights representation, the arbitrary nature of the sign, hybridity, and indeterminacy. Set on and near the Fine Day Reservation, a fictionalized version of White Earth, the text foregrounds metonymy and play in a song Arthur Boozhoo sings as part of a magic trick he performs:

Sleep, peels, angles of angels sing of sign,
sword of words, elm smells concrete, encore
on the corner, a northern ornithologist, jest
in case, sends a letter which ends in ways to
sway opinion to slice the union onion with a
sword of words, without tears.
    The Light People, 21

Boozhoo's song shares with a postmodern aesthetic a certain play with words and the chain of signifiers, and its playfulness does so in order to, as in the case of the shredded correspondence over which it is sung, make something whole (Henry, 21). A sword of words can heal, then provided those words are offered in a playful, tricky spirit, one captured in Boozhoo's very name with its echo of the Anishinaabe trickster Naanabozho and the Shinnob greeting designed to invoke, call out, and at times call on trickster.

The embodiment of trickster discourse, *The Light People* early on establishes the primacy of openness and a willingness to keep from locking onto and into a final answer. Searching for what became of his father and mother, of who they were and are, and thus of what his place is in the kinship structure of the Anishinaabe nation, Oskinaway, in the words that close the text's first paragraph, "came to no final conclusion" (Henry, 3). In the text's first and most fundamental playful move, Oskinaway's name both phrases the desire of the dominant culture to have the *indian* gone once and for all and suggests that it is via trickster, the figuration that "denies presence and completion" (Vizenor, *Narrative Chance*, 192), that such a desire is circumvented. In its place, the text ultimately offers one of the foundational phrases of the Republic, "We the people," appropriated to stand for the Anishinaabe.

The diviner and medicine man Jake Seed makes clear that openness and uncertainty are connected to seeking, finding, and healing. He tells Oskinaway and his grandparents:

You know what can be done, Jim. Sometimes memory runs away from us and even the spirit can't find the trail. In some cases people leave things in a particular place and wander further and further away from that place with the false knowledge that what they left will always be there. Sometimes, then, the lost must want to return, before their knowledge makes them forget what they left. Still, I go by what I am given. I never know how these things will turn out. [Henry, 9–10]

The passage tacitly stresses possibility and contingency, the need to keep an open mind and judge and act case by case. This prohibits the formation of any terminal creed that would imagine that there is a fixed and final answer ahead of time as to how "things will turn out."

As Seed's helper, Arthur Boozhoo arrives at the home of Oskinaway's grandparents wearing clothes that are a mixture of the non-Native and the Native. His baseball cap bill is trimmed with beadwork, his black suit coat features both a picture of a white eagle on its back and the traditional Anishinaabe woodland vine-and-leaf pattern on the front. If the jacket and cap together highlight hybridity, then the slogan on the T-shirt Boozhoo wears beneath his jacket indicates that stories and orality are a way to save the natural world as well as how to teach and heal: "save a tree / tell a story" (Henry, 11). Here too we see a link with the postmodern, which Hassan sees as tending toward parataxis rather than hypotaxis. Such a tendency, Betty Booth Donohue notes, shapes D. L. Birchfield's *The Oklahoma Basic Intelligence Test* (1998). Moreover, both Birchfield's first text and Henry's *The Light People* are multigenre offerings; their hybrid nature effectively calls into question the boundaries between genres and their efficacy. Given such questioning, it is telling that Henry's first book, a collection of poetry, is entitled *Outside White Earth* and his most recent offering, 2007's *The Failure of Certain Charms and Other Disparate Signs of Life*, includes a poem written from the edge: "Postmodern Rez Edge Inhalation: Paint Thinner Sublime."

While Birchfield's 2004 novel *Field of Honor* does not test the boundaries of genre, it does sound a note of survivance while calling into question, and thus asking the reader to think differently about, the received narratives of the *indian*, Europe, and America. The novel begins with a clear declaration of time and place—"15 October 1976 / Valley of the McGee / Ouachita Mountains / Southeastern Oklahoma" (*Field of Honor*, 3)—and then proceeds to pull the ground out from under our feet, literally and figuratively, as Patrick Pushmatha McDaniel stumbles upon a subterranean world populated by Choctaw, Natchez, and Catawba Natives. A young Natchez named Little Elroy recounts for McDaniel a brief history of his people, of the underground world called Ishtaboli, and of the Choctaw. Choctaw tribes from Okla Alabama to Okla Tannap call Ishtaboli home. These ancient groups give the lie to the dominant Euro-American tendency to lump all groups of a Native nation together as one tribe. Schooled by the dominant society, it makes sense that McDaniel would ask, "All these other tribes are Choctaws, too?" It makes equal sense that, schooled from another perspective, Elroy replies, "'Down here they are still Choctaws. Up on the surface, back in time, down through the centuries, a lot of Choctaw tribes pretty much tried to stop being Choctaw. . . . By the time of Indian Removal, in the 1830s, only the Okla Falaya, the Okla Hannali, and the Okla Tannap, up on the surface, were still willing to admit they were Choctaws. But, anciently, all of the others were Choctaws, and they all speak some dialect of Choctaw, and this place down here is an ancient place'" (Birchfield, *Field of Honor*, 112). What Elroy reveals, for McDaniel and the reader, should remind us that, as Michelle Raheja notes, "prior to 1492 Native American community identity was often flexible, communities and families sometimes splintered for a variety of reasons and formed new bands, nations, and confederacies" (3). Such flexibility and play ran counter to European and Euro-American desires to fix the *indian*.

In the ancient place that is Ishtaboli, children are taught "German history" from its beginning: the invasion of the English Islands by the European Germans, the invasion of North America by English-Island Germans, and critical civil wars between Germans that have affected the Choctaw—beginning with the "first North American German Civil War" of 1776 to 1784. In the words of McDaniel's young guide, "It is our misfortune that our continent is being invaded by such a barbarous, warlike people and that there is no way to escape their incessant and bloody civil wars, which now threaten all life on the planet" (Birchfield, *Field of Honor*, 124).

The stakes, then, are incredibly high. Given that, isn't it about time that we turn to Native literatures in all their telling diversity? Let the last word be Vizenor's. The first haiku in the Spring section of *Cranes Arise* (1999) is tethered to the headwaters of the Mississippi. Off the reservation, Lake Itasca is not outside the ancestral homeland of the Anishinaabe. It is where Nightbreaker goes after he has been diagnosed with a cancer that is linked to his exposure to radiation. He builds a cabin by the lake, and there he heals thanks to "meditation, native medicine, and the annual stories of survivance at the headwaters" (*Hiroshima Bugi*, 18). Place, home, and what grows there can heal, stories can heal. Native stories and Native storiers open for us:

> *lake itasca, minnesota*
> spring fever
> basho wades in the shallows
> cranes arise

NOTES

1. Throughout I am following Vizenor's practice of italicizing and lowercasing the word *indian* in order to designate the construction created and perpetuated by the dominant society; for more on this point, see below.

2. Warchitecture names the systematic and calculated attempt to destroy the cultural identity and collective memory of a group by targeting sites of significant cultural and collective importance. In Sarajevo, this meant targeting mosques, the Oriental Institute, and other important buildings in addition to Vijecnica. As "war against architecture," warchitecture constitutes "the destruction of the cultural artifacts of an enemy people or nation as a means of dominating, terrorizing, dividing or eradicating it" (Bevan, 8). See, for instance, Bevan, *Destruction of Memory*; Zeco, "The National and University Library of Bosnia and Herzegovina"; and Herscher, "Warchitectural Theory."

3. On the intersection of modernism and Momaday see, for instance, Schubell, *N. Scott Momaday;* Isernhagen, "N. Scott Momaday and the Use(s) of Modernism"; and Larry Landrum, "The Shattered Modernism of Momaday's *House Made of Dawn."*

4. Later that decade, Hassan wondered if theory should not, must not, devote itself "to grasp[ing] the creative moment of difference, of ontological diversity itself" ("Literary Theory in an Age of Globalization," 3).

5. See Johnston, *Ojibway Heritage,* pp. 11–12.

6. See, for instance, Vizenor, *The People Named the Chippewa* and Erdrich, *Books and Islands in Ojibwe Country.*

7. Hassan makes a distinction between postmodernism as it exists in terms of and in relation to philosophy, architecture, and the arts, especially, and between it in terms of and in relation to globalization, networks, technology, the media, and consumerism. He terms the latter "postmodernity." It bears remarking that when postmodernism makes an explicit appearance in *Hiroshima Bugi*, it does so in terms of what Hassan labels "postmodernity": "Mount Fuji, a mighty, natural spirit, remains the same, only the views have changed since the occupation. Mifune would have a similar view of the mountain when he ran away from the orphanage. The Ginza today is a wild, postmodern, international trade center" (25). Situating the Ginza as it does, the text makes clear the play between the global and the local that is a feature of postmodernity even as it highlights postmodernism's connection to global networks of circulation and geopolitical processes. This note is sounded again later when the envoy quotes MacArthur's reported concern that "The only remaining danger with Japan was its potential export competence. . . . MacArthur worried that Japan, supported by 'a salary of famine (cheap wages),' would dominate Asian markets with 'junk' products" (102).

8. On the history of White Earth Reservation see, for instance, Meyer, *White Earth Tragedy,* and Winona LaDuke's historical novel, *Last Standing Woman.*

WORKS CITED

Bevan, Robert. *The Destruction of Memory: Architecture at War.* London: Reaktion, 1996.

Bhabha, Homi. *The Location of Culture.* New York: Routledge, 1994.

Birchfield, D. L. *Field of Honor.* Norman: University of Oklahoma Press, 2004.

———. *The Oklahoma Basic Intelligence Test: New and Collected Elementary Epistolary, Autobiographical, and Oratorical Choctologies.* Greenfield Center, N.Y.: Greenfield Review Press, 1997.

Blaeser, Kimberly. *Trailing You.* Greenfield Center, N.Y.: Greenfield Review Press, 1994.

———. "*The Way to Rainy Mountain*: Momaday's Work in Motion," 39–54. In *Narrative Chance: Postmodern Discourse on Native American Indian Literatures.*

Edited by Gerald Vizenor. Norman: University of Oklahoma Press, 1989, 1992.

Erdrich, Louise. *Books and Islands in Ojibwe Country.* Washington, D.C.: National Geographic Society, 2003.

Giamo, Benedict. "The Myth of the Vanquished: The Hiroshima Peace Memorial Museum." *American Quarterly* 55:4 (December 2003), 703–28.

Hassan, Ihab. "From Postmodernism to Postmodernity: The Local/Global Context." *Philosophy and Literature* 25:1 (April 2001), 1–13.

———. "Literary Theory in an Age of Globalization." *Philosophy and Literature* 32:1 (April 2008), 1–10.

———. *The Postmodern Turn.* Columbus: Ohio State University Press, 1987.

Henry Jr., Gordon. *The Failure of Certain Charms and Other Disparate Signs of Life.* London: Salt Publishing, 2007.

———. *The Light People.* Norman: University of Oklahoma Press, 1994.

Herscher, Andrew. "Warchitectural Theory." *Journal of Architectural Education* (2008), 35–43.

Hutcheon, Linda. "Postmodern Afterthoughts." *Wascana Review* 37:1 (2002), 5–12.

Isernhagen, Hartwig. "N. Scott Momaday and the Use(s) of Modernism: Some Remarks on the Example of Yvor Winters." In *Aspects of Modernism: Studies in Honour of Max Nanny.* Edited by Andreas Fischer et al. Tübingen: Narr, 1997.

Johnston, Basil. *Ojibway Heritage.* Lincoln: University of Nebraska Press, 1976.

LaDuke, Winona. *All Our Relations.* Cambridge, Mass.: South End Press, 1999.

———. *Last Standing Woman.* Stillwater, Minn.: Voyageur Press, 1997.

Landrum, Larry. "The Shattered Modernism of Momaday's *House Made of Dawn.*" *Modern Fiction Studies* 42:4 (1996), 763–86.

Lincoln, Kenneth. *Native American Renaissance.* Berkeley: University of California Press, 1983.

Lyotard, Jean-Francois. *The Postmodern Condition: A Report on Knowledge.* Translated by Geoff Bennington and Brian Massumi. Minneapolis: University of Minnesota Press, 1984.

Meyer, Melissa. *The White Earth Tragedy: Ethnicity and Dispossession on a Minnesota Anishinaabe Reservation.* Lincoln: University of Nebraska Press, 1994.

Momaday, N. Scott. *House Made of Dawn.* New York: Harper & Row, 1968.

Notre Musique (2004). Dir. Jean-Luc Godard. Perf. Sarah Adler, Nade Dieu, et al. DVD. Wellspring Media, 2005.

Owens, Louis. "'Ecstatic Strategies': Gerald Vizenor's *Darkness in Saint Louis: Bearheart,*" 141–54. In *Narrative Chance: Postmodern Discourse on Native American Indian Literatures.* Edited by Gerald Vizenor. Norman: University of Oklahoma Press, 1989, 1992.

Raheja, Michelle. *Reservation Reelism: Redfacing, Visual Sovereignty, and Representations of Native Americans in Film.* Lincoln: University of Nebraska Press, 2010.

Schubnell, Matthias. *N. Scott Momaday: The Cultural and Literary Background.* Norman: University of Oklahoma Press, 1985.

Sloterdijk, Peter. *Terror from the Air.* Translated by Amy Patton and Steve Corcoran. Los Angeles: Semiotext(e), 2009.

Tate, Trudi. *Modernism, History, and the First World War.* Manchester: Manchester University Press, 1998.

Toth, Josh. *The Passing of Postmodernism.* Albany: SUNY Press, 2010.

Vizenor, Gerald. *Cranes Arise.* Minneapolis: Nodin Press, 1999.

———. *Darkness in Saint Louis: Bearheart.* St. Paul, Minn.: Truck Press, 1978.

———. *Fugitive Poses.* Lincoln: University of Nebraska Press, 2000.

———. *Hiroshima Bugi.* Lincoln: University of Nebraska Press, 2003.

———. *The People Named the Chippewa.* Minneapolis: University of Minnesota Press, 1983.

———. "A Postmodern Introduction," 3–16. In *Narrative Chance: Postmodern Discourse on Native American Indian Literatures.* Edited by Gerald Vizenor. Norman: University of Oklahoma Press, 1989, 1992.

Vizenor, Gerald, ed. *Narrative Chance: Postmodern Discourse on Native American Indian Literatures.* Norman: University of Oklahoma Press, 1989, 1992.

Zeco, Munevera. "The National and University Library of Bosnia and Herzegovina during the Current War." *Library Quarterly* 66:3 (1996), 294–301.

13

Speak Memory

The Remembrances of Contemporary Native American Poetry

A. ROBERT LEE

Knowing the distance
is always vast, realizing
destiny is somewhere beyond,
we need memory to know the way
    Simon Ortiz, "Across the Prairie Hills"[1]

I understand now that all life has ceremonies connected
with it, and for us, without our memory, our old people,
and our children, we would be like lost people in the world
we live in, as well as in the worlds in which our loved ones
are waiting.
    Luci Tapahonso, "All the Colors of Sunset"[2]

My memory starts under the earth . . .
    Ray Young Bear, "Emily Dickinson, Bismarck
    and the Roadrunner's Inquiry"[3]

With electric everything and my computer whirring
I *work* my way through memories and philosophies . . .
    Kimberly Blaeser, "Dictionary for a New Century"[4]

Can there be doubt of the heft and press of memory, remembrance, within
Native American and First Nations authorship? Whether it is memory of
tribal genealogy in all its massive cultural plurality and timeline, or of the
happenstance of any one discrete life within that genealogy, it has operated
as a necessary dynamic. It has long been recognized that oral traditions of
creation myth, chant, song, and humor, along with trickster fable like coyote,
spiderwoman, and raven, implicate both speaker and listener in memory as

a form of template even as it is being reworked in the spontaneity of new voice.[5] In written tradition, poetry perhaps above all, the same often carries over equally: one recognizes the presence of trace, frame, or image, even as the poem assumes its own individual pitch. The upshot has been a body of Native-authored poetry, whose part in helping augment the sense of a Native American literary renaissance, and allowing for all other points of focus, lies precisely in its unique lanterns or theaters of memory.

Earliest life-writing, notably by Samson Occom, William Apess, or George Copway, already saw its task as one of right memory. "The proper term which ought to be applied to our nation, to distinguish it from the rest of the human family, is that of '*Natives,*'" Apess would write in 1829 in *A Son of the Forest.* Subsequent life-writings—from Luther Standing Bear's *My Indian Boyhood* (1925), to N. Scott Momaday's *The Names: A Memoir* (1976) and Leslie Marmon Silko's *Storyteller* (1981), to Jim Barnes's *On Native Ground: Memories and Impressions* (1997)—have been no less assiduous, or inventive, in their webs of remembering: first-person, familial, tribal, both historical and geographic, and in Gerald Vizenor's battling gamester term, even "postindian."[6] Discursive work makes its own contribution, whether a rallying like Vine Deloria's *Custer Died for Your Sins: An Indian Manifesto* (1969) or "nationalist" cultural ideology of the kind recently given collective expression by Jace Weaver, Craig S. Womack, and Robert Warrior in *American Indian Literary Nationalism* (2006). In the footfall of Apess, these endeavors not only shadow the remembered past but rewrite, and so reposition, that past.

The different waves of fiction offer necessary confirmation, from John Rollin Ridge/Yellow Bird's *The Life and Adventures of Joaquin Murieta, the Celebrated Bandit* (1854), with its nineteenth-century California derring-do, to N. Scott Momaday's *House Made of Dawn* (1968), with its Jemez Pueblo circular healing-narrative of Abel's wars in both the Pacific theater and on the domestic battlefield. In the efflorescence of novels to follow, Native memory can be said to have taken on a sumptuous variety of idiom, be it James Welch's rehistoricization of 1870s Blackfeet life in *Fool's Crow* (1986), Gerald Vizenor's postmodern reversal of the Discovery Story in *The Heirs of Columbus* (1991), Leslie Marmon Silko's hemispheric eco-epic of the indigenous Americas in *Almanac of the Dead* (1991), or Diane Glancy's polyphonic narrative of Cherokee removal and the 1838 Trail of Tears in *Pushing the Bear* (1996). Taken together, a veritable consortium of memory comes into play, each, however, given its own singular inventive filtering.

Native poetry has acted in shared spirit. The headpiece threads from Ortiz to Blaeser as to the presence of memory in their verse, and, by implication, in that of fellow Native poets, give witness. How, in the one reach, to find ongoing measure for the remembrance of pasts at once richly tribal-specific in custom, belief system, and language, not to say possessed of continental liberty, yet also subject to lost sovereignty, colonialism, allotment, disease, displacement, the one or another kind of self-fissure? How, in another, to re-member pasts-into-present, or just a live present, altogether more personal in signature? Whichever the case, in poetry as in other Native writing, the avoid-ance of victimry has been the almost-unwritten rule. Odds, setback, there obviously has been, but also resilience, continuity, or in another widely taken-up Vizenor term, survivance.[7] Nor has all been tribe- or reservation-centered. Cities, lives in transit (sometimes adrift), domestic as well as foreign wars, the penitentiary or campus or hospital, even countries outside the Americas, as to be sure the perennials of identity, relationship, and location, have each provided their respective sources of Native remembering.

The challenge has been to make memory itself memorable, a reflexive affirmation derived from the poetry's very making. Stylings in this respect have taken on every form, free verse or prose poem, epic or sonnet in length, and whether belonging to the themed collection, the miscellany, the self-chronicle, or chapbook. In "A Share of the Stair (or As I Talk I'm Becoming What I Say)," Diane Glancy offers well-taken touchstones:

> Memory is a moraine. A little clutter of stones the glacier left
> when it retreated. . . .
> You see memories are shape-changers moving among us. So we
> create when we remember.[8]

Moraine, retreating glacier, memory as shape-changer, and the rubric of we create when we remember undoubtedly carry general import. But each gives an especial pointer to the way authorship, and Native authorship not least, in-scribes remembrance, for few American histories have had greater existential cause, or a longer resident chronology, to speak memory in all its different registers, and for sure, through the particularity of poetry.

The verse collections in view—*from Sand Creek* (1981) by Simon Ortiz (Acoma Pueblo), *Rooms: New and Selective Poems* (2005) by Diane Glancy (Cherokee), *Blue Horses Rush In* (1997) by Luci Tapahonso (Navajo), *Black Eagle Child: The Facepaint Narratives* (1992) by Ray A. Young Bear (Mes-quakie), and *Apprenticed to Justice* (2007) by Kimberly Blaeser (Anishinaabe), respectively—offer a spectrum of confirmation. All these poets can look to a further repertoire, literary careers of long-standing across prose and drama as well as verse genres. In settling upon a single volume by each, however, the bid is to seize upon poetries, and their different ways of speaking to memory, in their own deserving register.

Simon Ortiz's *from Sand Creek* offers an apt departure point with its inspired interplay of two war memories: the 1860s massacre of Cheyenne and Arapaho in tribally named Kiowa County, southeastern Colorado, and the Vietnam War in the persons of Native ex-combatants recovering at the VF hospital,

Fort Lyons, Colorado, during the 1970s, whom he names affectionately in his dedication. The preface leaves no doubt of the overall resolve:

> How to deal with history. That was the question on my mind when I began to write *from Sand Creek*. By *history* I meant the history that included me personally as a Native American, the history that included Native people and culture, the American history that I and other Natives sometimes felt foreign to.[9]

Ortiz so fashions a volume of dual memory, the one historic calamity "creatively" remembered in the other. The upshot, undoubtedly, is a major sequence at once tribute, riposte, scrupulously imaged meditation, and one of Native poetry's genuinely consequential landmarks.

"Grief memorizes the grass" (11) reads an opening line. Well it might, as Ortiz precisely, and clinically, first sets out the bloodbath of Sand Creek (8). The ensuing lines summon the November 29, 1864, slaughter of the peaceably encamped tribal members—105 women and children and 28 men—at the hands of the well-armed Reverend Colonel John W. Chivington and his Colorado Volunteers, in spite of the flag given in 1863 to the leader of the Southern Cheyennes, Black Kettle, by President Lincoln as token of federal protection. To which is added the rider, "By mid-1865, the Cheyenne and Arapaho People had been driven out of Colorado Territory" (8). This remembrance is to be seen from the vantage point of more search-and-destroy history, that of Vietnam, and in its wake, Native soldier-veteran rehabilitation at Fort Lyons by Ortiz and his fellow war wounded, suffering as much from damage to mind and nerve as to body.

Both histories, the collection underscores, have inflicted grievous damage, tribespeople of two eras caught in historical wound, the one an America-at-home of Manifest Destiny and the other an America-abroad of military conflict. Both bespeak iconic yet "raw" memory, "red-eyed and urgent" (11). The introduction of the figure of Toby personifies the feeling of self-erasure ("Yes, / he is Indian. / He hides and tends/ the shape of his face"), war trauma that causes his tongue to be "frozen," "frantic" (13). "Remember My Lai" (15), also brought up at the outset, is made to parallel "Remember Sand Creek" (15). This ligature of Native veteran, Vietnam and its fallout, and the antecedent Sand Creek massacre holds throughout, a continuity of damage to be set against redemptive "open plains and mountains" (31), "horizons" (41), an America of best Nature and promise. As if to further bind each of the defaults, Ortiz also deploys (and italicizes) one of the great animal figurations ("Buffalo ghosts" [21]), their power and their defeat, as remembered throughout tribal history: "*Buffalo were dark rich clouds moving upon the rolling hills and plains of America. And then the flashing steel came upon bone and flesh*" (20).

These parallels of era, and personnel, are again underlined as the voice of the poem recalls Sand Creek when driving across the Kansas border into Colorado:

Memory
is stone, very quiet,
like this,
a moment clenched tightly
as knuckles
around gunstock
around steering wheel. [23]

Clenched knuckles might readily stand in for clenched history. Black Kettle ("principal elder" [8]) assumes his place as the cheated interlocutor of Southern Cheyenne welcome and reconciliation to arriving frontier America (79). A run of further links comes into play. Sand Creek itself is said to anticipate 1901 and the expulsion of the Utes from Colorado (24). Oklahoma and federal removal policy are given due mention ("Ghosts Indian-like / still driven / towards Oklahoma" [25]). Paiute defeat in Nevada is invoked ("a warrior chief was assassinated by the cavalry, cut into stewing pieces, fed to the other chiefs, and a treaty was signed" [28]). Black Elk's famous declaration invites surprise: "It's almost inexplicable that Black Elk could say the dream was ended" (40). Kit Carson ("Carson caught Indians, / secured them with his lies" [53]), and Andrew Jackson before him ("ruminating, savoring / fresh Indian blood" [17]), are seen as malign players, antifigures, in the usual triumphalist roll call of frontier American history.

This same litany, with Sand Creek itself always as centerpiece, connects into the remembrance of Vietnam and its damaged Native returnees in the VA hospital ("Lie awake, afraid. / Thinned breath" [55]). "Very quiet," "stone" (23) may be the now-joined and retrospective memory of American West and Mekong Asia, but only as indeed "clenched tightly" (23). Ortiz's remembering of the veterans (to include himself), both in his own personal voice and in their own remembering, gives the sequence its live human presence. Toby, as inaugural figure, haunts the La Junta Café, is advised by VA doctors "not to worry" though "sick" with evident post-traumatic stress disorder, stares into a window neurasthenically, and in memorial tribal manner "closely tends to his shadow" (13). He serves, symptomatically, as the first among others.

W. and Nez are to be heard singing within a Rocky Mountain vista of "Land and sky; flowers and generations" (26). For Ortiz, their melody has the effect of "summoning eternity," even though they themselves "did not know how / they were patriots" (26). Billy disappears ("Like his words, / he could be anywhere" [61]), a wounded drifter seeking "shadows" and for whom "Memory was his lost trail" (61). The Polka Dot Kid, another of their fellow hospitalized, has ended confused, in a skid-row hotel not knowing whether it is Amarillo or Denver. Dusty plays piano before the start of the movies at the VA hospital, his fingers blunt ("Throbbing / bullets and aches" [69]) and for whom "Memory . . . rattles in dry cells" (69). Apache, a Korean War veteran, dreams freedom even in his confusion. "The "man / who cried for his mother" causes Ortiz's own throat "to constrict" (85). Oklahoma Boy sits slumped ("There is beauty / in his American face, / but the dread implanted / by the explosive / in Asia denies it' [93]), a depression-sufferer and yet, however distantly, a successor warrior to each of those who survived Sand Creek.

Yet as much as, for each, the silhouette of Sand Creek is replayed in World War II, Korea, and Vietnam, or white settlement is remembered ("Swedes, Germans, / Mennonites, Dutch, / Irish, escaping Europe"), or costs persist of self-loss, depression, alcoholism, and the "persuasion and force" (62) of the hospital, so there are also pointers to better health, better sources of memory. They lie in Sand Creek's "own flowers/and new grass" (9), the magpie (19), "corn" (32), "rain" (33), "quilts" (35), "young blood" (35), and both the legacy of Black Kettle ("He swept his hand / all about them. / The vista of the mountains / was at his shoulder" [79]) and the exemplary call of Walt Whitman, however traduced, to an America of spiritual health ("Whitman was a poet I loved" [80]).

Likewise if blood, the stigmata wounds not only to tribal body but to tribal land, is to be remembered as plentiful ("*The blood poured into the plains, steaming like breath on winter mornings*" [66]), so there is hope of cyclical repair ("*The breath rose in clouds and became the rain and replenishment*" [66]). "Spring wind," alongside "flowers" and "new grass" (9), gives promise. For all, thereby, that *from Sand Creek* unsparingly memorializes historic Native injury, and its traverse from one American era to another, it also reminds of Ortiz's equally unsparing memorial belief in the continuing Native wellsprings of life.

An observation in *Claiming Breath* (1992), Diane Glancy's "diary of personal matters," gives a frame to her poetry overall. Mindful of her mixed-blood Cherokee and white Arkansas family legacy, and a life of domestic gains and losses, she speaks to how, for her, memory mandates a changed kind of poetry: "Only poetry or a form of new writing captures the thoughts that entomb the mind \ the disorder of memory, the un-chronological order."[10] This might be regarded as Glancy's own version of Ezra Pound's "Make it New," an entrance point, itself poetically articulated, to *Rooms: New and Selected Poems*, in which memory is worked one way and then another in seizing upon the contrariety within the terms and conditions of her life. For her, that embraces Native-white identity, an unbreakable allegiance to Bible Christianity, the memory of parents and daughter-wife-mother gendering, the circuits of road travel and classroom across Minnesota, Oklahoma, Kansas, and Missouri in her role as English and creative writing professor at Macalester College and elsewhere, and always the call to literary word. Each of these facets presses into different, though often overlapping, verse remembrance.

"Here I Am Standing Beside Myself" (initially published in *Lone Dog's Winter Count*, 1991) can act as an axial composition from *Rooms* in this regard, a prose-poem of movingly focused memory-images as to background, history, family, name. Opening with an injunction to search memory ("Just look at the family album" [65]), it speaks immediately of her "white mother" and sisters and her father and brother with the skin of sparrow hawks on their heads. The latter detail links to two other observations, suitably accoutered with snippets of Cherokee. The one bears on flight, fugitive migrancy: "My father said his grandfather fled Indian Territory <*kuna'yeli st'di*> [claw-scratch-like] when he'd done something wrong" (65). The other implies margin: "We were outcasts now as well as Indian. & only part of them. Outcast of outcasts" (65). But a ripple of counter-memories enters the reckoning. Under the rubrics, "It's when I remember . . ." (65) and "The feeling we weren't but really were" (65), they lead into what might be thought a Native aide-memoire: cornbread soaked in squirrel-grease, Cherokee hymns, a corn-god Jesus, moon and sun deities, and a raccoon turtle deer nibbling her feet. These all come into the speaker-poet's mind as she curls into herself (legs pulled up, fingers inside out, arms in chest and "my ears & nose into my head" [65]). This is memory as albumed Native absence and presence, two languages, and a self of displaced but restorative connections. It is also a world of remembrance made over into strong poetry.

"Tuning," sonnet-length, and initially published in *The Shadow's Horse* (2003), does allied imaginative duty.[11] The speaker alludes to early "exile" life, tough, economically at the sharp end, one of tract housing and hands-on physical labor. That has meant, for her father, the stockyard and slaughterhouse "yarding" of cows and pigs, and for her mother the move from farm to city. It has meant the family moves (Kansas, Indianapolis), her child's eye view of them above her in flight as she makes houses in the sand, and the haunted feeling that "something terrible" in the past has caused the family to move.[12] This she links to her Native heritage—"My father's Cherokee heritage tucked under / some sort of shame" (31). She ends by calling "to them above me," in afterlife as in plane as it were, to aid not only the will-to-memory but to making coherence of that memory. How, runs the poem's implicit question, and in accord with its title, to "tune" memory toward a decisive understanding of an at-an-angle past, white-Native and blue-collar, with its tableau of girlhood, flits, animal rendering, abattoir, and Native shadow?

This plait of remembering takes on almost startling force in her sixpart "The Stockyard Series: *Remuda*," also originally issued in *The Shadow's Horse*.[13] Each part again takes up family memory, her father's Depression-era cattle work in the stockyards, the cattle headed for slaughter, packinghouse, and meat cars, Indian buffalo, and the *remuda* with its memorial reference to cowboy roundups and horses. But these remembered scenes she also suffuses with a fervent Christian eschatology, Glancy's remembrance of how the whole bloody process for her has called up martyrdom, heaven and hell "as if Christ stepped from his cross" (33). This is a Bible-Pentecostal Christ of "creative" remembering amid the world's flesh and offal—"Christ in the convent / sacrificed like cattle" (33), beasts whose voices are "Gregorian chants" (34), a "processional" (36) of "cattle crowned with thorns" and "hogs crucified" (36), and where the long-ago stockyard memorializes not only her deceased father but a "Christ of manure" (37). These flights of image, sacrificial life into death and death into resurrection, make for vistas not unakin to those of Gerard Manley Hopkins in "The Wreck of the Deutschland" or Flannery O'Connor stories like "Greenleaf" or "A Good Man Is Hard to Find," memory at once visionary, little short of apocalyptic.

Native heritage especially focuses Glancy's field of memory in *Rooms*. "Portrait of the Artist as Indian" (64), initially in *Lone Dog's Winter Count*, can be thought symptomatic, a laconic about-face to high art in which Native butchering craft is placed in the ascendancy over James Joyce or Henry James. As the titular Native woman of an earlier time field-dresses her buffalo, so, reflexively, she can be seen to be field-dressing history. Buffalo hide is carefully severed, "pouches, vessels, the stomach, liver, / bladder" (64) are extricated, "meat on sticks" is dried upon a line, and ribs are cut. The working gloss points up the poem's iconographical meaning—"She dismantles the carcass / the way old stories are carried in the heart" (64). Entrails washed, hide tanned, a medicine pouch made of ears: the unwasteful Native art of life is so remembered, and transposed, as also the Native life of art.

"Prayers and memories protect us" reads Luci Tapahonso's "A Birthday Poem" in *Blue Horses Rush In*,[14] a verse-and-story collection in line with her earlier and much-acclaimed *Sáanii Dahataał/The Women Are Singing* (1993). In the limning of her Navajo/Diné world, with its home center for her of Shiprock (or *Tsé Bit'a'i*), New Mexico, where she grew up bilingually in a clan-extended family, Tapahonso could hardly not write from a deep force of memory. Her ambit as poet, even so, has not infrequently extended beyond *Dinetah* (meaning "Navajo Country," as she explains in "In 1864," one of her best-known poems in *Sáanii Dahataał*, with its intimate memory of the brutal, displacing "Long Walk"). "The Pacific Dawn," also from *Sáanii Dahataał* (53–54), speaks of how Hilo's Hawaiian colors, volcanoes, and currents "force themselves into my memory" (54). "In Praise of Texas," from *Blue Horses Rush In* (11–13), offers a playful litany of the Lone Star State through its airports, the country-and-western songster George Strait, a fond moment with her husband, and a plane's eye view of "scattered herds of horses" (13). But of all the several geographies in her poetry, it is the remembrance of *Diné* birthplace and birthright (and in particular of *Hózhó*—the Navajo ethos of balance, harmony) that most draws her interest.

"A Birthday Poem" memorializes both. Opening lines speak of sunrise as "a brilliant song," its "sacred beams" at once "gifts," purveyors of "Hózhó," and a means whereby "Diyin" (holiness—*diyin dine*—are Navajo god-presences) is to be recognized (79). The speaker's prayer goes up for not only Hózhó but for its attainment through "precise prayers/and stories to ensure balance," together with a tranche of "the humor Diné/elders relish so" (79) and the continuing renewal of "soft hills, plains, and wind" (79). Driving through Kansas, she thinks of the Diné Night Ceremony, the Fourth World, and right prayers as bulwarks against succumbing to "foreign ways" and being "overwhelmed" by the world (80). To which end, always to be remembered, "each morning we pray to restore Hózhó, Hózhó, Hózhó, Hózhó" (80). The poem thereby itself becomes restorative prayer, the remembered figuration of "each morning" birth and rebirth. Memory here is sacral, the Diné spiritual pathway into life's true balance.

That same process, the poem as self-enactive ritual of memory, holds for "Rain in the Desert" (21–22). That "Rain in the desert is overwhelmingly beautiful," as announced in the opening line (21), is given confirmation in "early morning scents," "city shine," "crisp air," and Apache Country's "White Mountain people drinking coffee and cooking breakfast over an open fire" (21). The Pueblo Grande Museum in Phoenix, and its architectural park, is invoked, the grates and pipes muddy under each downpour and the homeless trying to catch drinking water. But from out of this mix of climate and place the poem moves to remember "the spirits of the Hohokamki" (21), ancestral Sonora Desert and Salt River agricultural people and forerunners to the O'odham.

The poem gives its own memory to ongoing Hohokamki presence: "Do they hover under the city, alongside the sewer lines, / or in the scrappy trees left in the Park of Four Waters?" (22). Do they not see, it asks, present-day joy in the falling rain, the refreshed air? Did not the Hohokamki, too, set out vessels to catch the rain, drink the water, and use it for crop-raising, cooking and the mud-and-color ceramics and paintwork whose fashioning bequeaths their creative signature down through the ages? The irony is not lost on Tapahonso of how, under all the architectural apparatus, the canals "which were witnesses / to the ingenuity and success" of the Hohokamki "are now lined with cement" (22).

But it is a legacy given ongoing continuity by the rain-nourished trees close to hand, each a species of natural memory-chamber:

The old gnarled trees also bear centuries of memories—
Of disasters, of celebrations, of transitions of all types (22).

The poem's closing line, "That the trees and the land survived is a wonder in itself" (22), underlines precisely these "centuries of memories" of the Hohokaki as ancestral culture, their cultivation of earth, creative artifacts and buildings, great systems of irrigation canal, and very emblem in the name Four Waters. The trees, gnarled, time-marked, icons of benign and unbenign transition, give abiding memorial, and wholly in keeping, from within each ongoing cycle of rain-in-the desert.

In his poem "the birds are housed in a small glass house," Ray A. Young Bear calls poetry "the act of remembering."[15] It could hardly better apply to *Black Eagle Child: The Facepaint Narratives.* Cast in the reflexive persona-voice of Edgar Bearchild as he remembers his rite of passage into a writer's adulthood amid tribal family and community, it works at full-length as a ply of free verse, diary, letters, dream, ceremony, and 1960s-and-after allusion to popular culture and music. That the text derives closely from, even as it rewrites, Young Bear's own Mesquakie/Sauk and Fox life in, and occasionally beyond, the Iowa settlement (not reservation) in Tama County, is unmistakable. But the lines of memory throughout are also, in Glancy's helpful phrase, shape-changed, full of monitoring invention.

This holds whether Young Bear has Edgar remember the gallery of events within his career, or call up America as literal politics and history, or put sequences in Mesquakie alongside English. The effect is to transform the oral life-story of Black Eagle Child Settlement ("twelve-hundred plus populace" [205]) into scriptural form, yet to retain immediacy, a book of remembered but still actively speaking voice. Across the span of November 1965-Winter 1989 (with publication in 1992), the sixteen wry-funny, ironic, sometimes angry, memory-panels turn circular even as they look to be sequential. In this way, tribal-centered, and always toughly unsentimental in its ledgering, *Black Eagle Child* rounds into the ongoing memorial whole. The very conception is usefully signaled halfway into the story. In 1975, in his twenties and like his begetter, Edgar applies for a creative writing fellowship from the Athens-based Maecenas Foundation. He sees this as written "sarcastically" (139), a "vindictive application" (141). But pitched antagonistically or not, the coordinates go right to the center of *Black Eagle Child*:

> Because no other voice should ever/can ever
> replace the original voice of the American Indian
> poet, especially one who resides at the place
> of his birth and not in the city of academia,
> I merely seek to compose meaningful narratives
> as experienced within the Black Eagle Child Nation.
> For too long we have been misrepresented
> And culturally maligned by an ungrateful country
> Of Euro-American citizens who have all but burned
> Their own bridges to the past. I will not tolerate
> Such transgressions of my being and character. [139–40]

How, then, for Edgar as memorialist best to remember his Black Eagle Child Settlement life? The response is to give voice to past but also contemporary ancestry, his wise-traditional grandmother ("or Nokomis" [56]), his parents Tony and Clotelde Bearchild, his partner/wife Selena Buffalo Husband, his uncle Winston Principal Bear, different Paintface relatives but his cousin Ted above all, and each different growing-up and adult compeer from Settlement to College and back to Settlement. Other dynasties enter, notably from the Kingfisher, Sturgeon, Hummingbird, Fix-King, and Beaver clans. Masquakie and Fire-Keeper/Star-Medicine creation stories and star and ghost mythologies preside even as they vie with missionary but distant "white" Christianity: "To me, / the Spirits were ever-present regardless / of ceremony" (61). An Iowa geography fills out tribal housing, nearby Why Cheer township (a possible echo of Gerald Vizenor's What Cheer?), the schools, diagonal railway tracks, river bottoms with their periodic flooding, and in the distance Grinnell and Des Moines.

Above all, Settlement life yields episode and contradiction: "While we were a 'tribe' in every respect, / it was unconscionable to help another / individual, family, or clan achieve / any degree of success in their public endeavors" (2). At the same time, it looks to the kind of continuity advocated, in due paradox, at Thanksgiving by the ceremony-presiding grandfather of his cousin Ted Paintface: "He concluded / Indians basically had little to be thankful for / on this national holiday, but what was crucial / was continuation of our culture" (18). Each fold of this community life, its intimacies, the breakages and gains, the occasional uproariousness—to extend to the various initials denoting status like EBNO ("Enrolled but in Name Only" [95]) or EBMIW ("Enrolled but Mother Is WHITE" [95]) and Henrietta Youthman's language confusion as to whether or not a white farmer is talking dirty to her (224)—not only fill but give lived variety to the text's overall memory. Young Bear leaves little doubt that memory does not equate with eulogy but owes duty to tribal life as web, contra flow, unyielding turns of irony.

In the opening sequences, *Black Eagle Child* looks to the pluses and minuses of ceremony. The Thanksgiving party at Weeping Willow Elementary uses improvised gifts of painted eggs and mission surplus. Edgar recalls his familiarity with drink-to-death friends. In the company of Ted, and Ted's war-hero uncle, Clayton Carlson Paintface, there is the hallucinogenic *na qwa o ni* "praying ceremony" (38), otherwise known as Star Medicine yet with a picture of Jesus Christ on the wall, presided over by Ted's grandfather. Its mix of high solemnity, Black Eagle "word-songs" (26), Edgar's upset stomach on eating the relevant herbs and the need to urinate, "visions and ghosts" (40), and assortment of motley-dressed tribal celebrants like John Louis and Percy Jim offer a richly turned one kind of memorial of the Settlement.

At a three-year gap, Edgar invokes the memory of his autobiographical launch into writing, a sci-fi fantasy of extraplanetary Scandinavian settlers in the Midwest decried by his writing professor at Luther College (53), lost writing notes, and failed first-love with Dolores Fox-King as the Supremes' "Baby Love" plays on the car radio. Other remembered highlights from the period call up Junior and the "precocious" Charlotte (73); visiting Ontarios, whose ancestor-village simply and mysteriously died; the story of Brook Grassleggings who inveigles Junior into a love tryst only to be revealed as a hermaphrodite (93); Edgar's time in student and LSD "Jefferson Airplane" mode at Pomona College ("it was an era of war-protest—and drugs" [111]) and his mother's affecting letters with small cash enclosed; and, in Ted Paintface's voice, the recall of California drift and intending return to Black Eagle Child; a despairing white man's offer to have himself killed for money; Edgar's "Journey of Words" (135); and, in Carson Two Foot's voice, the memory of 1908 allotment practice and meager government payouts. Each is told accoutered in asides, tics, and flourish of memory, Edgar's voice both in full disclosure and in the margin.

Edgar's immediate chronicle continues in the maybe out-of-body experiences with Selene near his geodesic riverfront home (built courtesy of Maecenas Foundation money). Is it a light cluster supernatural or some random strobe ray? He remembers Yakima Pat "Dirty" Red Hat, revered tribal singer killed in a crash in 1975 and celebrated by the group, The Young Lions ("we sang songs of commemoration" [191]). He recalls the vexed Grassleggings dynasty as presided over by its hugely overweight, waddling witch-broodmare mother ("Mathylde Hi-na—better known as Patty Jo" [95]), who somehow doubles as a curandera, and her differently fathered hooligan offspring. He thinks back to his role in the *Black Eagle Child Quarterly* as tribal publication and its report of Claude Youthman throwing a cantaloupe in court when arrested for contesting Iowa state's reneging on construction of twenty new Settlement houses (224). He also remembers the publication, with the teacher Lorna Bearcap, of the Weeping Willow Manifesto against petty tribal sleaze politics. Finally, he has a vision of the tribal-haunted alcoholic decline and expiration of Ted Paintface.

This overall miscellany of remembrance ("Twenty-four hours after anything occurred, it was recollected" [197]), peopled in the Settlement's flawed-yet-vital BEC humanity, gives *Black Eagle Child: The Paintface Narratives* a status to relish. If the different strands each have their own logic (and sometimes illogic), they become wholly of a piece. The result cannot be considered other than one of Native authorship's major memory-texts.

It could not be more appropriate that Kim Blaeser's *Apprenticed to Justice* should open with "Family Tree," an "all my relations" poem of mixed-blood genealogical memory.[16] To the one side is the German legacy, the "boxer grandfather," sire of six big-handed, beer-drinking sons and a father given to crooning "*Mona Lisa, // Mona Lisa, men have loved you* [sic]"(3), and the never-met grandmother, genetically large-thighed like the speaker, given to a sweet tooth, and begetter of sauerkraut-and-venison sausage family recipe. To the other side are the Chippewa grandmother, midwife, herbalist, mother of twelve with two babies lost to influenza, a son killed in war, other "limbo Indians turned to alcohol" (3), "My Indian grandpa" (3), squinting out from old photographs, working rocky allotment land, and "my first memory at two" (3). Through them is bequeathed the speaker's mother, born "in a reckless moon of miscegenation" (3), lifelong seamstress, a pattern maker of shirt and quilt. This calm poetic documentation, memory delivered in measured image and rhythm of disclosure, can be thought typical of Blaeser's poetry. Its strengths are untheatrical, those of patiently mediated recall and observation.

The remaining three stanzas fill out more of the family profile—the two uncles who fled Minnesota's Pipestone Indian boarding school, the aunt who lost fingers working at a laundry press yet mothered ("beaded, kneaded, quilted and braided" as the poem evocatively calls it) four children, and the houses and camps full of cousins, some on probation, some drunks, others softball players, all tender toward the speaker's own suckling children. But remembered beyond these, however intimate, is the great-grandfather, the dynastic link to an earlier Anishinaabeg (Chippewa-Ojibway) history. In him, memory is live presence, a veteran full of due honor to his tribal name and centered in an earth of fertile seed and pinecone:

> My great grandfather *Nii-Waan,*
> *Mii-nii-waan-noo-gwosh,* Lover of Natural Things,
> whose Antell heart I am said to bear
> who carried his name with humbleness
> as I try to
> and sometimes with rage
> fire brown eyes sharp as any weapon
> who cupped his hands around fertile seeds
> brown fingers the pinecone
> shelled house of protection. [4]

The language remains exact and yet lyric in its evocation of the great-grandfather, Elmer Antell—a man both humble and fierce, eyes as weapons and yet protective. Blaeser's careful working of lineage back to the family's oldest personally known figurehead fills memory with live presence. "Family Tree," its calling-up of warmths and losses, is unmistakably a poet's remembering.

This same deliberation of meticulously styled memory persists throughout *Apprenticed to Justice.* It shapes additional family portraiture like the prose-poem "Shadow Sisters," with its 1951–1992 chronology of Anishinaabe tribal women's lives from reservation hard times to casinos and new tribal college students, in all "celebrating 500 years of survival" (9).[17] It marks out "A Boxer Grandfather," with Ben Blaeser in his nineties flooring the drunken farmer who insults his daughter-in-law at the local pool hall. In return, the speaker's mother wryly, fondly, lets him cheat at two-handed solitaire all afternoon.[18] It runs through "Memories of Rock," a day out in the Boundary Waters Canoe Wilderness (BWCA) with son Gavin pebble-skipping upon Minnesota's Farm Lake and finding "a perfect triangle stone" (34).[19] The stone's "tiny black mystery" (34), sinking from sight, does perfect memorial service for permanence amid "the honeycomb patterns of ripple and reflection" (34). It is a style of memory that appositely holds sway in "Haiku Journey" (48–49), a four-season sequence of remembered seventeen-syllable landscapes.[20] Spring life and flowers give point of departure ("gathering crows," "may's errant mustard"). Summer vaunts its animals and birds ("turkey vulture," "snowy egret"). Fall yields wind and sky ("empty garbage cans dance," "sky black with migration"). Winter, finally, dispenses the bareness of twig and just a few deer ("lace edges of ice," "words turn with weather"). The gathered outcome is Nature as felt pageant, a kinetic, intimate memory-landscape.

More explicitly Native-themed poems take memory in yet other directions. "Indian in Search of an Entourage" cryptically summons savagist mystique, albeit modern-style: "He was an Indian / blown into town on a white girls dream / wearing destiny like a ten-gallon hat."[21] Figured throughout the poem as though both actual and fantasy Indian with Geronimo-length hair, his fusion of all the roles—singer, poet, preacher, powwow dancer, politician, Native language speaker, and night dancer—gives due recognition even as it gently mocks. Cat's eyes and Jim Thorpe physique, an ability to "sing Indian / dress cowboy / talk justice" (61), he is both reality and image, "mascot" more than team member and "not-quite new-age, not-quite-for-sale / Indian" (61). His is to be remembered as "small fame . . . on his chiseled cheekbones" (61), that indeed of the unentouraged Native, not quite in, yet not quite out of history. The poem's ironies work to advantage, memory as a way into picturing the paradox of the one Indian cajoled or choosing to play the other Indian.

"Goodbye to All That," with its Robert Graves title and diptych form, looks to a past and present in White Earth history.[22] In the first part, memory travels back to when the Anishnaabeg fought the Dakota Sioux "over whitefish and beaver territory," to "histories of dog-eaters and Chippewa Cows," and to the ensuing European intrusion with its "smallpox survivors" and "French fur traders" (66). Each has a successor population of "trackers and scouts in new bloodless legal battles" (66). Memory, however, is not allowed to be sentimental. How best, asks the second part, and as new remembering, to deal with "the follies of White Earth tribal leaders" (67), a Chair "under the influence of civilization" (67) who drives a pickup down the railroad track, who fails to check and aid "rabid casino bucks" (67), or who does not give actual and political nutrition to the community?

A shared press of history lies behind "Housing Conditions of One Hundred Fifty Chippewa Families," an at-length meditation on the 1938 report by Sister M. Inez Hilger as to the resistance of the reservation to moving from *"old ramshackled, tar-paper-covered homes"* into *"those fine new houses / the Indian Bureau built for Indians."*[23] The poem ponders how the good Sister's paper tabulations, her Order of St. Benedict "tight-lipped post-allotment spirituality" (83) could ever or even halfway have met the "white clay" and woodland cultural heritage of the Anishinaabeg, the chant and drum of "each Midé wiwin elder" (83). This is to give remembrance to two orders of life, one of ledgers, tabulation, the other in its outward poverty and fracture of inner unbroken tribe.

That same remembered continuity runs through Blaeser's title poem, "Apprenticed to Justice," a salute to both the memory of "this history of loss" and at the same time "fertile ground / from which we will build / new nations."[24] Each Anishinaabe and White Earth marker, "teeth marks on birch bark" (104), "Medicine voices" (104), "camps" (106), "red nations falling / when they are remembered" (106), and "new nations / upon the ashes of our ancestors" (106), make for a composite call to memory of the past. But that reads also, and in terms full of impetus, as poetry with its own memory of the future.

Memory throughout these different authorships, a quintet of poetic voices, inevitably differs in direction and image. There can be no doubt, however, of a shared will to imagining, the plurality of Native heritage remembered for its transition into contemporaneity, time-now. The virtuosity that has entailed in these poets, and in the literary generation to which they belong, has been a hallmark of the flowering widely acknowledged as a Native literary renaissance. In Ortiz, Glancy, Tapahonso, Young Bear, and Blaeser, and those who have been their cowriters of poetry, Native writing has mainstays, necessary memory-voices.

NOTES

1. Ortiz, *After and Before the Lightning*, p. 22.

2. Tapahonso, in Joy Harjo and Gloria Bird, eds. *Reinventing the Enemy's Language*, p. 325.

3. Young Bear, in Niatum, ed., *Harper's Anthology of 20ᵗʰ Century Native American Poetry*, p. 272. Republished in Young Bear, *Invisible Musician*, p. 22.

4. Blaeser, *Apprenticed to Justice*, p. 84.

5. In her preface to *Blue Horses Rush In*, Luci Tapahonso gives a perfect account of how oral storytelling can work: "Obvious advantages of oral storytelling are the expressions of the teller, the responses of the participants, and the gestures as well as the inflections in the voices. Although many of the stories or jokes that can be told can be translated and relayed fairly well in written form, the clear sense of

voices and characters is diminished in some ways, so that even though it's obvious when I tell a story that I'm not the protagonist or other person, the reader of the story may interpret it otherwise" (xiii).

6. For a full exploration of the term's implications, see Vizenor and Lee, *Postindian Conversations*.

7. See, in this respect, the essays collected in Vizenor, *Survivance*.

8. Glancy, *Rooms*, p. 118.

9. Ortiz, *from Sand Creek*. In context the phrase reads: "How to deal with history" (6).

10. Glancy, *Claiming Breath*, p. 54.

11. Glancy, *Rooms*, p. 31.

12. "Here I Am Standing Beside Myself," as quoted before, helps explain the point: "My father said his grandfather fled Indian Territory . . . when he'd done something wrong" (*Rooms*, 65).

13. Glancy, *Rooms*, pp. 33–38.

14. Tapahonso, *Blue Horses Rush In*, p. 79.

15. Young Bear, unpublished poem, cited in Robert Franklin Gish, *Beyond Bounds*, p. 86.

16. Blaeser, *Apprenticed to Justice*, pp. 3–4.

17. Ibid., pp. 5–10.

18. Ibid., p. 11.

19. Ibid., p. 34.

20. Ibid., pp. 48–50.

21. Ibid., p. 61.

22. Ibid., pp. 66–67.

23. Ibid., pp. 79–83.

24. Ibid., pp. 104–106.

WORKS CITED

Apess, William. *A Son of the Forest: The Experience of William Apes, A Native of the Forest, Comprising a Notice of the Pequot Tribe of Indians, Written by Himself.* New York: published by the author, 1829, 1831, Publisher G. F. Bunce.

Barnes, Jim. *On Native Grounds: Memoirs and Impressions.* Norman: University of Oklahoma Press, 2004.

Blaeser, Kimberly. *Apprenticed to Justice.* Cambridge: Salt Publishing, 2007.

Deloria, Vine. *Custer Died for Your Sins: An Indian Manifesto.* New York: Macmillan, 1969.

Gish, Robert Franklin. *Beyond Bounds: Cross-Cultural Essays on Anglo, American Indian & Chicano Literature.* Albuquerque: University of New Mexico Press, 1996.

Glancy, Diane. *Claiming Breath.* Lincoln: University of Nebraska Press, 1992.

———. *Lone Dog's Winter Count.* Albuquerque: West End Press, 1991.

———. *Pushing the Bear: A Novel of the Trail of Tears.* New York: Harcourt Brace, 1996, 1998.

———. *Rooms: New and Selected Poems.* Cambridge, UK: Salt Publishing, 2005.

———. *Shadow's Horse.* Tucson: University of Arizona Press, 2003.

Harjo, Joy, and Gloria Bird, eds. *Re-inventing the Enemy's Language: Contemporary Native Women's Writing of North America.* New York: W. W. Norton, 1997.

Momaday, N. Scott. *House Made of Dawn,* New York: Harper & Row, 1968

———. *The Names: A Memoir.* New York: Harper & Row, 1976.

Niatum, Duane, ed. *Harper's Anthology of Twentieth-Century Native Poetry.* San Francisco: HarperCollins, 1987.

Ortiz, Simon. *After and Before the Lightning.* Tucson: University of Arizona Press, 1994.

———. *from Sand Creek.* Tucson: University of Arizona Press, 1981.

Ridge, John Rollin (Yellow Bird). *The Life and Adventures of Joaquin Murieta, the Celebrated California Bandit.* 1854. Reprinted, Norman: University of Oklahoma Press, 1977.

Silko, Leslie Marmon. *Almanac of the Dead.* New York: Simon & Schuster, 1991.

———. *Storyteller.* New York: Little, Brown/Arcade, in arrangement with Seaver, 1981.

Standing Bear, Luther. *My Indian Boyhood.* New York: Houghton Mifflin, 1925.

Tapahonso, Luci. *Blue Horses Rush In: Poems and Stories.* Tucson: University of Arizona Press, 1997.

———. *Sáanii Dahataał/The Women Are Singing.* Tucson: University of Arizona Press, 1993.

Vizenor, Gerald. *The Heirs of Columbus.* Hanover: Wesleyan University Press/University Press of New England, 1991.

———, ed. *Survivance: Narratives of Native Presence.* Lincoln: University of Nebraska Press, 2008.

Vizenor, Gerald, and A. Robert Lee. *Postindian Conversations.* Lincoln: University of Nebraska Press, 1999.

Weaver, Jace, Craig S. Womack, and Robert Warrior. *American Indian Literary Nationalism.* Albuquerque: University of New Mexico Press, 2006.

Welch, James. *Fools Crow.* New York: Viking, 1986.

Young Bear, Ray A. *Black Eagle Child: The Facepaint Narratives.* New York: Grove Press, 1992.

———. *The Invisible Musician.* Duluth, Minn.: Holy Cow! Press, 1990.

14

The Re-membered Earth

Place and Displacement
in Native American Poetries

KIMBERLY M. BLAESER

These are the visioned names of places
here and not here, part of that other way,
like opening your eyes in another's dream.
                    Joe Bruchac, *No Borders*

I am conscious of my life as a journey, and what I write is a map.
                    Simon Ortiz, *After and Before the Lightning*

CULTURAL GROUND-INGS

When N. Scott Momaday's landmark work, *The Way to Rainy Mountain*, declared in 1969, "Once in his life a man ought to concentrate his mind upon
the remembered earth," the alignment of Native place and nature remained
largely intact in the cultural imagination (83). Paula Gunn Allen's 1980 statement, "We are the land. To the best of my understanding, that is the fundamental idea embedded in Native American life and culture," reinforced
long-held ideas about the grounding of Native culture and identity in nature
and natural cycles of seasons ("IYANA," 191). But trot out some of the recent
poems and poetry collections from Native writers, and the anticipated understanding of geographical place begins to shift. In her 1999 collection, *From
the Belly of My Beauty*, Ester Belin employs the acronym U.R.I. for Urban
Raised Indian, and writer Diane Glancy claims, "My sense of place is in the
moving" (Castanier, 1). The contemporary Native American poetry series edited by Cherokee author Janet McAdams for the British press Salt Publishing
may bear the title *Earthworks*, but the books in the series provide complex
representations of place and displacement in Native experience, from Allison Hedge-Coke's *Blood Run*, with its focus on the destruction of Native
mounds, to the work of Deborah Miranda, whose vivid survival poems depict

an American trailer-court experience or an inner-city relocation neighbor-hood.[1] Actually, although Indigenous peoples of North America do descend from, and continue traditions of, "land-based" cultures or geographical com-munities, place in Native literatures has always involved more than the easy stereotypes reservation, reserve, or Indian territory might suggest. The rela-tionships, both ritualistic and practical, involve deep and dynamic currents of engagement, elements of which involve or give rise to literary creations.

In his 1983 *Native American Renaissance,* Kenneth Lincoln likewise rec-ognizes that "Native American peoples acknowledge specific and common inheritance of the land. They . . . observe natural balances in the world and idealize a biological and spiritual principle of reciprocation" (16). When his discussion turns to the relationship between place and Indigenous literatures, Lincoln quotes Octavio Paz's comment about Native arts as being "Firmly planted. Not fallen from on high: sprung up from below" (*In Praise of Hands,* as quoted in *Native American Renaissance,* 16). A longer version of this state-ment by Paz is used again by Duane Niatum when he characterizes Native poetry in his introduction to the 1988 *Harper's Anthology of 20ᵗʰ Century Na-tive American Poetry,* one of the notable anthologies of the era. Niatum states that among both "ancient and modern themes" in Native writing "none of them may be more important than a sense of place, land and geography" (x). When he elaborates on this Native sense of place, Niatum first quotes Jar-old Ramsey, who distinguishes the Indigenous sensibility from the "vaguely guilty and nostalgic sense of place and feeling for landscape we inherit from Romanticism," and then introduces Paz's ideas of "a mutually shared physical life that is firmly planted, not fallen from on high. So instead, it springs up from below" (*Reading the Fire,* as quoted in *Harper's Anthology,* x; *In Praise of Hands,* as quoted, xi). The distinction, Niatum claims, involves "a living heri-tage of place and tradition" and a "sense of coming *from* the land not *to* it" (xi) (my emphasis). It is this elemental difference in perception that he believes informs the performance of Native American poets.

This cultural perception, of course, exists in the oral foundational litera-tures of Native nations, and both the writing generally identified as part of the Native American Renaissance and the ensuing growth of publishing in Native poetry since that time owe much of their distinctness and viability to these long-standing, multidimensional, oral literatures of the many Indig-enous tribes of the Americas. Within and through such oral performances, the land knowledge and interdependent place-based relationships were given voice and the people sought continuance. In any of hundreds of traditional texts we can examine the embedding of the various tribes' bio-knowledge and place-consciousness in, for example, the ceremonial song poems.

Among those that readily demonstrate a heightened awareness of the inter-weaving of place and the sacred is the Havasupai "Medicine Song" transcribed in Leanne Hinton and Lucille Watahomigie's collection, *Spirit Mountain: An*

Anthology of Yuman Song (108–14.). In the volume, the song/poem (derived from a performance by Dan Hanna) includes native language and English as well as "Singing," "Translation," and "Speaking" versions presented side-by-side in an attempt to convey something beyond the flat-page textual reality. The song/poem relates an account of travel by the speaker to a familiar healing place where the speaker's "illness is absorbed" (114).

In an incantatory fashion, the language invokes landscape, recounts journey, and suggests a long-standing and ongoing relationship with the natural elements as the speaker attests:

> The land we were given
> The land we were given
>
> It is right here
> It is right here. . . .
>
> All around our home
> All around our home. . . .
>
> Down at the source
> A spring will always be there
>
> It is ours
> It is ours
>
> Since a long time ago
> Since a long time ago. [108–109]

In addition, the inclusion of details such as "Red rock . . . Streaked with brown . . . Shooting up high" and lines describing the vital motion of the land—"At the edge of the water / Water foam forming . . . Swirl, swirling . . . Silt layers forming . . . Ripple, rippling"—work to convey attentiveness and an intimacy with the landscape. Likewise, when the song/poem uses first-person plural and then first-person singular, the "we" and "I" as well as the possessive "our" and "my" language reflects a familiarity and a sense of community.[2] Finally, the speaker continually employs a kind of verbal gesture to invoke what is present, identifying each named feature or creature as "here" or "right there": "The spring that heals / It is right there." This poetic technique creates an immediacy that, together with the we-speak, imaginatively "places" the reader/listener in the physical and spiritual spaces of the poem. Then, included or implicated in the knowledge and acts of relatedness, we, too, might respond in kind or experience an understanding of traditional reciprocity. The editors acknowledge the supraliterary goals of the traditional songs and retain similar goals for the collection of translations: "We have tried to preserve the song in ways that will turn the hearts of readers, as it turned the hearts of men and women before they began to forget" (3).

Although various traditional performances, from Anishinaabe dream songs to Yaqui deer songs, demonstrate earth consciousness and connectedness in different ways, embedded in the mythic and ceremonial literature of most tribes of North America are tenets of right relationship with the natural universe. As Hinton and Watahomigie explain:

> Traditionally, oral literature was not merely a means of entertainment. . . . The traditional tales and songs helped people to learn about the world and their place in it, how to behave toward other people, and how to lead a life harmonious with nature. It also taught people how to respect other species and how to respect the places on the land, by telling their own place in the pattern of the universe. [6]

Many tribal literary works, then, came into being to explicate and teach important cultural groundings.

POETIC EMBODIMENTS

In both their scholarly and creative work, contemporary Native writers also reinforce these groundings. Eloquent discussions of this ancient Native understanding of humankind's interdependence with nature have been offered over the years by many Indigenous writers, including (in addition to Momaday, Allen, and Niatum) Simon Ortiz, Leslie Silko, Louis Owens, Marilou Awiakta, Gerald Vizenor, Basil Johnston, and Linda Hogan.[3] In the 1998 volume, *Speaking for the Generations*, for example, Ortiz explains that not only do Native Americans insist on "a concept of self that is absolutely tied to the interdependence of land and people" but professes: "In fact, they [land and people] are one and the same essential matter of Existence. They cannot be separated and delineated into single entities. . . . Without land there is no life, and without a responsible social and cultural outlook by humans, no life-sustaining land is possible" (xiii, xii).

Within the contemporary collections of Native poetries, we find a virtual symphony of poems that arise out of Native cultural experience of place or placement or that voice the various aspects of our interdependent relationship with the rest of the natural world. These include works celebrating seasonal cycles such as Jim Northrup's "mahnomin," a poem detailing the ritualistic annual harvest of wild rice; Joe Bruchac's series of "Seven Moons" poems and the poetry in his book *Thirteen Moons on Turtle's Back* that use the Abenaki names of the moon cycles ("Ktsi Manido, Great Spirit Moon," "Mskikoiminas, Strawberry Moon," etc.) and characterize that season and its activities in the poems; and Gerald Vizenor's many haiku collections built around images of the four seasons of the year.[4] Other works by Indigenous writers that decry or warn against environmental destruction might fit neatly under the label of "eco-poetry." The writing of Warm Springs poet Elizabeth Woody, which addresses the degradation of the traditional salmon ecosystem in the Northwest, clearly falls into this category. Indeed, Ursula Le Guin has described Woody's activist writing as "poetry, doing the work of poetry, legislating" (book cover, *Luminaries of the Humble*). Among the many examples of poems focusing on environmental issues are Marilou Awiakta's playful "Mother Nature Sends a Pink Slip" in which Homo sapiens receive a "termination" notice because of their bad behavior and "Memo to NASA," which suggests the environmental earth model—"Con-quer . . . Conquer . . . / Con-quer . . . Conquer"—will be continued in outer space where the speaker envisions plans to "stripmine the moon" and "hang guns on the stars" (*Selu*, 88, 86). A yet more somber poem, Mary TallMountain's "The Last Wolf," depicts a lone surviving wolf making his way through the ruins of civilization to the speaker of the poem, whose ominous response lingers hauntingly when the poem closes: "Yes, I said / I know what they have done" (*Nothing but the Truth*, 554).

Other poems interweave traditional tribal knowledge with contemporary lifeways or conditions. For example, Heid Erdrich, one of a generation of new writers who follow on the heels of the Native American Renaissance writers covered in Kenneth Lincoln's book, attempts just such a complex representation in "Ojibwe: First Rice." The poet invokes teachings, renders evocative images of wild ricing, offers subtle commentary on the significance of the seasonal and ritualistic actions, and ultimately, implies a spiritual worldview. The slight eleven-line poem creates a sensibility conscious of both history and continuance.

In the opening three lines, Erdrich crafts sensory-laden images of wild rice and its locale as she describes manoomin ready for harvest:

> The grain should be green as river rocks,
> long as hayseed, with the scent of duckweed
> and sweetgrass that grows along the lake's banks.
>   [Blaeser, *Traces*, 68][5]

The poem next describes the "offering" of the title, the gift given in gratitude for the "first rice" of the harvest season:

> First *manoomin*, feast plate laid for the spirits—
> Berries and tobacco offered with song.

The closing six lines provide context and commentary, as the poem builds to a spiritual crescendo. Erdrich recalls:

What it must have meant to give
what little the people had to give:

Then, as she names the gift—"herbs left in thanks"—and enumerates the blessings for which the people made this offering, she includes among the benefactors not only those past tribal members but, with employment of the future tense—"food that will sustain us"—she suggests a tribal continuum that includes a contemporary "us." Thus she both re-members the past actions, reading their simple valor, and voices the contemporary connection to those same acts.

The last movement of the poem builds sonically, linking the phrases by repetition of words, sounds, and pattern, thus verbally embodying the very interlocked reality it so emphatically expresses:

herbs left in thanks for the food that will sustain us,
for the water that gives up that food,
for the world working the way it should
—living and full of living god.

The poem closes with a succinct representation of a tribal worldview, acknowledging as it does the vital world around us and the important sense of spiritual balance. It is in many ways a creed, a poem expressing a system of beliefs and showing those beliefs in action.

LAND LANGUAGES

Like Erdrich, Jeannette Armstrong also expresses a sense of contemporary continuity with older teachings. Her claims, however, extend the idea of reciprocity even to the practice of language. The title of her essay, "Land Speaking," encapsulates Armstrong's thesis: "Language was given to us by the land we live within" and "there is a special knowledge in each different place" (175–76). Therefore, according to Armstrong, "all indigenous people's languages are generated by a precise geography and arise from it," and we, as Native people, "listen intently to its teachings" and "invent human words to retell." (178, 176). Hence, we become "an inextricable part—though a minute part—of the land language" (178).[6] For a poet particularly, such an understanding of the land as source for language itself carries great significance and might indeed imprint the poetic focus, voice, and performance, as it does in Armstrong's case.

The First Nations poet's work frequently engages ideas of tribal continuance, tradition, and memory, and often finds the grounding for intergenerational threads of culture in the Indigenous relationship to place. Okanagan she describes as a "vocally rooted" language that "recreates sounds of the land in its utterance" and "re-sounds patterns of action and movement," thus translating earth voices for communication with humans (187–88). What Armstrong calls a "musical coherence" she sees reflected in or carried into the oral language in a way that is diminished or entirely lacking in a text-based language. Divorced from the body, text alone falters in attempts to cue alterations of volume and pitch and makes even elements like tempo, beat, and rhythm more difficult to render. Her writing in English attempts to "retrieve" that musicality and to "construct bridges" between the different cultural realities (189, 192). In her use of synaesthesia in a poem like "Frogs Singing," we can see this attempt embodied. Building the poem partly on an extraordinary experience of her sister, Delphine, Armstrong first suggests "star rhythms sang to her pointing their spines of light." This motion/sound then "filled her body with star song." Next, she implies a continuity between the "star song" and frogs singing: "frogs joined the star singing / they learned it / long ago" (188–89).

In addition to engaging a variety of poetic techniques to translate "land speaking," Armstrong and other tribal poets sometimes approximate this older earth language by employing pure sound, vocables instead of "dictionary" words of either Native language or English, or their poetry itself admits the ineffable reality of the natural world. In her cocreated volume, *Secrets from the Center of the World*, Creek poet Joy Harjo pairs poems with the dramatic landscape photographs of Stephen Strom in another effort to embody or speak earth's mysterious being. But in the opening poem, she acknowledges the ultimate futility of human language/her poetry to translate the essence she gestures toward: "Words cannot construct it, for there are some sounds left to sacred wordless form" (2). In a later poem, she again admits the limits of her own poetic translations, even as she suggests the sacredness and beauty all around her, claiming, "The land is a poem of ochre and burnt sand I could never write, unless paper were the sacrament of sky, and ink the broken line of wild horses staggering the horizon several miles away" (30).

Her poetic works in this collection also underscore a worldview similar to that expressed by Armstrong, one that understands earth as origin for being and as the source for speech. She writes, for example, "The earth has dreamed me" and "It is true the landscape forms the mind. If I stand here long enough I'll learn to sing" (50, 22). She also voices other overlapping ideas about place and identity, which become common themes in Native poetry—the notion of shared being, the possibility of transformation, and a symbolic or metaphorical expansiveness or certain kind of enlightenment or immanence. We see elements of all of these in the following prose poem:

If you look with the mind of the swirling earth near Shiprock
you become the land, beautiful. And understand how three
crows at the edge of the highway, laughing, become three crows
at the edge of the world, laughing. [4]

A similar kind of expansive understanding is suggested in the title poem, when Harjo writes, "My house is the red earth; it could be the center of the world" (2).

The singing of ourselves into or as located within the "center of the world" seems at the heart of the work of many Native poets. In *A Good Journey,* Simon Ortiz's poem "Back into the Womb, the Center" records a journey into Cochiti Canyon and includes this description of the encounter: "I knew that we were near / one of the certain places / that is the center of the center" (*Good Journey,* as included in *Woven Stone,* 210). Throughout his poetic career, N. Scott Momaday, too, has frequently alluded to that essence Harjo calls "sacred wordless form" and to the notion of arrival at a place of centering. In "Meditation on Wilderness," he writes of moving "to the other side of sound," of "keeping still" and "waiting," of being "drawn to the center of this dark surround" (*Again the Far Morning,* 65). When the poem continues, claiming "The sacred here emerges and abides," and later, "Here is the house where wilderness resides," the "here" of these lines is at once the specific physical environment Momaday describes in the poem and the metaphorical "center" that we reach through our own spiritual readiness. In "We Have Seen the Animals," he characterizes that arrival at the center in other ways: as "an arc / of time beyond the reckoning" and as having "ventured past the thing / that mere mortality confines"; in "Notebook," as "a quiet beyond language" (*Again the Far Morning,* 121, 131). Again and again in his poetry, Momaday links the physical experience of place and the ineffable. He does not confine his notion of "center" as tied to a specific place, but instead to an experience of the spiritual reality through the vehicle of the natural, as when he writes: "Beyond every tree on the plain is a clear dawn and eternity" (*Again the Far Morning,* 131).

The idea of place and the evocation of our placement resounds across poems by various tribal voices. What I have called expansiveness and immanence, the sense of universal vitality, a relatedness among all elements of the natural world, and an indwelling of power or sacred being that exists outside notions of hierarchy and within which we as human beings reap understanding and blessings—these ideas in variation appear again and again. Osage writer Carter Revard, for example, gathered old and new works together under the title *How the Songs Come Down,* opening with the poem, "Coyote Tells Why He Sings" in which he vividly describes the origin of sounds in place. He first enumerates the natural sounds—"Thunder," "drops . . . crashing down," "sounds of leaf-drip, rustling of soggy branches in gusts of wind," "the rill's tune," "a rock drop," "ripples gurgling"—and then attests to the dramatic impact of those natural phenomenon when he writes, "The storm made music, when it changed my world" (3). The rich and effusive poems that follow include a virtual field guide of the ecosystem and attest in various ways to the mysteries and gifts that abound in our world. In "What the Poet's Cottage in Tucson Said," Revard writes of elements that await their cue to "dance like

Talking God / down from heaven / and bring Mozart's / melodies back" (64). The title of another poem, "Snowflakes, Waterdrops, Time, Eternity and So On," suggests the wide range of Revard's vision, and in it he writes both of the world's wondrous cacophony and of the ultimate collapse of difference into singularity. Through his breathless rush of language, he seems to attempt to mirror the teeming variety he finds in the everyday world:

> this world I know's
> a curious place, but who'd have thought those still
> white mountaintops could capture difference,
> those moving ocean waves identity,
> while in between, the levity of clouds
> keeps turning snow to rain and rain to snow,
> and gravity's weird force has got us all
> aspiring to disappear into
> a singularity: who would believe
> how those great powers wring
> the music out of water over stones,
> the rainbow out of waterfalls that silver
> a mountainside with streams like veins
> in a maple leaf keeping delighted eyes
> from April sun—
> green leaf trembling up here from loam
> which over there has been called forth
> as columbine and ponderosa: Listen, how all
> those Trickster seeds and Coyote clouds, those
> big bangers say
> let there be light,
> and darkness fountains dawn like
> a trumpet's golden one-way where breath
> goes in, Mozart comes out. [78]

The closing lines of the entire collection, too, in a generous sweeping gesture picture many places and the universal songs that cut across distinctions of geography and being:

> Deep
> in the blue Antarctic seas, high
> in the green Guatemalan jungle, here
> in these cracked English words,
> can you hear them sing,
> the hummingbirds, the humpback whales,
> a neutron star, a human soul? [160]

So, like Armstrong, Harjo, Momaday, and many other Indigenous writers, Revard, too, in his poetry explores the idea of earth voices and our human relationship to them.

SACRED GEOGRAPHIES, SACRED JOURNEYS

Traditional relationships to place in Native cultures also involve reverence for particular sites, teachings about sacred geographies, and ritual journeys that are a part of the cyclical lifeways in a geographical region. Bonds to place sometimes have their basis in origin stories, which relate a supernatural happening that took place there or that map the territory of the tribe, identifying terrestrial boundaries as marked by sacred mountains or rivers, for example. Places may also come to hold significance as sites for star observation, as ceremonial grounds, as the source of important herbs or a healing spring, or as a resting place for the dead. They may as readily be associated with evil as with good, and in either case may be linked with particular figures or deities. Tribes build place associations through seasonal harvests, yearly cycles of weather, ritual journeys, and sky patterns. This multifaceted sense of tribal homeland that informs cultural and personal identities of Native peoples, this evolved kinship with place continues to embed itself in all the creative arts, sometimes linking them one to another. In poetry, elements of sacred geographies and sacred journeys become frequent subjects as well as the basis for form in some works.

The title of Ofelia Zepada's collection *Ocean Power* and several of the poems in the collection, for example, allude to her Tohono O'odham (Papago) dessert tribe's sacred four-day journey to the Gulf of California to gather salt and to the rituals performed to invoke rain. Many of Zepada's poems in this volume involve an awareness of, or interaction with, the weather, demonstrating both an intimacy with geography and the adaptations made for survival. Hers is a "land of hot dry air / where the sky ends at the mountains" (83). She writes of "relatives and family" who "participated in the ritual of pulling down the clouds and fixing the earth," and she acknowledges "all those who knew how to live toward the direction of the ocean" (5). The opening poem, "Pulling Down the Clouds," includes Tohono O'odham mingled with English, and the first stanza is presented as chant in language that gestures toward ritual, toward activity:

Ñ-ku'ibadkaj 'ant 'an ols g cewagĭ.
With my harvesting stick I will hook the clouds.
'Ant o 'i-wañ̃'io k o 'i-hudiñ g cewagĭ.
With my harvesting stick I will pull down the clouds.
Ñ-ku'ibadkaj 'ant o 'i-siho g cewagĭ.
With my harvesting stick I will stir the clouds. [9]

Just as the language binds the poem to a particular tribe, the imagined ritual binds it to that nation's particular geography.

In tribal pilgrimage, sometimes the sacred duty to return and retell holds as much significance as does the actual undertaking of the physical journey, since future continuance of the ritual depends upon the embedding of the pattern in tribal memory. The Tohono O'odham journey, for instance, which ethnographer Ruth Underhill explains had to be performed "four successive years— until the magic has been tamed," involved not only the difficult travel itself, but important verbal repetitions. Speeches she describes as filled with images of Coyote and arrival at the ocean are "recited year after year by the old men," and become "the patterns for dreaming" when, "The young man, exhausted with hunger and effort, awaits his vision with these pictures in his mind" (*Singing for Power*, 128). Zepada's poems, then, linked as they are to those older journeys, can be read as but another in a long line of cultural retellings.

As in Zepada's work, the account of contemporary experience is frequently linked to tradition, and poetic journey accounts are often made in tandem with the historical, with telling linked to actual travel or to early spoken accounts. N. Scott Momaday's *The Way to Rainy Mountain*, Simon Ortiz's *Going for the Rain*, Linda Hogan's *Calling Myself Home*, all record physical pilgrimages taken as the travelers retrace ancient pathways or sacred journeys, hearkening after a connection that will in some way mark or heal their own passage.[7]

In the simplest view, Momaday's book describes a pilgrimage the author made to his grandmother's grave in which he travels the same path his Kiowa forebears traveled more than three hundred years earlier when they migrated from the Yellowstone River to Oklahoma, a journey "carried out over a course of many generations and many hundreds of miles" (3). In the prologue to the book, Momaday alludes to the many levels of journey inherent in the text, characterizing it as being made "with the whole memory, that experience of the mind that is legendary as well as historical, personal as well as cultural" (4). The tripartite structure of this well-known book itself demonstrates the layers of connection, including, as it does, linked passages of myth, history, and personal experience. In the volume, Momaday also implies his intention to pass on the essence of this journey or the idea of journey to the reader via the text when he writes: "the journey herein recalled, continues to be made anew each time the miracle comes to mind" (4).

The text of *The Way to Rainy Mountain* is filled with observation and knowledge of place as well as with the braiding of the present place with the mythic and historical. Momaday retells, for example, the legend of Devil's Tower in which seven sisters climb a stump to escape a bear and are borne into the sky to become the stars of the Big Dipper. He then underscores the important inheritance of myth when he writes, "From that moment and as long as the legend lives, the Kiowas have kinsmen in the night sky" (8). Although some passages in the Momaday text have been seen as prose poetry, because the majority of the book is narrative prose, I use it here primarily to illustrate the relationship between contemporary writing and oral traditions and between contemporary, historic, and mythic journeys. A final passage from the book also offers a straightforward statement about a lived relationship with place. Here Momaday writes about the depth of his acquaintance with the lands of New Mexico: "I came to know that country, not in a way a traveler knows the landmarks he sees in the distance, but more truly and intimately, in every season, from a thousand points of view. I know the living motion of a horse and the sound of hooves. I know what it is, on a hot day in August or September, to ride a horse into a bank of cold, fresh rain" (67).

Like Momaday does in *The Way to Rainy Mountain*, Simon Ortiz entwines his own odyssey with the mythic understanding of an older tribal journey in the 1976 poetry collection, *Going for the Rain*. Ortiz's book records a literal journey he made in the southern and eastern United States and braids the telling of that pilgrimage to "look for Indians" with a ritual going "for the shiwana" or rain spirits (*Woven Stone*, 37).[8] Ortiz creates the form for the collection from the pattern of ceremonial journey, including four sections, or movements, in the volume—"The Preparation," "Leaving," "Returning," and "The Rain Falls"—and actually opens the collection by quoting from a traditional song:

Let us go again, brother; let us go for the shiwana.
Let us make our prayer songs.
We will go now. Now we are going.
We will bring back the shiwana.
They are coming now. Now, they are coming.
It is flowing. The plants are growing.
Let us go again, brother; let us go for the shiwana (37).

Filled with the poetry of place, the book depicts Ortiz, or his persona, "Passing through Little Rock," "Crossing the Colorado River into Yuma," "West of Ocotillo Wells," "Crossing the Georgia Border into Florida," and going "All the Way to New York City" (98, 103, 69, 74, 87). Some poems offer lyrical descriptions of landscape, some a litany of names: Casa Grande, Dateland, El Centro, Tuba City, Gallup, Amarillo, Tucumcari.[9] Ultimately, the volume recalls the object of the poet's quest, the rain spirits, the cleansing rains of tradition and symbolic rebirth. In lines of "Passing through Little Rock" Ortiz voices this longing:

I just want to cross the next hill,
go through that clump of trees
and come out the other side

and see a clean river,
the whole earth new
and hear the noise it makes
at birth. [98]

The poem "East of Tucumcari" depicts the narrator's arrival home to see "the brown water / falling from a rock" where "it felt so good / to touch the green moss" and "smell / the northern mountains / in the water" (116). Just as the works of Zepada and Momaday involved a metaphorical doubling of meaning, the "homing in" of the narrator in Ortiz's poem involves the cyclical return to place as well as the symbolic return to remembered ceremony.[10]

In Linda Hogan's 1978 *Calling Myself Home*, we find the functioning of a more subtle journey motif. The volume recalls the voluntary migrations of Hogan's Chickasaw ancestors as they followed the leadings of a sacred pole to guide their journeys. "Chickasaw / chikkih asachi," she writes in "Blessing," means "they left as a tribe not a very great while ago." And she recalls this migratory spirit of her Indian ancestors in a voice of mild lament: "They were always leaving, those people" (27). The cultural legacy of *Calling Myself Home* also includes the forced migration the Chickasaw would endure as a result of the U.S. government's policies of removal under Andrew Jackson. Finally, the movement of Hogan's own family into and out of Chickasaw territory in Oklahoma during her childhood also informs the collection. The pilgrimage implied in the poems of *Calling Myself Home* then involves a coming home to both the physical landscape of Oklahoma as well as an overcoming of the sense of perpetual homelessness described by Hogan—"From my family I have learned the secrets / of never having a home" (17)—by learning to feel at home in one's self.

In the title poem of the collection, she writes of returning to "our land" and of the "dry river . . . bed . . . the road I walked to return" (6). In this poem and elsewhere, Hogan characterizes return in terms of memory and history as well as in terms as of actual place. She uses various images to convey a sense of incalculable age: old bones, something buried or residing in another, an arrowhead, the dried-up land. She writes of "the old turtle," with "small yellow bones of animals inside" (3), "the dry pond / old bowl of earth" (4), "trees" that "have been in this place so long" (4), and "turtle, old as earth" (5). In the title poem she writes:

We are plodding creatures
like the turtle
born of an old people.
We are nearly stone
turning slow as the earth.
Our mountains are underground
they are so old. [6]

The movement in *Calling Myself Home* is toward this awareness of long-standing history, as much as toward the land itself. The poetic journey traces an idea of being invested in an ancient cycle of being. The individual identity of the narrator is again and again subsumed in the vast age of the earth, in the larger "we" and "our" of the poems.

Hogan's poems also repeatedly convey an understanding of our role as builders and rebuilders of our own belonging, and ultimately, the home to which Hogan calls her persona and her readers is not a specific building or even a singular place on the globe; she calls us to an understanding of home as our own ongoing journey, as the relationships we nurture within and without. In poems throughout the book she uses the image of the turtle, which, of course, is that mythic "home" of Indian people who reside "on turtle's back," and which recalls the Chickasaw use of turtle-shell rattles in ceremonial healing.[11] Finally, in Hogan's hands, the metaphor opens to revelations of how "we" who are all searching for a sense of home ground, can learn to create or carry our own place on this earth, how we can learn to embody belonging. "Wake up," she tells us, "we are women. / The shells are on our backs" (3).

The sense of sacred journey and sacred geography that permeates the works of Zepada, Momaday, Ortiz, and Hogan likewise continues to inform the writing of the new generations of Native writers. However, the loss that gives rise to the search in Hogan often becomes more emphatic in the writing of these poets, poets like Chumash Deborah Miranda and Huron and Tsalagi Allison Hedge-Coke. In the title poem of Miranda's collection *Indian Cartography*, the lament is for remembered ground, a valley that has literally disappeared under Lake Cachuma when the Santa Ynez River was dammed. The narrator imagines her father, who knew this lost geography, "looks down into lands not drawn / on any map," perhaps seeing the "shadows / of a people" their "mouths still opening, closing / on the stories of our home" (76–77). In another poem in the volume, "Burial Ground," Miranda implies memory might become a source for renewal. She writes, "I know how the earth remembers / the bones of a river," and suggests that "silence ripples subversively beneath the land" as "always the voice of a river seeks / an instrument for return" (97). The river's hoped-for return stands in metaphorically, of course, for Native people's own struggle for return or renewal. But just as the flooded valley in "Indian Cartography" cannot truly be recovered, Miranda's vision of the reclamation of culture, too, remains in question. The poems in this collection waiver between the reality of "4000 graves / out back behind the Mission," and "a tenuous truce / with history," between an attempt to "find my way / by echo" and "a course that flows directly / into the heart's homeland" (73, 68, 4, 98).

The sacred grounds lost and remembered in Hedge-Coke's recent *Blood Run* are destroyed or looted mounds from an Oneota site located at the current South Dakota/Iowa border. The volume recalls the more than four hundred original mounds, now decimated by development, farming, desecration, and dismantling for artifact theft until reduced in number to the mere seventy-eight remaining today. Through personae poems, the author reanimates the life of the community of Blood Run, but more impressively, accomplishes what scholar Chadwick Allen calls a "literary resurrection of a destroyed snake effigy mound" ("Serpentine Figures," 807). Allen analyzes the mathematical patterning of individual poems and their placement within the collection to demonstrate the way Hedge-Coke's form actually "simulates earthwork technologies" (807).[12] The link to sacred geography here is both philosophical and physical.

The volume also performs as a remarkable example of poetry of witness, embodying many voices from the scene—river, deer, corn, clan sister, tractor, skeleton, etc. Among this dialogic rendering is a group of poems from the voice of the mounds themselves. In the serial representation we can trace the changes. At various times the mound personae say, "In our day / we were many / so many landscape / appeared pleated, puckered," "we are the love of man honoring mystery," "I endure wrath of the till," and "We sorely await Reclaiming" (52, 55, 58, 64). Indeed, only part of Hedge-Coke's purpose in creating *Blood Run* was literary. As the last line alludes to real-time action in the physical world, so, too, does Hedge-Coke's book call for just such activism. She states in the acknowledgments: "This volume was written in effort to move the state and its citizens to protect, preserve, and honor an Indigenous mound site" (94), and she invites participation. Traditional oral literatures had both affective and effective intentions; many of the contemporary works of witness and resistance involving sacred lands also aspire to both beauty as literature and usefulness in the world.

DESTRUCTION, DISPLACEMENT, AND NATIVE DIASPORA

As both Hedge-Coke's and Miranda's works demonstrate, given historic disruptions, place consciousness in Native poetry involves complex representation. Abenaki writer Joe Bruchac claims that "travel" in contemporary Native poetry includes "sacred journeys and pilgrimages on the one hand to tragic tales of displacement on the other—Trails of Tears and Long Walks that ancestors survived and their descendants will never forget" (Francis, *On the Good Red Interstate*, inside cover blurb). The relationships with place, therefore, are not necessarily represented as positive or fulfilling, nor are they always figured as rural. Native Diaspora, the historical displacement of Native peoples through military conflict, removal, or U.S. government programs like Relocation or Canadian government policies like those pertaining to "Road Allowance People," together with everyday migrations or moves for military service, education or employment—these physical disruptions inform Native ideas of place in the poetry from the Native American Renaissance and beyond. Struggle for territory or verbal sparring about the "proper" use of land or ideas about "ownership" likewise inform much contemporary poetry of place, as do awareness of the destruction to tribal homelands and the irreparable damage done to the natural environment and its creatures.

The works addressing themes of destruction, displacement, and Native Diaspora range widely in form, perspective, and intention, with the youngest generation of Native poets especially working to express their new vision of the urban rez. Place as memory or absence, urban homeland, homelessness, and the travel from and return to "native" place, all become a frequent focus in contemporary aboriginal poetry and impact the patterns of the texts. Within the vast array of subjects, the works by early Native Renaissance poets often keyed on historical destruction and its aftermath. The harsh facts of the great land grab in history frequently lead to visions of survival and resistance, whether these involved cultural adaptations or activism on behalf of the tribes or the environment. New places and the re-membering of the past also figure prominently as poetic acts and subjects. Across this thematic wordscape the ideas of pan-Indianism and tribalism also play out as decades turn. Poetic dispersion seems to have followed on the heels of Native Diaspora, but despite the many strands and new perspectives within the body of Indigenous poetry, the preoccupation with place and displacement continues.

This preoccupation early on involved historical events and political circumstances surrounding land possession. These may be the central subject of poems such as several written by Jack Forbes, including those in the early chapbook, *Naming Our Land, Reclaiming Our Land,* or they may become the implied backdrop for work focused on contemporary conditions or relationships, as is true of the deeply place-conscious work of Blackfeet writer James Welch, and also true of several poems written about Alcatraz Island by Hopi poet and artist Wendy Rose.[13] In "When American Was a Brown Woman," Forbes uses rapid-fire language and slang to call into question the United States's own fast-talking claiming and renaming of various parts of the continent, including the sections of California taken from Mexico and the aptly named "Lone Star Republic—Texas" (1-2).[14] The title of James Welch's only collection of poetry, *Riding the Earth Boy 40,* alludes to another cog in the machinery of Manifest Destiny—the legislated allotment of tribal lands.[15] The "Earthboy 40" refers to the forty acres along Milk River assigned to an individual named "Earthboy," and another poem in the volume, "Range 18," refers to one of the parcels of allotted land that was divided into larger sections for use in raising cattle. The history of colonization is thus embedded both in the place and the poetry.

However, Welch's poetry does more than offer a symbolic reference to U.S. assimilation policies; in striking detail it limns their particular effects as played out in Montana Indian country. Elements of landscape—plains, buttes, ranges, reservoirs—inhabit Welch's poetry, together with wildlife from the region—hawks, antelope, horses, trout, coyotes. Family names—Lame Bull, Blackbird, Bear Child, Horseman, Heavy Runner—accumulate together with Montana place names—Moccasin Flat, Harlem, Mount Chief. Regional features and images populate the poems until, as scholar Sidner Larson notes, "Place is the steady, walking base to which events of life are syncopated" ("James Welch," 308). Then, within this sensually imagined place, Welch introduces memorable scenes, images of desperate poverty, and a tribal inheritance both pitiful and quietly enduring. In the poem "Christmas Comes to Moccasin Flat," for example, Welch particularizes poverty with images of people who "sit in chinked cabins, stare out / plastic windows and wait for commodities" and of "candles bought on credit" because of the "poor price for calves" (26). He communicates the underlying despair and desperation with references to "warriors face down in wine sleep" and "drunks" who "drain radiators for love or need."

If Forbes's poems offer political commentary on the history of land theft and Welch's offer moving images of the conditions those historic changes have brought, other Native "place" poems, including Wendy Rose's Alcatraz poems, come from the front lines of Native attempts to reclaim tribal lands. The title of one of her poems, "Caged Wings: First Impressions from the Boat, Alacatraz Island/Indian Land, 1970," suggests its immersion in the struggle for reclamation. Lines from the poem describe "a song at our center / and a campfire crackling / with the rags and branches that built it / to keep out the Coast Guard, make bright / the night that would hide / helicopters and guns," clearly depicting the contemporary military standoff (*What Happened*, 3). Alcatraz, of course, became a symbol of Indian resistance and the struggle to reclaim Native lands.

Poems about Alcatraz, land, and ideas of ownership are also among the works in collections by Mohawk poet Peter Blue Cloud/Aroniawenrate. Frequently anthologized is Blue Cloud's playful "The Old Man's Lazy," which dramatizes competing understandings of relationship with, or "use" of, the land (*Clans of Many Nations*, 123–26). Through the voice of "the old man" we are introduced to "the Indian Agent" who questions the Indian's character, suggesting he "has no pride, no get up /and go" because he sees the narrator's place as "overgrown" and offers suggestions on how it should be "fixed" up and "made use of" (123). Meanwhile, the old man notes how the agent "steps / all through the milkweed and / curing wormwood," implying the agent's disregard for these healing plants (123). The poem closes with a suggestion of the "uses" the old man derives from the land: "Each day / a different story is / told me by . . . / the rain and wind and snow, / the sun and moon shadows, / this wonderful earth, / this Creation" (125–26).

In addition to their sometimes dry sense of humor, Blue Cloud's works representing the natural world are also marked by experiments in voice and form. Like Hedge-Coke, his poetic repertoire includes personae poems and characterizations of various elements in nature from turtle to wolf to crow to milkweed. He also has a number of multivoiced poems, some with vertical parallel presentation in which one portion seems to be intended to serve as an underchant to the narrative progression prominent in the other section. Indeed, "White Corn Sister," the poem that opens *Clans of Many Nations*, is identified as "a play for voices" (15–33). Clearly, these experiments bring the poetry closer to the performance reality of traditional oral works. Meanwhile, the bodies of the poems are filled with naturalistic details, insinuations of the indwelling life, and a unique imaginative perspective, as demonstrated in this brief passage from "Sweetgrass": "hearing frog song and / watching a cattail bending / to the weight of a light question / a red-wing blackbird asks" (*Clans*, 106).

The delicate and vital images from Blue Cloud's work are balanced by a realism, sometimes by a touch of fatalism, as the poet acknowledges the damage done to Native nations and to the environment by rogue capitalists. In "Wolf," for example, the poet does not flinch from graphic images of wolf cubs killed by cyanide or a male wolf left with a stump of a leg by a trap. He offers images of the "protruding, blackened tongues" of dead wolves and names the "alien blood lust," the "rifle shot and snapping jaws / of steel traps and poisoned bait, / the bounty hunter and fur trapper / predators / of greed," and lists the lost—buffalo, beaver, fox, mountain cat, grizzly, antelope, elk, moose, caribou—who "have gone into death the prime breeders / to fashion garments of vanity" (*Clans*, 61–66). Blue Cloud's human or animal personae often stand apart from the environmental drama, casting a light.

Other Indigenous poets shine their literary light on urban conditions—the impersonal poverty and discrimination many displaced Native people experience in cities across the Americas. Chief Dan George was one of the early First Nations poets to write on this subject. His poem "To a Native Teenager" addresses an imagined youth who longs for big-city life. Apparently drawing from his own experience, the male speaker of the poem offers an account of various qualities of his rural home, all lacking in the city life in which he now finds himself trapped. This cautionary poem means to save another from following his path. He writes, for example:

> Again and again your eyes will try to see
> the evening dripping off the sun
> like wild honey and your nostrils
> will quiver for the scent of water
> that tumbled through the canyons
> of your childhood. [*Native Poetry*, 10]

Another Dan George poem, "Keep a few embers from the fire," uses fire to symbolize place and tradition and, though separation and loss are implied here, too, the speaker of the poem seems to hold out hope for survival and continuance:

> Keep a few embers
> from the fire
> that used to burn in your village,
> some day go back
> so all can gather again
> and rekindle a new flame,
> for a new life in a changed world [*Native Poetry*, 9]

Likewise addressing displacement, but with greater force, Simon Ortiz also writes of urban despair in poems such as "Relocation" and "Time to Kill in Gallup."[16] The first title alludes to the U.S. government policy of the 1950s that placed reservation peoples from across the nation in alien city environments, and the poem laments its effects:

> So I agreed to move
> I see me walking in sleep
> down streets, down streets with gray cement
> and glaring glass and oily wind,
> armed with a pint of wine,
> I cheated my children to buy.
> I am ashamed.
> I am tired.
> I am hungry.
> I speak words.
> I am lonely for the hills.
> I am lonely for myself. [*Going for the Rain*, 76–77]

The images from Gallup include those of "a toothless woman / Gumming back sorrow" who "gags on wine" and of "The children / who have cried too many times / would only dig more graves, / lean on church walls / for warmth." Ortiz alternately describes the city streets as "barren / fronts for pain" and "never useful / for anything /except tears" (*Woven Stone*, 247–50). Through these desperate urban scenes he layers longing and images of homeland. In "Leaving America," for example, the speaker tells of a bus depot acquaintance, Roy, who is "going home" and here the modest description of home nevertheless comes across as inviting. When Roy lists the qualities—"It's got red and brown land, / sage, and when it rains, / it smells like piñon / and pretty girls at Squaw Dance"—the narrator's simple assent speaks emphatically of his understanding: "I know" (*Woven Stone*, 97). Indeed, home here is so distinct from the urban environment (in this poem the Kansas City bus depot) that Ortiz suggests by the poem's title that it is not even part of the larger America.[17]

Whether or not they focus on the seedy aspects sometimes included in Ortiz's urban vision, many Native poets still express a dis-ease or sense of alien-nation in urban America as well as in "the heartlands." In her poem "Long Way from Home," for example, Cree writer Emma LaRoque captures the academic disconnection often experienced by Native scholars who find themselves in "hallways pallored by / ivory-coloured thoughts" (*Native Poetry in Canada,* 159). The speaker in LaRoque's poem numbers herself among Native groundbreakers who sought to use education to "make a difference," but she finds instead "I did my footnotes so well / nobody knows where I come from" (162). Like Ortiz's persona, Roy, LaRoque's, too, finds comfort in images of home places: "blueberry hills" and "Ama's red river jig" (161).

Although Choctaw poet Jim Barnes's 1982 collection, *The American Book of the Dead,* includes images of his several home places, overall the poems resist easy alignment between home and contentment. The book, which like Hogan's *Calling Myself Home,* might be considered the record of a personal quest, includes more than twenty autobiographical poems that trace a cross-country odyssey highlighting locations and scenes from Barnes's childhood in Oklahoma, his adult wanderings in various parts of the country, especially Oregon and California, and his ultimate return to his adult home in Missouri. But individually and en masse they do not find solace in place, instead they figure the journey as a fateful and futile search for belonging.

Barnes, who offers particularly accomplished and moving lyrical poems built with precision, voices at intervals throughout the collections variations on this tangible angst, on an unresolved, unspecified longing: writing of "an affliction so general you find no name," of "a pilgrim looking for a mecca he'll never find," of how "a constant fear swells in your groin," of knowing "all the ghosts are dead, / except the one never laid to rest" (64, 70, 89). Despite this seeming restlessness, Barnes's poetry is deeply grounded physically. He builds a remarkable sense of place(s). But, as scholar Elizabeth Blair has noted, "Commitment to place is often neither comforting nor simple" ("Jim Barnes," 31).

The buried history of America contributes to the discomfort of Barnes's persona in *The American Book of the Dead.* The speaker's struggle becomes particularly clear in two poems that follow one another in the collection: "Under Buffalo Mountain" and "Autobiography, Chapter XIV: Tombstone at Petit Bay, near Tahlequah" (36–37). In the first, Barnes writes of "where the Choctaw stopped, forever" and of the way "blood hides / in these hills and haunts." In the second, the speaker finds an "obelisk" dated 1839 and inscribed with "one faint vertical word, *child,* in Sikwayi script."[18] After this find, he voices this characteristic lament:

Years, you've quested in these hills, a running search
for something still you cannot name—something
holy, proof of migration or lost Phoenician sailors. [37]

When later in the poem Barnes writes, "The obelisk casts a shadow longer than its length," the reader has no doubt that the metaphorical shadow belongs to history, a history of destruction and dispossession.

Like those of Barnes, the poems of Paiute Adrian Louis, though with a different poetic timbre, also voice a sense of alienation and personal angst. Louis, however, ultimately casts a cynical eye not only on middle America, but on Native America as well and, with a rapier-sharp wit, he slashes all dearly held illusions about tribal places. Like Ortiz, he personifies a flawed America, writing, for example: "America has always been blind to the past, / and because of this, it has no soul" (*Vortex*, 18). His poems image the inane Wonder Bread, Campbell soup everyday of the Dakotas, Nevada, Nebraska, and Minnesota, the mindless Kmart consumerism, and the cable-channel mentality, the homeland in which "The communal eyeballs of American are being blurred blind by television" (*Evil Corn*, 116). But Native people in Louis's America also seem to have lost soul balance. When his personae, these "children of Crazy Horse," speak "There's something about being Indian" lines in his poems, the nostalgic/elegiac tone is always ironically undercut by images of the "fire water world," of "Rez gangbangers," of "shootings to the left / and stabbings to the right" (*Fire Water World*, 6, 13, 23; *Ceremonies*, 15). Still, Louis assigns historical blame for Native dis-ease, and links the contemporary circumstances of Indian lives to the history of invasion. "The reservation of the mind," he suggests, is always haunted by the memory of "one mass grave that America gave / to those eighty-four warriors / and their sixty-two women and kids" and by the knowledge that "by treaties they possessed our souls" (*Fire Water World*, 3, 64).[19] While Louis's poems demonstrate this unsettling awareness of the physical and spiritual displacement of Native peoples, they remain largely silent on the possibility of recovery or reclamation.

Many younger poets like Sy Hoahwah and Sherwin Bitsui, in the disillusionment of their vision, seem heirs of Louis's hard candor.[20] Like Louis and Ortiz, Comanche poet Hoahwah, in his recent collection, *Velroy and Madischie Mafia*, articulates a sense of alienation and renders a vivid picture of existence within a subculture of the larger America. Hoahwah's "Comanche County" is landscape haunted equally by death and beauty, and the ghosts that weave casually in and out of the arresting poems belong as much to the present as the past. The book embodies a tribal reality of meth labs, Zippo lighters, crow calls, and fancy dancing in which "boys neither go to heaven or hell / but into ghost stories" (5). Through juxtaposition of seemingly incongruous images—eagle medicine and Ecstasy, a war shield and a "bible thick as buffalo meat"—the collection replaces popular clichés of historical destruction, tragic

Indians, and vanishing culture with a sharp-edged portrayal of contemporary continuance in Indian country (33). By crossing new mythologies of Indian Mafia with older tribal narratives and traditions, the lyrical accounts imaginatively render a strange hybrid culture.

Navajo Bitsui's work, too, is invested in offering a new vision of Native America. His first book, aptly entitled *Shapeshift*, has been described as "articulating the challenges a Native American person faces in reconciling his or her inherited history of lore and spirit with the coldness of postmodern civilization" (cover blurb). Imagistic descriptions of place spill into disjointed gatherings of startling associations in Bitsui's work. In "Drought," for example, he offers this shimmering and memorable picture: "the old woman digging roots from the arroyo bottom as the sun becomes a spiral trail marked on a sandstone cliff." Several stanzas later he creates an alternate sense of time and place with this list: "two moths shake their fist at a young boy who unplugged his father's reading lamp, a newspaper then makes the sound of autumn, / a silver horse snorts— / the dark windows remind him of his master's eyes, / *the shadow of crushed grapes*" (55). Bitsui's poetry is often reminiscent of Ray Young Bear's surrealistic representations of the Black Eagle Child settlement, especially in its inclusion of dream imagery as in these passages from "The Noose in My Dreams": "I heard songs when the cactus wren sipped nectar from the tongue of a cricket" and "I drive home / imagining a man suckling milk from the cliffs of Canyon de Chelly / and dream the awakening of knives inside of grandmother's cabinet" (45).[21] Clearly, his poetry traces an uneasy passage between very different worlds.

Like Bitsui, other young Native writers are seeking new styles for their poetic expressions of place. Among the interesting developments are hybrid forms including concrete or visual poetry and the Native hip-hop movement.[22] The late Marvin Francis from Heart Lake First Nation in Alberta drew upon his experience as poet, playwright, actor, artist, and theater director when he created his "long poem," *City Treaty*. The work, as the title suggests, tries to create some kind of peace for Indigenous peoples living in urban spaces. A description of this zany, fresh text (or script for a performance or picture book of language) cannot do justice to the innovation Francis brings to the page. The book includes text boxes, symbols from dollar signs to crow's feet, stage directions, and textual variations of every imaginable sort. The thesis and the narrator's "point of view" are that "the landscape now has city" (69). Francis bears out this claim with an accumulation of urban reality: images of place such as "my usual back alley route, trash can trails"; depictions of activities such as "beer bottle picking" and "cruise crowds leather"; and the backbeat of social reality such as "the english dive into land they need / Steal Country Usually Because All is ours" (5, 41, 22, 8).[23] The "treaty map" of Francis's opus admits of many variants, motion as well as space, including "seasonal migration / human to city and back" in an effort to "cover all the territory" (67).

Ultimately Francis seems to want to name displacement just another Native place.

SPATIAL RACIAL ADAPTATIONS

In the twentieth and twenty-first centuries, the poetry of adaptation might compose another entire category in the discussion of Native writers and their relationship to place. Just as Dan George instructs us to "rekindle a new flame / for a new life in a changed world," Nora Marks Dauenhauer's poem, "How to Make Good Baked Salmon from the River," describes both change and continuity in a traditional activity performed in a new environment.[24] The best location for this cooking, the poem tells us, is "in a dry-fish camp / on a beach by a fish stream / on sticks over an open fire" (*The Droning Shaman*, 11). However, Dauenhauer's speaker must make it "in the city, / baked in an electric oven on a black fry pan" (11). Everything in the making of the salmon, from location to ingredients to accompanying activities, has substitutes lightheartedly introduced by the phrase "in this case." Throughout the poem Dauenhauer also intersperses teachings about thankfulness and respect, about right relationships:

> Shoo mosquitoes off the salmon,
> and shoo the ravens away,
> but don't insult them, because mosquitoes
> are known to be the ashes of the cannibal giant,
> and Raven is known to take off
> with just about anything.
>
> . . . And think how good it is
> that we have good spirits
> that still bring salmon and oil. [14]

The mention of the cannibal giant and Raven, by poetic gesture, alludes to the whole body of tribal story and traditions and we are meant to understand how each everyday activity is performed in the context of this intact social compact, this worldview. Ultimately, the poem suggests the mobility of these learned cultural groundings and the ability of these teachings to transform experience in new locations.

Of course, the poets and poems of Native America, or even the Native American Renaissance period, cannot be read as expressing a single or unified perspective when it comes to an understanding of place and displacement, but the many voices do illustrate certain continuities. The literatures of Native peoples emphatically demonstrate that place impacts spirit and experience. They also seem to suggest that belief systems can color experience of place. Indeed, Native poets have sometimes self-consciously named or claimed places inherently incongruous to a sense of Native-ness or located their Indigenous identity within unlikely cultural territories, perhaps implying that Native place is anywhere Indians live—or die trying. Native poetry often seems to decry the notion that the spatial is inherently racial, and to suggest rather that expectations about racial placement are socially and politically constructed, or socially constructed for political reasons. However, many poets and poems also seem to confirm a particularly Native understanding of the many places on the globe Indians find themselves, and to align that understanding with the acts of placement—in other words, with relationship, with reciprocity.

And, yes, many Native writers simultaneously attest that particular power may reside within specific places. What, then, is the possibility of the essence of place being carried over hundreds of miles of removal trails and then across generations, even across realms of being into new alien languages and forms? Scholars might call this cultural adaptation; Native nations might name it an act of survival. And some artists from tribal nations apparently believe that there is enough substance or soul in a place to even imbue writing with a vibration, a meaning—words like earth, homeland, *aki, endaad, akiiwan.*

NOTES

1. Miranda, *The Zen of La Llorona.* See, for example, "Almost a Pantoum for My Mother," in which Miranda writes, "The trailer court's sooty asphalt swam in oily rainbows" (13); or "After San Quentin," which includes these lines: "We are his inmates, the trailer / our prison" (14). In "Steele Street," Miranda creates a vivid sense of the "the geography of my life": "The old working class houses, cut or uncut grass, / salmon-pink roses unpruned. Under our feet, cracked / asphalt and old brick, dirt and sewers, / layers of civilization's debris. / The city's archeology, muffled histories / of a relocated tribe" (70).

2. Among the lines in the song, which include "I' and "my," are the following: "I sit down" and "Where my illness is absorbed" (112, 114).

3. See, for example, Awiakta, *Selu;* Momaday, "Native American Attitudes to the Environment"; or Owens, "Everywhere There Was Life: How Native Americans Can Save the World," in *Mixedblood Messages.*

4. The Bruchac "Seven Moons" series quoted from is in *No Borders. Matshushima* offers both fine examples of Vizenor's haiku and one of the essays in which he describes both the haiku and the Anishinaabeg dream-song traditions.

5. Erdrich's poem was later included in her collection *The Mother Tongue,* under the title, "First Rice" (32).

6. I refer you to Armstrong's longer discussion in "Land Speaking," which includes several other significant claims regarding the relationship between land and human language. She suggests, for example, that if or when we move over

time, "the land [changes] changed the language"; and she attests to noting in her own travel the alignment between "physical differences" and alterations in language (175, 179).

7. For a longer discussion of sacred journey in Native literature, see Blaeser, "Sacred Journey Cycles," pp. 83–104.

8. Ortiz spoke about his journey to "find Indians" in an oral performance of his work given on November 19, 1975. An audiotape of the reading is available from the American Poetry Archive at San Francisco State University. References given are for the reprint of *Going for the Rain* in *Woven Stone*.

9. Like many Native writers, Ortiz links place and identity. Indeed, his collection *A Good Journey* contains a poem composed primarily of place-names. After the listing of names, "Some Indians at a Party" concludes, "That's my name, too. / Don't you forget it" (88).

10. I allude here to William Bevis's use of the phrase in "Native American Novels: Homing In."

11. See Norma Wilson's discussion of this healing ceremony in *The Nature of Native American Poetry*, p. 91.

12. Allen's article explains that Hedge-Coke accomplishes this by "citing the terrestrial form and celestial alignments of the majestic Serpent Mound extant in southern Ohio" (807).

13. Rose's poems refer to the Indian occupation of Alcatraz Island by Native activists, including AIM members, beginning in 1969 and lasting for fourteen months.

14. Lines from Jack Forbes's poem include, for example, this slang harangue: "Hey bro do you dig / there was a little time / just a little under / a century and a half ago / that / Tejas and Nuevo Mexico / and Utah / Nevada and Idaho too / were not a part of the United States / so tell me, bro, / was the Lone Star Republic—Texas—part of America then?"

15. The Dawes Allotment Act of 1887 was used to break up Indian land by assigning individual parcels (allotments) of land and to allow so-called excess land to be purchased by the government and opened for white settlement.

16. The work of Ortiz is infused with place consciousness. Another strong work is *from Sand Creek*, which recalls the killing of 133 peaceful Arapaho and Cheyenne by the troops of Colonel John Chivington at Sand Creek, Colorado.

17. Ortiz's mentions of America are often barbed. In *Going for the Rain*, the poem "East of San Diego," for example, offers this warning: " Keep to the hills / and avoid America / if you can" and *from Sand Creek* includes these lines: "This America / has been a burden / of steel and mad / death."

18. Sikwayi is another name for Seqouyah (also, George Guess), who is credited with creating the Cherokee syllabary.

19. Louis's reference in the "one mass grave" lines is to the 1890 massacre at Wounded Knee Creek.

20. Other younger poets who likewise offer a fairly strong critique of contemporary conditions in Native America include Sherman Alexie, of course, as well as Mark Turcotte, Eric Gansworth, and Margo Tamez.

21. Young Bear, *Black Eagle Child.*

22. Scholar Karen Drane's Ph.D. dissertation, "Aural Traditions: Indigenous Youth and the Hip-hop Movement in Canada," covers interesting ground in its discussion of the apparently self-conscious claiming by hip-hop emcees of Native space in the city. She identifies her research as partly focusing on "the new ways urban spaces are being thought about and named by Native youth" and explores their "localized lexicons" (7).

23. Francis's use of the "scuba" acronym here, as he depicts the urban landscape and the way "the english dive into land," recalls Gerald Vizenor's retelling of the Anishinaabeg creation myth in which he pictures "earthdivers . . . Metis, tribal tricksters and recast cultural heroes" diving into "unknown urban spaces now, into the racial darkness in the cities" and calls for "the white world to dive like the otter, beaver, and muskrat in search of the earth, and federal funds" (*Earthdivers*, ix, xvii). Both employ the earthdiver myth to critique the colonial design.

24. Dauenhauer dedicates her poem to Simon Ortiz, having written it after the fashion of his own "how-to" poem: "How to make a good chili stew—this one on July 16, a Saturday, Indian 1971," from his *A Good Journey* collection. Ortiz's poem begins very like Dauenhauer's in its sense of playful accommodation: "It's better to do it outside / or at sheepcamp / or during a two or three day campout. / In this case, we'll settle / for Hesperus, Colorado / and a Coleman stove" (*Woven Stone*, 174).

WORKS CITED

Allen, Chadwick. "Serpentine Figures, Sinuous Relations: Thematic Geometry in Allison Hedge Coke's *Blood Run.*" *American Literature* 82 (2010), 807–34.

Allen, Paula Gunn. "IYANA: It Goes This Way." In *The Remembered Earth: An Anthology of Contemporary Native American Literature.* Edited by Geary Hobson. Albuquerque: University of New Mexico Press, 1980, 191–93.

Armstrong, Jeanette. "Land Speaking." In *Speaking for the Generations: Native Writers on Writing.* Edited by Simon Ortiz. Tucson: University of Arizona Press, 1998, 175–94.

Armstrong, Jeannette, and Lally Grauer, eds. *Native Poetry in Canada: A Contemporary Anthology.* Orchard Park, N.Y.: Broadview Press, 2001.

Awiakta, Marilou. *Selu: Seeking the Corn-Mother's Wisdom.* Golden, Colo.: Fulcrum, 1993.

Barnes, Jim. *The American Book of the Dead.* Urbana: University of Illinois Press, 1982.

Belin, Ester. *From the Belly of My Beauty.* Tucson: University of Arizona Press, 1999.

Bevis, William. "Native American Novels: Homing In." In *Recovering the Word: Essays on Native American Literature.* Berkeley: University of California Press, 1987, 580–620.

Bitsui, Sherwin. *Shapeshift.* Tucson: University of Arizona Press, 2003.

Blaeser, Kimberly. "Sacred Journey Cycles: Pilgrimage as Re-turning and Re-telling in American Indigenous Literatures." *Religion and Literature* 35:2–3 (Summer-Autumn), 2003, 83–104.

————, ed. *Traces in Blood, Bone, and Stone: Contemporary Ojibwe Poetry.* Bemidji, Minn.: Loonfeather Press, 2005.

Blair, Elizabeth. "Jim Barnes." *Dictionary of Literary Biography: Native American Writers of the United States.* Edited by Kenneth M. Roemer. Detroit: Gale Research, 1997, 30–34.

Blue Cloud, Peter. *Clans of Many Nations.* Fredonia, N.Y.: White Pine Press, 1995.

Bruchac, Joseph. *No Borders: New Poems.* Duluth, Minn.: Holy Cow! Press, 1999.

————. *Thirteen Moons on Turtle's Back.* N.Y.: Penguin, 1997.

Castanier, Bill. "Shattering the Silence: Author Glancy Speaks for Sacajawea." *City Pulse* (February 17, 2010). http://www.lansingcitypulse.com/lansing/print-article-4002-print.html.

Dauenhauer, Nora Marks. *The Droning Shaman.* Haines, Alaska: Black Current Press, 1988.

Erdrich, Heid. *The Mother's Tongue.* Cambridge, UK: Salt Publishing, 2005.

Forbes, Jack. *Naming Our Land, Reclaiming Our Land.* Bandon, Ore.: Kahonkok Press, 1992.

Francis, Lee. *On the Good Red Interstate.* San Francisco: Taurean Horn Press, 2002.

Francis, Marvin. *City Treaty.* Winnipeg, MB: Turnstone Press, 2002.

George, Dan. "Keep a few embers from the fire." *Native Poetry in Canada: A Contemporary Anthology.* Orchard Park, N.Y.: Broadview Press, 2001, 9.

————. "To a Native Teenager." *Native Poetry in Canada: A Contemporary Anthology.* Orchard Park, N.Y.: Broadview Press, 2001, 9–11.

Harjo, Joy. *Secrets from the Center of the World.* Tucson: University of Arizona Press, 1989.

Hedge-Coke, Allison. *Blood Run.* Cambridge, UK: Salt Publishing, 2006.

Hinton, Leanne, and Lucille Watahomigie, eds. *Spirit Mountain: An Anthology of Yuman Story and Song.* Tucson: University of Arizona Press, 1984.

Hoahwah, Sy. *Velroy and Madischie Mafia.* Albuquerque: West End Press, 2009.

Hogan, Linda. *Calling Myself Home.* Greenfield, N.Y.: Greenfield Review Press, 1978.

LaRoque, Emma. "Long Way from Home." *Native Poetry in Canada: A Contemporary Anthology.* Orchard Park, N.Y.: Broadview Press, 2001, 159–63.

Larson, Sidner. "James Welch." *Dictionary of Literary Biography: Native American Writers of the United States.* Edited by Kenneth M. Roemer. Detroit: Gale Research, 1997, 308–15.

Lincoln, Kenneth. *Native American Renaissance.* Berkeley: University of California Press, 1983.

Louis, Adrian. *Ceremonies of the Damned.* Reno: University of Nevada Press, 1994.

———. *Evil Corn.* Granite Falls, Minn.: Ellis Press, 2004.

———. *Fire Water World.* Albuquerque: West End Press, 1989.

———. *Vortex of Indian Fevers.* Evanston, Ill.: Northwestern University Press, 1995.

Miranda, Deborah. *Indian Cartography.* Greenfield Center, N.Y.: Greenfield Review Press, 1999.

———. *The Zen of La Llorona.* Cambridge, UK: Salt Publishing, 2005.

Momaday, N. Scott. *Again the Far Morning: New and Selected Poems.* Albuquerque: University of New Mexico Press, 2011.

———. "Native American Attitudes to the Environment." *Seeing with a Native Eye: Essays on Native American Religion.* Edited by Walter Holden Capps. New York: Harper & Row, 1976, 79–85.

———. *The Way to Rainy Mountain.* Albuquerque: University of New Mexico Press, 1969.

Niatum, Duane. *Harper's Anthology of 20th Century Native American Poetry.* New York: Harper & Row, 1988.

Northrup, Jim. "mahnomin." *Walking the Rez Road.* Stillwater, Minn.: Voyageur Press, 1991, 98.

Ortiz, Simon. *After and Before the Lightning.* Tucson: University of Arizona Press, 1994.

———. *from Sand Creek.* New York: Thunder's Mouth Press, 1981.

———. *Going for the Rain.* New York: Harper & Row, 1976.

———. *A Good Journey.* Tucson: University of Arizona Press, 1984.

———. *Woven Stone.* Tucson: University of Arizona Press, 1992.

———, ed. *Speaking for the Generations.* Tucson: University of Arizona Press, 1998.

Owens, Louis. "Everywhere There Was Life: How Native Americans Can Save the World." In *Mixedblood Messages: Literature, Film, Family, Place.* Norman: University of Oklahoma Press, 1998, 218–36.

Paz, Octavio. *In Praise of Hands: Contemporary Crafts of the World.* Greenwich, Conn.: New York Graphics Society, 1974.

Purdy, John, and James Ruppert, eds. *Nothing but the Truth: An Anthology of Native American Literature.* Upper Saddle River, N.J.: Prentice Hall, 2001.

Ramsey, Jarold. *Reading the Fire: Esssays in the Traditional Literatures of the Far West.* Lincoln: University of Nebraska Press, 1983.

Revard, Carter. *How the Songs Come Down.* Cambridge, UK: Salt Publishing, 2005.

Rose, Wendy. *Hopi Roadrunner Dancing*. Greenfield, N.Y.: Greenfield Review Press, 1973.

———. *What Happened When the Hopi Hit New York*. New York: Contact II Publications, 1982.

TallMountain, Mary. "The Last Wolf." In *Nothing but the Truth: An Anthology of Native American Literature*. Edited by John Purdy and James Ruppert. Upper Saddle River, N.J.: Prentice Hall, 2001, 554.

Underhill, Ruth. *Singing for Power: The Song Magic of the Papago Indians of Southern Arizona*. Berkeley: Regents of the University of California, 1938. Reprinted, Tucson: University of Arizona Press, 1993.

Vizenor, Gerald. *Earthdivers: Tribal Narratives on Mixed Descent*. Minneapolis: University of Minnesota Press, 1981.

———. *Matshushima: Pine Islands*. Minneapolis: Nodin Press, 1984.

Welch, James. *Riding the Earth Boy 40*. Revised edition. New York: Harper & Row, 1976.

Wilson, Norma. *The Nature of Native American Poetry*. Albuquerque: University of New Mexico Press, 2001.

Woody, Elizabeth. *Luminaries of the Humble*. Tucson: University of Arizona Press, 1994.

Young Bear, Ray. *Black Eagle Child: The Facepaint Narratives*. Iowa City: University of Iowa Press, 1992.

Zepada, Ofelia. *Ocean Power: Poems from the Desert*. Tucson: University of Arizona Press, 1995.

15

Telling You Now

The Imagination within Modern
Native American Autobiography

A. ROBERT LEE

Every writer is forced to rely, at some point, on the imagination.
The skill with which he can do that determines his success as
a writer. I can take credit for setting down those Kiowa stories
in English, in *The Way to Rainy Mountain*, but I didn't invent
them. The imagination that informs those stories is really not
mine. . . . It's an ancestral imagination. It's important to understand that dimension. But in the secondary materials and in that
third voice, which is personal reminiscence, I brought my own
imagination to bear.

N. Scott Momaday, Ancestral Voice (1989)[1]

There are stories that take seven days to tell. There are other
stories that take you all your life.

Diane Glancy, The West Pole (1997)[2]

Something strange appears when we look at certain autobiographies of Indian people: the notion of identity, of how the individual is related to the world, people, self, differs from what we
see in "Euro-American" autobiography.

Carter Revard, Family Matters, Tribal Affairs (1998)[3]

Native American life-writing has long come accoutered in controversy. How
much, how little, is first-person authorship entitled to reveal of ceremony,
spirituality, origin myths, clan naming, and custom? Is there a risk of vaunting
self-identity above shared larger genealogy, the betrayal of tribal-community
etiquette? Oral tradition, the governance of the spoken word, is axiomatic in
Native tradition. Yet how writerly, not to say readerly, is a Native author allowed to be? If an estimated more than two-thirds of Native Americans now
live in the townships or cities, be it by choice or by historic BIA termination

and relocation policies, how to balance duty to tribal rite of passage or origins or homeland with, in an increasingly deployed term and in all its pluses and minuses, urban-cosmopolitan (not to say international) modernity? It can little surprise that Native autobiography since indeed N. Scott Momaday's *The Way to Rainy Mountain* (1969), and its follow-up replete in sepia visuals in *The Names: A Memoir* (1976), has been a spate. In giving attention both to the kinds of modern life-writing, and to a number of its highlights, the emphasis falls upon the qualities of imagination—of textual fashioning—within each.

If written Native autobiography had its beginnings in the Christian-convert texts of Samuel Occom, William Apess, and George Copway, memorial threads as it were, those since Momaday have utterly diversified the legacy. Not only has that meant full-length prose narrative, albeit often with insets of corroborative poem or photograph, but full-length verse composition—few of late more consequential than Ray Young Bear's *Black Eagle Child* (1992)—and essay contributions of the kind in *I Tell You Now* (Swann and Krupat, eds., 1987), *Native American Autobiography* (Krupat, ed., 1994), and *Here First* (Krupat and Swann, eds., 2000). Further issues of interpretation and status have been quick to arise, not least of which are those as to whether any one Native voice can be assumed to carry representative, synecdochic weight, the single figural voice speaking for the many.[4]

For Elizabeth Cook-Lynn, be the domain autobiography, fiction, or verse, and as she develops it in *Why I Can't Read Wallace Stegner and Other Essays* (1996), *New Indians, Old Wars* (2007), and her *Wicazo Sa Review* and other discursive work, the desideratum calls for a voice at once rigorously tribalcentric, pledged to speak overwhelmingly to historical redress and the restoration of sovereignty. Jace Weaver, Craig Womack, and Robert Warrior, whether in the various studies under their own name or the jointly authored *American Indian Literary Nationalism* (2006), less prescriptively have argued for "intellectual sovereignty." They speak of a Native literature and its voicing rooted in tribal family, clan, and language, yet without denial of access or input by Euro-American and other reader-writer communities. In Paula Gunn Allen, especially *The Sacred Hoop* (1986), gynocentric voice—for her spiritual, life-bearing—invites its full reckoning, be it Leslie Marmon Silko in the Laguna Pueblo "war-zone" storying of *Ceremony* (1977) or Wendy Rose, whose mixed Hopi-Miwok-European womanhood and its rejections by a preemptive mainstream she notably locates in the sweet-and-sour contributions to *The Halfbreed Chronicles and Other Poems* (1985).

Gerald Vizenor has long pitched for a postindian aesthetic of voice, free of undue filo-piety, with roots in both Native (especially Anishinaabe) tricksterism and reflexive textual circlings from Beckett to Baudrillard. Rarely has that more been on display than in his autobiography and its very titling, *Interior Landscapes* (1990). In this he is joined by Louis Owens, the syncretism of whose background (Choctaw-Cherokee, Irish, Cajun, Mississippi-Protestant) feeds imaginatively into the various life-writings in discursive collections like

Mixedblood Messages (1998) and *I Hear the Train* (2001). Whichever holds, few would deny that the issues join: authenticity, subject position, cultural ideology, genre, and nowhere more so than in first-person life-writing.

The roster of recent Native autobiography approaches a plenitude not only in span but variety, those to be thought "literary" in the sense of belonging to a genuine creative oeuvre and those given to different kinds of other regime—visionary, political, the once-off memoir, or the arts- and media-based life.[5] Carlos Castaneda's *The Teachings of Don Juan* (1968), massively popular on publication and whether true-life or imaginary, set forth as though in apprentice-voice a shamanistic agenda, the proposed segue into the ways and wisdom of *brujería*. Reservation leadership and AIM pan-tribalism equally have engendered their own share of life-writing, albeit often coauthored, be it Wilma Mankiller's *Mankiller: A Chief and Her People* (1993), with its first-person Cherokee history; Ladonna Harris's *Ladonna Harris: A Comanche Life* (2001), with its Oklahoma portrait of a life's tribal activism and marriage to Fred Harris as senator and presidential candidate; or Russell Means's *Where White Men Fear to Tread* (1995) and Dennis Banks's *Ojibwa Warrior* (2004), with their memorialization not only of the activism that led to AIM's founding in 1968 and the 1973 occupation of Wounded Knee, but each personal itinerary of BIA schooling, rez life, FBI surveillance (in Banks's case his eleven years of being a fugitive), and respective drink afflictions, marriages, and family. The plethora of once-off memoir spans a wide tribal spectrum, from a First Nations Cree self-portrait like Jane Willis's *Geniesh: An Indian Girlhood* (1973) to Beverly Hungry Wolf's life within Blackfoot gynocracy in *The Ways of My Grandmothers* (1980). In *My Life as a Hollywood Indian* (1982) Iron Eyes Cody, albeit actually of Sicilian background and thereby one in a line of notable faux Indians, throws an ironic light on the whole panorama of media "Indians" and not least his own duly tearful 1970s "Keep America Beautiful" cameo.

Mixed-blood lives yield a near-discrete body of self-texts, reflective of much self-fissure and yet achieved self-composure, to include Maria Campbell's *Halfbreed* (1973) as a Vancouver-set chronicle of a Métis history at the margins of racism, drugs. and prostitution; Vincent L. Mendoza's account of Creek-Mexican ancestry and life before and after Vietnam in *Son of Two Bloods* (1996); Tiffany Midge's *Outlaws, Renegades and Saints* (1996) as the verse autobiography of Sioux and city legacy; and Linda Hogan's *The Woman Who Watches Over the World* (2001) with its redemptive Chickasaw chronicle of illicit early love, alcoholism, injury, and the adoption of Lakota sisters. *As We Are Now* (1997), under the editorship of the novelist William Penn—of Nez Perce and Osage ancestry (some Osage have questioned this)—plied into a likely Quaker-Pennsylvania family, adds to the gallery. Native authorship looks to Craig Womack's Creek and Cherokee two-spirit self-portrait ("Howling at the Moon"), Kim Blaeser's rumination on her Anishinaabe-German background and upbringing on Minnesota's White Earth Reservation as against Chicago as metropolis, and her Newberry Library fellowship ('On

Mapping and Urban Shamans"), and Inez Petersen's sally at identification and misidentification by dint of a family legacy at once Quinault and Danish ("What Part Moon").

Collaborative or "as told to" writings, with footfalls in vintage earlier landmarks—controversially *Black Elk Speaks* (1932) as Oglala Sioux witness under editorial rearranging of John Neihardt—have met with different kinds of continuance. However distinct each from the other, these have subsequently included Mary Crow Dog's *Lakota Woman* (1990), with Richard Erdoes, unyielding in its account of abused girlhood, boarding school, reservation drugs and drinking, and AIM marriage and politics with Leonard Crow Dog; and Greg Sarris's *Keeping Slug Woman Alive* (1993), a virtual if not actual autobiography in the guise of an essay-sequence, his adoptive California upbringing under the guidance of the Cache Creek Pomo weaver-medicine woman Mabel McKay. Script, profile, interior self-imagining, they again extend the remit of Native life-writing. Each, variously, helps locate the inflections of a Native-lineaged self not only inside, but reimagined and reordered, as autobiographical text.

In her chapbook, *Claiming Breath* (1992), Diane Glancy, who describes herself as of "Arkansas backhill culture mixed with Cherokee heritage,"[6] imagistically formulates yet another style of first-person voice, hybrid yet perfectly whole as to its operating terms and conditions: "I want to explore my memories & their relational aspects to the present. I was born between 2 heritages & I want to explore that empty space, that place-between-two-places, that walk-in-2-worlds. I want to do it in a new way."[7] She, like Momaday, Silko, and Vizenor, gives emphasis to the discrete literary imagination as much as any mere factuality in the life being inscribed. She is not alone. One can readily turn to Janet Campbell Hale in her fashioning of a drift-life as a Coeur d'Alene–ancestried woman in *Bloodlines* (1993) or to writer-professors like Carter Revard in his Osage-Ponca self-chronicles of Oklahoma and geographies far beyond in *Family Matters, Tribal Affairs* (1998) and *Winning the Dust Bowl* (2001) and Jim Barnes in the beautifully styled intimacy of Choctaw-Welsh legacy played into a wholly modern life in *On Native Ground* (1997). Glancy, in other words, is far from alone in assuming a stance that is nothing if not aware of its own authorial poetics and even ventriloquism. In alighting upon a selective gallery of what invites being designated *literary* autobiography, to include Momaday's autobiographies, the aim is to give recognition to imaginative virtuosity, the shaping art and language, of texts never other than integral to the larger renaissance of Native American expression.

Whichever emphasis is to be allowed in Momaday's life-writing, his Kiowa origins and its creation story, Navajo and Pueblo upbringing, or sense of the Southwest as iconographic, there can be no doubt as to his recognition of its conscious call upon imagination.[8] This is far from opting for some mere aesthetics for its own sake, quite the reverse. His texts, like those of Silko, Vizenor, Glancy, and others, use their very inventedness to underwrite wholly tribal-specific culture even as they explore the contours of self. In his celebrated 1970 essay, "The Man Made of Words," in an account of the effect of a meteor storm in 1833 as an abiding disaster omen to the Kiowa, Momaday gives a succinct touchstone as to how fact and imagination fuse in acts of story: "Do you see what happens when the imagination is superimposed upon the historical event? It becomes a story. The whole piece becomes more deeply invested with meaning."[9]

The Names is yet more explicit in leaving no doubt of tribal-specific situatedness yet also of the narrator-self in view: "In general my narrative is an autobiographical account. Specifically it is an act of imagination. When I turn my mind to my early life, it is the imaginative part of it that comes first and irresistibly into reach, and of that part I take hold. This is one way to tell a story. In this instance it is my way, and it is the way of my people."[10]

At one level the story follows a clear enough chronological line: the Momaday born of Kiowa father and part-Cherokee mother, raised on Navajo and Jemez Pueblo reservations where his parents were teachers, and the eventual Stanford Ph.D. with a dissertation written under the direction of Yvor Winters on the New England poet Frederick Goddard Tuckerman, and, by his own acknowledgement, an abiding interest in the strategies of voice and image of Emily Dickinson. But the text also hints of collage, a careful inter-ply of time-schemes and memory. In this it continues on from *The Way to Rainy Mountain* in which Momaday highlights his own life journey against that of the Kiowa people from Montana to Oklahoma, and told as a series of twenty-four triads: personal and family history, calendar history, and tribal-mythic history. The effect is one of contending, yet brilliantly complementary, narratives; something analogous happens in *The Names*—his own "isolated, yet fragmented and confused, images" (61) played against the journey he undertakes to Tsoai, Wyoming's Devils Tower (literally rock-tree in Kiowa), in quest of beginnings and heritage. Imagining, or "reflections" (161) as he calls them, in turn, takes on a quite special force throughout *The Names*.

However literal the sweep of New Mexico, Oklahoma, Arizona, and the Dakotas as Indian Country, or of the lives and family played out within their sound and sight, he could not more insist on, for him, their inwardly memorial and visionary resonance. He so speaks of his closing journey to Tsoai as implicating him in a double response: "I saw with my own eyes and with the eyes of my own mind" (167). A better reflexive marker would be hard to invoke, for each phase of *The Names* works in precisely this manner, the present-day actual with the past-time actual, the present-day imaginary with the past-time mythical. Time, place, tribe, origin, genealogy: Momaday has each deftly circle round, and into, the other, within the one coordinated autobiographical disclosure.[11]

First there is the summoning of his mixed genealogy. For his paternal Kiowa people, he begins from their creation myth as the Kwuda who emerged from a hollow log, itself to become the motif also at the close of *The Names*— "a fallen tree, the hollow log there in the thin crust of ice" (167). The remembrance to follow includes his naming ceremony as Tsoai-talee by Pohd-lohk, step-great-grandfather; the life of Mammedaty, his horseman grandfather buried at Rainy Mountain Cemetery; and his father, Huan-toa, or Alfred Morris Mammedaty, caught on the cusp of prior tribal and modern 1920s life, wanderer, teacher, and watercolorist (and who would use Al Momaday as his *nom de peinture*). His maternal Cherokee-white line he invokes through his beauteous mother, Natachee, her grandmother Natachee, and the marriage into the Galyan-Scott-McMillan dynasty with its different roots in Anglo and Scots-Irish Appalachia and Cajun Louisiana. This signifies family as literal mosaic, fragment and photograph, yet also, and more fugitively, as fictions of, and in, memory.

It leads him to call up the last Kiowa sun dance in 1887; life in Navajo country, or *Dine bikeyah*, in the 1930s; his white grandfather, Theodore Scott, photographed at Fort Sam Houston playing the banjo of his hill forbears; and Jemez Day School as among his "most vivid and deeply cherished memories" (117–18). Each, along with the references back to Kiowa tribal devastation brought on by smallpox in 1839–40 and measles in 1892, or his childhood sense of query to the point of near-bafflement as to "'how to be a Kiowa Indian" (101), or his first horse with its harking back to the Kiowa as a horse culture and its change of visual line for him ("I had a different view of the world" [155]), provokes a reach into fact and but also a call to imagination ("I lay the page aside, I imagine" [93]).

Landscape, equally, is made subject to these double auspices, a Southwest at once actuality and yet vision, the one given time and yet always a species of meta-time. Whether Jemez Pueblo, or Gallup in New Mexico with its iconic Route 66, or Rainy Mountain and its cemetery or, en route to the Kiowa homeland, Tsoai, the literal topography takes on its own imagist wrap, an implied immanence to township, mesa, desert, and horizon. The account of Monument Valley works typically, landscape if in shape and timeline best accommodated in Navajo then whose perfect linguistic fit Momaday seeks to emulate in his own prose:

> The valley is vast. When you look out over it, it does not occur to you that there is an end to it. You see the monoliths that stand in space, and you imagine that you have come upon eternity. They do not appear to exist in time. You think: I see that time comes to an end on this side of the rock, and on the other side there is nothing forever. I believe that only in *dine bizaad*, the Navajo language, which is endless, can this place be described, or even indicated in its true character. Just there is

the center of an intricate geology, a whole and unique landscape which includes Utah, Colorado, Arizona, and New Mexico. The most brilliant colors in the earth are there, I believe, and the most extraordinary land forms—and surely the coldest, clearest air, which is run through with pure light (68–69).

The sustained imagining of the Southwest's geology, its time, air, and light, as of the tribal and family lineages it has hosted that are shown to have been bound into, and around, the name Navarre Scott Momaday, gives *The Names* its distinction. At every turn the self is imagined as having been absorbed into the nonself of landscape, natural chronology, optics, temperature, even language, not to say the hollow log of Kiowa origins and the lives that have been lived in its footfalls. It makes for autobiography simply luminous in the telling.

In a 1986 interview, Leslie Marmon Silko gives her version of the place of story in Laguna community life and tradition: "The key to understanding storytellers and storytelling at Laguna Pueblo is to realize that you grow up not just being aware of narrative and making a story or seeing a story in what happens to you and what goes on all around you all the time, but just being appreciative and delighted in narrative exchanges."[12] If the observation holds for spoken storytelling, that of live mouth and ear, so it can be said to have been adapted to modern, and even postmodern, Native autobiography. *Storyteller*, certainly, itself could not be better thought of than as an endeavor to shadow these spoken "narrative exchanges," the text as enactive, at once celebration and mural, story cycle, and text-and-image collage.

Silko acknowledges at the outset her own paradox of *writing* oral heritage through the figure of Aunt Susie, protectress, Carlisle-educated teacher, and archivist of Laguna life and family:

> This is the way Aunt Susie told the story.
> She had certain phrases, certain distinctive words
> she used in her telling.
> I write when I still hear
> her voice as she tells the story. [7]

Oral-written, the speaking voice overheard as it were, makes a perfect point of entry. Each component text within a text, to include the unfolding photography, speaks in equal weight with the other, the effect one of a longitudinal or simultaneous voice, none unduly more privileged than the other.

The pattern is established at the outset. Aunt Susie herself, and Great Grandma A'mooh and Grandpa Hank, speak as though live, a continuum, to which Silko supplies a species of gloss in interlocutions like "Storyteller"

(17–32) and "Storytelling" (94–98). The point is made explicit in "The Story-teller's Escape" (247–53):

> With these stories of ours
> we can escape almost anything
> with these stories we will survive.

Silko's white Marmon family is given equal play alongside her Laguna family, rarely more touchingly than in the story of Grandpa Marmon's refusal to bow to anti-Indian prejudice in an Albuquerque hotel: "These are my sons," he tells the manager in a proud show of paternity [17]. Real-life history weaves into poem-chronicle or legend throughout. Aunt Susie's story of the drowned children who become butterflies (7–15) offers an opening instance. The Yellow Woman episode (54–62) gives a story of present-day love told as coyote myth. The episode of the golden-feathered rooster, which Silko unfolds in a letter to the poet James Wright, develops into a wonderfully Aesopian story (226–27); likewise the comic-absurd story, "Uncle Tony's Goat" (171–76), as retold from the Acoma poet Simon Ortiz.

The actual includes references back into history: "Grandpa Stagner had a wagon and team and water drilling rig. He traveled all over New Mexico drilling wells" (88). Or into the near-contemporary, like the police encounter and death in "Tony's Story" (123–29). Or into personal memory as when the author remembers an encounter with a bear: "When I was thirteen I carried an old .30-30 we borrowed from George Pearl" (77–78). The mythic can be a Pueblo creation story ("The world was already complete / even without white people. / There was everything / including witchery" [130]); a vignette of tricksterism ("One time / Old Woman Ck'o'yo's / son came in/from Redleaf town. . . . He asked the people / 'You people want to learn some magic?'"[111–21]); a Mexican-Pueblo courtship told as coyote fable ("Coyote holds a full house in his hand," [257–65]); a corn fertility parable ("The Go-Wa-Peu-Zi Song" [158]); or a Spider Woman sexual drama of love and fate ("Estoy-eh-Muut and The Kunideeyahs" [140–54]).

Silko also extends her range beyond the pueblo: "The Hills and mesas around Laguna/were a second home to my father" (160). She writes in a letter to Lawson F. Inada in September 1975: "The purple asters are growing in wide fields around the rocks past Mesita clear to the Sedillo Grant" (170). Centered on Laguna pueblo life as it may be, *Storyteller* also has no shortage of allusion to Hopi, Navajo, Sioux, and Apache culture. There is typically an opening image of "a tall Hopi basket" with its inlaid woven grasshopper or Hummingbird Man (1) and "A Geronimo Story" (212–23) as the near-mythic cavalry pursuit and escape version of the legendary Apache fighter yet also magical and holy deer-man.

Throughout, Silko keeps her reader-listener aware of the protocols in play. Introducing a Laguna-Keres myth to do with Acoma place, she issues a reminder of how story, tribally, is by necessity a shared circle and consent:

The Laguna People
always begin their stories
with "humma-hah":
that means "long ago."
And the ones who are listening
say "aaaa-eh." [38]

Yet, equally, she reserves her own margin to adapt, transform, collate, as imaginative form requires and as, in fact, oral tradition itself has always allowed: "I know Aunt Susie and Aunt Alice would tell me stories they had told me before but with changes in details or descriptions. The story was the important thing and little changes here and there were really part of the story. There were even stories about the different versions of the stories and how they imagined these differing versions came to be" (227). This could also virtually serve as *Storyteller's* prospectus, Silko's authorial guidance as to the interaction of oral and written, Native-spoken and Native-scriptural, in the delivery of her own self-telling.[13]

The opening, full-page, black-and-white photograph in Gerald Vizenor's *Interior Landscapes* offers "Clement Vizenor and son Gerald, in Minneapolis, 1936." As an image of parent and child affection, it looks replete. Smiling, open-shirted, a father in a fedora holds his two-year-old in protective arms. The boy, bright-eyed, wrapped, although the subject of the camera, appears to be monitoring its very action. Behind them lie piled-up bricks and two stern, crumbling houses, one with a curtained window. The picture, however, contains more than a few dark hints of prophecy.

First, Clement Vizenor, "crane descendant" (3) and "reservation-born mixedblood in dark clothes" (22), Chippewa house painter and feckless ladies' man from White Earth, Minnesota, within a year would be found murdered with his throat cut on another Minneapolis street. Police left the murder as "unsolved," a brawl perhaps, or a jilted husband's revenge, at any rate one more "Indian" who had got himself killed and bequeathed himself only in name. Fatherless, his son would be quickly deposited with relatives, or fostered out, by his feckless yet eventually three-times-married Swedish American mother, Laverne Lydia Peterson. It was a young life that was anything but protected, despite the benign intervention of his feisty, irascible Anishinaabe grandmother, Alice Beaulieu, herself, in trickster fashion, to enlist his aid in persuading a blind younger man not only of her enduring physical beauty but to become her husband. Vizenor's self-authoring in life, as later in script, becomes as much necessity as calling.

That process finds its life shape as he evolves from Minneapolis "mixed-blood fosterling" to leading Native American writer-professor, from the Boy Scout who camps on grounds "stolen from tribal people by the federal government" (62) to adult enrolled member of the Chippewa White Earth Reservation. Throughout all of *Interior Landscapes* he emphasizes yet further paradox: the G.I. who is sent to Korea, and by chance of having a name at the end of the alphabet, is assigned to a unit in Camp Chitose, Japan, and transmutes from soldier into author ("Mount Fuji over my typewriter . . . my liberation was the military in Japan" [128]); the mixed-blood Native American who fantasizes a new life as a reincarnated Lafcadio Hearn; and the returnee soldier who, on demobilization, studies for a technical qualification at New York University but who, after Asian areas studies at the University of Minnesota, becomes successively city activist, journalist, professor, respectively, at Bemidji State, the University of Minnesota, Santa Cruz, Oklahoma, Berkeley, and in due course the University of New Mexico—and one of the most published writers in the Native literary canon.

The other kind of self-authoring finds its shape in the "Vizenor" of his books. The classroom Minnesota youngster who dreamed up Erdubbs Mac-Churbs as his alter ego storyteller, and an early manifestation of his taste for baroque naming, has become one of the most international and voluble of Native authors. A literary output of over thirty volumes accrues to his name. This, and each other paradox, *Interior Landscapes* makes into the one narrative spectrum, a present of interacting pasts. The span runs from "Families of the Crane," with its allusion to Anishinaabe clan systems, through to "Honor Your Partners," partly a credo of Vizenor's own postmodern improvisations and tactics and partly an account of the violent, and anything but communitarian, threats against him from AIM members for having dared criticize their politics of Red Power as radical chic. The twenty-nine "autobiographical myths and metaphors," or first-person fictions, each dated yet gapped one from another, serve as interfoliations, discrete yet at the same time complementary panels of memory.

Not inappropriately, he sees himself early on in the Earthdiver role of Anishinaabe Creation myth, a postmodern Earthdiver, however, as likely to call upon Eudora Welty, Michel Tournier, Primo Levi, William Scheick, or Michel Foucault, all of whom supply prefatory quotations, as upon tribal legends of Naanabozho, generic begetter of the Anishinaabe. This tribal-cum-postmodern blend, in fact, becomes the very hallmark of *Interior Landscapes*. A reference to Ishi, last of the Yahi, eventually the residential maker of museum artifacts in San Francisco, foreshadows his own academic tenure at Berkeley. Anishinaabe legacies of nature, pictographs carved on bark, he connects to his lifelong taste for the dynamic stillnesses of haiku and for Matsuo Basho as haiku master. He ponders another kind of connection between Hollywood and "The Indian" in recalling that his mother, a frequenter of Depression-era movies, fell for his handsome mixed-blood father because of a resemblance to George Raft. His father's death likewise calls up an overlap of two worlds: "Clement William must have misremembered that tribal web of protection when he moved to the cities from White Earth Reservation" (26).

One-time classroom daydreaming finds its army counterpart when he tells a none-too-interested officer in Japan, "I want to be a writer" (126). As he moves into authorship, so he finds himself more and more authored by his own truest subject: Native America in all its historic mixed-blood windings. Patronizing white school authorities metamorphose into "the new fur traders" (185), a nice reference back to an ancestry that calls up his own Métis or French Canadian Chippewa family, the Vezinas, whose name was mistranscribed into Vizenor by a then–Indian agent. Vizenor's own "trickster signature" (263) as storyteller, two centuries on, might well be thought a textual making good. In the National Guard he thinks himself "a mixedblood featherweight" (80), his boxing that of a kind of shadow tribal warrior. "Death Song for a Rodent," a vignette of his remorse on shooting a squirrel, again suggests a linkage between past and present, the modern hunter in disregard of Anishinaabe woodland etiquette.

As journalist, his purview widens to include reporting the suicide of a twelve-year-old Dakota Sioux boy, Dane White, also inadequately parented, and then detained in a prison cell for school truancy to quite disastrous effect; the murder trial of Thomas James White Hawk, a killer for sure, yet on Vizenor's long-held reckoning, also a victim of "cultural schizophrenia" (289); and, in "Avengers at Wounded Knee," his keen understanding of the Seventh U.S. Cavalry's massacre of Big Foot and his Minneconjou Sioux (nearly three hundred in all) at South Dakota's Wounded Knee Creek in 1890, and yet, at the same time, his unpious take on the Dennis Banks's style of warrior bravura during the 1973 protest, with its drugs, guns, and even limousine service, which he calls "a revolutionary tribal caravan" (237). He re-creates his own haunting by skinwalkers, or tribal poltergeists, in a Santa Fe room where, previously unknown to him, there had been painful deaths. He also recalls an article he once wrote for the *Minneapolis Tribune* that indicted a University of Minnesota archaeological dig as tribal desecration. With just the right working blend of seriousness, yet trickster provocation, he proposes a "federal bone court to hear the natural rights of buried human bones" (258).

These interfolding domains of Native and white, city and reservation, America and Japan, street and campus amount to a life remembered always as simultaneity and yet contradiction. In this, they take their cue from an observation by N. Scott Momaday, his greatly admired cospirit: "Story-telling," he quotes from Momaday's address to the First Convocation of American Indian Scholars, is "a process in which man invests and preserves himself in the context of ideas."[14] The point holds exactly for Vizenor's own "survival trickeries on the border" (73). He indicts fixed categories of "Indian" as Hollywood or TV silhouette, or as social science case study, or, perhaps above all, as prime exhibit in the annals of victimry. *Interior Landscapes* unravels a life consciously imagined in all its contradance: self-possession as textual process, Native modernity from out of Native ancestralism, city from reservation, Indian, in the term Vizenor has made quite his own, as postindian.[15]

In opening *Bloodlines: Odyssey of a Native Daughter* with a familiar dedication, "For All My Relations," Janet Campbell Hale speaks ancestrally, a Native tie of history. Two insets follow, first the memory of a village Coeur d'Alene raven prophecy as to the arrival of three Black Robes ("By then everybody knew who the terrible enemy was"),[16] then a turtle-clan dream of rejoined family despite having been "stepped on, broken into a million little pieces" (xxxi). Throughout the life account that follows, these Native flows and contraflows are plaited into a quite personal focus, a balance sheet of loss and gain, scar and healing, historic mainstream racism but also unblinkered recognition of Native miscreancy. Each, in different filterings of memory, can be said to represent how Hale develops her own version of Momaday's "being what we imagine."

At an immediate level, *Bloodlines* could not more be portraiture of life caught within poverty, the marred childhood of a hostile mother and often absentee father, alcohol, disruptive flits ("twenty-one schools in three states" [34]), the marital violence of her second marriage ("I was absolutely destitute, staying not at a battered wife's shelter but at a welfare hotel" [80]), and vulnerable single-mother struggles of food stamps and tenancy ("We had to move again—this time to a ratty suite above Mission and South Van Ness" [100]). Itinerancy, son in tow, means townships and cities across California, Washington, Idaho, and Oregon and from Tijuana to Vancouver. Eventually, a Berkeley and UC Davis education yields a pathway into self-possession and, with it, fulfillment of the aborning urge to a virtuosity of written word long presaged in her childhood poetry and stories that will eventually secure for her different visiting writer-professor academic berths.

The setbacks, even the intermittent returns to the Yakima Reservation in Wapato, underline her sense of the irony of a heritage whose Coeur d'Alene name translates from the French as "heart of steel" (145) as does the history of the name Campbell anglicized, and so appropriated, as a version of her great-grandfather's name of Cole-man-née (170). Even so, Hale makes her own counter-appropriation not only in *Bloodlines* but in her novel, *The Jailing of Cecelia Capture* (1985), which shares a fair degree of autobiographical material. The outcome is a life told to its own commanding rhythm, through its own self-aware authorial lens. However much seeming straight-from-the-heart chronicle (it has received praise as oral narrative), it actually draws upon a savviest sense of design, the alignments and contrasts of an author-autobiographer always shrewdly in control. The eight "autobiographical essays" (xxii) are to be seen as orchestration, each panel a monitoring time-present adroitly folded into time-past.

It is in this respect that *Bloodlines* as overall autobiographical text gives ground to Hale's observation that "real life comes into play only insofar as it can serve the purpose of art" (15). An early sequence she titles "Autobiography in Fiction" brackets childhood's first doodlings in "three Big Chief tablets" to the "much later . . . writer of novels" (4), even imagining what it would be to invent a persona called Julia whose life would shadow her own. Julia, too, is to be seen as mixed-blood, ageing, given a drinking problem, with a brother in Vietnam, and finally confronted with her mother's hospital frailty, even as her own daughter grows out of girlhood. To good purpose the text speaks of "fiction tapestry" (11), "fiction and fact" (12), "re-arrangements" (12), as if to underline awareness of the account's scripting, its deliberateness of imaginative pattern. It makes a perfect route-marker, working rules-of-the-game, for how the autobiography unfolds, the protocols that have gone into its writing and which by implication hold for its reading.

Like Maxine Hong Kingston's *China Men* (1980), *Bloodlines* does a subtle trade in historical family. The mother's setbacks ("We're so poor, Mom and me, so damned poor" [30]) play against her capacity to demean Hale ("a master, an absolute master of verbal abuse" [60]). The Coeur d'Alene and Kootenay legacies turn and re-turn, mother, father, sisters, in-laws, the promised but never delivered tribal help, the memory of being cruelly excluded from a family Fourth of July celebration, and her own final call to "mother" her own illness-shrunken mother: "My mom is gone. In the end there are no resolutions. Only an end" (86). The few respites achieved in childhood and adolescence transition into her being "a young welfare mother" (96), belted in the eye by her second husband, and then both amazed and hushed by the family at the discovery of being descended from Dr. John McLoughlin, "Father of Oregon" (139). The image of the Chippewa wife of this touted Irish American pioneer is foisted on the young Janet as a model of what it is to be a "good Indian"—meaning compliant and "white," whose marriage, together with McLoughlin himself as both great man yet unexemplary in his treatment of extended family, she researches on a Newberry Library fellowship in 1984. Excavating this genealogy reenforces her resolve to contest all versions of the "good Indian": "I didn't care to be a good Indian" (113). McLoughlin, and his role in her history, she further delineates through Gram Sullivan, shared descendant and kinswoman and, as Hale imagines her, her story—even her facial appearance—a species of persona, herself mirrored in earlier incarnation.

A speaking tour takes Hale to Bear Paw, Montana, where she conjures into being her own Coeur d'Alene grandmother's unwitting part in the flight of Chief Joseph and his Nez Percé in 1877: in imagination "I saw her, my grandmother" (152). The two stories elide, her grandmother's, her own, even the detail of seeing where the anti-Indian bullets of racists have nicked the memorial plaque of Joseph's surrender. A 1992 visit to the Coeur d'Alene Reservation in Idaho ("I live in New York with my third husband" [163]) reminds of her father's Coyote stories but also his random and sometimes drink-fueled mistreatment of her. The remembered fantasy of a childhood ideal Native homeland contrasts with the actuality of "my poor, transient childhood" (186). Back in Spokane, she sees (but leaves unnamed) the film *Thunderheart*, the 1992 Michael Apted/Val Kilmer screen story of a part-Sioux FBI agent sent down to solve a murder in tribal South Dakota. "On the rez he learns Who He Is" (187), she observes laconically, with capital letters for emphasis. It points both to her own hard-fought intimacies of Native legacy and a latest "Indian" story line she dubs "action-packed and full of clichés" (187). Among Native-authored autobiographies, *Bloodlines* assumes a rare virtuosity in imagining the gaps between the two.

If there is an unmistakable ebullience to Carter Revard's poetry and essays, it equally suffuses his autobiographical writing, two volumes given over to a life span from childhood in his Osage-Ponca 1930s Oklahoma Dust Bowl dynasty through to emeritus professorship of medieval literature and linguistics at Washington University in St. Louis, Missouri. His prolegomena, "To the Reader," in *Winning the Dust Bowl*, gives off an indicative density of allusion:

> This book tells of growing up in a mixed-blood family of Indian and Irish and Scotch-Irish folks. . . . It moves from Oklahoma to Oxford to the Isle of Skye, to Jerusalem, Paris, and the Isle of Patmos, to Knossos, Bellagio, St. Louis, Cahokia Mounds, and California. These are stories of Poncas and Osages, of the American Indian Movement and urban Indian centers. Some are powwow stories, some Oxford fables; some talk of racing greyhounds and stealing watermelons, others of bootlegging and bankrobbing.[17]

Revard rarely delivers less than the full menu. Witness *Family Matters, Tribal Affairs* in kind with *Winning the Dust Bowl*, and with due recognition that the latter assumes more of a collagist styling as interstitial verse, photography, and diary. His different speculative panels possess their own winning variety, Oklahoma land-and-oil politics to Old English prosody, growing deafness and memories of sound to Las Vegas as neon kitsch. The sum translates into life-writing always busy but not at the expense of genuine aplomb.

Each major way station in Revard's history gets due accord, starting from Pawhuska, Osage capital and his Oklahoma Indian Agency birthplace. Revard hardly shies from due acknowledgment of a life fed by learning, books, libraries, and an eventual creative and scholarly repertoire of his own. Early

Buck Creek country-schoolhouse learning and a University of Tulsa scholarship lead into his Oxford Rhodes Scholarship and Yale Ph.D., followed by several decades of academic life in St. Louis. But if the portraiture necessarily includes the campus, the library holdings of fabliaux and manuscript, it also moves well beyond the professorial c.v. *Family Matters, Tribal Affairs* vows "a community of words on Indian ground" (x). *Winning the Dust Bowl* speaks of placing "a meadow . . . of history and autobiography" around poems that look out to "people, places, and happenings from 1931 to the present" (xiii). The use of meadow as image nicely points beyond academia.

The Oklahoma dynasty in which "there was always plenty of trouble and strife" (*Family Matters*, 11) gives a further nonacademic touchstone. Early in life he is required to give carcass feeds and dawn exercise to greyhounds owned by the Kendall family, who employ him in occasional work. Teenage is "full of miserable moments," boy-consciousness, smallness in competitive sport (*Family Matters*, 63). His recollections step back, a touch Bonnie and Clyde-ishly, to both bootlegging relatives and Uncle Carter Jump's parole after an attempted bank robbery. A key figure is Aunt Jewell, Ponca matriarch, whose subtle ancestral humanity and ministrations he eulogizes in the poem "An Eagle Nation." His Osage "Thunder-ceremony" naming as Nom-peh-wah-the he invokes with pride, the very touchstone of heritage. His recognition of AIM and the significance of the Wounded Knee/Pine Ridge Occupation in 1973 bespeaks a politics far from those of any university. To be factored in is the plethora of overseas travel, the UK of Cotswolds and Hebrides, the Mediterranean of Lake Como and rural Greece, and his own ongoing activism at the St. Louis–based American Indian Center of Mid-America (AICMA). Throughout, and in splashes of color, there is the relish of animal and avian life, coyotes and birdsong, interests imaginatively further developed in a body of later verse addressed to Jurassic and related evolutionary genetics.

This abundance, however, is carefully framed, each volume unfettered by mere chronology. In this respect, *Family Matters* can typically engage in a reverse "Columbus- discovers" map ("Report to the Nation: Repossessing Europe"), with the author positioned as scriptural Coyote—*Special Agent Washazhe No. 2,230*. With just a footfall of Twain, Revard guys Europe as high civilization, a seeming "report" on new-old territory to mirror the colonialism that seized Native lands in the Americas. In "How Columbus Fell from the Sky and Lighted Up Two Continents," he ponders "Columbianism" as discovery myth in the contexts of both Osage and Navajo creation myth and Milton's *Paradise Lost*, nothing if not a reach into paratextuality. *Winning the Dust Bowl* opts as much for autobiographical commentary as history, each poem indeed glossed for occasion and context. "Training Greyhounds" so balances the account of hard-chore kennel work with a verse racetrack story. The seven-part "Indian Survival" links Osage-Ponca cultural and sovereignty history to each particularizing poem. Coyote fare underwrites the Ponca nation's unvanished continuance as expressed in a closing poem like "After Sand Creek," with its allusion to tribal song: "*We recognize that song. It's one that we still sing*" (203). Revard's best forte, throughout, lies in bringing to the chronicles of his life a matching poetics, his own tease of fashioning.

The subtitle to Jim Barnes's *On Native Ground: Memoirs and Impressions* lends the working key, memory as theater given a poet's tuning—his "inland sky," as he engagingly calls it, in one of the interfoliated poems (37). Like Revard, Barnes has lived a life of teaching and books and yet also of pursuits far beyond. His east Oklahoma birth in 1933 to a family at once Anglo-Welsh and Choctaw finds definition in the hard-scrub landscape of LeFlore County's Fourche Maline bottoms and Holson Creek hills. Childhood and World War II coming-of-age takes its place inside topography of smallholding, tenant sharecropping, animals, fish and birdlife, arrowheads, bones, and petroglyphs. Chafed, a touch stir-crazed, he steps west in 1951–59 to lumberjack in Oregon before college study both in Oklahoma and Arkansas. Thereafter, he becomes the professor-author and writer-in-residence at Truman State University (cofounding *The Chariton Review)* with a late stint at Brigham Young University, and with intervening writing and translation fellowships in Bellagio, Lausanne, Paris, and Munich. This trajectory of "Indian Country" Oklahoma, Northwest logging, and Missouri classroom, Europe as repository of Homeric Greece, *Rinascimento* Italy, a France of Baudelaire, the Impressionists and Picasso through to the latter-day Metro—together with French Switzerland and Barvaria's Villa Walberta—he makes over into quite formidably elegiac narrative.

Not the least of his "memoirs and impressions," reflexively one might say, lies in setting forth desiderata for "the art of making"—"irony," "vantage point," tone"—qualities, he suggests, to take the writing "beyond subject" (235) and "against pretentious self-absorption" (191). In part this is the poet speaking, in part the seasoned magazine editor. His own autobiography acts on these prompts to a tee: contemplative ("The Fourche Maline River and Holson Creek flow through much of what I have written" [3]), honed ("I fell in love with the art of writing twenty years before I knew what had afflicted me" [49]), and if elegiac then without saccharin ("I was raised in Choctaw country . . . and count myself one-eighth *Chahta*. I was raised on the language and foods, practically all that was left us then of the culture" [117]). Choctaw and related seams supply history, and also image, throughout *On Native Ground*, whether mounds, bones, trails, arrowheads, or even books: "I am reading Angie Debo's *The Rise of the Choctaw Republic* [of] when the Choctaw Nation was struggling for national autonomy" (97). But they do so also within each other's domain: the still larger "Great Southwest" (115), the sumptuous Cascades and alluvial Willamette Valley (though he writes, "I knew, finally, that I would not find in Oregon what I had left Oklahoma for" [134]), together with the Paris that stirs his poetry, *le midi*, the Montreux of authors as divergent as Hemingway, Rousseau, Dostoevsky, and Rilke, and the Bellagio where by Lake Como and the castles his imagination summons Pliny and Dante.

In other words, Barnes gives simultaneous place to "Indian Country," the America of the Pacific Northwest, and Europe as cultural encounter and voyage: all play their part in forging the remembered "geography," past and present, of the self so adroitly summoned in *On Native Ground*, itself, as Barnes fully acknowledges, its own further act of self-authorship. This goes a long way in giving his autobiography its measure, a Native-heritaged writer bound into mixed Choctaw family origins yet if wholly alert to the one signature then unwilling to let that be all-defining. His stance as author, moreover, invites controversy: "There have been many, many anthologies . . . to tell us just who are the American Indian writers, just who this and who that, along with pedigree. . . . But we must not be misled. The writer is first a writer, second a Native American, a black, a Chicano" (122). Such may not be a prospectus to win over all hearts and minds.[18] But it speaks to, and from, a conviction as to the exigency of imagination in all consequential domains of authorship.

On Native Ground, assuredly, works to act upon Barnes's own sense of the need for exactitude of word, image, craft. From the opening vignette of hearing the roar of a mountain lion as an Oklahoma five-year-old to his return to the Sommerville family plot in 1995, there can be no doubt of how readily he himself makes each serve the contour of his life. Whether telling the blacksmith's Choctaw story of "how crow got black" (19), the "Indian" iconography of Deadman's Trail (70), shopping in otherwise historic Bellagio ("It is a tourist town, with tourist prices. . . . Even a mixed-blood from Oklahoma can tell that" [169]), or of a fond visit to Gertrude Stein's Rue de Fleurus (209) , there is the contemplative verve, the formidable lyricism. Furthermore, and indicative of the whole, his travels beyond Oklahoma in no way diminish attachment to origins of family, inheritance, place. "Wherever I go," he observes in typical mode, "it seems I never get too far from home but what I am reminded of it" (259).

Momaday's construing of *The Names* as "an act of imagination," like his dictum "We are what we imagine" in the much-celebrated 1970 essay "The Man Made of Words," provides the most apposite of sight lines not only for his own but almost all autobiography.[19] Quite inevitably this entails a degree, often very large, of reflexivity, the transcript from life endemically given to signaling its own process of composition. Even those autobiographies of American selves already greatly public and so assumedly agreed-upon, be it Benjamin Franklin, Henry Adams, Henry James, or Gertrude Stein, in fact do not disguise their own circling awareness of the identity being magicked on to the page. Richard Poirier's diagnosis of "the performing self," at once "self-discovering" and "self-watching," wholly applies.[20] In Native autobiography, however, even another self-tier presses, that of at the same time *un-writing* an identity-category long installed as shadow, harlequinade. To write, to compose, any one Native self, and quite beyond wrangles about tribal-communal fealty over the "western" desideratum of the singly disclosed self, is to write against simulacrum, the preemptive myth that has passed into history as "Indian identity."

Were one to seek the yet fuller compass of modern Native autobiography, the more than forty essay-chapters of the Swann-Krupat anthologies, *I Tell You Now* and *Here First*, enter the reckoning. Mary TallMountain to Joy Harjo, Sherman Alexie to Ofelia Zepeda, on the coeditors' description, bequeath "collective memoir," a formidable column of life-writing. But amid the stories told, and the encircling issues of identity, oral-scriptural inheritance, colonialism, family, reservation and city, sovereignty, and protocols of appraisal, it is hard not to be struck by the emphasis on imagination—Momaday's bringing "my own imagination to bear."

From quite another angle, Susan Sontag, in her preface to Roland Barthes's *Writing Degree Zero*, offers the greatly useful general reminder that "the choices made by the writer always face in *two* directions: towards society and towards the nature of literature itself." [21] It may be that a celebrated French semiotician, not to say an equally celebrated American admirer like Sontag, would be the last to come to mind in an account of Native American autobiography. But the point being made strikes a right chord. These texts, "literary" autobiographies if that is not to prejudice matters, indubitably carry their sense of history—tribal-existential and self-existential. But they equally exhibit, indeed depend upon, a force of telling, their efficacy as design, self-inscriptive voice, and always imagination. It is in this respect, as in the lives and the ambit of "Indian" history, culture, or region they seek to encode, that they make their wholly indelible contribution to the Native American Renaissance.

NOTES

1. Woodward, ed., *Ancestral Voice*, p. 57.

2. Glancy, *West Pole*, p. 70. Cited also in King, *Truth about Stories*, 122.

3. Revard, *Family Matters*, p. 126.

4. As in all indigenous self-expression, moreover, whether oral or scriptural, issues of language options and rights press hard, the effect of global English or Spanish upon the nearly three hundred Native languages across the Americas, especially and ironically on those that have proved the most durable like Navajo and Cree, Anishinaabe and Cherokee, Mayan and Inuit.

5. Relevant historical mappings of Native life-writing, early to modern, include [Sweet-]Wong, "Native American Life Writing," and Wong, *Sending My Heart*

Back across the Years; Johnson, "Imagining Self and Community in American Indian Autobiography"; Bumble, *American Indian Autobiography*, and Bumble, *An Annotated Bibliography of American Indian and Eskimo Autobiographies*; three works of David Murray: *Forked Tongues*, "Authenticity and Text in American Indian, Hispanic and Asian Autobiography," and "From Speech to Text"; Krupat, *For Those Who Come After*; and Bataille and Sands, eds., *American Indian Women Telling Their Lives*.

6. Glancy, *Claiming Breath*, p. 22.

7. Ibid., p. 4.

8. Portions of the accounts of Momaday, Silko, and Vizenor rework material published in my own *Multicultural American Literature*.

9. Momaday, "Man Made of Words."

10. This is taken from Momaday's italicized frontispiece to *The Names*.

11. Hertha Dawn Wong gives a useful account of the cyclic journey, and structure, within *The Names*: "The narrative movement of the work is from the mythical past to the Kiowa-personal to the imaginary mythical past reimagined in the present. This process parallels the very nature of autobiographical activity in which one filters past experience into the present moment. At the same time, the focus shifts from tribal to family to individual back to the family and tribal." *Sending My Heart Back across the Years*, p. 177.

12. Kim Barnes, "Leslie Marmon Silko Interview," pp. 83–105.

13. It may be worth noting that Silko ran into trouble with some Lagunas for alleged misappropriation of myth in her novel *Ceremony*.

14. Momaday, "Man Made of Words."

15. The term "postindian" and the view of Native legacy it encodes is explored in Vizenor and Lee, *Postindian Conversations*.

16. Hale, *Bloodlines*, p. xv.

17. Revard, *Winning the Dust Bowl*, p. xiii.

18. One writer to whom this would appeal, however, is David Treuer in his battling *Native American Fiction*.

19. Momaday, *Indian Voices*.

20. Poirier, *Performing Self*, p. xiii.

21. Barthes, *Writing Degree Zero*, preface by Susan Sontag, p. xiv.

WORKS CITED

Allen, Paul Gunn. *The Sacred Hoop: Recovering the Feminine in American Indian Traditions*. Boston: Beacon Press, 1986.

Banks, Dennis, with Richard Erdoes. *Ojibwa Warrior*. Norman: University of Oklahoma Press, 2004.

Barnes, Jim. *On Native Ground: Memoirs and Impressions*. Norman: University of Oklahoma Press, 1997.

Barnes, Kim. "A Leslie Marmon Silko Interview." *The Journal of Ethnic Studies* 13 (Winter 1986), 83–105.

Barthes, Roland. *Writing Degree Zero.* Preface by Susan Sontag.New York: Hill and Wang, 1968.

Bataille, Gretchen, and Kathleen Sands, eds. *American Indian Women: Telling Their Lives.* Lincoln: University of Nebraska Press, 1984.

Bumble, David, III. *American Indian Autobiography.* Berkeley: University of California Press, 1988.

———. *An Annotated Bibliography of American Indian and Eskimo Autobiographies.* Lincoln: University of Nebraska Press,1981.

Campbell, Maria. *Halfbreed.* New York: Saturday Review Press, 1973.

Castaneda, Carlos. *The Teachings of Don Juan: A Yaqui Way of Knowledge.* Berkeley: University of California Press, 1968.

Cody, Iron Eyes. *My Life as a Hollywood Indian.* Edited by Colin Perry. New York: Everest House, 1982.

Cook-Lynn, Elizabeth. *New Indians, Old Wars.* Urbana: University of Illinois Press, 2007.

———. *Why I Can't read Wallace Stegner and Other Essays: A Tribal Voice.* Madison: University of Wisconsin Press, 1996.

Crow Dog, Mary, with Richard Erdoes. *Lakota Woman.* New York: Grove Weidenfeld, 1990.

Glancy, Diane. *Claiming Breath.* Lincoln: University of Nebraska Press, 1992.

———. *The West Pole.* Minneapolis: University of Minnesota Press, 1997.

Hale, Janet Campbell. *Bloodlines: Odyssey of a Native Daughter.* New York: Random House, 1993.

———. *The Jailing of Cecelia Capture.* New York: Random House, 1985.

Harris, LaDonna. *LaDonna Harris: A Comanche Life.* Lincoln: University of Nebraska Press, 2001.

Hogan, Linda. *The Woman Who Watches Over the World: A Native Memoir.* New York: W. W. Norton, 2001.

Hungry Wolf, Beverly. *The Ways of My Grandmothers.* New York: William Morrow, 1980.

Johnson, Kendall. "Imagining Self and Community in American Indian Autobiography." In Eric Cheyfitz, ed., *The Columbia Guide to Native American Indian Literatures of the United States.* New York: Columbia University Press, 2006, 357–409.

King, Thomas. *The Truth about Stories: A Native Narrative.* Minneapolis: University of Minnesota Press, 2003.

Krupat, Arnold. *For Those Who Come After: A Study of Native American Autobiography.* Berkeley: University of California Press, 1985.

———, ed., *Native American Autobiography: An Anthology.* Madison: University of Wisconsin Press, 1994.

Krupat, Arnold, and Brian Swann, eds. *Here First: Autobiographical Essays by Native American Writers.* New York: Random House/The Modern Library, 2000.

Lee, A. Robert. *Multicultural American Literature: Comparative Black, Native, Latino/a and Asian American Fictions.* Jackson: University Press of Mississippi, 2003.

Mankiller, Wilma, with Michael Wallis. *Mankiller: A Chief and Her People.* New York: St. Martin's Press, 1993.

Means, Russell. *Where White Men Fear to Tread.* New York: St. Martin's Press, 1995.

Mendoza, Vincent L. *Son of Two Bloods.* Lincoln: University of Nebraska Press, 1996.

Midge, Tiffany. *Outlaws, Renegades and Saints: Diary of a Mixed-Up Half-breed.* Greenfield Center, N.Y.: Greenfield Review Press, 1996.

Momaday, N. Scott. "The Man Made of Words." In *Indian Voices: The First Convocation of American Indian Scholars.* Edited by Rupert Cosco. San Francisco: Indian Historian Press, 1970, 49–84.

———. *The Names: A Memoir.* New York: Harper & Row, 1976.

———. *The Way to Rainy Mountain.* Albuquerque: University of New Mexico Press, 1969.

Murray, David. "Authenticity and Text in American Indian, Hispanic and Asian Autobiography." In *First Person Singular: Studies in American Autobiography.* Edited by A. Robert Lee. London: Vision Press, 1988, 177–97.

———. *Forked Tongues: Speech, Writing, & Representation in North American Indian Texts.* Bloomington: Indiana University Press, 1991.

———. "From Speech to Text: The Making of American Indian Autobiographies." In *American Literary Landscapes: The Fiction and the Fact.* Edited by Ian F. A. Bell and D. K. Adams. London: Vision Press, 1988.

Neihardt, John. *Black Elk Speaks.* New York: William Morrow, 1932.

Owens, Louis. *I Hear the Train: Reflections, Inventions, Refractions.* Norman: University of Oklahoma Press, 2001.

———. *Mixedblood Messages: Literature, Film, Family, Place.* Norman: University of Oklahoma Press, 1998.

Penn, William S., ed. *As We Are Now: Mixblood Essays on Race and Identity.* Berkeley: University of California Press, 1997.

Poirier, Richard. *The Performing Self: Compositions and Decompositions in the Languages of Contemporary Life.* New York: Oxford University Press, 1971.

Revard, Carter. *Family Matters, Tribal Affairs.* Tucson: University of Arizona Press, 1998.

———. *Winning the Dust Bowl.* Tucson: The University of Arizona Press, 2001.

Rose, Wendy. *The Halfbreed Chronicles and Other Poems.* Los Angeles: West End Press, 1985.

Sarris, Greg. *Keeping Slug Woman Alive: A Holistic Approach to Indian Texts.* Berkeley: University of California Press,1993.

Silko, Leslie Marmon. *Ceremony.* New York: Viking Press, 1977.

———. *Storyteller.* New York: Little, Brown/Arcade, in arrangement with Seaver, 1981.

Swann, Brian, and Arnold Krupat, eds. *I Tell You Now: Autobiographical Essays by Native American Writers.* Lincoln: University of Nebraska Press, 1987.

Treuer, David. *Native American Fiction: A User's Manual.* Minneapolis: University of Minnesota Press, 2006.

Vizenor, Gerald. *Interior Landscapes: Autobiographical Myths and Metaphors.* Minneapolis: University of Minnesota Press, 1990.

Vizenor, Gerald, and A. Robert Lee. *Postindian Conversations.* Lincoln: University of Nebraska Press, 1999.

Weaver, Jace, Craig S. Womack, and Robert Warrior, eds. *American Indian Literary Nationalism.* Albuquerque: University of New Mexico Press, 2001.

Willis, Jane. *Geniesh: An Indian Girlhood.* Toronto: New Press, 1973.

Wong, Hertha Dawn. *Sending My Heart Back across the Years: Tradition and Innovation in Native American Autobiography.* New York: Oxford University Press, 1992.

[Sweet-]Wong, Hertha Dawn. "Native American Life Writing." In *The Cambridge Companion to Native American Literature.* Edited by Joy Porter and Kenneth M. Roemer. Cambridge: Cambridge University Press, 2005.

Woodward, Charles L., ed. *Ancestral Voice: Conversation with N. Scott Momaday.* Lincoln: University of Nebraska Press, 1989.

Young Bear, Ray. *Black Eagle Child: The Facepaint Narratives.* Iowa City: University of Iowa Press, 1992.

16

Theater Renaissance

Resituating the Place of Drama in the Native American Renaissance

GINA VALENTINO

When Kenneth Lincoln's *Native American Renaissance* was published in 1983, there was only a handful of studies devoted to Native American literature in general and fewer still devoted to contemporary Native American literature, Alan R. Velie's *Four American Indian Literary Masters* (1982) being the most notable. Lincoln's monograph was groundbreaking, and it remains foundational to Native American studies. Like any piece of literary criticism that has been successful in identifying the parameters of a particular tradition, Lincoln's *Native American Renaissance* has ended up generating certain critical orthodoxies. The first of these is that Indian writers began to emerge only in the 1960s. The second is that the Native American Renaissance (NAR) truly took off when N. Scott Momaday's *House Made of Dawn* won the Pulitzer Prize in 1969. Momaday's success helped pave the way for other writers—namely, James Welch, Leslie Marmon Silko, and Simon Ortiz—to be recognized and published. The third is that the writers of the NAR shared a commitment to orality. As Lincoln himself puts it, "The Native American renaissance here targeted, less than two decades of published Indian literature, is a written renewal of oral tradition translated into Western literary forms. Contemporary Indian literature is not so much new, then, as regenerate: transitional continuities emerging from the old" (8).

Lincoln's book became highly influential in shaping the reception of the body of texts he wrote about: works published in English by Native authors from the 1960s to the publication of Lincoln's monograph in 1983. Other critics began to expand the reach of the term "Native American Renaissance," and it eventually came to include any work written after the publication of Momaday's *House Made of Dawn* in 1968. Moreover, authors not originally included in Lincoln's original study have been added to the cadre of renaissance authors. Craig Womack addresses a key problem about how the term is used in literary criticism when he writes, "Most approaches to the 'Native

American Renaissance' have proceeded as if the Indian discovered the novel, the short story, and the poem yesterday" (3). Part of the problem here might lie with the word "renaissance" itself, for it suggests a prior period comparable to the Dark Ages, when artists of color were operating in some unlearned void. Furthermore, the term also highlights the fact that contemporary minority authors are often seen as lacking the long-standing literary traditions afforded to white European artists who can claim to trace their artistic genealogies back to Homer. Finally, there is also the question of market: was it that Native authors hadn't been writing or was it that "renaissance" simply indicated the emergence of a white literary marketplace in which Native writings were suddenly in vogue?

Despite such caveats, there is nonetheless something useful about the idea of a "Native American Renaissance": it indicates that something profound did happen in Native American arts beginning in the 1960s. Indeed, one does catch glimpses of what drama could mean for understandings of the renaissance in Lincoln's observation that "Dramatists remember ritual priests and cultural purveyors of daily tribal life" (42), a comment that is not followed up with any real discussion of plays. As influential as Lincoln's work has been, this omission has had a profound effect on scholarship that takes up the NAR. In the following pages, I hope to suggest how this critical gap might be remedied (and to reorient Womack's critique) by fleshing out a key term missing from Womack's list of genres and also from Lincoln's monograph: Native American drama.

As it turns out, there are some basic ways in which the concerns of Native American drama are also those of the renaissance as Lincoln rendered it. Native American drama has a shared sense of Native community and belief in what Lincoln calls "kinship and tribal ways" (13). Native drama was also an amalgam of Anglo and Native cultures. Perhaps more than novels and arguably more than poetry, drama carried an immediate respect for "the values and perceptions in older oral literatures underlie contemporary Indian writing" (Lincoln, 41). Moreover, Native American drama during the renaissance worked to "transcend factional differences in a shared struggle for Cultural Survival and rebirth" (Lincoln, 13).

The emergence of drama in such sites as the Institute for American Indian Arts, the Native American Theater Ensemble, and Spiderwoman Theater should be seen as part of a cultural formation that includes writers like Momaday and Silko, given that all of them share certain aesthetic, cultural, and political concerns. To some extent, dramatic works have tended to be left out of most mappings of the renaissance. Also the perspectives of a foundational figure in Native American drama, Hanay Geiogamah, are a valuable asset in considering how contemporary Native American drama might be reinvigorated by a renewed integration of dance, which would deepen its ceremonial dimensions.

NATIVE AMERICAN DRAMA DURING THE
RENAISSANCE: A STORY OF THREE TROUPES

Although it is not as well known as the story that begins with publication of *House Made of Dawn*, there is another story that is often told about the reawakening of Native American aesthetic culture in the late 1960s.[1] This story—the story of Native American drama—is often said to begin in New Mexico at the Institute for American Indian Arts. Founded in 1962, the institute established a performing arts program in 1969, the year that Scott Momaday, recently given a doctorate by IAIA, won the Pulitzer Prize for *House Made of Dawn*. In July of that year, Lloyd K. New, an instructor at the institute, wrote *Credo for American Indian Theatre*. New called for the formation of contemporary Indian theater: "No pure traditional form of Indian theater presently exists—one must be created" (3). While words such as "pure" and "traditional" today might be challenged (in part because writers of the renaissance helped to refigure Native notions of purity and tradition), New nevertheless was calling for a revolution in Native performing arts. He asserted that this new theater would have to be on built on a Native political and artistic foundation. "New ethnic cultural forms," he asserted, "must result from the forces and ideas within the ethnic group itself" (3). Indian theater, then, was to stem from Native communities. The Institute for American Indian Arts would function as a place to develop talent and train Native artists. New continues,

> Indian theater ultimately will be born from this group of sophisticated Indian artists. Until their statement is made and heretofore new theatrical form is evolved we can only view present dramatic manifestations of Indian life, the religious ceremony, the grandstand performance, the Indian powwow as the raw material from which Indian theater will evolve. [3–4]

As New conceived it, contemporary Native drama from the outset would be fashioned from ceremonial practices. As an extension of tribal ritual, then, it was imagined that both the performers and audience of this new theater would be Indian. The IAIA performing arts program lasted only a few years, but it laid the groundwork for other theater to follow. Some of the students trained at the institute there were part of the Native American Theater Ensemble, which formed in New York City in 1972.

While still a journalism student at the University of Oklahoma, Hanay Geiogamah (Kiowa/Delaware) began to consider seriously combining his activism with his interests in the performing arts. Geiogamah considered enrolling at the Institute of American Indian Arts but decided instead to focus on forming a sustainable Native theater in Oklahoma, the Living Indian Theater. While this first attempt at forming a theater wasn't as successful as Geiogamah had hoped, it provided useful experience for his next project, the Native American Theater Ensemble. After a short-term stint at the Bureau of Indian Affairs (BIA) and securing a grant from the National Indian Youth Council, Geiogamah was free to realize his vision of an all-Native theater company. Launched in 1972, the American Indian Theater was the first of its kind. The founding ethos of the theater can be found in Geiogamah's grant proposal:

> For decades Indians have been portrayed in films and television in a manner entirely derogatory to their cultural and mental well-being. Who on this earth can enjoy seeing themselves and their race portrayed as fiendish savages and murderers who scream blood-curdling yelps as seemingly their only form of vocal communication? It is thought by many American Indian leaders and activists that this unabated, corrupt use of American Indians by the American dream makers has been a major factor in the deepening cultural and spiritual malaise of American Indians. [Pinazzi, 178]

The American Indian Theater Ensemble was cosponsored by Ellen Stewart, the director of La MaMa Experimental Theatre Club in New York City. During its second season, the ensemble renamed itself the Native American Theater Ensemble (NATE). From 1972 to1974, while at La MaMa, NATE produced *Body Indian*, and early versions of *Coon Cons Coyote* and *Foghorn*, along with other works such as Robert Shorty's *Na Haaz Zaan* (Geiogamah, "Introduction," 3). Geiogamah describes his guiding methodology in this way: "Does the play speak effectively to Indians? Can Indians understand what is happening on stage? If there is a message, is it communicated clearly and effectively in Indian terms? Are the characters and dialogue culturally authentic?" ("Introduction," 5). Each of these plays utilized the group's ethos that, though all were welcome, NATE existed to create Native theater for Native audiences.

NATE garnered invitations to perform across the United States and did so at reservations, Native American cultural centers, universities, and other performance venues. The pivotal year for the ensemble was 1973. In that year, they were invited to work with the English director Peter Brook during his summer workshop at the Chippewa Reservation at Leech Lake, Minnesota. That fall, the group traveled to Berlin to work with the Berliner Ensemble, the renowned theater group founded by Bertolt Brecht and Helene Weigel in 1949. These two opportunities stand out as moments when the ensemble came into direct contact with avant-garde Western theater. The results were apparently mixed. Brook was more interested in having his own actors learn "primitive" techniques from the ensemble than engaging with Native theater on its own terms (Pinazzi, 180). The ensemble's time in Berlin was more beneficial. The group worked with the Berliner Ensemeble on their staging of Brecht's *The Guns of Frau Carrar* and rehearsed Geiogamah's *Coon Cons Coyote* and *Foghorn*.

While 1973 was a highly productive and successful year, it also marked the beginning of NATE's decline. In 1974 NATE halted preparations to stage *49*, a play destined to become one of Geiogamah's most famous works. While never officially abandoned, NATE's performance schedule became increasingly sporadic until it eventually became dormant. Geiogamah himself remained an active playwright during this time and served as artistic director for Native Americans in the Arts from 1980 to 1982. In 1980 the University of Oklahoma Press published Geiogamah's *New Native American Drama: Three Plays*, which was the first such collection by a Native American playwright (Haugo, 339). Several members of NATE went on to form theater companies around the United States. Among them were the Navajo-Land Outdoor Theater (1973); the Red Earth Performing Arts Company (1974); and Spiderwoman Theater (1975) (Darby, vii).

Spiderwoman Theater was founded by Muriel Miguel and her sisters, Gloria Miguel and Lisa Mayo. Spiderwoman Theater was the first radical feminist ensemble to address Native issues. The company took its name from the Hopi creator-goddess who taught her people to weave. Josephine Mofsie (Hopi), a close friend of the sisters, and fellow performer, once told the Spiderwoman story to Muriel Miguel while finger weaving. The name signaled a Native feminist genealogy that served to honor their friend and encapsulate the ethos of the group. Spiderwoman Theater was in many ways shaped by the Third World Feminist/Women of Color movement and also by experimental theater. It aimed to express the desire of Native women to tell Native stories from their perspective. Much like the Native American Theater Ensemble, Spiderwoman was a collaborative effort that brought Native issues to stage. However, whereas NATE brought together actors who shared both race and a common political concept of Native experience, Spiderwoman brought together a *multiracial* group of actors and therefore prioritized a solidarity based on gender politics over one based on racial solidarity.

This is not to say that racism wasn't a concern. Just as the sisters confronted sexism and violence in their experience of the AIM movement, mainstream feminism left little room for racial difference. Miguel and other women of color were excluded on the one hand by a racial movement that thought little about gender politics and, on the other, by a gender movement that was often blind to issues of race. Spiderwoman Theater continued to delve deeply into these complex issues and began to home in on issues in Native America. As Ann Haugo notes, "by the time the company developed *Winnetou's Snake Oil Show from Wigwam City* (1988) the focus was on Native politics, though always also from a feminist perspective" (342).

In addition to its emphasis on building a multiracial coalition, Spiderwoman differed from NATE in the kind of theater it produced. Spiderwoman Theater's signature style is on crafted improvisational performance, a process they call "storyweaving." Storyweaving is a method by which the members outline stories based on their own and collected histories:

We work onstage as an ensemble, basing our productions on life experiences. We translate our personal stories, dreams and images into movement, and refine them into the essential threads of human experience. In seeking out, exploring, and weaving our own patterns, we reflect the human tapestry, the web of our common humanity. Finding, loving, and transcending our own flaws, as in the flaw in the goddess's tapestry, provide the means for our spirits to find their way out, to be free. [Haugo, 341]

By working together, the ensemble allows these stories to develop and evolve, to become deftly structured, interwoven performance pieces. Creating this kind of structure allows for in-the-moment improvisation and creation to occur. As Christy Stanlake explains, "[S]toryweaving connects people by creating a tapestry of narrative which sometimes has no articulated meaning but must be felt instead" (113). Storyweaving calls for the audience and performers to experience nonlinear connections and fluid interrelations. Like NATE, Spiderwoman became a catalyst for other theater companies, including the lesbian company Split Britches, founded by Lois Weaver and Peggy Shaw.

RETHINKING THE RENAISSANCE FROM THE PERSPECTIVE OF DRAMA

It is clear that it is the collaborative aspect of drama that constitutes its most vital difference from the literary genres that Lincoln identified as representative of the renaissance. Whereas we tend to regard the novel, the short story, or the poem as the product of a singular, solitary figure—Momaday, Silko, or Harjo—drama is by its very nature a collaborative project. Even though Native American drama in the 1970s could not have emerged without such important players as New, Geiogamah, and the Miguel/Mayo sisters, it simply would not have existed without the various actors, dancers, musicians, directors, producers, stage crews, choreographers, lighting designers, artistic directors, donors, funding sources, and, perhaps most importantly, *audiences* that enabled plays to be performed. The complexities of production may offer a practical explanation for why drama and performing arts are hard to sustain in Indian country, given the difficulties inherent in an art form that is so multifaceted and ephemeral. As Hanay Geiogamah has observed,

A novelist writes something and it gets put in a book and it's there and it's easy to reproduce it and circulate it and get it all around. A play, a ceremonial performance, has to be produced, has to be performed, has to be kept alive, toured, presented, shared. A play that speaks to Native American people in general, Native America in general is all over the place all over the country. How you going to get it there? [Author interview]

NATE and Spiderwoman Theater offer examples of collective authorship. In the case of the NATE, Geiogamah worked closely with the actors, which created a free-flow of ideas and created space for improvisation. The plays and performances throughout the Native American Renaissance allow actors great license. Many of the works call for improvisation on a set theme, mean- ing that each performance will be different. With this in mind, the audience becomes a community for that performance. The interplay between scripted words, performers, and audience creates and interprets the meaning of the play. In this way, drama has a singular connection with tribal oral traditions.

Perhaps this is why Native theater escapes heated discussions regarding identity and authenticity. Questions about Native artistic and racial authentic- ity are not readily found in Native American drama. A critique that springs up about the NAR involves concerns about Native authors' adoptions of Western artistic forms. For example, does *House Made of Dawn* contain an unhealthy ventriloquism of European modernist forms? NATE and Spider- woman were able to create and perform in the oral traditions that Momaday and Silko worked hard to re-create on the page. In the case of Spiderwoman Theater, whatever acculturation occurs happens in the ethos of storyweaving and it happens directly on stage. Racial influence travels in multiple direc- tions and is actively and visibly incorporated into the creative process. If the Miguel/Mayo sisters are "whitewashed," then we might say that everyone else in theater is "redwashed," because their acts of creation depend on the others around them. Spiderwoman Theater works in part by acknowledging what is already racially present. Ceremonial orality, then, has not been entirely lost during the renaissance, or merely adapted to written forms, since it contin- ues to flourish and be transformed in multiple theatrical venues and sites of performance.

Drama expands our understanding of the forms of Native nationalism that have been dominant during the period of the Native American Renaissance. NATE was composed of Native performers from multiple nations and they performed works that drew from their tribal legacies. For example, *Na Haaz Zaan* is a contemporary retelling of the Navajo creation story. Momaday, as a Kiowa/Cherokee writing about Jemez Pueblo formed *House Made of Dawn* within a pan-tribal framework, so at some level the NAR has always been pan-Indian in scope. However, the nature and process of NATE's drama and performance render a plurality of Native national voices and allow them to interact in a complex manner. Native drama and performance on stage are a microcosm of the types of ritual that occur during intertribal powwows and ceremonies. NATE was a space for artists to express both Native unity and Native national difference.

In the principles and practices that defined Spiderwoman Theater, we see a feminist and transnational expansion of the coalitional ethos of NATE's pan-tribalism. Spiderwoman Theater expanded Native pan-tribalism to in- clude transnational indigeneity. Gloria and Muriel Miguel and their sister Lisa

Mayo are Rappahannock, a tribe from Virginia, and Kuna, a tribe located in the San Blas Islands off the coast of Panama (Haugo, 340). The sisters' mixed, transnational, indigenous background served as a creative impulse for their work. Storyweaving, the theater's foundational creative principle, derives from transnational feminist philosophy. In Spiderwoman's hands, storyweaving is a feminist Native epistemological creative process in which every member of the company participates. In this way, Spiderwoman Theater combines transnational Native ideologies and Third World feminism. The political fight for indigenous rights was, at the time of the renaissance, just as it is now, a global struggle. Foregrounding these dimensions of the cultural works that were produced during the early stages of the Native American Renaissance enables us to see the period in much the same way that Karen Tei Yamashita asks us to see the Asian American movement in her most recent novel, *I-Hotel*—as transnational even in its foundational moment.

A NEW RENAISSANCE:
NATIVE AMERICAN THEATER TODAY

An earlier generation of critics in commenting on the NAR erred in confining their discussions to the novel, the short story, and the poem. As we come to terms with what Native American literature in the later stages of the renaissance, it looks as if we need to do so in ways that address more fully the vitality of Native drama.

As a professor at the University of California, Los Angeles, Hanay Geiogamah continues to be a tireless advocate for Native American theater. Geiogamah has a radical vision that lays bare the connection between tribal sovereignty and Native American performing arts:

> There are 512 or so Indian tribes in the United States today. If each of these tribes was to establish and sponsor its own tribally oriented theater company, and each company produced just one new work based on that tribe's history, culture, heritage, whatever, we would have 512 new works for the theater. Can you imagine that? Five hundred and twelve new Indian plays! And if only half of them were to do this—in, say, some nearly fantastical, dream-come-true kind of thing—then there would be 256 new Indian plays. The theater can really help us stop the erosion of our Indian way of life. Theater is one of the most accessible of the performing arts. We really ought to get started on this right away. There can and ought to be a whole bunch of new Indian theaters. [D'Aponte, 1]

For Geiogamah, Native American performing arts is about tribal self-determination. It allows Native people to tell their stories directly. As

Geiogamah said years ago, "If you don't do it, then the white people will do it for you. That I found out. . . . They'll tell your story for you. They'll tell you who you are. They'll tell you what you are if you let them" (Darby, vii). Geiogamah's plan for Native theater combines grassroots organization on behalf of the arts with tribal governance. Economic and creative development, ideally, would be in the hands of Native people.

Geiogamah's vision of Native theater includes developing critical inter-pretative strategies rooted in Native philosophical and creative traditions. Founded by Geiogamah and Jaye T. Darby, Project HOOP (Honoring Our Origins and Peoples through Native American theater), in conjunction with the UCLA's American Indian Studies Center, publishes edited collections of plays by authors such as William S. Yellowrobe, Jr., and Bruce King. Project HOOP is also at the forefront of Native American studies by publishing groundbreaking anthologies such as *Keepers of the Morning Star: An Anthology of Native Women's Theater*, and critical collections that span all aspects of performing and developing Native theater.

Along with Project HOOP, Geiogamah has served as director of the American Indian Dance Theater. As he did with NATE, Geiogamah has further developed his art in a collaborative, pan-tribal context, this time incorporating aspects of traditional movement and dance to bring narrative to stage. Geiogamah's theater has changed since the early 1970s to a view of theater that he calls Ceremonial Performance:

> At the time of the Renaissance book we were trying to do [W]estern Native theater. We were trying to write plays like playwrights and stage them like they do in regular theaters. Which is fine. There's nothing wrong with that. And plays like that can be considered Native Theater. They are Native theater. . . . But there's another Native theater that I think of was always there and that's the performance aesthetic and style that I'm trying to aim for now. And I had a lot of that in my, instinctively and intuitively, I had that present in my work. I just wasn't aware of that. Author interview]

Ceremonial performance unites tribal traditions, collective memories, and storytelling with Native spiritual practices and aesthetics. Geiogamah's goal is to highlight Native theater as a ritualistic practice and thus bring it out of a purely Western framework, both in staging and interpretation. As Geiogamah puts it,

> We are re-inventing Native theater. Because there's always has been a Native performance aesthetic. We lost most of that. Most of that was not available to us and it's not been available to us because it died out, when everything else died out. We cannot say that we know what it

used to be. We have bits and pieces and fragments like we have with the Greek theater that are helpful to us. But from those we able to able to sort of Rosetta stone it in a sense and be able to extrapolate this and interpolate this and match this and that and come up with things that we know that we can compare with our own understanding of who we are now in a style that probably was in our predecessors, our ancestors. [Author interview]

In looking to the past, Ceremonial Performance suggests one of the futures toward which Native American theater is moving.

Spiderwoman Theater now has the distinction of being the oldest continuously run women's theater collective in North America. The long-standing success of Spiderwoman Theater and its members has helped pave the way for a new generation of Native women in the performing arts.[2] The Native American Women Playwrights Archive (NAWPA) began, like most of these things do, out of need. At Miami University of Ohio, John Allen Johnson, a graduate student of mixed Cherokee and African American heritage, wanted to find plays written by Native American women and was having a hard time locating primary sources. Working in conjunction with William Wortman, the humanities librarian at the university, they began to build a collection of original materials written by Native American women.

The NAWPA continues the tradition of a shared Native genealogy for community and activism that began with the Native American Theater Ensemble. The goals of the NAWPA fit precisely Jace Weaver's definition of communitism—a combination of community and activism. The archive seeks "to identify playwrights, collect and preserve their work, try to make it widely known, and encourage performance and continued creativity" (NAWPA). Since its conception in 1996, the archive has expanded to include plays and performances by LeAnn Howe, Diane Glancy, JudyLee Oliva, Monique Mojica, and many others. The NAWPA also houses the Spiderwoman Theater papers. As part of the mission to build a community of writers and performers, the NAWPA also invites playwrights at any stage in their development to submit their materials.

Technology is playing an important role in linking Native communities with Native scholarship and Native performing arts. As much as possible, the Native American Women Playwrights Archive includes many of their resources online. This open access to materials is an increasing trend for Native American performing arts as a "workaround" for dwindling resources in often increasing hostile environments. Additionally, Alexander Street Press offers *North American Indian Drama*, an online collection of over two hundred plays, to libraries on a sliding scale (Stanlake, 14–15). Not surprisingly, Hanay Geiogamah is also involved in this Native technological artistic revolution with innovative web conferences and workshops that reach Native populations in ways unavailable in the 1970s. In his view:

Technology is coming in to help that too now. Technology. That's one of the reasons we started experimenting with the Project HOOP national video conference. We can now do things with technology. We can have a performance like say here and we're going to be doing it here. We're going to be experimenting here . . . and we're going to hook up with 33 tribal colleges. We don't have to go to all those colleges. Here this is, so let's get everything we can out of this experience, academically, teaching, everything, because there's not money that's needed to support . . . the people who are going to be doing the play to take them to all those places. [Author interview]

Native dramatic artists and their allies are implementing twenty-first-century strategies of what Geiogamah calls "survivability," a concept that is akin to Gerald Vizenor's survivance. Survivability gives name to the capacity of Indians to live with tragedy and find ways to renew and care for oneself and community. As Geiogamah describes it, survivability is "gritty, physical, psychologically reflective, and even ongoing in interpretation. It is a key component of creativity" (Geiogamah and Darby, *American Indian Performing Arts*, 108). Survivability's dramatic incarnations are, finally, something that critics will have to reckon with more fully in order to come to terms with Native American literature after the renaissance.

NOTES

1. There is a generally agreed-upon narrative about the origins of Native American drama in this period. For accounts, see Haugo's "Native American Drama," Pinazzi's "The Theater of Hanay Geiogamah," Darby's "Introduction," and chapter 1 in Stanlake's *Native American Drama*.

2. Muriel Miguel's new work, *Red Mother*, a performance based partly on Brecht's *Mother Courage*, premiered at La MaMa in June 2010. Gloria Miguel has worked with playwright (and daughter) Monique Mojica and director Floyd Favel Starr to develop indigenous dramaturgy with *Chocolate Woman Dreams the Milky Way*. Spiderwoman Theater continues feminist Native activism with *The Elder Project*, a series of performances and conversations with Native elders in New York City and the development of *Women in Violence II*.

WORKS CITED

D'Aponte, Mimi Gisolfi, ed. *Seventh Generation: An Anthology of Native American Plays*. New York: Theatre Communications Group, 1999.

Darby, Jaye T. "Introduction: A Talking Circle on Native Theater." In *American Indian Theater in Performance: A Reader*. Edited by Hanay Geiogamah and Jaye T. Darby. Los Angeles: UCLA American Indian Studies Center, 2000, iii–xv.

Hanay Geiogamah. Interview with author, January 19, 2011.

———. *New Native American Drama: Three Plays*. Norman: University of Oklahoma Press, 1980.

———. "Old Circles, New Circles." In *American Indian Theater in Performance: A Reader*. Edited by Hanay Geiogamah and Jaye T. Darby. Los Angeles: UCLA American Indian Studies Center, 2000, 283–87.

Geiogamah, Hanay, and Jaye T. Darby, eds. *American Indian Performing Arts: Critical Directions*. Los Angeles: UCLA American Indian Studies Center, 2009.

———. "Introduction: The New American Indian Theater." In *Stories of Our Way: An Anthology of American Indian Plays*. Edited by Hanay Geiogamah and Jaye T. Darby. Los Angeles: UCLA American Indian Studies Center, 199, 1–6.

Haugo, Ann. "Native American Drama." In *A Companion to Twentieth-Century American Drama*. Edited by David Krasner. Oxford: Blackwell Publishing, 2005, 334–51.

Howard, Rebecca. "Introduction." In *Footpaths and Bridges: Voices from the Native American Women Playwrights Archive*. Edited by Ahirley A. Huston-Findley and Rebecca Howard. Ann Arbor: University of Michigan Press, 2008, 1–10.

Lincoln, Kenneth. *Native American Renaissance*. Berkeley: University of California Press, 1983.

Momaday, N. Scott. *House Made of Dawn*. New York: Harper & Rowe, 1968.

Native American Women Playwrights Archive. Miami University of Ohio. Web. Accessed July 29, 2011.

New, Lloyd K. *Credo for American Indian Theater*. In *American Indian Theater in Performance: A Reader*. Edited by Hanay Geiogamah and Jaye T. Darby. Los Angeles: UCLA American Indian Studies Center, 2000, 3–4.

Pinazzi, Annamaria. "The Theater of Hanay Geiogamah." In *American Indian Theater in Performance: A Reader*. Edited by Hanay Geiogamah and Jaye T. Darby. Los Angeles: UCLA American Indian Studies Center, 2000, 175–94.

Stanlake, Christy. *Native American Drama: A Critical Perspective*. Cambridge: Cambridge University Press, 2009.

Velie, Alan R. *Four American Indian Literary Masters: N. Scott Momaday, James Welch, Leslie Marmon Silko, and Gerald Vizenor*. Norman: University of Oklahoma Press, 1982.

Womack, Craig S. *Red on Red: Native American Literary Separatism*. Minneapolis: University of Minnesota Press, 1999.

17
Reading around the Dotted Line

*From the Contact Zones to the Heartlands
of First Nations/Canadian Literatures*

DAVID STIRRUP

Kenneth Lincoln's *Native American Renaissance* (1983) celebrated the ways in which, after more than a century of sporadic production,[1] Native writers not only found voice in numbers but also began to develop a poetics that both embraced technical and formal developments of twentieth-century literary modernisms *and* reflected continuity with the oral tradition—a "new nativism with its organic forms and subjects" (Lincoln, 7). This gathering of voices, perhaps the most significant aspect of the "renaissance," represented a critical shift. It did not merely intervene in the historical and literary record, but forced its reappraisal, initiating genuine reflection on the colonially constituted nature of the image of Native peoples in the United States. It contributed, too, to the continuities of indigenous cultural expression in ways imagined by the non-Native "nativists," but all the more powerful for its vital place "at the functional heart" of tribal identities (Lincoln, 6–8, 12).

Which is why, in its turn, *Renaissance* is curious for its *exclusion*—albeit a historically moderated exclusion—of Native voices from outside the United States, as if networks of indigenous cultural production and influence extend only to the boundaries of the modern nation-state. Conversely, in many works of criticism focused on Native American literatures, the odd figure is thrown in without due consideration of those problematic borders. The mixed-blood poet and performer E. Pauline Johnson, for instance, described in some widely disseminated accounts of the "Native American Renaissance" as a failed progenitor,[2] was born a British subject in one of the three colonies that became the Federal Dominion of Canada in 1867. As Carole Gerson and Veronica Jane Strong-Boag note, U.S. critics' "enthusiastic quest for Native American literary history has pulled Pauline Johnson into the United States canon, where she now appears in reference books specifically designated 'American.' The author of the 1903 poem 'Canadian Born,' which proclaims 'The Yankee to the south of us must south of us remain,' would probably not be amused to be included in the *Oxford Companion to Women's Writing in the United States* (1995)" (133). Long held up as a Canadian treasure, Johnson is extracted from that particular literary nationalist narrative with difficulty.[3]

Elsewhere, Thomas King, California-born Greek-Cherokee, is regularly dropped in to discussions about Native American literary production without reference to his explicit decision to move to Canada in 1980, and later to become a Canadian citizen. His situation is instructive with regard to the various constructions at play here—from marketing categories to the nation-state—since, as a Canadian citizen, where the Cherokee have no precolonial stake, King is a "Canadian writer and a Native writer, but he cannot be a Canadian Native writer" (Andrews and Walton, 605). The irony of that scenario is otherwise implicated, by King himself, in the globalized discourse of the post-/trans-national. He regularly navigates the Canada-U.S. borderlands in his fiction, holding up a lens to the imposition of that "figment of someone else's imagination" (102) as it bisects and disrupts, or is resisted and transcended by, communities and individuals. A fuller appreciation of indigenous literary production in North America, then, demands acknowledgement of the broader nexus, reflecting (insofar as Lincoln's interest is Anglophone writing) on writing in English produced by Native writers in Canada, and engaging with the ways in which those literatures both exist within and resist the nation-state parameters.[4] This chapter will first situate Canadian Native writing in a dual context, addressing the paradigmatic (locating this discussion in the broader debate around "New" American studies) and historical (emphasizing the decades immediately before and after the "pivotal" moment of Momaday's first novel). The remainder of the chapter will delineate, by genre, a selective narrative of those contributions.

CONSIDERING THE POST-/TRANS-NATIONAL

Introducing *Post-Nationalist American Studies*, John Carlos Rowe and his contributors note that "as a critical perspective, post-nationalist American Studies values . . . scholars whose concept of the nation and of citizenship has questioned dominant American myths rather than canonized them. . . . [I]t builds upon previous work, within and outside of American Studies, that is critical of U.S. hegemony and the constructedness of both national myths and national borders" (Curiel et al., 3). In his own essay Rowe insists, "The Native American [along with other ethnic minority] perspectives must be represented in such studies . . . in keeping with the comparatist aims of the New American Studies" (Rowe, 28). And yet a brief flick through the book's index reveals no entry for "Native American," "First Nations," "Indigenous," or "Aboriginal"—no "Indian," "American Indian," "North American Indian," "Inuit," or "Métis"; this, despite a chapter on the Joaquin Murieta myth, including Cherokee writer John Rollin Ridge's *The Life and Adventures of Joaquin Murieta* (1854). Furthermore, while several essays address nation-state borders, none apparently are that interested in the cross-border land bases of several First Nations, not to mention the cross-border territories of many more Native peoples whose cadastral boundaries were set short of the line in deliberate acts of division and containment.

A stark presentation of the artificiality of the nation-state border, it is a very real reminder, too, of the different colonial experiences of Native peoples throughout the Americas, even down to the inclusion or exclusion of Native voices within projects that purport to examine the "hemispheric" or "transnational" trends of the literatures of the Americas. Given postnationalism's stated interest in models that deconstruct the nation as concept, this omission is surprising at best. Native voices truly cross the 49th parallel in ways that Rowe seems vaguely ambivalent about;[5] that they "de-center" the United States in the broader American studies conversation is beyond question. That they do so more thoroughly than the "New" American studies, which inevitably *returns* to the nation in one form or another (see, for example, Siemerling and Casteel, 10) is also likely, and yet these issues have largely been overlooked. Recently, scholars have begun to address some oversights, not least in the comparative terms of indigenous nationalisms;[6] but Native peoples themselves have traversed "the line" since long before Canada and the United States—indeed the 49th parallel itself—were imagined. In recent history, the involvement of Native Canadians in the American Indian Movement presents a potent political instance, while the influence of First Nations figures such as Basil Johnston and Edward Benton Banai on Anishinaabeg audiences in the U.S. Midwest offers a cultural instance of the same. Meanwhile, the fact that the Canadian grassroots movement Idle No More has had an impact south of the Canada-U.S. border, without being taken up as a wide-scale movement in the same way, speaks both to cross-border affinity and affiliation and to the legacy of those different experiences of colonialism.

Jim Northrup, in his *Rez Road Follies* (1997), writes of a powwow held in International Falls, Minnesota, in the early 1990s to commemorate the 1794 Jay Treaty, bringing together roughly two thousand Anishinaabe people from the United States and Canada. Such events celebrate, among other things, the work of Tuscarora chief Clinton Rickard and his "fight for the line" through the Indian Defense League of America. That this raises clear questions about citizenship—the IDLA was established to contest the imposition of U.S. citizenship, particularly pertaining to free passage across the border—is further treated by a range of writers on and near the border. They include Thomas King, whose "Borders" addresses this very issue; Louise Erdrich, who raises important questions about maternity, identity, and belonging via a border crossing in her *Books and Islands in Ojibwe Country* (2003); and Onondaga artist and author Eric Gansworth, across whose oeuvre the border takes on significance in various, often paradoxical, ways.[7] In all of these examples— just a few of many—the question "Canadian or American?" is subordinate to indigenous identities, and is even rendered irrelevant by the broader narratives of emplacement in Native literatures, presenting a serious challenge to the national (and even postnational, which depends on a "national" against which to be "post") literary project.

Renaissance, as mentioned, sets its parameters almost exclusively at the borders of the United States, excepting the odd surreptitious "crossing." Ignoring Pauline Johnson, for instance, Lincoln refers to Ontario-born George Copway—largely for his friendship with Longfellow. The major exception is chapter 6, devoted to Howard Norman's translation of the Mushkegowuk (Swampy Cree) *The Wishing Bone Cycle* (1976). That this transcription and translation of "Swampy Cree Narrative Poems," unlike all examples of the written literature covered in the book, is a production external to the United States, is a curious quirk. Its problematic nature is inadvertently expressed by a reviewer: "The powers that be in literary studies . . . that define the writers to be studied and who set the agendas for our anthologies, have not worked especially hard to provide Americans with a full sense of *this nation's* rich native literary traditions" (Bloodworth, 94; emphasis added).

This elision of the nation-state border and the subsuming of Native literatures into a U.S.-bound national narrative is explicit. More to the point, it is explicitly imperialistic.[8] But there is another layer of more implicit difficulty in the assumption (undoubtedly indirect and unintentional, but still misleading) that at this point in U.S. history, oral literatures are either past, appropriated devices of a literary aesthetic, or "other," extranational but ripe for appropriation. With Howard Norman, a non-Native, at the helm, too, we might reflect on the ways in which even the most sympathetic of intentions has the capacity to elide and obscure the realities of performance and production.[9] So what does it say of Canadian Native printed literature in the 1960s?

1968: THE "LEAP" YEAR

Delineating Canadian Native writing in the 1960s, Hartmut Lutz quotes Métis writer and activist Howard Adams's response to his suggestion that there was little aboriginal writing in the '60s:[10] "No, there was no literature! Native people were not at all at that level of concern. . . . You cannot talk about culture or literature when you are hungry. So, there was no way! I had tried it, and I would only get insulted from my own people. So, there was no way that we would talk about literature at all" (Lutz, 167).

Lutz lists some of the major determinants of that scenario, particularly outlining the effects of extreme poverty, displacement, enfranchisement,[11] and the residential school system. Pointing out that "Colonialist 'de-education' left the majority of schooled Natives literally speechless," Lutz articulates an essential truism at the heart of Adams's absence: "Native writing reflects this process." And yet this is only a partial truth, as his illumination of the proliferation of writings by, about, or including First Nations people in the '6os testifies. It begins, arguably, with George Clutesi's (Tseshaht) 1967 *Son of Raven, Son of Deer: Fables of the Tse-Shaht People,* the first collection of Native stories produced specifically *by* a Native writer/editor in Canada. Clutesi's second book, *Potlatch* (1969), "combines formal oratory and poetry of the Nootka, translated/recreated in English, with varying narrative points of view that integrate historiography, myth, ritual, drama and forms of short story" (Lutz, 183). Echoing, in that description, Momaday's *The Way to Rainy Mountain* (1969), the formal diversity of the book is "in keeping with typical sixties experiments" but as "an outgrowth of the multi-media tradition of the Potlatch itself" rather than as any deliberate engagement with the literary avant-garde (183). In fact, Lutz describes Clutesi's prose as "Victorian."

Quite explicitly, then, the emergence of a Native voice fully in control of his/her own production in Canada stands suggestively in continuity with the oral tradition on which Clutesi draws, and which proceeds alongside the printed text: "[T]he advent of Native written literature did not . . . mark the passing of Native oral literature. In fact, they occupy the same space. . . . And, if you know where to stand, you can hear the two of them talking to each other" (King, 101–102). The appearance of these books at the same time as Momaday's text is a salient reminder of that fact, as well as of the broader contexts of *that* text's production. Far from absent, if the Native Canadian novel was not to appear for over a decade yet, the oral tradition was nevertheless alive and well and, in such forms, flourishing in print in the 1960s.

Of course, despite the asserted "speechlessness" (a necessary indictment of the residential school system, but also an inadvertent perpetuation of the "vanishing Indian" myth), Clutesi has textual forebears, such as the aforementioned Johnson (whose 1911 *Legends of Vancouver* was republished, coincidentally, in 1961), or Kah-Ge-Ga-Gah-Bowh (George Copway). More important, Lutz says, "The examples of Nuligak [*I, Nuligak,* 1966], [James] Sewid [*Guests Never Leave Hungry,* 1969], [Maria] Campbell [*Halfbreed,* 1973] and others indicate that Native writing in Canada developed according to a pattern outlined in the United States some years earlier, with an ever increasing number of Native persons acting as authors, collectors, editors, and publishers" (179).

Three key areas of production in First Nations, Métis, and Inuit writing see pivotal moments in the 1960s, in fact. As noted, *I, Nuligak,* the first Inuit autobiography, was published in 1966; non-Native George Ryga's *The Ecstasy of Rita Joe* (1967) dealt sensitively with Native themes, via Native actors, arguably opening up modern theater to many Native playwrights; and in 1969, Harold Cardinal published *The Unjust Society,* taking Canadian hegemony to task, and paralleling Vine Deloria, Jr.'s *Custer Died for Your Sins,* that hugely influential "Indian manifesto" published contemporaneously in the States. That Lincoln's choice would seem to establish a problematic divide between Native American voices (literary, self-determined, drawing from the oral tradition) and First Nations Canadian voices ("salvaged," represented/mediated, steeped *in* the oral tradition) is actually, and ironically, underlined by the fact that he does not address this issue. This mini-narrative of the '60s emphasizes the similarities and differences between Native literary production in the United States and Canada, while underlining the growing presence of Native-produced texts. Despite the apparent absence of a Momaday figure, the publishing scene in Canada, with its clear concentration on "traditional" materials and texts that "testify," was not so dissimilar from that in the United States. It is into the 1970s that the major difference emerges, with the rise in the United States of the likes of James Welch (novelist), Leslie Marmon Silko (poet, novelist, and storyist), and Gerald Vizenor (poet, prose writer, and scholar)—and the emergence of other young writers, such as Simon Ortiz, many of them similarly formally adventurous.

In Canada, by contrast, the 1970s is probably most clearly marked by the rise of two particular writers (neither of them, yet, a novelist), and a form that has notably thrived in Canada. Lee Maracle launched her publishing career in 1975 with *Bobbi Lee, Indian Rebel: Struggles of a Native Canadian Woman*; Basil Johnston, first published in 1971, began his best-known work— a series specific to Ojibwe oral tradition—with *Ojibwe Heritage* (1976)[12]; and First Nations drama arrived prominently in the work of playwrights like Nona Benedict (*The Dress*, 1973) and through the establishment of the Association for Native Development in the Visual and Performing Arts (Däwes).[13] The remainder of this chapter, then, will move away from chronology, favoring generic divisions between key areas of largely First Nations literary production post-1970. These divisions, though, very loosely follow a chronological development, as particular forms grew out of the bedrock laid in the 1960s. They are memoir and myth; drama; poetry; and prose fiction.

MEMOIR AND MYTH

In 1969, James Sewid (with James Spradley) published *Guests Never Leave Hungry: The Autobiography of James Sewid, a Kwakiutl Indian*, taking up the well-recognized form of the collaborative "auto"-biography. Problematic though this interface can be, it is worth remembering Jeanette Armstrong's prefatorial comment in another coproduction: "This book is spoken at a time when writing was not considered a 'useful' endeavour in the ongoing struggle of our peoples" (Maracle, 1990, 15). A few years later, in 1972, Anahareo (Gertrude Bernard) published the best-selling *Devil in Deerskins: My Life with Grey Owl*, an account of her time with the notorious "Eco-Warrior," Archibald Belaney. If these books share an (ironic) connection in the ways they address issues of cultural continuity amidst change, they do so within a tradition that has tended to perpetuate the sense of romance and victimry associated with the "vanishing Indian." In keeping with the politically assertive work of the likes of Deloria and Cardinal, however, the '70s also witnessed the nascence of a charged—*angry*—form of personal testament too.

In his introduction to the first paperback edition of *Renaissance*, Lincoln notes that "Native Americans are writing prolifically, particularly the women, who correlate feminist, nativist, and artistic commitments in a compelling rebirth" (1985, xi). Lincoln refers to the work, published in the year or so since the hardback publication of *Renaissance*, of two debut novelists (Paula Gunn Allen and Louise Erdrich), two poets (Joy Harjo and Linda Hogan), and two anthologies (Rayna Green's *That's What She Said* [1984] and Gretchen Bataille and Kathleeen Sands's *American Indian Women, Telling their Lives* [1984]). These publications mark a significant turn, as Bataille and Sands make clear. "American Indian women," they note, "have not been spared the attitude that until recently assumed the inferiority of all women."

And yet, as several commentators had already noted, and as Beatrice Medicine "ha[d] said repeatedly in lectures and in print . . . Indian women do not need liberation, . . . they have always been liberated within their tribal structures" (Bataille and Sands, vii–viii). But while Bataille and Sands argue that "The belief that Indian women do not need the feminist movement is consistent with the role Indian women have played within their societies" (129), Lee Maracle's *Bobbi Lee, Indian Rebel* focused more intensely and intently on the avowed rage (toward white Canadian culture) of a young woman. Like the contents of the Bataille and Sands anthology, *Bobbi Lee* (recorded and then transcribed with the aid of Don Barrett and Rick Sterling) was very much in the tradition of an "as-told-to" life story.

Far from proferring "witness" to the enrichment of women's culture, *Bobbi Lee* highlights the traumatic disruptions of colonial imposition experienced by Native women (and men). Referring to the standoff at Kanesatake between Mohawk activists and the Quebec police/Canadian military, Maracle provocatively suggests in her prologue to the 1990 edition, "Maybe bloodletting is what this country needs. Maybe if we just let the road to Oka run red with the blood of women, someone in this country will see the death and destruction this country has wrought on us" (6). This provocation precedes Jeanette Armstrong's foreword, in which she celebrates "the clear path toward transformation through personal resolve, resistance and clear thinking," figuring Maracle's commitment to (and influence on?) "the formative ideals that burgeon into a strong native political and cultural renaissance immediately following the period the book covers" (Maracle, 1990, 15–16). Maracle followed up *Bobbi Lee* with her collection of essays, *I Am Woman* (1988), with further observations, many excoriating, on "the impacts of colonialism on us, as [Native] women, and on myself personally" (Maracle, 1988, vii). Similarly, although Maracle concedes her obligation to endorse aspects of universal feminism in her preface to the second edition, the essays that constitute *I*

Am Woman represent her "personal struggle with womanhood, culture, traditional spiritual beliefs and political sovereignty" with a specific remit to "empower Native women to take to heart their own personal struggle for *Native feminist being*" (vii; emphasis added).

A contemporary of Silko, Maracle offered an honest, often eviscerating critique of colonial conditions that cut to the core of Native women's issues within the context of Native community more broadly. It matched the powerful plainspeak of Native women's voices in the United States such as those of Elizabeth Cook-Lynn and Paula Gunn Allen. Another first, Beth Brant, Maracle's elder by roughly nine years, addressed the question of Native women's writing in the context of her experience as a lesbian woman.[14] Her *A Gathering of Spirit: A Collection by North American Indian Women* (1988),[15] a collection of poetry, drawings, narrative segments, and interviews, was groundbreaking, the first to contain solely women's writing, about which Brant writes: "We are angry at white men and their perversions. . . . We are angry at Indian men for their refusals of us. For their limited vision of what constitutes a strong Nation. We are angry at the so-called 'women's Movement' that always seems to forget we exist. . . . We are not victims. We are organizers, freedom fighters, healers" (10–11). That she continues in the spirit of Maracle et al. is reinforced in numerous ways, but not least here: "I look on Native women's writing as a gift, a give-away of the truest meaning. Our spirit, our sweat, our tears, our laughter, our love, our anger, our bodies are distilled into words that we weave together to make power" (Brant, 1997, 176).

Resistance, on the one hand, also gives way to reclamation in this period, particularly through continued publication of collections of stories, traditional songs, and so on, and also through the "reclamation" of storytelling traditions in written form. Basil Johnston, in particular, has had truly "transnational" influence. Writing in the preface to *Ojibway Heritage* (1976), Johnston echoes one of the fundamental premises of Lincoln's readings—the primacy of orality, and its relationship to performance: "[I]t is in cerermony, ritual, song, dance, and prayer that the sum total of what people believe about life, being, existence, and relationships are symbolically expressed and articulated; as it is in story, fable, legend, and myth that fundamental understandings, insights, and attitudes toward life and human conduct, character, and quality in their diverse forms are embodied and passed on" (7).

Under a balanced remit of instruction and entertainment, Johnston's work, including many other books on Native life and Ojibwe culture (as well as five books in Ojibwemowin), represents one of the largest single archives for Anishinaabe cultural education. Equally instructive, of course, is the map in that first book (reproduced in subsequent books too) that illustrates the fullest understanding of "Ojibwe Country," a vast territory across the Canada-U.S. border, including much of the Great Lakes region, westward to Montana/Saskatchewan, as far south as lower Michigan, and up into northern Ontario.

Embracing the relationship between orality, the pictographic, and the performative, that map-in-context figuratively encapsulates the cross-border networks of Native literatures.

DRAMA

Turning more directly to performance, playwright Drew Hayden Taylor claims: "in terms of, I guess, per capita art form, it seems that theatre, for one reason or another, has become the predominant expressive vehicle for Canada's Native people. I believe the reason is that theatre is just a logical extension of storytelling" (144). It took time, though. In the United States, Lynne Riggs's *Green Grow the Lilacs* (to become the hit musical *Oklahoma!*) literally set the stage in the 1920s/1930s (Haugo, 189). Although it did not deal with Native themes, the follow-up, *Cherokee Night*, did, while Canadian theater remained dominated by non-Native representations of Native lives until the 1980s. Such portrayals—Sharon Pollock's 1973 play *Walsh*, for instance—while powerful and well-intentioned, often tended still to inadvertently silence Native voices. In its exposition of the treatment of Sitting Bull and his followers by Canadian authorities after the Battle of the Little Bighorn, *Walsh* navigates the fraught questions of territory and homeland caught up in the Dakotas' right to cross the border. While late-nineteenth-century policy effectively put an end to the ease with which "small groups of Sioux moved back and forth across the border" in the decade preceding Sitting Bull's 1877 flight (Nichols, 420), the play itself ultimately examines the frontier myth's epic tussle between "savagism" and "civilization" rather than the arguably more vital matter of the disruptions and continuities that follow.

The historic weight of that subject matter inevitably juxtaposes Sitting Bull's aspirations in Canada with Canada's treatment of him, presenting a kind of missed opportunity for the Canadian national psyche. Insofar as historical revisiting is a common theme for Pollock, it arguably has more to do with examining the official record of Canadian or North American history than with representing the immediate experience of Native lives, histories, or cultural/intellectual legacies. George Ryga's *The Ecstasy of Rita Joe* (1967) had seemed to represent a '60s turning point of sorts, with aboriginal actors at least taking center stage, but the balance still favoured non-aboriginal playwrights. Besides the odd early exception, such as George Kenny's *October Stranger* (1977),[16] and the formation of the Association for Native Development in the Performing and Visual Arts (1974), the gradual emergence of theater companies and playwrights began to redress that balance toward the end of the period covered by *Renaissance*. And again, as W. H. New notes, where prose fiction brought attention to Native writing in the United States, it was theater that effected this breakthrough in Canada (370). In the first instance it was through the establishment of Native Earth Performing Arts by Denis

Lacroix and Bunny Sicard, and Debajehmujig, founded in 1984 by Shirley Cheechoo and others at M'Cheeging First Nation on Manitoulin Island.[17]

Native Earth Performing Arts, established in Toronto in 1982, secured government funding in 1986 under a clear mandate, including pledges:

- to provide a base for professional/Native performers, writers, technicians and other artists
- to encourage the use of theatre as a form of commnication within the Native community, including the use of Native languages
- to communicate . . . the experiences that are unique to Native people in contemporary society.

That platform in turn produced a number of cowritten plays, examples of "collective creation," or collaborative developments between actors, before its first formally scripted production, *The Rez Sisters* (1986) by Tomson Highway, the company's musical director (*Canadian Theatre Encyclopedia*). As Taylor records: "For many of us within the Native community, Rez Sisters was the start of contemporary Native theatre, because that's where people first stood up saying 'Eh, what's this?' Native people are telling their own story and they're telling it well" (150). Despite an inauspicious start, Highway's play received strong reviews, becoming a success largely by word of mouth.

Lincoln's emphasis on the primacy of the oral tradition in the principal works he covers, as "a written renewal of the oral tradition translated into Western form," has been complicated by over three decades of analysis of ethnic and cultural hybridity, indigenous aesthetics, and political and cultural sovereignty. But its central premise—that contemporary Native literatures represent "continuities emerging from the old"—still has purchase, particularly in theater (8). Common views of the 'theatrical' in aboriginal terms prioritize the performative aspects of ritual and of the oral tradition, as Taylor notes: "To look back at the roots and origins of traditional storytelling—not just Native storytelling but storytelling in general—it's about taking your audience on a journey through the use of your voice, your body, and the spoken word. And going from that onto the stage is just the next logical progression" (140).

Another element for Taylor, the need to have grammatically perfect English to participate in the written arts, of course reflects back on Lutz's point about writing per se and the role of education in a Native literary tradition.

That Lincoln all but ignores theater is at least in part due to the *literary* focus of his text. As Haugo notes, "as late as 1995, only Hanay Geiogamah's *New Native American Drama: Three Plays* (1980) and a few individual titles had been published" (193–94). Lincoln's oral-to-text trajectory, then, inevitably skirts the stage. The inclusion of Canadian productions in the broader equation, however, tells a slightly different story, since, as Haugo notes, several Native Canadian playwrights had been published individually by 1995, while Caroline Heath had edited *The Land Called Morning: Three Plays* in 1986 (194).

This latter point falls outside the time span of Lincoln's argument, but it speaks profoundly to the legacy of the "renaissance" in Native Canadian theater, the depth of which is impressive. In the period since that production of *The Rez Sisters*, first published in 1988, a number of playwrights have had their work performed and published, including[18] Daniel David Moses, *Coyote City* (1988); Maria Campbell, with Linda Griffiths, *Jessica* (1989); Drew Hayden Taylor, *Toronto at Dreamer's Rock* (1989); Margo Kane, *Moonlodge* (1990); Yvette Nolan, *Blade* (1990); Shirley Cheechoo, *Path with No Moccasins* (1991); Monique Mojica, *Princess Pocahontas and the Blue Spots* (1991); Billy Merasty, *Fireweed* (1992); Marie Clements, *Age of Iron* (1993); Joyce B. Joe, *Ravens* (1996); Ian Ross, *FareWel* (1997, and recipient of the Governor General's Award in that year); Kevin Loring, *Where the Blood Mixes* (2008, and recipient of the Governor General's Award for 2009); Kenneth T. Williams, *Suicide Notes* (2007)[19]; and the list goes on. A significant number of these, including Taylor, Moses, and Mojica, along with Tomson Highway, have established solid international reputations, not least because "much cross-fertilization occurs in Native theatre, with actors, directors, and other artists frequently crossing the [U.S.-Canada] border to work on projects" (Haugo, 194). At a "political" level, in theater as elsewhere, though First Nations Canadians tend to navigate and negotiate the particular circumstances of Canadian colonialism, and Native Americans deal with the conditions of colonization in the United States, both past and present, "culturally some such divided groups might share important qualities and histories" (Haugo, 194). In the pan-Native arena, such "transnational" flows are recurrent and recuperative, while more locally, tribal continuities, convergent and parallel histories, and other kinds of affinities and affiliations, *particularly* common aesthetic trajectories, render the nation-state border a minor element in the stuff and substance of cultural production.

POETRY

In his chapter "A Contemporary Tribe of Poets," Lincoln places the output of Native American poets in their obvious literary context. Addressing the appropriation and celebration/mourning of Native American voices in American poetics, he asks:

And why all these dream words from would-be Indians? The myths and realities of white America's freedoms were bound up in contradictory myths of Indian culture and history: in the "free speech" of Native American oratory, freedom of movement in Native American migrations, freedom of definition . . . freedom of religious expression . . . free verse in the nonrhymed Native American chants metered to the subject sung, and freedom of space in the "wilds," the "plains," the mystic forests, the forbidding mountains and almost impassable deserts. [64]

A burgeoning American poetics—in the "discovery" mode of salvage ethnography, through an American symbolic, to the "poetic renewal" of Olson's "projective verse," the ethnopoetics of Jerome Rothenberg et al., and Gary Snyder's ecopoetics (Castro, *passim*)—marks the quest to liberate the American psyche through the co-option of an always already romanticized, always already elevated "primitivism." The irony, of course, as well as the echo of the palimpsestic narrative of settler colonization, is surface-level: "Native Americans lived here of their own volition, not wild but attuned with who and where they were. Native peoples lived at home in the American frontier. The pilgrims, homesteaders, pioneers, ranchers, city-builders, and now the poets watched at a distance in awe, fear, and envy" (Lincoln, 64)

McKenzie, among others, describes a similar process of "indigenizing" the national literature in Canada—part celebration, part appropriation. But if what Lincoln describes comes uncomfortably close to fetishisation, it is a form of icon building that is quickly collapsed in much Canadian Native poetry.

Addressing Canada's Mohawk "Princess," E. Pauline Johnson, by way of developing and nuancing that poet's own, wholly co-opted, voice, Joan Crate writes:

> Someone writes poems about me,
> words lying on the page, small corpses.
> She is afraid of my moist breath under her wrist,
> and ink mixing our veins.
> She reels me into the late twentieth century
> where I am quaint. . . . [27]

Crate reminds us that Johnson, that doyenne of Canadian verse (for her performance every bit as much as her poetry), both encapsulated and resisted the romantic version of the "Indian." Johnson's famous "The song my paddle sings," for all its natural idyll, contrasts starkly with poems like "A Cry from an Indian Wife" about the 1885 Riel Rebellion:

> Go forth, and win the glories of the war.
> Go forth, nor bend to greed of white men's hands,
> By right, by birth we Indians own these lands. [1996]

Reading back to that early era, then, the national boundaries were being challenged in a way that didn't simply assert Native presence; more than that, it *re*asserted aboriginal rights, figuring a kind of pan-Native nationhood in the rhetoric of resistance. How ironic that Johnson should ultimately be wholly subsumed for so long within a *Canadian* cultural nationalism; and it further ironizes the attempt to figure indigenous literary movements fully within those nation-state paradigms.

While Crate is an inheritor of Johnson's legacy, her first book did not appear until 1991, but the republication of Johnson's *Legends of Vancouver* thirty years previously heralded a period of poetic production (though it, itself, was prose) at the vanguard of the cultural revival of the 1960s. Figures including Duke Redbird and Peter Blue Cloud made their names in this period as political activists, later as poets and performers of other kinds. Redbird, for instance, is introduced in *Red on White* (1971), a multiform "autobiography," as "a mystic, a painter, a hypnotist, a businessman, a prophet, a poet, a politician, a writer, a sideshow freak, a lecturer, a playboy, an actor, a red-power militant" and more (Dunn, 1; also quoted in McKenzie, 77–78). Redbird's early work speaks directly to the spirit of resistance of late civil rights era:

I am the Redman
I look at you White Brother
And I ask you
Save not me from sin and evil
Save yourself. [Petrone, 1984, 175–76]

Blue Cloud, a participant in the claiming of Alcatraz by "Indians of all Tribes" in 1969, is described as "a moving force in the revival of Native culture and the stimulation of creative writing by Native people in the late 1960s and 1970s (Armstrong and Grauer, 24). His devotion to his people is paramount, elaborated in his poetry as a commitment to the political cause in a language both specifically cultural and universally significant. As he declares in "Alcatraz": "a tribe is an island / and a tribe is a people / in the eternity of Coyote's mountain" (Armstrong and Grauer, 25).

One of Canada's most famous Native spokespeople, Chief Dan George, came to prominence as a poet in the 1970s with the first of two best-sellers, *My Heart Soars* (1974). Meanwhile, Marion Sarain Stump, artist and writer, had published *There Is My People Sleeping* in 1970. According to McKenzie, "It is Sarain Stump's beautiful poem-drawings . . . that remain some of the richest finds in the literature of the Native Literary Renaissance" (78). Stump himself draws a direct correlation between image and text, describing in his work, "a fully formed pictographic tradition and how this concrete system serves as the basis for poetic artistry," suggesting that "for many Aboriginal writers who have either grown up with Aboriginal instruction or who have later educated themselves in Aboriginal ways of knowing, there might be some relationship between Stump's overtly visual poetic depictions and the concrete and tactile metonyms which dominate . . . so much of the poetry of the Native Renaissance" (McKenzie, 79). Given the relationship between the pictographic tradition and orality, this paradigm would seem to fit neatly into Lincoln's conceptual model.

This summary is, necessarily, brutally selective, but no poetry conversation is complete without acknowledgement of two hugely significant female writers, Rita Joe and Emma LaRocque. Joe is known for her advocacy of Native art and culture, and her poetry. She deals movingly with her experiences at residential school: "I lost my talk / The talk you took away. / When I was a little girl / At Shubencadie School" (28).[20] In *When the Other Is Me* (2010), LaRocque writes about the "inevitable Aboriginal contrapuntal reply to Canada's colonial constructs," pointing to the emergence of "a resistance born from the contested ground upon which we, the Canadian colonizer-colonialist and Native colonized, have built our troubled discourse" (3). Dealing with the specificity of Canadian-indigenous relations, LaRocque delineates the dialogue in which Joe participates in "I Lost My Talk." But LaRocque's words have purchase well beyond the boundaries of the nation-state when she writes: "the 'Indian' as an invention serving colonial purposes is perhaps one of the most distorted and dehumanized figures in white North American history, literature, and popular culture" (4). Both writers, then, have taken their places in the multivalent process of creating a literature that both furthers cultural modalities and provides counterpoint to the colonial processes of erasure and occlusion.

This particular thematic vein, resistant to the impositions and proscriptions of colonial languages, reflects that earlier conversation about autobiography. Marie Annharte Baker, for instance, whose first volume of poetry, *Being on the Moon,* appeared in 1990, writes in "Raced out to write this up":

> I often race to write   I write about race   why do I write
> about race   I must erase all trace of my race   I am an
> eraser abrasive bracing myself embracing

Grauer, in interview with Baker, declares, "As a reader, I feel liberated, given some space by Annharte's playful handling of a word that usually chokes, shames, and shuts down." Baker herself meanwhile notes, "There are so many class barriers besides racial ones that are employed to exclude the 'Other' in English. The colonial mindset of Canadian English usage avoids the diversity of spoken language" (Baker and Grauer, 2006). Such language strategies, again located within a Canadian cultural/linguistic context, nevertheless traverse the border, echoing what Ortiz (1981) sees as an "Indianizing" of English—a refusal to submit to the colonizer's language, embracing the play and power of the spoken/speechlike word. and also echoing what Gloria Bird (1993) identifies as a necessary strategy in the decolonization of the mind. Similar plays and ploys form part of the projects of numerous other poets, reveling in the fluidity and function of language—as story, vessel, weapon; in continuity, construction, and resistance—from Beth Cuthand (*Horse Dance to Emerald Mountain*, 1987) to Gregory Scofield (*The Gathering: Stones for the Medicine Wheel*, 1993); from Armand Garnet Ruffo (*Opening in the Sky*, 1994) to Kateri Akiwenzi Damm (*My Heart Is a Stray Bullet*, 1993); from Joanne Arnott (*Wiles of Girlhood*, 1991) to Marilyn Dumont (*A Really Good Brown Girl*, 1996). Common ground includes the complex networks of identity and community, the disruption of language and form, and the reimagining of traditional structures through story and tribal language.

THE NOVEL

It might seem strange to relegate the Native novel, the "renaissance" catalyst, to the closing pages of this chapter, but the truth is that in Canada it was a latecomer. Although some of Canada's best-known Native writers, such as Thomas King, Ruby Slipperjack, Eden Robinson, and Jeanette Armstrong, are prose writers, the first impactful First Nations novel (*In Search of April Raintree*, 1983) did not appear until some fifteen years after Momaday's *House Made of Dawn*. In fact, Inuit writers had the lead in this respect, with the appearance of Markoosie's *Harpoon of the Hunter* (1970), which, while not exactly well received (see Harry), nevertheless significantly precedes Beatrice (Culleton) Mosionier's *Raintree*. Indeed, *Raintree* itself is contemporaneous with Mitiarjuk Attasie Nappaaluk's *Sanaaq*, published in Inuktitut syllabics in 1984 (and in French translation in 2003).[21] Nevertheless, if *Raintree* marks the beginnings of a "new wave" of First Nations and Métis novels in English, it initiates a slow beginning.

Armstrong's *Slash* (1985), Slipperjack's *Honour the Sun* (1987), and Crate's *Breathing Water* (1989) follow *Raintree*, each in turn adding another dimension to the representation of indigenous experience in Canada. Where *Raintree* navigates the lives of Métis sisters amidst the dissolution of their family and the insufficiency of the social services, *Slash* develops the "space between the negative stereotype of the Indian and the romanticized popular view" in which the Native voice, renewed and recovered, inserts itself (Fee, 170). For Fee, "Although both *Slash* and *April Raintree* work through many fake ideas, the need to undermine the 'manichean aesthetic' is at the heart of each" (170), both with connections to *I Am Woman* and, later, Maracle's novel, *Ravensong* (1993). Slipperjack's novel explores poverty, alcoholism, and the threat of violence often indirectly, in the form of a coming-of-age narrative, while Crate's *Breathing Water* navigates an often bewildering urban space as a young mother struggles to reconcile past and present, the psychic legacy of her Native heritage and her present life.

It is implausible to pick out any of these novelists for the kind of singular influence Momaday has had—indeed, Momaday, Silko, Welch, et al. are as influential on First Nations/Métis novelists as anyone. Most recently, Joseph

Boyden (*Three Day Road*, 2005) arguably wears the influence of writers like Louise Erdrich most clearly, but his story of Ojibwe sharpshooters during World War I recounts a uniquely haunting tale of the line between camaraderie and alienation, fortitude and madness. In its description of fighting long before the United States entered the fray, it is a story that is uniquely "native" to Canada. Before Boyden, Lorne Simon (*Stones and Switches*, 1994) trod the tricky path between Christian values and Mic'maq culture, while Highway's *Kiss of the Fur Queen* (1998) reraised the specter of the residential school system for two boys ultimately redeemed by their developments in music and dance. Richard Wagemese (*Keeper'n Me*, 1994) and Richard Van Camp (*The Lesser Blessed*, 1996) have meanwhile invested similar themes—enforced separation and return, and adolescence—with considerable poignancy and penetration. But unlike those other genres I have related, almost all of this comes well after the period Lincoln covers, legacies of, but not participants in, that first wave of "discovery" by publishers of indigenous writing.

Even still, two of Canada's best-known Native literary exports are novelists. Eden Robinson, of course, best known for *Monkey Beach* (2000), has at least partially made a name for herself by resisting the kind of cultural representation highlighted so frequently here. In that novel, her mixture of Haisla myth with European folkloric motifs (such as leprechauns); an intense, almost cartographic exposition of the Northwest; and a deeply personal narrative of self-discovery by the novel's narrator invite *and* refuse culturally bound analysis. Elsewhere, the dirty realism of the story collection *Traplines* (1996), and in the reprisal of some of its characters in *Blood Sports* (2006), including the sociopath Jeremy, defies those who would seek to privilege Robinson's Haisla/Heiltsuk heritage over her artistic integrity. Robinson refuses, more successfully than many, to allow her fiction to merely become a repository for a kind of ethno-literary archaeology.

Thomas King, on the other hand, plays on that tendency in the critical archive in much of his fiction, returning us to the valency of the spoken word and to that border crossing (in all its connotations) with which I began. From his first novel, *Medicine River* (1989), King has sought out the seams and frayed edges of colonial legacy, drawing together an array of stereotypes and misconceptions, myths and apocrypha to rechart the terrain of colonial-Native relations. He picks apart the impact of the Indian Act, highlights the human cost of settlement and environmental heavy-handedness (one of many themes in *Green Grass, Running Water*, 1993), heaps satire on the self-importance of Christian epistemology, and even tackles the impact of the Canada-U.S. border (*Truth & Bright Water*, 1999), as what Hugh Keenlyside once called "physically invisible" but also "emotionally inescapable" (cited in Brown, 156). King's Canadian stature is both well deserved and somewhat ironic. His crossing from the United States to Canada in the early 1980s, an international move with transnational implications, is intractably bound in the nation-state politics within which cultures of national production are formed. It is, in that sense, an apt place to remind us of the parameters I explored at the beginning by way of a close to this chapter.

I want to do so, though, in the words of a First Nations writer, collaborating with a Canadian educator, in the introduction to their *Staging Coyote's Dream* (2003):

> *Staging Coyote's Dream* is the first collection of Native plays to be published in the land that is now called Canada, but it is not an anthology of "Canadian Plays," nor have we chosen to identify the plays collected here as "Native." The decision to use the term "First Nations," and the decision not to restrict the plays included to those produced within the geopolitical boundaries of Canada . . . claims the right of First Nations peoples not to be subject to the political or legislative regimes of later-day nations . . . lays claim to a history that long precedes contact or colonization, that has not been superseded, and that cannot be circumscribed. [Mojica and Knowles, iv]

The message is explicit and instructive, and it must resound long and loud through indigenous studies in North America, however scholars choose to frame the argument. I have outlined here a range of writers and writings that intervene in nation-state delimited conversations about Native North American literatures; that this chapter in turn itself maps out a "national" Native literature is, therefore, inevitable. In doing so, though, it selectively delineates a literary history that demonstrates the presence of literary voices above (literally) and beyond those contained by, and documented within, the Native American Renaissance and that register, in different ways, a presence aside from the measures of absence conferred by that project's parameters. Its point is precisely to note that the more one recognizes the wealth and range of indigenous writers for whom the 49th boundary is little more than a (post) colonial imposition, the more artificial that border appears, either as a barrier to physical passage *or* as a framing mechanism for any kind of intellectual project. That said, as this essay also reveals, merely eliding the border from a narrative of Native North American literary production is, in and of itself, an occluding gesture that ignores the *differences* between, and fails to account for the nuances of, the postcolonial experiences of Native peoples in the United States and Canada. It is a complex story that demands complex interactions with the implications of the nation-state boundary. Taking full account, then, of indigenous literary production north and south of the border poses a serious challenge not only to the reimagining of the nation-state *but also* to its deconstruction; it informs, too, a fuller understanding of indigenous nationhood and Native sovereignty in the context of continental networks of relations—through connections and continuities, in other words, that precede and transcend the "renaissance."

NOTES

1. There is plenty of well-known criticism of Lincoln's claim. Most of it galvanizes around the point that Native "literatures" do not begin and end with print, and that even then, Momaday has numerous antecedents. Nonetheless, Lincoln highlighted a critical mass, after 1968, of print publication of Native writers around a set of common themes.

2. The Wikipedia entry, for instance, reductively notes that Johnson, among some nine other writers who precede the "renaissance," had "not inspired other Natives to follow in their footsteps." Questionable though such sources are often held up to be, their ready accessibility makes them logical "first port of call" reference sites for many interested readers.

3. As commentators such as Gerson and Strong-Boag (2000) have noted, Johnson's Canadian legacy is itself fraught, the poet herself often "sanitized" to fit into a highly romanticized narrative and overlooked on a critical level. Highly compelling attempts at reasserting Johnson's importance beyond the colonial paradigm include Beth Brant's *Writing as Witness* (1994). The simple point, of course, is that any reduction of the complexities of Johnson's public identity will inevitably misrepresent her.

4. A fuller project still would include indigenous language, francophone, and hispanophone writing and the various borders and border crossings implicated there—more than a single article could contain!

5. Canadian studies scholars get justifiably exercised about phrasing such as "This new interest in border studies should include investigations of how the many different Americas *and Canada* have historically influenced and interpreted each other" (Rowe, 25; emphasis added), as if Canada is some kind of appendix to the "real" Americas.

6. See, for instance, Kit Dobson's comparison of Craig Womack and Taiaiake Alfred in his *Transnational Canadas*. Other scholars who take account of indigeneity in a hemispheric context include A. Robert Lee's four-volume *Native American Writing* (2011), Claudia Sadowski-Smith (including her *Border Fictions*, 2008), Shari M. Huhndorf (*Mapping the Americas,* 2009), and Rachel Adams (*Continental Divides*, 2009). These works tend to come either from indigenous studies or Canadian studies perspectives, and *not* from the heartlands of American studies, and they often tend to emphasize gestures of *remapping*.

7. As a member of the Haudenosaunee Confederacy, Gansworth's situation is most instructive, since the confederacy does not recognize the separateness of the United States and Canada, essentially considering them one continuous colonial power.

8. W. H. New later identified a "Native Canadian Renaissance" between 1960 and 1990. I would argue this reinforces the critique of the nationally bounded (or, shall we say, critically colonial) nature of academic treatment of Native writing.

9. This is neither an indictment of Norman (who grew up with and around the Muchkegowuks and was fluent in Cree) nor of Lincoln. It highlights, however, the ways partial stories rapidly become whole truths. Such anthologies, "unavoidably 'translating' some [texts] into the format of a different culture simply by converting them from oral to written form," common in Canada in the 1960s through the '80s (New, 6), were equally common in the United States.

10. There were actually a number of writers actively seeking publication between 1913 (Johnson's death) and 1960. The real issue was the lack of opportunity to publish. (See Edwards, who names Ethel Brant Monture, Edward Ahenakew, Bernice Loft Winslow, and others. Adams's sense of the impossibility of writing in the '60s equating to a lack of literature obscures, as a number of scholars in the United States have demonstrated in recent years, the continuity of oral traditions and the longer history of Native writing in Canada.

11. "'Enfranchisement,' one of the key issues of all Indian Acts and amendments, is a euphemism for loss of Indian status" (Lutz, 169). This persisted until 1960 (at the federal level, longer in some provinces), whereby individuals who left the reservation, who voted, or even sought higher education, were "enfranchised," and therefore no longer eligible for Indian "status."

12. Artist Norval Morrisseau's 1965 *Legends of My People, the Great Ojibway* is an important precursor to Johnston's work.

13. Like "renaissance," "emergence" too occludes prior dramatic and performative forms in Native cultures. The distinction here is of a practice that materializes in "mainstream" locations, or that develops either systematiclly or programmatically through social and community fora. Native theater *has* blossomed in the United States (see Haugo), but Cherokee actor Elizabeth Theobold wrote enviously in 1997 of what she saw as a Canadian Native "theater movement all their own" that was then absent in the United States (142).

14. Brant (whose mother is Scots/Irish) is a Bay of Quinte Mohawk (Tyendinaga), although she grew up in Detroit, Michigan. The Mohawks straddle the Canada-U.S. border (literally at Akwesasne), and Brant's work has similarly traversed national and cultural borders.

15. First published in 1984 as a special issue of the journal *Sinister Wisdom*.

16. An adaptation of one of Kenny's poems, cowritten by Dennis Lacroix (Taylor, 144), *October Stranger* was performed at an international theater festival in Monaco in 1977 (Taylor says 1979). It fell victim to the clichéd expectations of the non-Native audience. See Schäfer.

17. Debajehmujig moved to the Wikwemikong Unceded Reserve on Manitoulin in 1989, where it remains "the only professional theatre company located on an Indian Reserve" (Debajehmujig/Storytellers). Other companies have appeared in more recent years, including Nakai Theatre Ensemble in the Yukon and Crazy

Horse Theatre in Calgary, not to mention a number of Native film and TV production companies.

18. Only first plays are named here, and the dates correspond to first productions, except where noted.

19. *Suicide Notes* was first published in *Three on the Boards*.

20. Joe's first collected book was *The Poems of Rita Joe* (1978).

21. The separation of First Nations, Métis, and Inuit peoples (largely due to the differences in their legal and political treatment) is one of the several reasons the experiences of Native Canadians and Native Americans are not so easily conflated. Indeed, Ruffo draws attention to this, where he describes a fellow reader on an Australian tour:

> Her name was Rita Mestokosho, . . . an Innu poet from Ekuanitshit (Mingan), in the territory of Nitassinan, located on the east coast of northern Quebec. I also learned that Rita's first language was Innu, and French her second. As Rita was not fluent in English, she read nearly all her work in the Innu language. . . . It occurred to me then that here we were, an assembly of Native writers from Canada touring Australia with the goal of forging links with other Indigenous writers while "one of our own" stood on the periphery of our literary family, isolated by a linguistic barrier. To say the least, it was ironic (110–11).

WORKS CITED

Adams, Rachel. 2009. *Continental Divides: Remapping the Cultures of North America.* Chicago: University of Chicago Press.

Andrews, Jennifer, and Priscilla Walton. 2006. "Rethinking Canadian and American Nationality: Indigeneity and the 49th Parallel in Thomas King." *American Literary History* 18:3, 600–17.

Armstrong, Jeanette, and Lalage Grauer. 2001. *Native Poetry in Canada: A Contemporary Anthology.* Peterborough, ON: Broadview Press.

Baker, Marie Annharte, and Lally Grauer. 2006. "'A Weasel Pops In and Out of Old Tunes': Exchanging Words." *Studies in Canadian Literature / Études en littérature canadienne* 31:1. Reprinted online: http://journals.hil.unb.ca/index.php/SCL/article/viewArticle/10203/10554 (last accessed April 4, 2011).

Bataille, Gretchen, and Kathleen Sands, eds. 1984. *American Indian Women, Telling Their Lives.* Lincoln: University of Nebraska Press.

Bird, Gloria. 1993. "Towards a Decolonization of the Mind and Text 1: Leslie Marmon Silko's *Ceremony*." *Wicazo Sa Review* 9:2, 1–8.

Bloodworth, William. 1985. "Review: *Native American Renaissance*." *MELUS* 12:1, 93–97.

Brant, Beth. 1988. *A Gathering of Spirit: A Collection by North American Indian Women.* Ithaca: Firebrand Books.

———. 1994. *Writing as Witness: Essays and Talk*. London: The Women's Press.

———. 1997. "The Good Red Road: Journeys of Homecoming in Native Women's Writing." In *New Contexts of Canadian Criticism*. Edited by Ajay Heble, Donna Palmateer Pennee, and J. R. (Tim) Struthers. 1997. Perterborough, ON: Broadview Press.

Brown, Russell M. 1981. "Crossing Borders." *Essays on Canadian Writing* 22, 154–68.

Castro, Michael. 1991. *Interpreting the Indian: Twentieth-Century Poets and the Native American*. Norman: University of Oklahoma Press.

Crate, Joan. 1991. *Pale as Real Ladies: Poems for Pauline Johnson*. London, ON: Brick Books.

Curiel, Barbara Brinson, David Kaznjian, Katherine Kinney, Steven Mailloux, Jay Mechling, John Carlos Rowe, George Sánchez, Shelley Streeby, and Henry Yu. 2000. "Introduction." In *Post-Nationalist American Studies*. Edited by John Carlos Rowe. 2000. Berkeley: University of California Press, 1–22.

Däwes, Birgit. 2009. *Tricksters on Stage: Contemporary First Nations Theater and Drama in Canada*. http://www.canlit.ca/letter.php?page=archives&letter =24 (last accessed March 24, 2011).

Debajehmujig/Storytellers. "Brief History." www.debaj.ca/content/Artistic-Direc tor?q=content/About-Company-History (last accessed January 11, 2011).

Dobson, Kit. 2009. *Transnational Canadas: Anglo-Canadian Literature and Globalization*. Waterloo, ON: Wilfrid Laurier University Press.

Dunn, Marty. 1971. *Red on White: The Biography of Duke Redbird*. Toronto: New Press.

Edwards, Brendan Frederick R. "'Yours Aboriginally': Twentieth-Century Aboriginal Authorship in Canada." *Historical Perspectives on Canadian Publishing*. http://digitalcollections.mcmaster.ca/case-study.quotyours-aboriginally quot -twentieth-century-aboriginal-authorship-canada (last accessed April 3, 2011).

Fee, Margery. 1990. "Upsetting Fake Ideas: Jeanette Armstrong's 'Slash' and Beatrice Culleton's 'April Raintree.'" *Canadian Literature*, 124–25, 168–80.

Gerson, Carole, and Veronica Strong-Boag. 2000. *Paddling Her Own Canoe: The Times and Texts of E. Pauline Johnson–Tekahionwake*. Toronto: University of Toronto Press.

Harry, Margaret. 1985. "Literature in English by Native Canadians." *Studies in Canadian Literature/Études En Litératture Canadienne* 10, 1 and 2. http://lib .unb.ca/Texts/SCL/bin/get.cgi?directory=vol10_1_2/&filename=Harry.htm (last accessed January 10, 2011).

Haugo, Ann. 2005. "American Indian Theatre." In Joy Porter and Kenneth M. Roemer, eds. 2005. *The Cambridge Companion to Native American Literature*. Cambridge: Cambridge University Press, 189–204.

Huhndorf, Shari M. 2009. *Mapping the Americas: The Transnational Politics of Contemporary Native Culture*. Ithaca, N.Y. Cornell University Press.

Joe, Rita. 1989. "I Lost My Talk." *Canadian Woman Studies* 10:2 and 3, 28.

Johnson, E. Pauline. 1996. " Cry from an Indian Wife." *The E. Pauline Johnson Project*. McMaster University. http://www.humanities.mcmaster.ca/~pjohnson /cry.html (last accessed April 10, 2011).

Johnston, Basil. 1990 [1976]. *Ojibway Heritage*. Lincoln, Neb.: Bison Books.

King, Thomas. 2005. *The Truth about Stories: A Native Narrative*. Minneapolis: University of Minnesota Press.

LaRocque, Emma. 2010. *When the Other Is Me: Native Resistance Discourse, 1850-1990*. Winnipeg: University of Manitoba Press.

Lee, A. Robert. 2011. *Native American Writing*. New York: Routledge.

Lincoln, Kenneth. 1985 [1983]. *Native American Renaissance*. Berkeley: University of California Press.

Lutz, Hartmut. 1997. "Canadian Native Literature and the Sixties: A Historical and Bibliographical Survey." *Canadian Literature/ Littérature Canadienne: A Quarterly of Criticism and Review*, 152–53. 167–91.

Maracle, Lee. 1988. *I Am Woman: A Native Perspective on Sociology and Feminism*. Vancouver, BC: Press Gang Publishers.

———. 1990 (orig. 1975). *Bobbi Lee, Indian Rebel*. Toronto: Women's Press.

McKenzie, Stephanie. 2007. *Before the Country: Native Renaissance, Canadian Mythology*. Toronto: University of Toronto Press.

Mojica, Monique, and Ric Knowles. 2003. *Staging Coyote's Dream: An Anthology of First Nations Drama in English*. Toronto: Playwrights Canada Press.

Native Earth Performing Arts. "About Us." www.nativeearth.ca/ne/about-us (last accessed March 1, 2011).

New, W. H. 2002. *Encyclopedia of Literature in Canada*. Toronto: University of Toronto Press.

Nichols, Roger L. 2010. "The Canada-US Border and Indigenous Peoples in the Nineteenth Century." *American Review of Canadian Studies* 40:3, 416–28.

Northrup, Jim. 1997. *The Rez Road Follies: Canoes, Casinos, Computers, and Birch Bark Baskets*. New York: Kadansha America.

Ortiz, Simon. 1981. "Towards a National Indian Literature: Cultural Authenticity in Nationalism." *MELUS* 8:2, 7–12.

Petrone, Penny. 1990. *Native Literature in Canada: From the Oral Tradition to the Present*. Oxford: Oxford University Press.

———, ed. 1984. *First People, First Voices*. Toronto: University of Toronto Press.

Rowe, John Carlos. 2000. "Post-Nationalism, Globalism, and the New American Studies." In *Post-Nationalist American Studies*. Edited by John Carlos Rowe. 2000. Berkeley: University of California Press, 23–39.

Ruffo, Armand Garnet. 2010. "Afterword." *Studies in Canadian Literature / Études en littérature canadienne* 35:2, 110–13. http://journals.hil.unb.ca/index.php /SCL/article/viewArticle/18325/19758 (last accessed April 4, 2011).

Sadowski-Smith, Claudia. 2008. *Border Fictions: Globalization, Empire, and Writing at the Boundaries of the United States*. Charlottesville: University of Virginia Press.

Schäfer, Henning. 2008. "Disappointing Expectations: Native Canadian Theatre and the Politics of Authenticity." In *Embracing the Other: Addressing Xenophobia in the New Literatures in English*. Edited by Dunja M. Mohr. 2008. New York: Rodopi, 307–26.

Siemerling, Winfried, and Sarah Phillips Casteel. 2010. *Canada and Its Americas: Transnational Navigations*. Montreal: McGill-Queen's University Press.

Stoddard, Grant. 2011. "The Lost Canadians." *The Walrus* 81, 24–31.

Taylor, Drew Hayden. 1997. "Storytelling to Stage: The Growth of Native Theatre in Canada." *The Drama Review* 41:3, 140–41, 144–52.

Theobold, Elizabeth. 1997. "Their Desperate Need for Noble Savages." *The Drama Review* 41:3, 142–43.

Wikipedia. "Native American Renaissance." http://en.wikipedia.org/wiki/Native _American_Renaissance (last accessed January 10, 2011).

18
Tribal Renaissance

KENNETH LINCOLN

> You have to listen. You have to know me to know what I'm talk-
> ing about.
>
> Mabel McKay to Greg Sarris

A backstory to the writing of *Native American Renaissance* seems called for.

July 1969. At twenty-five I came to UCLA in buckskins, boots, and a beard, my three-piece professorial suit at attention in the closet. Revolution darkened the air, and it seemed an odd time to join a retro English Department to teach Victorian studies, but that was my doctoral training and this was a job in California. The Vietnam War had turned full-throttle with an all-points draft, while John and Robert Kennedy, Martin Luther King, Jr., and Malcolm X were gunned down in cold blood. Fifty-eight thousand American soldiers were to be killed in Southeast Asia, along with some two million Vietnamese.

Spring 1970. Following the Cambodian invasion and the Kent State massacre, UCLA rioted. The students took over the men's gymnasium and drove back campus cops with chains and baseball bats. Faculty emptied classes. Three hundred LAPD in black-leather riot gear motorcycled in pairs down Sunset Boulevard and stormed the campus in vectors that swept the ivy halls clean as Clorox. Broken arms, powder burns, bruised butts and legs, cuff-chaffed wrists, and black eyes branded any student or faculty careless enough to be caught in the way.

Students demanded alternative educational classes, an end to the war, and radical social action. In this chaotic vortex I organized an off-campus seminar on "Native American Voices" in our beachside apartment. I'd grown up among South Dakota Sioux, met N. Scott Momaday during my Stanford undergraduate years, and knew that Nick Black Elk had been a holy man in my hometown. Other than starting my life among Pine Ridge and Rosebud Sioux kids, I knew little of American Indian cultures or histories at large, as with most Americans in the 1960s. My students were discussing Momaday's *House Made of Dawn*—the World War II veteran Abel from Jemez Pueblo relocated in the dark heart of downtown Los Angeles—when my wife came from the bedroom announcing that she was in labor. Our daughter was born the next night at 3 A.M. after thirty-two hours of intermittent maternal contractions. Rachel grew into my evolutionary touchstone for tribal kinship and white male reeducation, as her mother left us both for an alternative life never explained. She was done with the nuclear family, and we were on our own.

I mutated from three-piece suit back into blue jeans and harness boots, but at twenty-nine remained radically naïve, no more savvy than an earwig in our rumpled sheets. There were plenty of things awaiting my education in women's liberation, ethnic studies, political protest, societal change, child-raising, domestic chores, and the academy. They didn't show up in orderly fashion, nor did I learn them all at once.

Back home in Alliance, Nebraska, my adopted Rosebud Lakota brother, Mark Monroe, was organizing a south-of-the-tracks American Indian Center for equal rights, social justice, nondiscrimination, health care, feeding the poor, and economic opportunities. Mark's Indian people were dying thirty years younger than people in the Anglo mainstream, suffering the worst job numbers, medical statistics, educational failure, suicide rates, and homelessness in the country. Where was a tinhorn professor in all this turmoil, having grown up working-class WASP and high-plains Republican?

Historically by the sixties, the lower middle class of my background began to invade American institutions through college education—rising blue-collar barbarians at the gates. We heartland chumps had little idea what to do with corrupt power or social injustice or fallow tradition, except to protest and subvert it from within the system. We were new at the game of civil disobedience and got some things backwards.

A veteran of wars at home and abroad, Mark's grassroots social activism began with a "home and some hope," addressing indigent alcoholics—a frugal but nutritious meal a day at the Indian Center for those who washed in the creek and combed their hair to eat lunch, as well as anyone else who "declared a hunger." His programs branched out with medical busing to the reservation hospital, GED-test tutoring for high school dropouts, CEO job training for unskilled workers picked off barside curbs and subsisting as day laborers, bingo games, quilting bees, Indian Boy Scout troops, lot cleanups, community gardens, tribal arts workshops, a pine-bough Sun Dance Circle grounds, and alcohol and drug counseling along with a Nativist-tailored AA program called *Iktóme* for the two-faced Trickster. Mark and I wrote grants, harangued city fathers, petitioned United Way, canvassed churches, and generally stirred up enough Good Samaritan interest to underwrite our self-help programs on fraying shoestrings. My life pronged between UCLA Victorian studies and Native American cultural activism, on campus and back home.

The plot thickened when, untenured in 1975, I lit out from Los Angeles for the High Plains territories with eight students and my daughter on a four-month field trip into Sioux and pioneer heartland, eventually documented with Allogan Slagle in *The Good Red Road*. That trip widened our cultural parameters and focused my life work in American and Native American studies. Interdisciplinary training in British imperial Victorian studies provided strong methodology for comparative history, intercultural literacy, economic class structure, political maneuvering, and religious pluralism, but the university hardly needed more Dickens scholars. It was still obvious that Native American representation in academic circles amounted to less than zero. No professors, few staff, a handful of high school graduates recruited from Arizona water holes and the Sherman Indian School.

I came back to a deadlocked UCLA tenure vote, decided in my favor by a gay-rights chairman from my redneck home state. Questionably anointed, I had a job for life, a motherless five-year-old daughter entering kindergarten, and a suspect calling in American Indian studies. I stood at my own life crossroads of Western and Native cultures to take a deep, if uncertain breath. I had been trained at Stanford in American literature and humanities with a year abroad in Germany, then specialized at Indiana University in British literature and Victorian studies with a dissertation on Joseph Conrad's dark humor. My Native American education began at ground zero with Lakotas back home in Nebraska, and on my own I was reading everything in any discipline I could find about tribal cultures. I learned what I could about Indians where I could, from Mark's work in Alliance to the UCLA library.

Nationally, the occupation of Alcatraz was a few years smoldering, the American Indian Movement at full throttle, and Wounded Knee '73 still in the news. The federal government acknowledged 315 extant tribes with fewer than a million enrolled members. The National Congress of American Indians argued three times that number. Indeed, conservative data showed that over two thousand language cultures of thirty million to forty million peoples had inhabited the hemisphere before Columbus stumbled over them. So Vine Deloria, Jr., deep-fried anthropologists and missionaries in a 1969 *Playboy Magazine* article and heckled Christian conservatives in *An Indian Manifesto* that God just might be Red out West. *Custer Died for Your Sins,* AIMsters challenged, and the Christian call-out became a '70s bumper sticker. Cultural revolutions simmered at every crossroads.

The Nixon administration scripted a federal Indian policy ostensibly premised on sovereignty. The real issues were conscripting coal, oil, uranium, water, and land rights. Navajo tribal chair Peterson Zah charged that Peabody Power paid the tribe less than the price of a twelve-ounce Pepsi for a ton of Four Corners coal, the most polluted site on the globe. Tribal assets had long been easy pickings for traders, bureaucrats, and big business, but Indian people were dying at an alarming rate. The Native life expectancy was just over forty years and few Natives had gone to college, though more than half lived off-reservation. The times were changing.

Heathen and aboriginal had morphed into *American* Indian, as a century back Buffalo Bill Cody featured conquered Plains tribes in his Wild West

Show. Native peoples began problematizing academic "Indian" gloss and asking for regional and cultural specifics among hundreds of tribal communities. Who's Indian, whose Indian? By the 1970s Noble Savage translated into *Native* American by academic assignation, though few Americans knew of tribes beyond mounted warriors and Southwest planters. California was, and still is, the most Natively populated state in the Union—687,400 by the 2004 census count and a hundred thousand more today.

When I came back from the Dakotas in 1975, the reorganized UCLA Indian Center asked me to help turn an academic newsletter into a national research quarterly. Among the Pine Ridge Lakotas, giving back to people was called *helping out,* so I pitched in. Crossing disciplinary boundaries, cultural borders, and departmental norms wasn't easy. The university wanted published scholarship from our Organized Research Unit. Students asked for Native classes beyond traditional canons. Strapped Indian communities needed local services.

So I took over editing UCLA's *American Indian Culture and Research Journal*, still the longest-standing academic quarterly in the field, and initiated a Native American Poetry Series that eventually included Paula Gunn Allen, my Laguna colleague; Linda Hogan, Chickasaw ecological poet and friend from Colorado; Mike Kabotie, the Hopi silversmith, graphic artist, and poet, son of Fred Kabotie, the legendary painter; and Sherman Alexie, Spokane/Coeur d'Alene *enfant terrible* from the Pacific Northwest. Thirty-six years later the series has published fifteen volumes of emerging Native poetry.

My Native godfathers in this work were Vine Deloria, Jr., and Alfonso Ortiz. Vine came from my neck of the High Plains, Standing Rock where Sitting Bull was born and died. He had joined the Episcopal seminary to honor his father's work as the first Native to serve as a Christian priest in the Dakotas, but dropped out to serve in the army, then complete a degree in law school. I first read Vine's roast of anthropologists, missionaries, and bureaucrats in *Playboy Magazine,* as I worked vacations in the Alliance city engineering department to earn college pocket money in the late sixties. His chapter from *Custer Died for Your Sins* was the wryest voice I'd encountered since Mark Twain—attuned to the broadly educated reader, grounded in telling data, at once ironic and compassionate, the spoken voice hewn as writing blade. I followed his career from Alcatraz 1969 to Wounded Knee 1973, from *God Is Red* to *We Talk, You Listen,* from academic seminar to Jungian sensitivity training. Vine was always the smartest guy in the room, the wittiest and most informed in Indian affairs, the keenest to get things right.

A barrel-chested and big-hearted buddy from New Mexico's San Juan Pueblo, Alfonso Ortiz broke trail for some of my early publications, writing acute reader's reports that silenced mortarboard objections. We became dog soldiers in academic subversion, conference coyotes, and barbecuing fathers raising our children between ring-roads and the rez. Alfonso was a MacArthur "genius grant" Fellow specializing in social sciences, who always carried

T. S. Eliot's *Four Quartets* in his pocket, from Ford Foundation meetings in New York City to Siberian hunting camps across the Bering Straits. Al was another big brother shouldering to my rescue, a loyal trickster, a true friend. Alfonso, Paula, Logan, Scott, Linda, Vine, Joy, Bobbi, Mark, and countless Native others became "all my relatives" in the renaissance of American Indian studies.

The university inexplicably asked me to direct the Indian Center, but I was a single white guy raising a kindergarten daughter. Where were my Native colleagues? The chancellor would not grant me administrative leave time or child-care services, considered extracurricular. So I taught both British and Native classes, oversaw Indian Center publications, served on endless committees, wrote my books, battled for tribal rights back home, and bucked the administration for respect.

The English Department thought their Victorian studies flunky had gone feral. I had been hired to teach British literature, but UCLA seemed top-heavy with literary Anglophiles. One thing was clear: tribal cultures were entering a renaissance, a historical rebirth with scarce academic representation. Few faculty, if any, taught Native literatures, or wrote about the new writers, or parsed the politics of cultural renewal, as tribal peoples crossed margin to mainstream, reservation road to Main Street. My academic patrons dismissed the autodidactic work as countercultural heresy. One Restoration colleague suggested that I relocate into anthropology if I wanted to study aboriginals. An Americanist stopped me in the hall to insinuate that the speeches of illiterate hostiles like Red Jacket, Cochise, and Smohalla turned on the literary skills of army translators. I wondered how cavalry scribes could make up such eloquence as "From where the sun now stands I will fight no more forever," Chief Joseph's words as he surrendered the Nez Percé to General Bearcoat Miles in 1877. What would an academic insurgent do? Since at that time I was up against a tenure vote, senior colleagues warned of committing career suicide.

The promise of an academic *Journal* was integral to, if not the masthead of, the UCLA Indian Center, and the two were inseparable in my professional redevelopment. I am not a trained ethnographer, folklorist, historian, or linguist, but exposure to several dozen academic fields while editing the *American Indian Culture and Research Journal* educated me broadly. Interdisciplinary research in all aspects of Native American studies seasoned and sharpened the literary tools to write *Native American Renaissance* as my first book at the age of forty.

Besides stubborn idealism, I'm not sure whether my off-grid work or the *Journal* kept me going in those days. The headwinds were fierce. Lakota kinfolk Art Zimiga and Pat Locke were my tribal colleagues in re-education. We tried an experimental Hi-Potential Program of recruiting precollege Native students from desert springs, caliché basketball courts, and reservation special-ed programs, but reassessed academic outreach when the tutored students failed freshman entrance exams en masse. "This city is big enough to fill the Grand Canyon," a Navajo student told me upon leaving. How could his story be told in a fledgling academic quarterly dedicated to interdisciplinary Native scholarship or a book of literary criticism?

Despite the steady emergence of American Indian studies as an academic discipline nationally, the Indian Center wasn't firmly centered. We mashed through several directors and found no one to captain the canoe, until Gary Nash noticed an untenured Cherokee ethnomusicologist on our search committee. Charlotte Heth became our academic clan mother over the next decade, as Indian and non-Indian scholars began to constellate around solid research and teaching. We worked and recruited a colleague and a student at a time. Vee Salabiye, our Diné librarian, found a Hidatsa graduate student named Jim Young to help edit the *Journal,* and eventually the young Ojibwe sociologist from Harvard, Duane Champagne, took the director's reins. Duane's leadership carried the center and the *Journal* into international prominence—not without healthy debate. "The day-long cold hard rain drove / like sun through all the cedar sky / we had that late fall" is how Jim Welch recalls surviving Blackfeet winters in the blood. These were years of promise, grit, growth, turmoil, and enthusiasm filled with national symposia, administrative meltdown, intercultural dialogue, and guest lecturers that featured the likes of Vine Deloria, Jr., Alfonso Ortiz, Dave Reisling, Fritz Jennings, Bea Medicine, John Roulliard, Jack Forbes, Clara Sue Kidwell, Rupert Costo, and Wilcomb Washburn. It makes me smile inside to recall our debates. My San Juan coyote-amigo-in-arms, Al Ortiz, told me conspiratorially that, according to the Iroquois, you must have "skin seven thumbs thick" to do this work.

In 1977 I met Paula Gunn Allen, along with Joy Harjo and Barney Bush, at the first Modern Language Association (MLA) gathering of Native literary scholars and artists in Flagstaff. Paula buttonholed me with her black cigarette to gossip about Native networking, ethnic academic parity, and creative writing. Pugnacious, spunky, penetrant in her mixed-blood Laguna, Lakota, Scots, and Lebanese genius, Paula became my lifelong comrade and partner in poetic devilry. We drank more than a few bottles of Chardonnay, told outrageous lies and family tales, gossiped like ferrets, and laughed our way through academic stalemate, personal grief, and political outrage. Paula left San Francisco State, then UC Berkeley to join UCLA in the late 1980s, and my department has not been the same since.

Our upstart quarterly featured several of Paula's lively essays, and a maverick clutch of poems found their way into our Native American Poetry Series under the title *Shadow Country.* In 1992 Paula and I coedited a personal shortlist of three dozen contemporary tribal poets for *The Jacaranda Review* run by UCLA graduate students. Because of creative thinkers like Paula Allen, Linda Hogan, Mike Kabotie, Sherman Alexie, and Joy Harjo, Native verse has been a scholarly adjunct in the *Journal* for three and a half decades, and we have published fifteen poetry books in the Native American Series. "We lived with a hunger only solitude could afford," Bobbie Hill Whiteman wrote. Much of this early rough work found its way into *Native American Renaissance,* and this is the backstory of how that book got written.

Treaties were first designated "at-the-forest's edge" between pilgrim clearing and Native woods. Exchange "good goods" with us, the people asked newcomers. For Indian studies in the 1970s, reservation and urban borders marked the challenging draws of an intercultural, yet-to-be-mapped, crossover frontier—promising Native and newcomer dialogue stretching back tens of thousands of years, tribe to tribe, ethnic to émigré. Perhaps a human catalyst for a rebirthed Native/American studies lay in crisscrossing UCLA expertise with some forty campus colleagues from several dozen disciplines: to name but a few, Bill Bright in linguistics to Johannes Wilbert in anthropology, Melvin Seeman in sociology to Charlotte Heth and Ernest Siva in ethnomusicology, Kogee Thomas in library science to Carole Goldberg in law, Concepción Valadez in education to Jennie Joe in public health, Allegra Fuller-Snyder in dance to Bob Georges in folklore, Gary Nash and Norris Hundley in history to James Porter in music. These were intercultural, Nativist pioneers of the 1970s on campus, blooded and otherwise, scores to follow. They were my mentors, my friends, my beloved colleagues.

Teaching was the frontline reality check for all of us. A Native spark came from postradical students at large, so hungry for rhizomic local wisdom under the surface of imported American culture. Born of the spring 1970 campus riots, my first multidisciplinary catalogue offering of "Native American Voices" drew 127 aspirants from all disciplinary corners of the campus (and a few undisciplined hippies). *Old Shirts & New Skins,* Sherman Alexie quipped a generation later in our Native American Series. Certainly the UCLA tribal alchemy was jump-started early on by the personal Native genius of Allogan Slagle, N. Scott Momaday, Vine Deloria, Charlotte Heth, Paula Gunn Allen, Velma Salabiye, Jennie Joe, Alfonso Ortiz, Duane Champagne, Melissa Meyer, Hanay Geiogamah, Lee Ann Herald, Joy Harjo, Richie Stone, Lorenzo Baca, Dave Smith, Ruddy Buckman, Rebecca Tsosie, Greg Sarris, Rebecca Hernandez, and Paul Apodaca—Native students, staff, and faculty who touched me in deeply human and profoundly professional ways. Speaking their names is an epic roll call of heroes, explorers, coyotes, and savants.

By 1982 the center had started an American Indian Studies Master's Program, and a quarter century later we have graduated more than two hundred professionals in several dozen disciplines who serve as tribal judges and historians, work in public health and reservation resources, teach in public and private universities, write and lecture internationally. My first book, *Native American Renaissance,* was published in 1983 by the University of California Press. By the 1990s our Indian studies faculty offered major and minor degrees for undergraduates. These human successes are UCLA's legacy, our heritage keepers.

Certainly a small Native perk was sending professionals on missions back to the people and places we came from. Mine was payback Lakota respect to my adoptive Monroe family in northwest Nebraska—homage to the thousands of Pine Ridge and Rosebud Sioux who never graduated from high school, let alone went on to college. The interdependently poor Lakotas have no word for goodbye, and they'd rather see you come home. *Dok-shá*, Sioux 'Skins quip for "so long, bro"—literally, *pay you back later*. Dawson No Horse sang out in an all-night *yuwipi* ceremony thirty years ago at Lake Wakpamni in South Dakota, "We're gonna make it up as we go along, generation to generation, addin' on an' addin' on." I've never forgotten Dawson's healing faith or tribal vision or spiritual blessing.

As a national flashpoint of interdisciplinary Native scholarship, the *American Indian Culture and Research Journal* was our torch and beacon, and my literary work became an offshoot. Intellectual debates were feisty, cultural exchanges ran risky, and everyone learned something outside given disciplinary parameters. Whatever kept all the boundary-crossers and their hybrid scholarship moving, we survived. And some four and a half million Native Americans outlasted 97 percent genocidal slaughter over the past five hundred years of colonial invasion. These are not just postcolonial, but rather post-Holocaustal times, and local acculturations vary. The several million descendants of five hundred decimated cultures don't necessarily agree on regional terms of reconstruction or welcome no-bloods into the debated pan-Indian camp, but we're all still reconfiguring.

Native American Renaissance marked a neophyte's attempt to set benchmarks for writerly discussions to come. Early chapters surveyed Native American cultural history and tribal oral traditions, but the study focused on contemporary publication by Indians, as stated upfront. I couldn't cover the entire literary field, no more than any one scholar could do justice to the European Renaissance from England to Italy, so I focused on Native writers coming into print since N. Scott Momaday's 1969 Pulitzer Prize for *House Made of Dawn*. These artists were my college-educated contemporaries with similar creative training and modernist literary interests. I felt we shared some common ground beyond cultural gaps.

To answer skeptics carping that these tribal authors didn't spring out of nowhere, recall that the word "renaissance" means *re*birth, not initial conception. As *Native American Renaissance* acknowledges, literacy grows out of oral traditions. No text is penned in newfound literacy without speech, prayer, story, dance, and song layering the evolving print medium. Homer rose from ancient Greek song-poetry and epic narrative, Christian texts coalesced from Hebraic and Fertile Crescent religious complexes, and Virgil wrote from Roman papyrus and stones. The sixteenth-century European Renaissance revisited Greek and Roman classics to spring Leonardo, Michelangelo, Cervantes, Brueghel, Montaigne, Shakespeare, and countless other artists in regional cultural genius. None of this would have transpired without scientific and artistic breakthroughs ancient in the Middle East. Four centuries later, the Irish Renaissance allowed Yeats, Joyce, Synge, Shaw, Russell, and Wilde to emerge from Anglo suffocation with transcribed Celtic songs, stories, speeches, histories, and ethnic pride millennia in the making. The 1920s Harlem Renaissance was rebirthed from hundreds of evolving years among thousands of African tribal oral traditions brought in chains across the Big Water to the New World. None of these rebirths obviated what came before; each used prior cultural history to advance contemporary literacy. Shakespeare, Yeats, and Langston Hughes served their people and times as imaginative pioneers in ongoing cultural rebirthings.

I counted on echoes of F. O. Matthiessen arguing that the 1855 post-Colonial breakaway from British and European royalism—Emerson, Thoreau, Whitman, Melville, Hawthorne, Poe—constituted an *American Renaissance* of reasserted self-identity, regional speech, pioneer literacy, and national pride. Early on, the broad recognition of writers such as N. Scott Momaday, Jim Welch, Leslie Silko, Simon Ortiz, Paula Gunn Allen, Joy Harjo, Roberta Hill, Gerald Vizenor, and Jim Barnes only tipped the iceberg. Hundreds of Native writers were flooding into print in the 1970s, and hundreds more have continued to thrive for decades, looking forward as contemporary word-crafters in international print from oral traditions of tribal song-poetry, ceremonial dance, traditional prayer, historical narrative, cultural folklore, cautionary tales, how-to stories, and the ubiquitous trickster mixtures of comic folly and how-not-to allegories. The past informs the present, and little is lost, only transformed. All this is clearly stated in *Native American Renaissance* and my work beyond.

Other scholars and emerging creative talents were hot on the trail, Native and otherwise, and I followed up with academic and field research in *The Good Red Road: Passages into Native America* (Harper & Row, 1987), *Indian Humor: Bicultural Play in Native America* (Oxford, 1993), *Sing with the Heart of a Bear: Fusions of Native and American Poetry, 1890–1999* (University of California, 2000), and *Speak Like Singing: Classics of Native America Literature* (University of New Mexico, 2007). I went off-grid to publish a novel about off-reservation 'Skins in my Panhandle Nebraska hometown, *The Year the Sun Died* (PublishAmerica, 2006), and continued for over four decades in English to teach, edit, write, and serve on UCLA faculty committees for the American Indian Center.

Colleagues across the nation were trenching the front lines of a tribal literary assault on canonical privilege. Ken Roemer, Kay Sands, Andrew Wiget, Lavonne Ruoff, Michael Castro, Del Hymes, William Bevis, Alan Velie, Gretchen Bataille, Robert Bieder, Jim Ruppert, Michael Dorris, Jarold Ramsey, Barre Toelken, Keith Basso, and Gary Witherspoon, among other scholars, were doing the good, hard work of teaching and writing about specific texts and issues. John Bierhorst, Dennis Tedlock, Larry Evers, Ken Rosen, Joseph

Bruchac, Brian Swann, Arnold Krupat, Geary Hobson, Peter Nabokov, Duane Niatum, Jerome Rothenberg, Dexter Fisher, and John Milton were editing primary anthologies of literary and scholarly works for our interactive teaching and research. The new Native writers didn't come out of nowhere, and I was only one among many readers interested in tracking and celebrating a historical turning point. As stated, the controversial "renaissance" was an evolving rebirth of cultural awakening.

There were precious few Native literary critics, to be sure. My Native graduate students focused on the social sciences, for the most part. The English majors I trained, such as Allogan Slagle, Rebecca Tsosie, Lee Ann Herald, and Richie Stone, went on to law school, with the exception of Judith Volborth, the Apache poet, and Greg Sarris, who eventually returned to UCLA with a Stanford doctorate in modern thought and culture and taught next-door to me in the 1990s, in tandem with Paula Gunn Allen, Hanay Geiogamah, and Joy Harjo. Greg has produced novels, stories, criticism, plays, movies, and Native anthologies, while serving as elected tribal chair of the Graton Branch of Coastal Pomo/Miwok for twenty years running. We still talk regularly.

Ours was a time of great energy and enthusiasm; this was revolutionary work in the academy, as a cultural and political renaissance swept reservation and off-reservation life. It seemed no secret that tribal voices were re-emerging across the land, and writers sharpened the cutting edge of ongoing cultures, from Vine Deloria, Jr., and Paula Gunn Allen, to Scott Momaday and Alfonso Ortiz, to Louise Erdrich and Luci Tapahonso, to Sherwin Bitsui and David Treuer today. The inevitable scrum for recognition and promotion ensued, and several generations of talents and opinions have broken more trail into the twenty-first century. Over a thousand Native writers are in print today. They have spawned a cottage industry of born-again critics.

I don't want to debate who's in or out, blooded enough or not, pioneer or postcolonial, but rather to honor the great-hearted reawakenings among Native cultures during our lifetime. In October 2009, UCLA celebrated forty years of American Indian studies with a national symposium. To support the Indian Center and its enduring work, my doctoral student Kathleen Washburn and I were asked to select and edit thirty-one historic essays from the *American Indian Culture and Research Journal* to be published for the symposium in *Gathering Native Scholars: UCLA's Forty Years of American Indian Culture and Research.*

Since people hear what they want and want their own heartsongs within earshot, let me speak from *Native American Renaissance* forward now, citing literary voices about race, language, and culture, testifying to half a century of Native witness in my academic career. Let's "sing with the heart of a bear" at our honoring the best, on and off the rez. At the heart of any tribal language, singers give lyric accent to narrative speech. Where I come from, Lakota *wichasa wakan* allow Old Man Bear to chant through the heart's eye, *cante ista.*

"For reals," the Navajo kids say near my present home among northern New Mexico Dinétah. Call mine an elder's search for homeplace, voice, and kinship, back to my raising up times with Lakotas in northwest Nebraska, forward to teaching UCLA American Indian studies for over forty years, and nearing retirement to Santa Fe, New Mexico, among Southwest desert nations. I live a stone's throw from the Institute of American Indian Cultures in the Rio Grande's fertile crescent of Native nations. "Once in his life a man ought to concentrate his mind upon the remembered earth, I believe," is how N. Scott Momaday ends *The Way to Rainy Mountain.* At my age, any number of remembered Native earths means dreaming culture as personal heritage, making a grounded life worth living, and witnessing injustice as shared public grief. The Navajos designate this *Hozhó*—truth, beauty, balance, goodness—along with an old-fashioned sense of fair play, dignity, and justice. We can't go forward as a people without hope; we must remember genocidal crimes against all humanity in order not to repeat them. We should make due reparations. And let us not forget the responsibilities of history, the personal trials of time, the cultural riches of communal memory. Nick Black Elk, a Lakota healer in my hometown, remembers his Great Vision: "[W]hen I looked behind me there were ghosts of people like a trailing fog as far as I could see—grandfathers of grandfathers and grandmothers of grandmothers without number. And over these a great Voice—the Voice that was the South—lived, and I could feel it silent. And as we went the Voice behind me said: 'Behold a good nation walking in a sacred manner in a good land!'" Call this what the poets call the heroic survival of tribal peoples never meant to survive. In this sense Americans are all miners' canaries.

Tribal literacies are laced with constructive narratives and cautionary tales, raven creation stories and coyote gaffes. Biological evolution keys on species-crossing and gender-pairing; ethnocentrism rejects the Other as outsider. Remember the old-time tribal grace of hospitality to strangers. "Shake hands hello," the Diné say. Try fantasizing cultural fusion while resisting racial xenophobia to stretch the tribal hemispheres of the mind toward that troubling concept of reconciliation. Speak the tongues of your people and compassionately translate those of others. Anyone who does not know a second language, Goethe said, does not know his own. And that includes the language of other-than-human beings like animals, plants, crawlers, stars, spirits, and stones. *"Do we ramble when we speak in tongues?"* Sherwin Bitsui shape-shifts from Diné to English. The Navajos say that beauty begins at the tip of the tongue and leaves its mark in the trail of the wind.

Borders are the doors of cultural interface, mutual learning, and exogamous action, not comfort zones of the moral majority, regardless of tribe, wealth, or skin. Place human margin over public mainstream, extracurricular courage over centrist assumptions. "The morning was clear. A good road led on. So there was nothing to do but cross the water, and bring her home," Lipsha personally decides his belonging at the end of Louise Erdrich's *Love Medicine*. Race means more an active social construct than a biological quantum, and fusions outsource curiosities for trial-and-error treks through the unknown. Venture something, think outside the box, travel by heart and mind, maybe write a poem on race as faux wrestling. "Because My Father Always Said He Was the Only Indian Who Saw Jimi Hendrix Play 'The Star-Spangled Banner' at Woodstock," Sherman Alexie riffs in *Old Shirts & New Skins*. Conceive ethnicity as a calling in the blood and grease for the soul's skillet. "That night the moon slipped a notch, hung / black for just a second, just long enough," Jim Welch sings blue surviving, "for wet black things to sneak away our cache / of meat. To stay alive this way, it's hard."

Imagine tribal community to be a thing of deep roots, living names, interactive animisms, and dissolving horizons. Find your homeplace, what the Lakotas call *tióte,* your ancestral past and callings beyond. Regard cultural politics as a poor excuse for tribal kinship, sovereignty as every citizen's legacy. Who's in or out is not so important as who's listening and learning, finally, and who's paying attention and why. Respect the old ones, help the unfortunate, protect the young. Honor all life and oppose its abuses. Beyond ethnic nationalism, Red-on-Red exclusions beget White-on-White backlashes. Indeed, everyone's blood is red. "You don't write off all white people," the mixed-blood healer Betonie says in Silko's *Ceremony,* "just like you don't trust all Indians." Think of the *musteno*'s agile strength and Mendel's botanical experiments with crossing petunias, nature's hybrid seed strengths; consider the inbred travesties of European royalty. Trust sunrise and stone voice, celebrate moon Beautyway and star Spiritway, honor bear heart and coyote wit, smell sage incense and cedar smoke. And consider narrative as a prose gloss on the heart's true lyrics, so witnessed in Joy Harjo's "Eagle Poem":

> We are truly blessed because we
> Were born, and die soon within a
> True circle of motion,
> Like eagle rounding out the morning
> Inside us.
> We pray that it will be done
> In beauty.
> In beauty.

Native American Renaissance? Indigenous resistance, resonance, and revival for all of us crossing into the circle of tribal circles.

The controversy around my 1983 *Native American Renaissance* tilted on Leslie Silko's sniping that tribal cultures didn't spring out of nowhere. The "reborn" translative argument for oral cultures evolving into modernist literacy, beginning with N. Scott Momaday's Pulitzer Prize for *House Made of Dawn*, got lost somewhere. The Nativist field and literary legends in the making—Scott Momaday, Simon Ortiz, Paula Gunn Allen, James Welch, Leslie Silko, Joy Harjo, Linda Hogan, and Louise Erdrich—began to gain national recognition by the late 1970s. What accounts for the interglobal currency of Native writers from James Welch and Louise Erdrich through Sherman Alexie and Sherwin Bitsui, as chronicled four decades later in *Speak Like Singing: Classics of Native American Literature*?

Momaday's *The Way to Rainy Mountain* fused Hemingway's spare genius with the cultural insights of Clyde Kluckhohn and Isak Dinesen in an ethnographic memoir setting the benchmark for the genre. Never had tribal thought, folkloric recall, and frontier history been so seamlessly woven together. So, too, the 1969 Pulitizer Prize–winning *House Made of Dawn* was unlike any novel I had ever read, and its mysterious alterity spun me back to Sioux differences in Alliance. Perhaps the narrative runs closest to Faulkner's unregenerate South in swirling tone, impressionist images, and fractured structure. The story of Abel's desert mountain origins in New Mexico, his war nightmares in Germany, his drunken violence toward an albino witch, his relocation in the Native slums of downtown Los Angeles, and his ceremonial run back to his grandfather showed me that here was an authentic and deeply damaged Native America, still coming home. It was the job of the novelist to document this cultural history personally, the work of the critic to bring attention to the creative spark and cultural contexts. The challenge of all Americans was to heal the country and its people, particularly Natives in America. This work would go on for a lifetime and beyond.

Jim Welch's 1974 Montana tour de force, *Winter in the Blood*, cut through the patriotic fustian and sentimental crap of a bloodless American frontier with searing candor. The nameless Blackfeet narrator staggers from bar to bar, chasing an Indian girlfriend who stole his rifle and razor. He uncovers the tragic deaths of his brother, Mose, and father, John First Raise. He details the spit-dirt epiphanies of ranch life on the plains through Indian eyes and laughs purgatively in the face of evil banality. He buries his nameless grandmother with her tobacco pouch for the spirit journey. Kin to Ray Carver and John Steinbeck, Welch's novels and poetry changed American literature the way Balzac changed French reading, or Eliot fractured English pastoral verse with urban wasteland detritus. There was no going back from these literary visions.

After publishing James Welch and Hyemeyohsts Storm, Harper & Row in 1975 launched a Native American literary series with sixteen Native poets in *Carriers of the Dream Wheel*, the first such anthology of contemporary verse by Native Americans across the country (average age thirty-one at publication). Acoma Pueblo word mason Simon Ortiz built walls by hand with his father while cobbling the lines of his free-verse, confessional poetry. Joy Harjo blazed an androgynous trail for women warriors who had their own horses.

Scott Momaday latticed his tensile lines with meter and rhyme, and Bobbi Hill cadenced her stanzas with the breath-metrics taught her at the University of Montana by Richard Hugo, who was also blank-verse mentor to Jim Welch. Among the hundreds of gifted Native poets, Choctaw Jim Barnes, Oklahoma poet laureate thirty-four years later, scalloped his lines with stone-carved totems and finely rhymed metrics: "Two fish, / definitely carp, / picassoed in stone." Barnes writes in traditional forms, counting his measures, constructing narrative lyrics that draw a fine thread from Wordsworth and Frost to Seamus Heaney and James Welch. Jim Barnes grew up Gaelic-Anglo-Choctaw in what was once Indian Territory, and in some respects still cores the Native heart of things, a living frontier of catfish sloughs, heaving prairies, canebrake thickets, tufted skies, squirrel hollows, émigrés and relocated Natives, mixed-blood croppers and dirt-poor hamlets. His "Contemporary Native American Literature" speaks for the rebirth of tribal literacy in our time:

> For one thing, you can believe it:
> the skin chewed soft enough to wear,
> the bones hewn hard as a totem
> from hemlock. It's a kind of scare-
>
> crow that will follow you home night.
> You've seen it ragged against a field,
> but you seldom think, at the time,
> to get there it had to walk through hell.

The range of this tribal gathering was staggering; the birth of a Native American Renaissance was clearly upon the land and people. Leslie Silko's *Ceremony* in 1977 protested war with the healing pilgrimage of a mixed-blood Laguna veteran Tayo finding his way home through nurturing women and compassionate men, procreatively empowering goddesses and wily healers. No one has ever written so indigenously from the Southwest landscape of desert bajadas and mountain meadows, dry arroyos and spring ponds, dragonfly and coyote, sagebrush and ocotillo cactus.

One woman's voice rises above some thousand Indian writers in the country, her lyric pitch grounded in narrative grist. By now, Louise Erdrich has published thirteen novels, seven young adult/children's books, two works of nonfiction essays, three books of poetry, one short story collection, and two books coauthored with Michael Dorris. No less than Momaday, Welch, or Silko, Erdrich's narrative poetry sisters her lyric prose with verse outtakes from the novels. Her poetry collection *Jacklight* debuted the same year as the novel *Love Medicine* in 1984, a year after *Native American Renaissance*. In a narrative ribboned with love as medicine, Erdrich combines Native American resurgence with feminist liberation. She fuses tribal rebirth with a woman's nurturing sexuality and comic trickster graces. Love softens the edges of human pain; mothering rescues the lost, abandoned, or bastard child. Forgiveness and understanding keep people together, for the most part, family-focusing human priorities. Love then is the reality of human interaction, intimacy the glue, romance the bonding "dream stuff." And the seductive come-hither of play and coy intrigue of courting hooks the reader—engaged, amused, intrigued, and tolerant of six first-person participant narratives. The interwoven distances of eight third-person points of view blend intimacy with authorial omniscience. The author shifts inside, outside, and through the three interlocking generations of Kashpaw/Nanapush/Lamartine Métis or mixed-blood Indians, comic epic romance across half a century of tribal history—an expanded, updated way to Turtle Mountain, all as collective family stories about love's mixed medicines.

Poetic prose crosses into prose poetry, as Erdrich's cultures mix German-American and pantribal Chippewa-French complexes. Clichés of noble savage, dusky maiden, and ruthless pioneer give way to the reality of mestizo, literate, Indian-White collaboration on the Midwest's High Plains. Erdrich's verse seems more character-as-plot than Momaday's modernist lyrics or Welch's chiseled metrics. Her poetic settings trail the breakdown lanes of North Dakota from Dairy Queen to deep woods, even more prosaically than Silko's Southwest riparian arroyos or Linda Hogan's Oklahoma home-bound verse, still remaining mythic and modern from spotlit northern clearings just outside the forest's edge. Her diction turns on prosaic building as in Paula Gunn Allen or the younger Sherman Alexie, but hers is more a thickening texture using rhythm to cadence lines. Her metaphors layer naturally with daily rural lifeforms of turtle, cow, deer, mustang (horse and car), cane, or geese. Her poetic tools—heightened diction, rhythmic tension, imagistic mystery, cadenced memory—all work to serve the verse-story as character-and-place on the go, as her baker's dozen novels register working-class epiphanic dramas of cousins and kin, love and disease, old and new combinations of Native American lives. Over a quarter century of publishing, she has proved the most prodigious and nationally recognized Native writer of the tribal renaissance.

A mixed-blood artist conscious of Indian-Anglo fissures, Linda Hogan writes herself into one person, Chickasaw relocatee to Nebraska pioneer, as a modern *Native* American. Chickasaw descendent, she reads the landscape for signs of life damage and renewal. Hogan listens to the land's rhythms and feels for its wounds, talks with and about plants, and especially animals, in her poems and novels. Combining spiritual intuition with environmental activism, the poet listens over technology that deadens hearing. She asks blessing, grace, and courage from her totemic guardians—bear, wolf, raven, whale, coyote, blackbird. No less than any spiritual scientist—caretaker of the natural world and natural part of humans—she listens and observes the Other for empathic understanding and interspecies exchanges. Stories, places, events, revelations—from animal magic, to historical markings. to strange happenings—tie her people tribally together. Her writing has evolved over four decades, from steadily emerging poems, richly documented novels, trenchant environmental essays, and a post-traumatic memoir, *The Woman Who Watches Over the World*. Linda Hogan has proved herself one of the most prolific and committed writers of the tribal renaissance.

Greg Sarris, of mixed Pomo/Modoc heritage, has written literary criticism, cultural biography, prose fiction, stage drama, political discourse, and screenplay, while chairing the re-acknowledged Federated Indians of Gratan Rancheria for over twenty years and teaching in three universities. He advanced in record time from a 1991 Stanford doctorate in modern thought and literature to full professor of English at his alma mater, UCLA, while coproducing film documentaries, publishing his own work, and anthologizing California Indian writing. He held a creative writing and literature chair at Loyola Marymount University, then a tribally endowed chair at Sonoma State University in northern California, where he was born. The critical essays in *Keeping Slug Woman Alive* (1993) set an academic benchmark for Native resistance to acculturation. The next year *Weaving the Dream*, the life story of Mabel McKay, legendary Pomo basketmaker and tribal medicine woman, was published by the University of California Press in their Portraits of American Genius Series, centering Native healing in today's world. Sarris adapted an award-winning screenplay, *Grand Avenue*, from his collected short fiction about Santa Rosa, California, by the same title, and then wrote a three-generational novel, *Watermelon Nights*, about off-reservation coastal Indians scrapping for ethnic self-respect in a world that had forgotten about them. No one ignores or forgets about this writer, teacher, and activist. His talents are broadly diverse, his energy unflagging, and his work always moving forward. Sarris is presently writing children's literature based in California cultural history, working on a collection of prose fiction, and battling as veteran tribal chair to build the first Native-run casino in the Bay Area.

Leading a second wave of writers, Indian X-generation Sherman Alexie tears the scabs off frontier history, from his early short fiction, *The Lone Ranger and Tonto Fistfight in Heaven*, to his recent collection, *Blasphemy*. He holds out for a Native uprising in the popular arts and feeds off public controversy—glossy magazine articles that taunt White Men who can't drum or dance, trickster movies that turn Westerns inside out and stereotypes upside down, short stories that cut to the ethnocentric chase, novels that fuel fictive race riots in Seattle, poetry that challenges all the rules of form and manner with censored diction, pop clichés, and edged syntax. Alexie is the *enfant sauvage* of contemporary ethnic writing, Native trickster with wicked lip—breed Spokane and Coer d'Alene, nobody's Tonto, nobody's tenth little Indian. The cheeky gadfly speaks for a grunge generation of off-reservation, mainstream-schooled Native activists who want to make movies, reclaim tribal rights, update history, play in rock bands, court fame, and publish in high-paying magazines.

Sherwin Bitsui was born in 1975 in Fort Defiance, Arizona, in the heart of Dinétah. This youngest member of the Native renaissance writes with the incendiary charge, visionary drive, musing spirit, and language passion of an emerging classical poet. The poet does not offer set text, sculpted as the lines set up, so much as crystalline catalysts or generative "seeds," he says, to take root and grow in intercultural landscape between town and tribe. In 2005 Bitsui was chosen by the Poetry Society of America among the twenty best emerging poets nationwide. Radioactively charged and formally unstable by ordinary verse standards, his lines leap as surds in sequence, and he thinks through irreducible images. "Do we ramble when we speak in tongues?" His verse fractals defy pattern and break trail through a contemporary wasteland of *Shapeshift*. His debut book of poems is a landmark gathering for yet a third generation of artists reborn over half a century of the tribal renaissance.

Listen to Native and nonblooded voices asking some hard, provocative questions around progressive tribal literacy today. Where have we come? What have we learned? What lies ahead? Is there a future for Native American literature outside chosen privileges of the few who eschew cultural crossings or interethnic collaboration?

One imminent, ongoing fear is that the populist academy will co-opt and colonize Indian studies away from the flesh-and-blood cultures. Indian nations require honorable respect, practical research, and pragmatic follow-up to maintain sovereignty and to evolve intertribally. Paranoia is no Native fantasy or tribal stranger: there are legitimate fears about head-tripping theory and forgoing immediate needs of health care, basic education, land, timber, hunting, fishing, and water rights, economic development, gaming sovereignty, literacy and professional opportunity, spiritual continuity, erasure of stereotypes, religious freedom, ancestral repatriation, historical continuity, and reasonable accommodation to change. Academia festers with careerism, and given notable exceptions, those who can't teach or do research get paid extra to boss the place or make trouble. Remember you don't trust all Indians or write off all whites.

The fallout can be disastrous to multicultural discourse and interdepartmental programs as separatism drives a stake through cooperative progress. Dissed whites take flight when essentialists claim academic blood rights or Red-for-Red dog soldiers look down on faux kinship. I am exhausted calling out the Lakota blessing *Mitak' oyasin* or "All My Relatives," though I still believe we're all in this together. Pay attention to elder wisdom and grace. "Search yourselves, in your lives, for the meaning," the Pomo dreamer Essie Parrish told a young Greg Sarris—don't drop words "here and there like old clothes." It's not too much to ask for decency and civility, as three decades ago

Charlotte Heth gathered scholars, leaders, and students at the UCLA Indian Center—a rebirth of reason and compassion for all-nations discussions of critical Native concerns. "Blessed / are those who listen," Linda Hogan writes of her ghosted Chickasaw ancestors, "when no one is left to speak."

These days Craig Womack argues for closed ranks in *Red on Red: Native American Literary Separatism* (1999) and joins his cohorts, Jace Weaver and Robert Warrior, in *American Indian Literary Nationalism* (2005), as Elizabeth Cook-Lynn trashes "reconciliation" between Natives and newcomers in *Anti-Indianism in Modern America* (2001). As pack leader, Womack aligns ethnic cleansing of Native American studies with the 1813–1814 Muskogee Red Stick War, when Creek purists with red-painted war clubs murdered hundreds of their own suspected tribal collaborators and all the whites they could lay hands on, resulting in a decade of bloodshed and the violent intervention of Andy Jackson's federal troops. The internecine Creek war guttered in a disputed 1825 Treaty of Indian Springs, the execution of Chief William Macintosh by his own people, and pyrrhic tribal meltdown. "Integration, acceptance, and assimilation to literary norms will no longer be our highest goal," Womack trumpets in separatist bravado. "Native critics will turn toward more disruptive tactics." Indian academic beware: could Puritans burn the wrong witches or Skinwalker essentialists terrorize hapless locals? Who will be left to read Native writers? In a pedagogic civil war, whatever the disputed stakes, the tribe's own people may get trapped behind the Buckskin Curtain or outside the essentialist tarp, since many (including Womack by his own admission) are not natively literate speakers, let alone readers, and more than half the Creek Nation is no longer indigenous to southeast Oklahoma. Dissing others, my ex-UCLA Muskogee colleague, Joy Harjo, says, poisons her own mixed Red-White bloodlines. "I've gone through the stage where I hated everybody who wasn't Indian, which meant part of myself," she tells Joe Bruchac in *Survival This Way*. "We're not separate. We're all in this together."

Stop and think about all this. The old-timers have learned that Indian cultures are indeed tenacious, but friable and susceptible to co-option within and without. We have learned that trash talk whips like wildfire through delicate alliances across cultural divides. We have learned that "blood" purity can be used as racial ploy, no less than ethnic eugenics. Genealogy is but one of many cultural links with historic custom, marital fusing, adoptive kinship, clan crossing, tribal relocation, and community service in determining "the people." Everyone counts when human capital is critical. We have learned despite the obvious shortcomings of academics, churchmen, and politicians—as Vine Deloria checked his own diatribe on Custer dying for our sins—that religion, government, and the university offer high-density cores to discuss issues, hash out policies, initiate necessary research, and apply tried-and-true innovative, or hybrid, approaches to solve mutual problems, from reservation to urban Indian. Along these tribal lines our work showcases critical research for scientific scrutiny, community use, and public debate. We simply cannot waste these Native resources.

The intelligence cache is immense. Our rebirthing students are our future, and their work proves or disproves our scholarly and human vision. Empowerment seems key—power to all the peoples—and Indian power flows selfless as a medicine pipe. Tribal living teaches giving back. One hard lesson comes with learning to discern friends from enemies, true allies from subversives to the common cause. "Reinventing the enemy's language," as Joy Harjo has documented, does not turn on trashing people of good heart and keen mind, whatever skin. And don't forget to smile. The Navajo poet Sherwin Bitsui says that if he could be reborn as an action hero, he'd come back as Captain Asterisk.

We have known the rise and fall of scores of Indian studies programs nationally. Directors, movements, charismatics, policies, tropes, born-agains, spiritualists, and autodidacts fire up and flame out. Scholars change their minds, colleagues shift allegiances, tribal councils try new approaches, politicians promise, stonewall, and betray historic concerns. Scholarly books argue every shift of angle in the four-winds circle. Journals, broadsides, newsletters, petitions, dissertations, and manifestos come and go. Student movements muster and melt down as graduates move on and greener thinkers enter the debate.

Elders see progressive minds trying to bring retrograde thinkers up-to-date. Hip 'Skins rake tribal mossbacks. Innovators work with traditionalists, and at times everyone gets more than a little impatient with the loss of faith, or lack of progress, or contaminated purity of intent. An exasperated Paula Allen once told me she'd had it with tribal backbiting and narrow-minded gossip, and she was turning in her Indian card. Near the end of his life at a Nativist conference in Albuquerque, Vine Deloria, Jr., referred to quibbling scholars as academic house pets. Casualties of the cause, some quit the good fight or think they can find better things to do. Some just give up and go away. These losses are heartbreaking.

Ours is a time of retrospective accounting, a crisis of self-identity for the newly initiated, a lifelong haul for those in the middle. Consider data for renewed hope. Over fifty thousand Native students are enrolled in higher education today, and over a thousand writers are in print. In my literary field N. Scott Momaday, Joy Harjo, Louise Erdrich, Paula Gunn Allen, Gerald Vizenor, Linda Hogan, Leslie Silko, Greg Sarris, Luci Tapahonso, and Sherman Alexie command hundreds of thousands of readers at home and abroad. Native thinkers have received Fulbright, MacArthur, Ford, Rockefeller, Guggenheim, Wordcraft Circle, American Book Award, National Endowment for the Arts, American Council of Learned Societies, Modern Language Association, National Book Critics Circle Award, Native Writers' Circle of the Americas, and Pulitzer Prize distinctions. Over a thousand tribal cultures from Alaska to Alabama are reclaiming silenced languages, repressed histories, co-opted politics, forbidden religions, stolen land and mineral rights. Recognition and respect have been hard won and long coming.

The average Native life span has risen twenty years over the past forty years, family incomes more than doubled, health services multiplied, and education profiles moved steadily upward. Diabetes, alcoholism, malnutrition, illiteracy, obesity, domestic violence, suicide, and heart disease statistics have fallen dramatically, as frybread and Coors are countered by Native grains and game. Health centers have proven a life option to bars. Hollywood potboilers and sports mascots have been scrubbed of clichés and stereotypes. The Stanford Indians are today the Cardinal, the Jeep Cherokee has morphed into a Hummer. Yet rust never sleeps: Red Man chaw, Crazy Horse beer, Washington Redskins, and Apache helicopters still buzz around. Some reservations are not low-income, but still no-income economies. Ill-gotten or not, gaming has brought three hundred tribes windfall revenues to critical needs around health care, schools, hospitals, housing, transportation, community services, and public interaction. With still a ways to go, things are getting better.

Take none of this for granted. We are either heading toward a future of cross-cultural respect and collective learning, human empowerment and individual distinction, or end times for all. The average Pine Ridge male lives only a fraction longer than do Haitians in the Western Hemisphere.

Thirty years ago, on Second Mesa, the Hopi elder Thomas Banyaca, Sr., warned me on the good red road that one day it would "all come crashes," if we two-leggeds don't wake up and pay attention. Ghost Dancers may skirmish with the Rapture. Just as the world can no longer wait for palliatives to nationalist slaughter, religious hijacking, racial discrimination, resource squandering, and global warming, so Indian studies needs a healthy dose of self-examination, a clear-eyed recommitment to the needs of all the people (not just my people), and a reinspired idealism to hang tight when things get rough, "for reals."

Four decades of Nativist research in my lifetime range from history to public health, literature to biology, political science to linguistic translation, religion to repatriation, Red blues to tribal ceremony. The international ethnic debate still offers an all-tribal symposium for democratically airing differences, clearing cultural debris, and striking new trails through old controversies. Our diverse life work has deepened by way of its all-color voices. Our spirits have risen with its inspirations.

Today we can see an ongoing tribal renaissance through to renewed beginnings for all our children's children. This is the way we all got started. This is the courage of the ancients and the wisdom of the elders. This is the hope of the young. And such is the spirit of the cultural offerings gathered for all the people. "Grandfather, pity me," the High Plains Sun Dancers chant. "I want to live." *Hetchétu alóh!*

The Things I Love about Pine Ridge, South Dakota, are
the yucca hills
clumped with buffalo grass
and soapweed
swaling above pothole lakes
the long-hair ponies
running away in the wind
and the wind soughing
through heart-shaped cottonwood leaves
the Cuny Badlands
with open sandstone lesions
and clay thumbs
along drybed alkali creeks
the scrub pines
and jacktail deer
the prairie chickens
and dung mice
the sky the sky the sky
massed with blue
and fractured clouds
all colors of loss and light

the charcoal roadside junked cars
torched for the hell of it
and speed limit signs
bullet-riddled as spent beer cans
the Jack and Jill derelicts
with sandpaper eyes
and more fisted scars
than tears at Wounded Knee
the memories of bloodshed
that weep the stars down
and the terrors
that pitiful few remember
the old friends
walking stoned from grade-school
and the five stillborns
my brother buried by hand
saber thoughts
ripping conscience from indifference
and blanket-ass jibes
turned the other way
the country's manifest avarice

for territorial freedom
and gutless chicanery
that came flooding after

the wagon wheels
deep in the rut of greed
and cindered teepees
slant in the lying wind

the survival of a people
butchered with bison
the swarming homesteaders
still not at home

the whole goddamn pack
of rabid swindles and lies
and the fact
that we're here today to talk about it.
        Kenneth Lincoln

Contributors

Kimberly M. Blaeser, a professor at the University of Wisconsin, Milwaukee, teaches creative writing, Native American literature, and American nature writing. Her publications include three books of poetry: *Trailing You,* winner of the first-book award from the Native Writers' Circle of the Americas, *Absentee Indians and Other Poems,* and *Apprenticed to Justice.* Her scholarly study, *Gerald Vizenor: Writing in the Oral Tradition,* was the first Native-authored book-length study of an indigenous author. Of Anishinaabe ancestry and an enrolled member of the Minnesota Chippewa Tribe who grew up on the White Earth Reservation, Blaeser is also the editor of *Stories Migrating Home: A Collection of Anishinaabe Prose* and *Traces in Blood, Bone, and Stone: Contemporary Ojibwe Poetry.* Blaeser's poetry, short fiction, scholarship, and personal essays have been widely anthologized, with pieces translated into several languages and works included in exhibits and publications around the world, most recently in Norway, France, and Indonesia. Blaeser's recent scholarly publications include "Cannons and Canonization: American Indian Poetries through Autonomy, Colonization, Nationalism, and Decolonization" in *The Columbia Guide to American Indian Literatures of the United States.*

John Gamber, assistant professor of English and ethnic studies at Columbia University, received his B.A. from the University of California, Davis; his M.A. from California State, Fullerton (both in comparative literature); and his Ph.D. in American studies from the University of California, Santa Barbara. He has coedited *Transnational Asian American Literature: Sites and Transits* (2006) and published articles about the novels of Gerald Vizenor, Louis Owens, and Craig Womack. His current project examines the role of waste and pollution in late-twentieth-century U.S. ethnic literatures.

Linda Lizut Helstern is an associate professor of English at North Dakota State University, where she teaches Native and environmental literature and creative writing. She is the author of *Louis Owens* (2005) and numerous essays on contemporary Native writing. Her essays on Owens have appeared in such journals as *ISLE (Interdisciplinary Studies in Literature and the Environment), Southwestern American Literature,* and *Studies in American Indian Literatures.* The recipient of a North Dakota Humanities Council Remele Memorial Fellowship for research and public humanities, she has guest-edited a special issue of *Southwestern American Literature* on the atomic Southwest and is currently working on a project related to Native literature and traditional environmental knowledge.

Kathryn Hume is Edwin Erle Sparks Professor of English at Penn State University, University Park. She started academic life as a medievalist, but her more recent work has been on contemporary fiction. That includes *Pynchon's Mythography: An Approach to Gravity's Rainbow* (1987), *Calvino's Fictions: Cogito and Cosmos* (1992), *American Dream, American Nightmare: Fiction since 1960* (2000), and—more practical—*Surviving Your Academic Job Hunt: Advice for Humanities PhDs* (2005, rev. ed. 2010). Cornell University Press published her *Aggressive Fictions: Reading the Contemporary Novel* in 2011. Authors of special interest to her include Vonnegut, Coover, Pynchon, Reed, Burroughs, Kennedy, Vizenor, Wideman, and Powers.

Connie A. Jacobs has specialized in American Indian literature, an interest springing from her doctoral studies and dissertation on Ojibwe poet and novelist, Louise Erdrich. She is the author of *The Novels of Louise Erdrich: Stories of Her People* (2001) and a coeditor, along with Greg Sarris and James Giles, of *Approaches to Teaching the Works of Louise Erdrich*, published by the Modern Language Association (MLA) in 2004. Her forthcoming publication is *Re-Mapping Indian Country: New Stories for the Literary Canon*, coedited with Debra Barker. Her publishing and conference work includes not only that on Erdrich but also on Diné poets Esther Belin and Luci Tapahonso. Jacobs was a member of MLA's Committee on Community Colleges and is the outgoing vice president for the National Association of Ethnic Studies. She is the current president of the Durango Adult Education Center. She is a professor emerita at San Juan College in Farmington, New Mexico, where she was cofounder of the college's honors program and served as English Department chair.

Cristopher LaLonde is the author of *William Faulkner and the Rites of Passage* (1996) and *Grave Concerns, Trickster Turns: The Novels of Louis Owens* (2002), as well as numerous essays on Native American literature. He has published especially on Gerald Vizenor. He focuses on the "ceded landscape" and "literary activism" in his writings. He is professor of English and director of American studies at the State University of New York at Oswego.

A. Robert Lee was professor of American literature at Nihon University, Tokyo, until 2011, having previously taught for nearly three decades at the University of Kent, UK. His thirty or so book publications include *Designs of Blackness: Mappings in the Culture and Literature of Afro-America* (1998); *Multicultural American Literature: Comparative Black, Native, Latino/a and Asian American Fictions* (2003), which won an American Book Award in 2004;

United States: Re-viewing Multicultural American Literature (2009); *Gothic to Multicultural: Idioms of Imagining in American Literary Fiction* (2009); *Modern American Counter Writing: Beats, Outriders, Ethnics* (2010); and the sets *Herman Melville: Critical Assessments* (2001) and *African American Writing* (2013). His Native American work embraces *Shadow Distance: A Gerald Vizenor Reader* (1994); *Postindian Conversations* (1999) with Gerald Vizenor; *Loosening the Seams: Interpretations of Gerald Vizenor* (2000); *The Salt Companion to Jim Barnes* (2009); *Gerald Vizenor: Texts and Contexts* (2010) with Deborah Madsen; and the four-volume set, *Native American Writing* (2011). He has also published essays on Diane Glancy, Carter Revard, Simon Ortiz, Stephen Graham Jones, and D. L. Birchfield, as well as on Native fiction, poetry, and autobiography.

Kenneth Lincoln grew up in northwest Nebraska south of Wounded Knee. He taught contemporary and Native literatures for forty years at UCLA and retired to Santa Fe, New Mexico, in 2011. Since *Native American Renaissance* (1983), he has published *The Good Red Road: Passages into Native America* (1987), *Indi'n Humor* (1993), *Sing with the Heart of a Bear: Fusions of Native and American Poetry, 1800–1900* (2000), and many books in American Indian studies, as well as novels, poetry, and personal essays about Western Americana His latest books are *White Boyz Blues* (2007), *Speak Like Singing: Classics of Native American Literature* (2007), and *Cormac McCarthy: American Canticles* (2008).

James Mackay is a lecturer in comparative literatures at European University Cyprus. He edited *The Salt Companion to Diane Glancy* (2010), part of a series of companions to individual Native poets, and also edited a special issue of *Studies in American Indian Literatures* (23:4) that focused on tribal constitutions as literary documents. Forthcoming publications include the monograph, *Kleptographers*, for the University of Minnesota Press, on acts of imposture and exaggeration in works by purportedly Native writers; the coedited collection *Tribal Fantasies: Native Americans in the European Imaginary, 1900–2010* (with David Stirrup) for Palgrave; and a coedited issue of the *European Journal of American Culture* on Native American/European interactions (also with David Stirrup). His work centers on American Indian writing and literary theory, particularly regarding intersections of identity, nationality, and indigeneity. He has published articles on Gerald Vizenor, Diane Glancy, Anglo-Welsh poetry, hard-core pornography, Darwinist literary theory, digital humanities, and recent Native American travel poetry. He writes regularly for the *Guardian Online* on indigenous affairs.

Carol Miller holds a Ph.D. in American literature is from the University of Oklahoma, and she is an enrolled member of the Cherokee Nation of Oklahoma. She is a Morse-Alumni Distinguished Teaching Professor (Emerita) of American Indian studies and American studies, University of Minnesota, Twin Cities. She is a former chair of both departments and currently lives in Grand Marais, Minnesota. Her previous essays include "Telling the Indian Urban: Representations in American Indian Fiction" in *American Indians and the Urban Experience* (Alta Mira Press), and "Authority: The Native American Voices of Mourning Dove and Ella Cara Deloria" in *Multicultural Education, Transformative Knowledge, and Action,* edited by James A. Banks (Teachers College Press). Her reviews of John Milton Oskison's *The Singing Bird: A Cherokee Novel* and Robert Conley's *Cherokee Thoughts* have appeared in recent editions of the *American Indian Culture and Review Journal.*

Kathryn W. Shanley is a professor of Native American studies at the University of Montana, Missoula, and serves as special assistant to the provost for Native American and Indigenous Education. She has published extensively in the field of Native American literature and has edited *Native American Literature: Boundaries and Sovereignties* (2001) and a special issue of *Studies in American Indian Literature* (*SAIL*) that honored James Welch (2007). With Laura Beard, she is also coeditor of *Intertexts,* a special issue on "Gender in Indigenous Studies" (Fall 2010). Recently published articles appear in the *Handbook of North American Indians* (2008); *Gerald Vizener: Texts and Contexts* (2010); and *American Indians and Popular Culture* (2011). In addition to service on the national level with the Modern Language Association and the Ford Foundation, Dr. Shanley served as president of the Native American and Indigenous Studies Association from 2011 to 2012. She is a proud member of the Fort Peck Assiniboine (Nakoda) Tribe.

David Stirrup is senior lecturer in American literature and director of American studies at the University of Kent, UK. His monograph, *Louise Erdrich,* was published by Manchester University Press in 2010. He coedited a special issue of the *American Review of Canadian Studies* on the Canada--U.S. border (Summer 2010), and a special issue of the *European Journal of American Culture* on Native Americans in Europe (with James Mackay, Fall 2012). He also is coeditor of the volume *Tribal Fantasies: Native Americans in the European Imaginary, 1900–2010* with James Mackay (Palgrave, 2013). Other published works to date include articles and book chapters on the prose and poetry of a number of Native writers (including Louise Erdrich, Gordon Henry Jr., Susan Power, David Treuer, Joan Crate, and Andrew Blackbird); on indigenous rights discourse in the rhetoric of the European far right; and on artworks by several Native and non-Native artists, including Andrea Carlson, Star Wallowing Bull, Jim Denomie, Alan Michelson, and Alex Mackay. Current projects include a book-length study tracing the image/mark in contemporary Anishinaabeg literature, and a volume of essays titled *Enduring Critical Poses: Beyond Nation and History* (SUNY Press), which he is coediting with Gordon Henry Jr. He is lead investigator on a three-year Leverhulme Trust–funded network project entitled "Culture and the Canada-U.S. Border," and is also coediting a volume of essays called *Parallel Encounters: Culture at the Canada-US Border* (with Gillian Roberts).

Rebecca Tillett is a senior lecturer in American studies at the University of East Anglia, working in the field of American literature, ecocriticism, and postcolonial studies, with special reference to contemporary Native American writers and filmmakers. Her research interests include the relationships between literature and the environment, with a particular focus on environmental racism and environmental justice. She is the author of *Contemporary Native American Literature* (Edinburgh University Press, 2007) and coeditor (with Jacqueline Fear-Segal) of *Indigenous Bodies: Reviewing, Relocating, Reclaiming* (forthcoming 2013, SUNY Press). She is currently editing a collection, *Howling for Justice: Critical Perspectives on Leslie Marmon Silko's Almanac of the Dead*, and is completing a monograph on the same topic. She has published on a range of contemporary Native writers, both in edited collections and in journals such as *Studies in American Indian Literatures, Feminist Review, ARIEL: A Review of International English Literatures, The European Review of Native American Studies, The European Journal of American Culture,* and *Comparative American Studies.* Her current research project explores community responses to environmental racism and demands for environmental justice in recent multiethnic fiction and poetry of the American Southwest. With her colleague, Dr. Jacqueline Fear-Segal, she founded and runs the Native Studies Research Network UK.

Gina Valentino is an assistant professor of English at the University of Rhode Island. Her research interests in contemporary comparative ethnic and literary critical studies include class mobility; globalization and neoliberalism; gambling and U.S. culture; Native American, African American, and Chicano/a literature. She is coeditor of *Transnational Asian American Literature: Sites and Transitions* (2006). Her current book project, *Hustling: Work, Survival, and U.S. Literature in the New Economy,* analyses race and working-class identities in late-twentieth-century U.S. ethnic literatures.

Alan R. Velie is David Ross Boyd Professor of English at the University of Oklahoma. His 1969 class on Native American writers was the first course in the world to deal with contemporary American Indian literature. He has lectured on Indian literature at universities in North and South America, Europe, and Asia. His books include *Shakespeare's Repentance Plays: The Search for an Adequate Form* (1973); *Blood and Knavery: English Renaissance Pamphlets and Ballads of Crime and Sin* (1973); *Appleseeds and Beercans: Man and Nature in Literature* (1974); *Four American Indian Literary Masters* (1982); *The Lightning*

Within: An Anthology of Contemporary American Indian Fiction (1991); *Native American Perspectives on Literature and History* (1995); *Native American Studies* (with Clara Sue Kidwell, 2005); and *Encyclopedia of American Indian Literature* (with Jennifer McClinton, 2007).

Jace Weaver is the Franklin Professor of Native American Studies and director of the Institute of Native American Studies at the University of Georgia. He is the multiple-award-winning author or editor of eleven books, including *That the People Might Live: Native American Literatures and Native American Community*; *American Indian Literary Nationalism* (with Craig Womack and Robert Warrior); *Other Words: American Indian Literature, Law, and Culture*; and *The Cherokee Night and Other Plays by Lynn Riggs*. He is a leading critic in the literary nationalist movement. His most recent works are *Notes from a Miner's Canary: Essays on the State of Native America* and *Red Clay, 1835: Cherokee Removal and the Meaning of Sovereignty* (with Laura Adams Weaver). He is currently completing *The Red Atlantic: American Indians and Transoceanic Exchange, 1000–1927* (under contract with the University of North Carolina Press). He splits his time between Athens, Georgia, and Tahlequah, Oklahoma.

Index

CPSIA information can be obtained at www.ICGtesting.com
Printed in the USA
LVOW08s0834231013

358214LV00003B/3/P

9 780806 144023